CREATIVITY AND TRADITION

STUDIES IN MEDIEVAL RABBINIC SCHOLARSHIP, LITERATURE AND THOUGHT

This publication has been made possible by
the generous support of
the Alan M. Stroock Fund for Advanced Research in Judaica

CREATIVITY AND TRADITION

STUDIES IN MEDIEVAL RABBINIC SCHOLARSHIP, LITERATURE AND THOUGHT

Israel M. Ta-Shma

Harvard University Center for Jewish Studies

Distributed by
Harvard University Press
Cambridge, Massachusetts and London, England
2006

Library of Congress Cataloging-in-Publication Data

Ta-Shma, Israel M.
Creativity and tradition : studies in medieval rabbinic scholarship, literature and thought / Israel M. Ta-Shma.
p. cm.
"Set in Germany, northern France, Italy, Poland and Spain"—Data sheet.
ISBN-10: 0-674-02393-5
ISBN-13: 978-0-674-02393-2
1. Rabbinical literature--History and criticism. 2. Hebrew literature, Medieval--History and criticism. I. Title.
BM496.6.T25 2006
296.109'02--dc22 2006049506

Cover illustration: *The Barcelona Haggadah*, an illuminated Passover compendium from fourteenth-century Catalonia. Courtesy of the British Library, London. ADD. 14761 Folio 65v. Presents a synagogue scene accompanying the initial word Halleluyah, "Praise the Lord" taken from the Psalms. A rabbi stands on a reading platform holding a Torah in front of four adults and three children.

Book production and design by CDL Press,
POB 34454, Bethesda, MD 20827

Dustjacket design: Catherine Lo.

Publisher: Harvard University Center for Jewish Studies.

ISBN 0-978-0-674-02393-2
ISBN 0-674-02393-5

Israel M. Ta-Shma
September 14, 1936 – November 4, 2004

TABLE OF CONTENTS

FOREWORD

Israel Moshe Ta-Shma was born in Tel Aviv in 1936, in a middle-class religious-Zionist family. He received his elementary education in an ultra-religious school, *Histadrut ha-Ḥaredim*, in Tel Aviv, which shut its doors more than forty years ago. While the curriculum included secular studies, as required by the educational system of the time, the emphasis was primarily on religious subjects. Later he attended the yeshiva high school *Ha-Yishuv he-Ḥadash* in Tel Aviv, and still later studied at the celebrated Hebron Yeshiva in Jerusalem. He received his *semikhah* (rabbinical ordination) from the Chief Rabbi of Eretz Israel at the time, Rabbi Isaac Herzog. After serving in the Israel Defense Forces from 1957 to 1959, he enrolled as a student in the Hebrew University of Jerusalem, receiving a Bachelor's degree in the Departments of Talmud and Classical Studies and a Master's degree in Talmud. In 1974 he completed his Ph.D. dissertation at Bar-Ilan University, under the supervision of the late Professor Y. D. Gilat. He used to say of his teachers: "Those who influenced my scientific and personal attitudes were the late Professors Ephraim E. Urbach, Shraga Abramson, and Yeshayahu Leibowitz, and my good friend and colleague Professor Yaakov Sussmann."

For some eighteen years, beginning approximately in 1963, Ta-Shma was the secretary and later deputy editor of the departments of Judaic studies in the *Enzikoklopedia Ha-Ivrit* (*Encyclopaedia Hebraica*), working under the editors, Professors Urbach and Leibowitz.

In 1974 Ta-Shma founded a journal of Hebrew bibliography entitled *Alei Sefer*, whose first ten volumes he was to edit. Three years later, he joined the faculty of Bar-Ilan University, teaching in the Department of Talmud. Beginning in 1981, he taught in the Talmud Department of the Hebrew University of Jerusalem, serving also for some twenty years as director of the Institute for Microfilmed Hebrew Manuscripts at the National and Hebrew University Library in Jerusalem. In 1982 he was appointed academic secretary of the *Mekitzei Nirdamim* Society—a voluntary society for the publication of medieval Hebrew manuscripts of scientific importance that would not normally be published by public or commercial bodies. Professor Ta-Shma retired in 1999 and from that time on devoted his time and energy entirely to research.

The bulk of Professor Ta-Shma's research concerned rabbinic literature in the Middle Ages and the Early Modern Era in Europe, that is, in the years 1000–1500, and in the development of halakhah in that period. He published ten volumes of research, as well as more than 170 scholarly papers. His published books (in Hebrew) are the following:

Rabbi Zerachya Halevy and His Circle—Rabbinic Literature in Twelfth-Century Provence, Jerusalem: Mossad Ha-Rav Kook, 1993, 200 pp.

Early Franco-German Ritual and Custom, Jerusalem: Magnes Press, 1999[3], 350 pp.

Talmudic Commentary in Europe and North Africa, Part I: *1000–1200*, Jerusalem: Magnes Press, 1999, 230 pp.; Part II: *1200–1400*, Jerusalem: Magnes Press, 2000, 220 pp.

Ritual, Custom and Reality in Franco-Germany, 1000-1350, Jerusalem: Magnes Press, 2000[2], 320 pp.

Ha-Nigle sheba-Nistar—The Halakhic Residue in the Zohar, Tel-Aviv: Ha-Kibbutz Ha-Me'uchad, rev. ed., 2001, 126 pp.

The Early Ashkenazic Prayer—Literary and Historical Aspects, Jerusalem: Magnes Press, 2003, 265 pp.

Knesset Meḥkarim—Studies in Medieval Rabbinic Literature, Part I: Germany, 420 pp.; Part II: Spain, 350 pp.; Part III: Italy and Byzantium (in print).

Ta-Shma's work *Talmudic Commentary in Europe and North Africa* earned him the Bialik Prize for 2001. One year later, in 2002, he received the prestigious EMET Prize for talmudic research, under the auspices of the Prime Minister of Israel, and in 2003 he was awarded the Israel Prize in talmudic research. The Israel Prize Committee explained their choice as follows:

> [Professor Ta-Shma's] research is unique in three respects: his proficiency in all areas of talmudic and rabbinic literature, whether in print or in manuscript; his brilliant insights and intuition, which enable him to integrate different realms of knowledge; and his extremely prolific research. His works demonstrate that Halakhah may be combined in research with culture and literature, creating a rich, detailed and at the same time profound picture of the spirit of the Jewish people in medieval Europe, a picture in which Torah study, Jewish law, custom, Kabbalah, and everyday life may be viewed against the background of contemporary Christian culture. Professor Ta-Shma is the only contemporary scholar who has focused on rabbinic literature and the rela-

> tionship between Halakhah and life in all the Torah centers of medieval Europe: Franco-Germany, Spain, Provence, Italy, Britain, and Byzantium. While systematically describing the characteristic features of each center and each period, he brings out the influences and mutual ties between places and times, his research thus revolving around the dynamism so typical of Jewish culture. His research methods have initiated a new era in the history of research in Judaic studies.

Many will also remember Professor Ta-Shma for his noble character. Prof. Jay Berkovitz, a close friend and colleague, offered the following reminiscence:

> Israel Ta-Shma dedicated himself tirelessly—even relentlessly—to the pursuit of truth. Blessed with prodigious talents that included a penetrating mind, an almost flawless memory, and incomparable self-discipline, he opened path- breaking vistas in the study of rabbinic culture. It is no exaggeration to say that his enormous contributions transformed the entire field of Jewish studies.
>
> Behind this towering intellect was a man of uncommon humanity, the embodiment of extraordinary generosity, personal warmth and integrity. From his desk at the Institute for Microfilmed Hebrew Manuscripts, or in his office at home, Professor Ta-Shma delighted in the opportunity to assist colleagues, from Israel and abroad, in their scholarly pursuits. Time and again, scholars would call upon his encyclopedic knowledge, wisdom, and critical acumen, which he offered generously and cheerfully. Without fail, he showed warmth, caring, and respect, especially to younger scholars for whom he was both cherished mentor and devoted friend. As a result, many in the early stages of their careers were able to find the direction they needed and, with his encouragement, also developed confidence in themselves and their own abilities. With these personal qualities and exceptional gifts, which had long become legendary in Jerusalem, Israel Ta-Shma epitomized the highest ideals of scholar, teacher, and friend.

Professor Ta-Shma considered the publication of the present volume as most important, as he wrote in the introduction a few months before his death. He had intended to dedicate the book to the memory of his late friend Professor Isadore Twersky, but was prevented by illness from wording the dedication.

We would like to thank Professor Jay Harris and the Harvard Center for Jewish Studies for publishing this book, and Professor Elchanan Reiner for helping us to prepare the book for publication after the author's death.

Professor Israel M. Ta-Shma passed away during the Intermediate Days of the Sukkot festival in autumn 2004. His presence is sorely missed. His family and friends will remember him as a loving, devoted husband and father, a modest and kind person, and, above all, a lover of the Torah and its students.

PREFACE

This brief preface is intended to clarify the underlying reasons for publishing this collection of my articles in English. I have now been studying medieval rabbinical literature for more than forty years, having published during that time many books and more than two hundred articles on several central aspects of the field: identifying books and authors and determining the authorship of books; researching early Ashkenazic custom and its dependence on the customs of the Land of Israel; the development of halakhah in the Middle Ages; Ashkenazic prayer and its history; and the history of the medieval European schools of talmudic exegesis.

Rabbinical literature in all its variety—exegesis of the Bible, the Talmud, the Midrash, prayer, and liturgical poetry; collections of responsa, halakhic monographs and anthologies etc.—as against mystical, kabbalistic, and philosophical literature, accounts quantitatively for the bulk of Hebrew religious literature written in Europe in the tenth to the fourteenth centuries. This corpus represents a tremendous wealth of wisdom, science, and general historical information, whose depths have yet to be plumbed by modern scholarship. For example, on the one hand, the great research projects of Professors Avigdor (Victor) Aptowitzer, Ephraim Elimelech Urbach, and Abraham Grossman, through their detailed analyses of the literature of early scholars in Franco-Germany and of the Tosafists and their schools, have laid solid historical foundations for our understanding of the history and culture of the Jews of France and Germany in the tenth to thirteenth centuries. On the other hand, Professor Yitzhak Baer's great studies of the history of the Jews in Christian Spain made very little (and rather superficial, at that) use of the material embedded in the responsa literature, and as a result created a greatly misleading historical portrait of that community. Until recently, very little had been done to investigate the history of the Jews of Provence other than the pioneering work of the late Professors Benedikt and Twersky; and almost nothing had been gleaned from rabbinical literature in regard to the early history of the Jews of Italy and

Greece-Byzantium. There are many reasons for this research lacuna, some of which I shall describe below. At any rate, as a result of this situation, historians have concentrated on processing the few already available data, adding, as if to compensate, general information and new perceptions derived from a broader perspective, based primarily on modern studies of the Middle Ages and of general medieval culture.

And that is not all. Very little has been done to elucidate the data base itself, that is to say, the extent of rabbinical literature written in medieval Europe, much of which—perhaps the great majority—has been lost in the intervening centuries. A *sine qua non*, if we are to advance the study of the historical background, is to determine how much material has been lost and thus to identify some of the surviving manuscripts, as convincingly proved not long ago in Dr. Simcha Immanuel's study of the lost books of the Tosafist period. A considerable amount of labor, devotion, and perseverance is required, and the rewards are not always immediately obvious; not surprisingly, Immanuel's book is the only work of its kind known to me.

Rabbinical literature is generally a formidable challenge for the average historian, because of its talmudic language—a combination of Aramaic, in a variety of dialects, and Hebrew, all written in the grammar and syntax customary in the Middle Ages, which permitted, for example, switching subject in mid-sentence without any prior warning. An even more difficult problem is the legal nature of most of the subject material, which is a closed book to anyone unfamiliar with the style of study and casuistry of the Talmud and its early commentators; familiarity is generally acquired only by a lengthy spell of yeshiva study—something that is not part of the training of the average historian. More often than not, unqualified readers' efforts to cope with these medieval texts result in a misreading of the text and accordingly in erroneous conclusions.

But the main point has yet to be made. Over the past few decades, as communication and publishing technologies have advanced by leaps and bounds, thousands of "new" medieval Hebrew manuscripts have been discovered, preserved in dozens, perhaps hundreds, of public and private libraries the world over. A major contribution in that respect has been the publication of dozens of excellent catalogues and, in particular, developments in microfilm photography. As far back as the 1950s, the Jewish National and University Library in Jerusalem established an Institute of Microfilmed Hebrew Manuscripts. In the fifty years of its activity, the Institute has located and microfilmed all the Hebrew manuscripts in the world, as far as we know today; it has conclusively identified and catalogued—according to several major rubrics—more than half. After the fall of the Iron Curtain and the collapse of the Soviet regime, the treasures of Hebrew manuscripts in Eastern Europe were also thrown open, and their photographic reproductions are readily available to modern scholars in the Institute's drawers. This project has doubled the amount of literary material currently available to scholars, opening up new possibilities for the discovery of material relevant to the history of the Jews in the Middle Ages (as well as in later periods), mainly in Europe. This scientific wealth is all being kept, for the present, in Jerusalem, but centers of Jewish research in other parts of the world are gradually expanding their microfilm libraries, subject, of course, to budgetary constraints. Any scholar who knows what manuscript he or she needs will be able to access it in a matter of minutes, but the study of rabbinical literature requires a systematic survey of *all* the material in order to filter out the new, unknown material; this cannot be done, of course, in a few minutes, sometimes not even in a few years.

In addition, medieval authors would frequently publish—that is, arrange for the official copying and dissemination of—revised versions of their own works, having retracted some of the things they wrote previously, or as a means of debating with opponents who in the meanwhile had published objections to and critiques of the original works; sometimes they merely wished to add new material. Corrections and additions were inscribed in the margins of the original version and the copyists were expected to interpolate them, omitting the earlier, original passage that the author wished to delete or replace. This frequently produced different versions of the same book, all with the same title and the same headings, which in the course of time came into different people's hands. The question is not one of, say, version A versus version B; but of a multiplicity of versions, some complete and some fragmentary, depending on the quality of the copy given to the copyist. This, in turn, elicits the need for a systematic review of all the ostensibly parallel versions of the same book that do not seem to differ in any essential respect.

One important corpus, all of which is now available in microfilm at the Institute, consists of the documents from the Cairo Geniza, which are currently scattered over several countries in Europe and the United States. This body of material comprises about a quarter of a million fragments, some short, some of medium length, and some relatively long, in different states of preservation, some clearly reflecting early and highly significant copies of rabbinical material from the eleventh century and later. The great majority of this material is relevant primarily to rabbinical literature in the Orient, while the material reproduced from the great western libraries, as already mentioned above, largely reflects western material. In recent years, a rich fund of (mainly) European rabbinical material has come to light on leaves (generally parchment) torn by Christian hands from manuscripts stolen from Jews (or purchased from them cheaply in the early days of printing) and then used to bind archival material, as well as religious and other literature. This was a particularly common practice in central Europe in the fourteenth and fifteenth centuries. The Institute of Microfilmed Hebrew Manuscripts has gone to considerable lengths to locate archives and major libraries possessing large amounts of such material, and much money has been invested in photographing both sides of the many thousands of such leaves. The study of this corpus, now known as the "European Geniza," is still in its infancy; as yet, these reproductions are available only at the Jewish National and University Library in Jerusalem, and they are still in the course of being properly identified and catalogued.

These are just a few of the difficulties facing scholars working in the area of medieval rabbinic literature, in view of which the study of this voluminous material and the effort to extract from it reliable historical information, indeed, present a formidable task. As a consequence, most historians working in medieval Jewish history consciously ignore this indispensable corpus; instead, they tend to return again and again to the available source material, which generally reflects the efforts of previous generations of scholars, whose yeshiva education provided them with the tools to deal with the comparatively limited amount then available. Present-day historians generally prefer to advance more sophisticated historical and sociological theories, reflecting the significant progress since made in those areas, and to reexamine the old texts with a view to achieving a new, improved understanding of their content. These theoretical studies are based on ideas now current in modern scholarship in general, and they no doubt expand our horizons and add an important and profound dimension to our understanding of the broader historical processes, often deepening and sharpening the sometimes naïve, superficial conclusions drawn by previous generations of scholars. Nevertheless, these modern studies not infrequently come aground on new data from the more complete body of available sources. A good many attractive theories have been refuted on the strength of knowledge culled with much effort and perseverance from the new source material; while the results sometimes seem slight and marginal in proportion to the work invested, they are of immeasurable importance for the establishment of historical truth, supposedly the ultimate goal of every scholar and historian. In the final analysis, it is the facts that provide the final yardstick for the validity of theories, and not vice versa. No particular intellectual effort is required to bring up new theories, and for each such theory there is generally a counter-theory based on a different reading of the same sources, perhaps from a different angle and on the basis of different basic assumptions, depending on the author's predilections. However, putting these theories on a firm, factual basis is a rather different story, involving diligent detective work and endless patience.

Most of my articles, by far, were written in Hebrew. This is primarily because the study of medieval rabbinical literature requires a careful reading of Hebrew sources, which reflect three different periods in the history of Hebrew language, grammar, and syntax: (1) talmudic sources from the rabbinic period; (2) Hebrew as commonly written by Torah scholars in the Middle Ages ("rabbinical Hebrew"); and (3) Modern Hebrew as spoken in present-day Israel. To my mind, it is pointless to put such material before any reader who lacks a good command of the language; a person incapable of reading the research in Hebrew will hardly profit from its translation into English. This, at least, was my personal view over the years, and I acted accordingly.

However, there are exceptions to any rule. In time, some twenty studies came up, as it were, for publication; some were, in fact, originally written in English for delivery as lectures at conferences outside Israel, while others had been translated and published in English on various occasions. Of the conference studies originally written in English, some were, in fact, published in the conference proceedings; but most of them have never seen the light of day, in English or in Hebrew, and are being published for the first time in this volume. Articles translated into English after publication in Hebrew were reworked prior to translation, and generally contain additional material compared to the Hebrew originals.

I have lately been busy collecting the best of my articles, updating them and rearranging them in accordance with the state of our present knowledge, completing the necessary bibliographical basis, taking the opportunity to respond to colleagues who have referred to my work in their own studies—for better or for worse. The whole project, which I have divided into five well-defined geographical units (Franco-Germany, Spain, Provence, Italy, Byzantium), has been undertaken by the Mossad Bialik publishing house, under the title *Kenesset Meḥqarim*. The first part, dedicated to France and Germany, was published on the eve of Passover 2004 and the second, dealing with the culture of Spanish Jewry, appeared a few months later, on the eve of the New Year festival that year. The last three parts are currently in the final stages of preparation. Since some twenty percent of my articles were written in English—or already translated—the project would not have been complete without publishing them separately, in a volume of their own; the fruit of those labors is hereby presented to the reader.

Israel Ta-Shma

CHAPTER 1

ASHKENAZI JEWRY IN THE ELEVENTH CENTURY

LIFE AND LITERATURE

THE FRANCO-GERMAN CULTURAL ARENA

The multifaceted literary creation of Ashkenazi Jewry, which was destined to influence the spiritual development of most Jewish communities in Europe, had its origins at the turn of the eleventh century, approximately seventy years after the first scholarly Jews (specifically, the Kalonymus family from Lucca, Italy) had established themselves in the Rheinland. R. Gershom b. Judah (known as Rabbenu Gershom, Me'or ha-Golah) led the yeshiva of Mayence; he was the first founder and perhaps the architect of the yeshiva in its classic European form.[1]

From the viewpoint of medieval Jewish intellectual history, Germany and northern France should be studied as one cultural area.[2] The Jews who lived in these two centers (separated by a clear political boundary dating from the early post-Carolingian period) had similar literary and halakhic traditions, similar social and religious ideals, and an identical framework of beliefs. To be sure, there were differences in custom between the Jews of the two countries, and

[1] We now have a thorough historical description of the developments in Ashkenaz in the eleventh century in Avraham Grossman's detailed and precise book *The Early Sages of Ashkenaz* (Jerusalem 1981) (Heb.). The present article, therefore, refers to the situation in a general manner; for detailed information, the reader is referred to Grossman's book. A much more detailed study of the topics treated in this article is printed in Hebrew in *Sidra* 3 (1987).

[2] Most of the problems raised here relate only to the Ashkenazi communities, but they are not limited to the eleventh century. They do not, as a rule, occur as communal phenomena in the Jewish diaspora lands under Muslim dominion except incidentally and tangentially. Their absence is not relevant to a portrayal of the Jewish community in the Orient or the Sephardic community as a whole. A portrait of this sort must be based on the entire range of traits that characterize the community under discussion, typifying it in a historical sense. We are still a long way from such a typology, both for the western and eastern diasporas. I have sketched a few lines toward a portrait of the early Jewish community of Spain in my article "Jewish Judiciary and Law in the Eleventh and Twelfth Centuries in Spain" (Heb.), *Shenaton ha-Mishpat ha-Ivri* 1 (Jerusalem 1974).

even between communities, but there were no conspicuous differences in their way of life, and their rabbis and scholars shared the same approach to the study of Torah.[3]

The spiritual center of this combined geographic entity shifted periodically: at times it was in Germany, at times in France, and there are periods when there were actually two parallel centers with notable differences in approach and attitude—differences that did not affect the basic outlook common to both, but nonetheless made for differing priorities in the social and religious spheres.

Rabbenu Gershom's disciple, R. Eliezer b. Isaac of Mayence (called R. Eliezer the Great), and the latter's disciple, R. Isaac b. R. Judah, succeeded Rabbenu Gershom as heads of the Mayence academy and established its fame. Eleventh-century scholars such as R. Isaac b. R. Elazar ha-Levi of Worms and R. Solomon b. Samson of Worms became leaders of the academy of Worms; others, at the end of the eleventh century, were at the head of the yeshiva in Speyer.

During that period the *yeshivot* of Germany also admitted young scholars from neighboring France, among them Rashi, author of the classic commentaries on the Bible and Talmud. When Rashi returned home about 1070, there began a gradual shift of the center of rabbinic scholarship from Germany to France. This shift was caused by four factors: (1) the circumstance that Rashi's commentary (*Kuntres*) on the Talmud was written and disseminated in France; (2) the scholarly activities of Rashi's disciples, sons-in-law, and grandsons, who taught in several French localities; (3) the new, revolutionary method of the Tosafists, formulated on the basis of Rashi's commentary and in keeping with the scholastic-dialectic trend that developed in France at the time; and (4) the decline of the important centers of Jewish learning in Mayence and Worms due to *gezerot tatnav*—the massacres of the year 4856 [1096] linked to the First Crusade, in which virtually all the leading rabbinic scholars active in these cities were killed.[4]

During the eleventh century, however, the German area was recognized as the main center of Jewish scholarship because of Rabbenu Gershom's presence, his teaching, and literary activities there, and also because of the continuous influx of Jews from Italy, which contributed exceptional spiritual resources to the growth of this new Jewish center, resulting in several generations of high-quality leadership.

The shift of the center of Jewish scholarship to France has an interesting parallel in general European history. During the period from ca. 950 to ca. 1050, culture in Germany had attained a level far superior to that of France. This development was due to the "Ottoman Renaissance," so called after the

[3] E.E. Urbach, *The Tosafists* I (Jerusalem 1980), p. 165 (Heb.).

[4] A. Grossman, *The Early Sages* (Jerusalem 1980), pp. 435–440 (Heb.).

Holy Roman Emperor Otto I (912–973), who imported a long line of theologians and other illuminati from northern Italy to strengthen the intellectual movement that he and his brother Bruno, Archbishop of Cologne (925–965), had vigorously supported. But beginning with the middle of the eleventh century this movement declined in Germany, while intellectual life in France gradually became stronger, until it reached its apex in what is now known as the "Twelfth-Century Renaissance," the roots of which are clearly planted in the mid-eleventh century.[5] The shift of the Jewish cultural center from Germany to France is congruent in its general lines to the process in the non-Jewish world, but it did not come about until half a century after the latter. The cause of this discrepancy lay in the unique character of the yeshiva, an institution of a type unknown to scholars at the German court. This talmudic academy made possible the education of a new generation of local scholars that was able to maintain and even raise the standards of its predecessors. Thus, only the combined four factors listed earlier could have forced the movement of the center of rabbinic scholarship from Germany to France. Such fortuitous (or perhaps not-so-fortuitous) similarities between events in inner Jewish life and historical developments in the surrounding Gentile world recur a number of times in the history of German Jewry, as shall be seen.

THE BABYLONIAN TALMUD AND ITS COMMENTATORS

As already indicated, the yeshiva, of which we have spoken so highly, was an original product of Ashkenazi Jewry. It bore little resemblance to its predecessors, the great academies of Babylonia, in curriculum, structure, or general objectives. Perhaps the Ashkenazi *yeshivot* had more in common with the *yeshivot* founded during that same period in northern Africa and Spain, though there was no historical connection between them and there is no reason to assume that they knew of one another except, perhaps, through vague reports.

We lack sufficient information to answer even a few of our questions about the structure of the early Ashkenazi *yeshivot*, their organization, and their means of economic support. However, it is clear that they were open all year except on the holidays and that their principal objective was the study of Torah for its own sake—the reading and interpretation of the various mishnaic, talmudic, and midrashic texts available to them. The students learned together under the guidance of a teacher (the rabbi), engaging in mutual discussion and debate and comparing all the texts in their possession. This was done with the

[5] This topic has been repeatedly discussed in the scholarly literature. For the most important comments, see C.H. Haskins, *The Renaissance of the Twelfth Century* (1976), ch. 2. The most recent summary article, which contains a comprehensive, annotated bibliography on all the specific issues that were explored within the framework of the larger topic of the "Twelfth-Century Renaissance," is Elizabeth A.R. Brown's review essay in *History and Theory* 19 (Nov. 1980), pp. 319–331.

help of a basic commentary that, begun by R. Gershom b. Judah and refined and enriched over years of study and discussion,[6] was attributed to a collective, anonymous authorship, such as "the Sages of Mayence" or "the Saintly Ones of Mayence." Such commentaries have come down to us in the form of various manuscripts on a number of talmudic tractates, on parts of *Seder Kodashim*, and on the tractates *Nedarim, Nazir, Hulin, Bava Batra*, et al., and are now printed in the standard editions of the Talmud under the title "Commentary of Rabbenu Gershom, Light of the Exile." A comparative study of the various versions indicates variant adaptations and chronological differences in various sections of the commentaries. It seems that the cycles of study at the Ashkenazi *yeshivot* were annual for certain subjects and longer for others. The material interpolated into the basic commentary is prefaced or followed by such notations as "another commentary" or "another explanation." It may be assumed that the students had before them, side by side, various versions of this collection of commentaries. In the spirit of their time, and in keeping with their great humility, individual sages are seldom mentioned by name. The Italian rabbis of the eleventh century refer also to these commentaries in the collective terms mentioned above.

Rashi, too, benefited from the Mayence and Worms commentaries when he prepared his own commentary on the Talmud. It seems that he refers to them when he speaks of, say, the "*yesod* of R. Isaac b. R. Judah," or the "*talmud* of R. Isaac ha-Levi." Rashi extracted the best from these materials: sifting, condensing, and, with his brilliant simplicity as a master of style and syntax, adding his own contribution. As a result of Rashi's work, these earlier collections of commentaries became superfluous and eventually fell into oblivion. It is obvious that, by the beginning of the twelfth century, only scant effort was expended on copying the commentaries of Mayence and Worms. That is why so few of them have survived; most of those that have come down to us are on tractates that Rashi failed to comment on or for which his notes had never reached the early copyists. It can be demonstrated that the great Ashkenazi scholars who were active during the first half of the thirteenth century no longer even recognized such early material as the work of their forefathers who had lived and taught two centuries earlier.

The studies at the *yeshivot* of Mayence and Worms included most of the rabbinic literature: halakhic and aggadic. We have, both in manuscript and in print, the commentaries of these scholars on *Genesis Rabbah* in several variants and traditions, with superimpositions identified by such annotations as "another commentary." We also have, in the same style, the commentaries of the early yeshiva scholars on the *Mekhilta* to the book of Exodus and on the Aramaic

[6] I. Ta-Shma, "R. Gershom Me'or ha-Golah's Commentary on the Talmud" (Heb.), *Kiryat Sefer* 53.

hymns recited on Shavuot,[7] based on rabbinic midrash and on selections from the Aramaic translations of the Bible. There is evidence that the very early mystical work *Sefer Yetzirah* was studied and commented upon at these *yeshivot*; so, too, was the prayer book with its major *piyyutim*. On the other hand, it is equally clear that the Bible was not studied as a separate subject at the *yeshivot* of that period; we have no record of any Ashkenazi attempt at biblical exegesis prior to Rashi. The primary initiative to write commentaries on the Bible, including the Pentateuch, was Rashi's innovation; and as he worked, he did not have before him any systematic written source material except for some lists of vernacular equivalents, scattered explanations, and French translations of various scriptural verses or verse fragments.[8]

The Mayence commentary on the Talmud is straightforward in its approach, with only a few passages involving dialectics. There is a tendency to present several alternative explanations side by side and in this context to employ, up to a point, the dialectical technique of question and answer. This tendency is also apparent in Rashi's commentary on the Talmud, which represents the summation of eleventh-century Ashkenazi commentary. What characterizes these commentaries, and what distinguishes them sharply from all commentaries written during the same period outside the area known as Ashkenaz—especially from the works of R. Nissim Gaon (ca. 990–1062) and R. Hananel b. Hushi'el (d. 1055/56), both outstanding leaders and talmudists in North Africa—is that in the Ashkenazi works the commentary is fully integrated with the talmudic text. The Ashkenazi commentary never constitutes a self-contained literary unit but is composed of isolated sentences that become coherent only when connected to phrases from the actual talmudic discussion (*dibbur ha-matkhil*). In many instances, the cited talmudic phrase is itself part of the interpretive language; but even when this is not the case, it is impossible to make any sense of the commentary if one does not read it together with the talmudic text to which it refers. Thus, the study of the Ashkenazi commentaries presupposes a familiarity with the talmudic text and is not a substitute for the knowledge of it.

In this respect, as already noted, the Mayence commentaries are unlike those of such non-Ashkenazi masters as R. Nissim Gaon, which offer a complete and handy paraphrase of the talmudic discussion from which the reader can get all the information he may want without having to refer to the talmudic text itself. The commentary by R. Hananel, R. Nissim's contemporary and fellow townsman, does not constitute a paraphrase like that of R. Nissim, because

7 I. Ta-Shma, "Al ha-Perush la-Piyyutim ha-Aramiyim she-be-Makhzor Vitry," *Kiryat Sefer* 57 (1982). On the newly discovered Mekhilta commentary, see id., "Perush Ashkenazi Kedum…," *Tarbiz* 55 (1986).

8 M. Banitt, "*L'eazim* in the Commentaries of Rashi and in the Old French Glossaries" (Heb.), *Te'uda* 4 (Tel-Aviv University 1986).

he regularly omits sections that he considers "simple" and comments on selected portions only. Nevertheless it, too, is based on the principle of paraphrase, albeit in abridged form. The Mayence commentaries, by contrast, assume that the student has the original talmudic text before him and that he is making an effort to understand it from "within." The commentary itself requires laborious study, as it is terse and its meaning not always readily apparent. Whoever is familiar with the commentaries of Mayence, as well as with those of Rashi, knows that their value is at its best in the review of material already known. They are of only limited use to the neophyte and the inexperienced, because they cannot serve as a substitute for a teacher and are hardly adequate preparation toward self-study of the Talmud.

LITERARY SOURCES

A survey of the library of primary and supplementary sources available to eleventh-century Ashkenazi scholars is surprising in the wealth and completeness of its material. Indeed, there was hardly any extant Hebrew volume of importance that it lacked.[9] Scholars had access to the Babylonian and Jerusalem Talmud, the halakhic and aggadic *midrashim*, the Babylonian Targumim, and the Targumim from *Eretz Israel* almost in their entirety with only a few exceptions, such as *Tanya de-vei Eliyahu* and *Pesikta Rabbati*. Students could also readily refer to mystical texts such as the *Sefer Yetzirah* and other ancient works of mysticism and magic such as the *Merkavah* (speculations, *nomina sacra*, and visions connected with the Throne of Glory and the Divine Chariot), the *Razim* (magical material), and the *Shi'ur Komah* (speculations on anthropomorphic aspects of the Deity) literature. They also had at their disposal *piyyutim* from *Eretz Israel* by Elazar ha-Kallir (Tiberias, seventh century) and Yannai (probably sixth century) as well as the early Italian *payyetanim* who followed in their footsteps.[9] Scholars were even familiar with parts of the Apocrypha and Pseudepigrapha, most probably in Hebrew translations.[10] They used the major works of the Babylonian Geonim (but very few of their responsa) from the early period of R. Saadia Gaon (882–942) and R. Ahai (eighth century), through the various geonic *Halakhot Pesukot* and *Halakhot Gedolot*, down to the works of R. Hai Gaon (b. Sherira; 939–1038), head of the academy of Pumbedita, and R. Samuel b. Hophni, the Gaon of Sura (d. 1013). The Ashkenazi students were also familiar with the *Ma'asim* literature of *Eretz Israel*,[11] which was then unknown in other Jewish centers and which we ourselves are only gradually discovering today through the treasures of the Cairo

[9] I. Ta-Shma, "Sifriyatam shel Hakhmei Ashkenaz Benei ha-Meah ha–11" (Heb.), *Kiryat Sefer* 60 (1985).

[10] A. Epstein, *Mi-Kadmoniyot ha-Yehudim* (Jerusalem 1957), pp. 130ff.

[11] B.M. Lewin, "Sefer ha-Ma'asim li-Vnei Eretz Israel," *Tarbiz* I (1930), p. 1; and most recently, M. Margulies, *Hilkhot Eretz Yisrael min ha-Genizah* (Jerusalem 1974), pp. 1 –16,

Genizah. They also knew such early Italian works as the books of Shabtai Donnolo (913–982 C.E.), one of the earliest Jewish writers on astrology and medicine, and the *Josippon* (an anonymous work on the history of the Second Temple, based on the work of Josephus), Assaph ha-Rofe (a Hebrew medical treatise), the Alphabet of Ben Sira, and some Hebrew writings of tenth-century Sephardim such as the Spanish philologists Menahem Ibn Saruq and Dunash Ibn Labrat. Even very new books composed at the end of the eleventh century, such as the *Arukh* (talmudic dictionary by R. Nathan b. Yehiel of Rome; 1035–1110) and the work of R. Hananel and R. Isaac b. Jacob Alfasi (1013–1103), reached them rapidly.[12] On the other hand, works written in Arabic, or Hebrew mixed with Arabic, like those of R. Samuel ha-Nagid (993–1056) and R. Isaac b. Judah Ibn Ghayyat (1038–1089), both of whom were active in Spain, were not known to them.

Side by side with this intellectual openness and readiness to absorb knowledge from many different sources in Babylonia, *Eretz Israel*, and Europe, the scholars of Ashkenaz showed remarkable selectivity in drawing upon (and citing from) this wide range of literature. We can distinguish clear preferences in their attitudes toward the various books. They viewed some of these works as authoritative and universally binding; other works seemed to them not authoritative but nonetheless valuable; and still others were rarely studied and simply put aside, to be viewed with reservations at best. The principal criterion established by the Ashkenazi scholars for their acceptance of a given work was the extent to which it adhered to the basic historical tradition of Ashkenazi Jewry. This criterion was applied to poetry and mysticism as well. Ashkenazi and Italian poets "were modest in their poetic forms and embellishments. No poetic school in the history of Hebrew literature...was more restrained in its forms. It is not that the *payyetanim* of Italy were ignorant of the classical formal embellishments, or that they refrained from resorting to them, but rather that they were 'miserly' in the use they made"[13] of them, because the character of their work was religious rather than playful. With regard to mysticism, this phenomenon has been noted by Prof. Joseph Dan: "*Hasidei Ashkenaz* had available to them only parts of the mystic works. Yet, they were selective even with the scarce material on hand. They chose what they considered close to their own spirit and paid no attention to ideas they felt to be remote from their own."[14]

1–7, (Heb. num.). Mordecai A. Friedman, "Marriage Laws Based on Ma'asim li-Vnei," *Eretz Yisrael* (Heb.), *Tarbiz* 50 (1951).

12 I. Ta-Shma, "The Dissemination of the Writings of R. Isaac Alfasi (RIF) and Rabbenu Hananel and of the 'Halakhot Gedolot' in France and Ashkenaz in the Eleventh and Twelfth Centuries" (Heb.), *Kiryat Sefer* 55 (1980).

13 E. Fleischer, *Shirot ha-Kodesh ha-Ivrit bi-Yimei ha-Beinaim* (Jerusalem 1975), p. 433.

14 J. Dan, *The Esoteric Theology of the Hasidei Ashkenaz* (Jerusalem 1968), p. 24, (Heb.).

Yet another element conspicuous to the student of the early Ashkenazi library is the tendency of the scholars to inject themselves directly into the texts of the books they studied. They did so by means of deletions, corrections, and interpolations, in which they were guided by such considerations as comparisons to parallel literature and their own differing internal traditions. The extent of the emendations introduced by the Ashkenazim into their talmudic texts has been known from early times; only Sephardi works were regarded as pristine and unaltered originals.[15] The Sephardi scholars maintained continuous contact with the Geonim of Babylonia and treated the geonic texts in their possession with respect, never altering the text without referring to earlier and authoritative manuscripts and paying serious attention to the traditions of the Babylonian Geonim. The sages of Ashkenaz, on the other hand, who did not maintain contact with the Babylonian center, were in the habit of adapting the texts to their own exegetic and halakhic tradition, which did not always correspond to that of the Babylonians.

They proposed alternative readings in the margins of their texts (*hakhi garsinan*), and these readings were then rapidly transferred to the body of the text by later copyists who wanted to shorten their labors.

One of the reasons for this attitude on the part of the Ashkenazim is rooted in their historical view of the formation of the Talmud. Based on their version of the Epistle of R. Sherira b. Hanina Gaon (ca. 906–1006), they believed that the Talmud had not been put into written form until a substantial time after it had been rehearsed at the academies of the great Amoraim.[16] This assumption had clear implications for the reliability of the phrasing and spelling of the traditional texts. However, this is not the only explanation for the attitude of the Ashkenazim; its deeper causes will be examined later in this study. In any event, the liberties they took with the texts led to a kind of vicious circle: if the text handed down to them was not particularly reliable because it presumably had been tampered with in the past, there was no good reason to refrain from further emendations as seemed necessary in an attempt to restore the text to its hypothetically original form.

This practice, which the Ashkenazi scholars applied to any literature they touched—the Babylonian and Jerusalem Talmud, halakhic and aggadic midrash, and even geonic and secular literature—reached such dimensions that already Rabbenu Gershom, who was active at the beginning of the eleventh century, deemed it necessary to anathematize the emenders of talmudic texts.

15 J. Sussmann, "Masoret Limud u-Masoret Nusakh shel ha-Talmud ha-Yerushalmi be-Sifrut ha-Talmudit," in *Researches in Talmudic Literature: A Study Conference in Honour of the Eightieth Birthday of Saul Lieberman, held June 13–14, 1978* (Jerusalem: Israel Academy of Sciences and Humanities, 1983), pp. 34–41.

16 J.N. ha-Levi Epstein, *Introduction to the Literate of the Amoraim* (Jerusalem 1962), pp. 613–615 (Heb.).

However, this was of little avail. Leading rabbis who followed Rabbenu Gershom found themselves faced with the same situation, and Rabbenu Tam, in the middle of the twelfth century, was actually compelled to reinstate the *herem*, because he considered the situation so dangerous. As he put it in his introduction to the *Sefer ha-Yashar*: "It is not enough that [emenders] have corrupted the interpretive [anonymous] talmudic texts. They have done so even [with] the words of Tannaim and Amoraim, and this is not proper for God-fearing men to do....May the Lord forgive Rabbenu Samuel; for every emendation by Rabbenu Solomon he produced twenty emendations; not only that, but he [actually] deleted what was [originally] written...." And so it came about that various books, including famous *midrashim*, developed a separate manuscript "tradition." This misled scholars into regarding such "ancillary" texts as a separate, ancient tradition, perhaps of *Eretz Israel* origin, which had found its way into Ashkenaz in a manner now unknown to us. However, this assumption is incorrect. One may hypothesize that dozens of fragments cited in various places by early Ashkenazi writers as "Jerusalem Talmud" or "Jerusalem Book," and not found in the present Jerusalem Talmud, are, in fact, remnants of varied material that originated in *Eretz Israel*, were added to the text of the Jerusalem Talmud for reasons of convenience and textual similarity, and were then passed down to posterity as part of the Jerusalem Talmud itself.[17]

By the period under study, and probably before, Ashkenazi scholarship was already completely anchored in the Babylonian Talmud, around which virtually all the spiritual activity of these scholars revolved. The Ashkenazim gave little time to the Jerusalem Talmud in their studies, and their prayers (except for the *piyyutim*) were classic Babylonian in form. Rashi and his mentors viewed the Babylonian Talmud as "our" Talmud.

But all this does not yet give us the whole picture. Closer study shows that the most important element in the religious life of the Ashkenazi scholars was that of custom and tradition handed down by each community and each family. The emphasis was on custom rather than on the learned, halakhic conclusions derived from discussions set down in the Babylonian Talmud. To be sure, the central importance of the Babylonian Talmud was never doubted in theory, but in practice each community was careful to adhere to the traditions of its own forebears, even where there was no talmudic basis for such traditions, and sometimes even when the custom implicitly or explicitly contravened the Talmud. In such cases of discrepancy the scholars of Ashkenaz strove to broaden their framework of supporting sources. In the words of Rashi's grandson Rabbenu Tam: "Whosoever is not familiar with the *Seder R. Amram Gaon* and *Halakot Gedolot* and *Seder Soferim* and *Pirkei de-R. Eliezer* and the

17 Sussmann, "Masoreth Limud," n. 128.

Midrash Rabbah and Talmud [read: *Tanhuma*][18] and other aggadic works should not undermine the words and customs of the ancients, upon whom we should rely in matters that do not contradict the Talmud but [only] amplify it. We have many customs that they have handed down to us" (*Sefer ha-Yashar*, Responsa, p. 81). When R. Meshulam b. Nathan of Melun (twelfth century) wanted to abrogate the benediction over the Sabbath lights, which has no source in the Talmud, Rabbenu Tam wrote to him: "If you do not believe in the words of the ancients and in our customs, then you also should not accept the Babylonian Talmud, because we find that the talmudic sages chose the Jerusalem Talmud....but our customs are Torah, and our customs in Babylonia follow the sages of Eretz Yisrael who are the principal decisors..." (ibid., p. 99). Elsewhere, he writes: "Their custom is Torah, for not everything was written down in the Talmud. Some things, such as the intercalation and the order of prayers and benedictions, and many things concerning modesty and abstinence have been handed down to us by oral tradition" (ibid., p. 85).

Some of the Ashkenazi scholars attempted to reconcile their customs with the Babylonian Talmud by such methods as dialectics or emendation, or by ingeniously adducing sources not indicated in the straightforward meaning of the talmudic text. During the first half of the twelfth century, R. Eliezer b. Nathan of Mayence (Raban) devoted an entire book to this subject. However, even if they did not succeed in their efforts to harmonize their customs with talmudic sources, they did not abandon their customs and, in fact, rejected the conclusions implied by the Talmud if the latter were at variance with their tradition.

In light of the foregoing, it can be better understood why the scholars of Ashkenaz permitted themselves so many liberties with the talmudic text. This problem is in need of further discussion.

MINHAG ASHKENAZ (CUSTOMS OF ASHKENAZ)

Minhag Ashkenaz differed from the customs of all other Jewish diasporas in both quantity and quality. Of course, habits crystallize wherever a certain routine of religious observance becomes established. In this respect, Ashkenaz was no different from any other diaspora. The difference to which we refer has to do with the value attached to custom in the spiritual (i.e., religious and intellectual) world of Ashkenazi Jewry by its leaders and its plain folk, as expressed in the rabbinic literature created in that part of the world.

Attachment to custom has several aspects, the first one being purely quantitative. In Ashkenaz, and only there, custom accompanies halakhah at every step, so that there is hardly a law that is not embedded in an elaborate network

[18] S. Abramson, "Notes on the 'Sefer ha-Yashar' of R. Jacob b. Meir (Rabbenu Tam) and Its Introduction" (Heb.), *Kiryat Sefer* 37 (1962), p. 242.

of custom that regulates the details not defined in the basic law and toward which that law seems to be neutral. Other Jewish communities, of course, also had their own usages and ceremonies, but they did not share the unique attitude of the Ashkenazi world toward custom. The Geonim, in their responsa, engaged in discussions of the halakhic and religious role of custom and the proper attitude toward it,[19] and the Talmud cites and discusses no small number of customs. *Pesahim* 4 devotes a detailed discussion to the halakhic status of local custom, in and out of the localities where the custom originated. As is well known, the prevalent view is that, from a historical perspective, custom is an important factor in the formation of halakhah in general; this was true especially for its period of crystallization during the latter part of the Second Temple era and the Tannaitic period.[20] However, there is no time or place in which the number of documented customs was as large as in Ashkenaz (both early and late), reaching a point where custom eclipsed the basic law like a dense shadow. Nowhere else are records found of such a deeply emotional relationship between the people and their customs.[21] Also, nowhere else was a mass of

19 The interested reader may obtain some impression of the range and content of the customs of the Geonim from the indexes accompanying the volumes of *Otzar ha-Geonim*, where Benjamin Menashe Lewin notes customs described by the Geonim. Among these the reader will also find North African customs concerning which the Geonim were queried. Thirty-seven customs that were widespread in North Africa were included as a group in the book *Megilat Setarim* by R. Nissim Gaon, as explained in its index: "And he even spoke of things that our rabbis, of blessed memory, were accustomed to do and of common practices for which no bases are known: he elucidated these and explained their meaning." See Shraga Abramson, *R. Nissim Gaon* (Jerusalem 1965), pp. 270–274 (Heb.). R. Nissim Gaon's viewpoint is reflected also in a statement cited by R. Maimon, the father of Maimonides. Jacob Toledano in *Sarid u-Falit* (Tel Aviv 1944), pp. 7–8, quotes as follows from a manuscript of *Hibbur ha-Tefillot shel R. Maimon*: "In discussing Hanukkah in his Arabic-language tract on prayers, R. Maimon writes: One should not make light of any custom, even a minor one. And whoever deems it right, let him take it upon himself to bake fancy cakes on Hanukkah." And Rabbenu Nissim wrote in *Megillat Setarim* that the same attitude should be taken toward all nation-wide popular practice with regard to such customs: "The custom of consuming a head [of an animal] on Rosh Hashanah, and milk on Purim and on the night following Passover... all such practices should not be belittled, and whoever established their conduct was diligent and alert, for [these customs] were derived from practiced principles. Popular practice should not be spurned. Already the Prophet said: 'Do not forsake the teaching of your mother' [Prov 1:8]–[which means] Do not abandon the law of your nation." Similar customs were mentioned also among the practices and stories traditionally told by the Geonim, the heads of the academies. See Shraga Abramson's comment in *R. Nissim Gaon*, p. 328, and his book *Inyanot be-Sifrut ha-Geonim* (Jerusalem 1974), p. 396.

20 E.E. Urbach, "The Derashah as a Basis of Halakhah and the Problem of the Soferim" (Heb.), *Tarbiz* 27 (1958), pp. 169–171. Perhaps some of the authority wielded by custom was due to the fact that the ancients perceived custom as reflecting early unwritten laws.

21 This article deals only with Ashkenaz—see n. 2 above; extraneous material is included only parenthetically. For purposes of superficial comparison, the reader is referred to the text

customs defined as "*minhag*" with a special status, nor did custom become the subject of a distinct genre of literature, approached from a specific point of view, at such an early date.

It is erroneous to think that this phenomenon characterizes Ashkenaz during the fourteenth and fifteenth centuries. These centuries are not unique in this respect; the institution of custom, with all its characteristic manifestations, was already in full bloom during the eleventh century. During the twelfth and thirteenth centuries the power of custom was significantly diminished under the impact of French tosafist methodology, but in the fourteenth and fifteenth centuries it made a comeback with the revolution that occurred in the method of Talmud study at that time.[22] The placement of the Talmud at the center of their intellectual efforts resulted, during the period of the *tosafot*, in a natural preference for the written and precisely defined law over traditional, oral, and flexible "custom-law" that had prevailed there during the tenth and eleventh centuries (and before). The decline of the innovative tosafist methodology during the fourteenth century brought about a revival of the old pre-tosafist conceptions.[23] The popular impression that the fourteenth and fifteenth centuries have a special status with regard to the power of custom in Ashkenaz derives from the fact that a greater number of literary sources are extant for that period, while far fewer texts have survived from the eleventh century; and even these are difficult to identify and interpret, suggesting that the roots of this phenomenon go back to the tenth century and before. However, this cannot

of an eleventh-century fragment from North Africa, which is included in a letter written by R. Hai Gaon in reply to one from R. Nissim Gaon of Kairouan. This fragment includes a rare expression of the closest attachment known to me of that culture area: "You wrote: It is our custom that we conclude every day our study at the synagogue with this dictum:... 'Disciples of the sages increase peace in the world'...whereas some students arrived from Egypt and stated that the rabbi [cf. D.S. Goitein, "HaRav: Beirur Parashah Setumah" (Heb.), *Tarbiz* 45 (1976)] who resided in Egypt composed something to be recited after the reading of the chapter...and we communicate it to our teacher...but we said that, for our part, we have the custom of our forefathers and we will not alter or change it. What is more, if we were to start reciting [his composition], he might compose another one like it the next day and tell us to recite that one. We have only the practice of the holy academy, and we wrote to our teacher so that he might write to us what the custom of the holy academy is, so that we might do likewise and [that he might] let us know whether we should abandon our custom and recite this ...." To which R. Hai Gaon replied: "That which was composed in Egypt is not ugly, but quite nice by itself. However, it is worthwhile and much better to adhere to the custom of the ancients, especially when there are those who refuse and contest...lest there be a quarrel ..." (*Otzar ha-Geonim*, Shabbat, p. 104, par. 320).

22 I. Ta-Shma, "Tosafot Gornish" (Heb.), *Sinai* 58 (1971). See also Ta-Shema, "Yediot Hadashot al 'Tosafot Gornish' ve-Inyanam" (Heb.), *Alei Sefer* 2 (1976).

23 This major issue is explained *in extenso* in my article "Halakhah, Tradition and Custom in Eleventh-Century Ashkenaz," *Sidra* 3 (Ramat-Gan 1987).

be substantiated due to absence of literary sources. It is no accident that the earliest surviving Ashkenazi book, the *Ma'aseh ha-Ge'onim* (printed in Berlin, 5661 [1900/01]), composed during the last third of the eleventh century by two rabbis, sons of R. Makhir,[24] summarizes Ashkenazi customs in the form in which they had become established by the middle of that century, especially in Mayence, Worms, and Speyer. The work has not come down to us in its entirety, but it is nevertheless clear from its known content that the number of customs practiced in the communities of Ashkenaz at the time was large and versatile enough to create a need for summarizing them in writing so that they might survive.

Until the sixteenth century this subject gave no rest to Ashkenazi Jewry, each century yielding its own varied literature on customs. This phenomenon has no parallel except perhaps in Provence, which, however, should be viewed as a cultural outpost of Franco-German Jewry. Moreover, until the fourteenth century, we know of no book written by a Jewish scholar outside the borders of this cultural area that deals specifically with customs. Only after the penetration of Ashkenazi influences into Spain during the late thirteenth century, especially after R. Asher b. Yehiel and his followers had settled there, did Sephardi Jewry begin to contribute some of its own books on custom, mostly by R. Asher's school and its later disciples.

It is, therefore, erroneous to link the proliferation of custom in Ashkenaz with the material and spiritual deterioration that took place there during the fourteenth century in the wake of the Black Death and the series of anti-Jewish decrees and expulsions that gradually led to the uprooting of Jewry from that area. To be sure, the general decline is reflected also in the realm of custom, just as it is in other areas of creativity, but the emphasis on custom cannot be attributed to this decline. On the contrary, the eleventh century, in which Ashkenazi custom was already in full flower, was one of the best periods in the history of the Jews in Germany in terms of personal and communal security, economic prosperity, and literary creativity. Adherence to custom does not necessarily attest to an intellectual decline, just as strict observance of the written halakhah and talmudic dialectic does not necessarily attest to a high intellectual level. A generation in a state of decline—like that of the fourteenth century—will show that decline in all its activities. By the same token, a generation on the rise, too, will manifest its blossoming in every aspect of its life.

It is also difficult for me to accept the following evaluation:

> The *Ma'aseh ha-Makhiri* [*Ma'aseh ha-Ge'onim*] serves as clear testimony to the attitude of self-abnegation that the scholars of Ashkenaz have developed toward their preceding generations, and that many scholars in Mayence at

[24] For a description of this book, see A. Grossman, "Bene Makhir ve-Sifram Ma'aseh Makhiri," *Tarbiz* 46 (1977); Grossman, *The Early Sages*, pp. 374ff.

> the end of the eleventh century specifically the sons of Makhir themselves, did not appreciate their own [scholarly] worth. This is the reason why they gave so much respect to accepted custom even if the rationale for that custom was unknown and shaky.[25]

The scholars of Ashkenaz did not submit to "preceding generations" in Ashkenaz, but solely to tradition. These sages never doubted their own intelligence and scholarship—not even where it forced them to doubt the theoretical value of a custom—but they still submitted to tradition.

The complete separation of academic study (*mitzvat talmud Torah*) from practical instruction is one of the basic pillars of Ashkenazi halakhah. This has nothing to do with any self-abnegation. This point can be clarified by means of a simple case in point cited from the *Sefer ha-Pardes* and parallel works:

> Because of this the Master ruled: Whoever recites the last blessing over wine taken in the middle of the meal...is praiseworthy...as we read in *Pesahim* [103b]. Thus you can see with your own eyes that one should recite the [last] blessing over the wine taken in the middle of the meal....And in the past we stood around our Masters table and urged him to recite this blessing before our eyes so that we might see the practical halakhah. But he refused to take the responsibility of establishing, in our presence, [what] the halakhah [should be] for all time to come. Nevertheless he used to say: "Whoever does so, may blessings rest upon his head" (p. 181).

In other words, the teacher is absolutely convinced that the blessing should be recited in the middle of the meal, and he even encourages his disciples to act in accordance with this view. Nevertheless, he refuses to change the prevailing custom openly, because it has become accepted as the tradition. If he had been in any doubt about his own scholarly competence, he would surely not have encouraged his disciples to rebel privately against this tradition ("Whoever does so, may blessings rest upon his head"). After all, these same disciples would be expected to hand down rulings of their own and lead in years to come.

This case in point also teaches us the extent to which the students were aware of the difference between the levels of theoretical study and practical ruling That was why they stubbornly insisted that their teacher translate his academic opinion into the language of action. But all in vain, as has been seen. Students acquired their academic skills from their teachers in the *beit ha-midrash*, but the practical skills of decision-making were acquired by constant personal attendance upon their teacher. Disciples were in their master's company—or at least in his immediate environment—even in intimate and unusual situations, to say nothing of the kitchen, the courtyard, and street, and on occasions of joy and sorrow, weekdays, Sabbaths, and festivals. Under these circumstances they could follow halakhic events in actual practice, and they

25 Grossman, *The Early Sages*, p. 369.

sometimes engaged in lengthy discussions with their master if they failed to understand his behavior or believed that it would have been proper for him to act otherwise.

To cite another case, this one from *Ma'aseh ha-Geonim* (no. 24): The teacher (Rabbenu Solomon b. Samson; cf. parallel in *Siddur*, ed. Moshe Hershler, pp. 278–79) is engaged in a discussion with one of his students (probably R. Nathan ha-Makhiri) about the correct time for destroying leaven when the eve of Passover falls on a Sabbath. The master finally concedes that his opinion tends toward that of the student, which is supported by the talmudic text; however, he cautions against departing from the custom of the fathers even if they deviated from what appears to be the straight meaning of the talmudic text.

To discuss additional cases in point would lead too far afield. But there is no justification for the statement "To investigate the basis of a custom is, in itself, illegitimate in the eyes of R. Nathan, lest it undermine its authority." On the contrary, R. Nathan's own *Ma'aseh ha-Ge'onim* is replete with attempts to uncover the origins of various customs; he never condemns such efforts. The case cited as proof of his unwillingness to delve into the origins of a custom refers not to an academic theoretical investigation of the basis of the custom but to attempts to abolish it in the questioner's locality. This is clearly implied in the last part of the question, as published in *Shibbolei ha-Leket* (Part 2, p. 115). Only this, and not inquiry *per se*, is what aroused R. Nathan's ire.

One important characteristic of Ashkenazi custom is its branching off in terms of geography. In addition to the fact that custom tends to branch out into every area of halakhah and to fill every vacuum therein, there is also a tendency here toward pluralism. In other Jewish diasporas, identical customs were generally observed by all the inhabitants or, at the very least, by those dwelling within well-defined political boundaries. Not so in Ashkenaz. The customs of Ashkenaz are generally confined to individual communities, and in each community they differ in detail from the ways of all the other Ashkenazi communities, even those in close geographic proximity. At the same time, an outstanding feature of *minhag* Ashkenaz—both early and late—is the fundamental uniformity of conception and outline, which runs like a scarlet thread through the multifarious local expressions of each custom. For example, all Ashkenazi communities (and Ashkenazi communities only) expanded the time limits of the mourning practices characteristic of the Ninth of Av back to the beginning of Av and to the seventeenth day of the preceding month of Tammuz, though they disagreed on details. These practices include such strictures as the prohibition against washing garments, getting haircuts, putting on new clothes, and getting married. Unified customs prevailed throughout Ashkenaz also with regard to the prohibition against eating legumes on Passover, the practice of *Tashlikh* on Rosh Hashanah, and various customs associated with the late afternoon of the Sabbath, which are connected with the common Ashkenazi belief that, as the Sabbath draws to a close, the tortures of *gehinnom* (Gehenna), which cease in honor of the day of rest, are resumed.[26] Those on earth observe these customs since they are responsible for the welfare of their deceased during these difficult hours of transition. The details of these rituals and their exact order diverge widely throughout the Ashkenazi community, but their essential unity is quite clear.

This phenomenon applies also to standard liturgy; main basic features stand out in all ramifications of Ashkenazi custom (e.g., all public worship on festivals includes *piyyutim*; there is a tendency toward esoterica and *Merkavah* mysticism; and the formulae of the Kaddish, Shemoneh Esre, Kedushah, and benedictions are identical). Nevertheless, it must be noted that, surprisingly, the general impression received from an examination of early Ashkenazi literature is that emphasis is placed precisely on differences. This emphasis results from a careful insistence on the preservation of differentiating characteristics. No apology is made—or considered necessary—with regard to this matter, nor is there any effort to point out fundamental unity. On the contrary, the impression one receives is that this background unity, which is clear to us today due to our broader perspective, was not recognized at all—or at least its importance was not recognized—in those early days.

The lush proliferation of customs in Ashkenaz came about because, from the very beginning, the Jewish communal organization of Germany (and France) was classically decentralized. Each Jewish community, great or small, was free to conduct its affairs according to majority rule and local rabbinic sanction. No community had the right to intervene in the affairs of another. This freedom is already set forth in the early eleventh century, in a responsum by the French R. Joseph b. Samuel Tov Elem, who writes: "As a rule, the ones cannot compel the others, even if they are greater and more numerous, except in cases of castigation for the abrogation of laws, or in cases where they can be caught and made to pay for such acts." This principle was reiterated by R. Judah ha-Kohen, author of *Sefer ha-Dinim*, and R. Eliezer the Great, one of the major Ashkenazi figures in the eleventh century.[27]

The historical foundations of this communal structure are rooted in an internal Jewish tradition[28] reflected in the Talmud, on the one hand, and in the influence of the decentralization typical of the disintegrating Carolingian Empire during the early Feudal Era, on the other. During that period, dominion in France was divided among a large number of local rulers who fought

26 J.L. Avida (Zlotnick), "Me-Aggadot ha-Shabbat u-Minhagah," *Sinai* 25 (1949).

27 A. Grossman, "The Attitude of the Early Scholars of Ashkenaz toward the Authority of the '*Kahal*'," *Annual of the Institute for Research in Jewish Law* 2 (1975).

28 I. Baer, "The Origins of the Organization of the Jewish Community of the Middle Ages" (Heb.), *Zion* 15 (1950). On the halakhic and legal implications of this organization, see M. Elon, *Jewish Law* 2 (1974), pp. 547–555 (Heb.).

each other fiercely to extend their power and influence, while the central authority of the king was thoroughly undermined. Though the situation was not quite as extreme in Germany, the real power there, too, was wielded on a local level. This was so especially because of the ancient tribal traditions that held sway there and because the local rulers fought against the fiat of the central unifying power.[29] Once again, there is an interesting correspondence between an internal Jewish development and a simultaneous process in general history, as indicated above.

"THE CUSTOM OF OUR FATHERS IS TORAH"

Aside from the basic similarity of concept and the geographic-cultural unity and continuity, is there a common denominator that unites the customs of Franco-German Jewry? The affirmative answer leads us to another characteristic unique in Ashkenazi custom: the unusual respect accorded to custom by all under its authority despite the many variants. No one doubted the validity of any custom indigenous to his home locality. Paradoxical though this may appear, persistent local divergences in custom do not indicate that the hold of the custom is weak. On the contrary, they show that the custom is important. Loyalty to local custom assures the preservation of each variant and subvariant; far from creating a breach in the authority of the custom, the variations, in fact, become its foundation. As Rashi put it "Israel in exile—if they are not prophets, they are sons of prophets, all adopting appropriate and correct custom, from which one should not deviate" (*Sefer ha-Pardes*, p. 302). Similarly, one of the sons of Makhir (or perhaps it was Rashi again) said:

> There are those who are stringent about not reciting the *zidduk ha-din* [after the death of a close relative] on Friday afternoon, beginning with the middle of the day [because mourning is not permitted on the Sabbath]. I see no reason for such stringency. But then Israel are sages, the sons of sages, and if they are not prophets, then they are sons of prophets, and their customs that they learned from their fathers is Torah, to which nothing should be added [and from which] nothing should be subtracted (ibid., p. 265).

In the hierarchy of talmudic halakhah (except for civil law, in which the litigating parties may set conditions that are at variance with Torah law) the place of custom, though integral to the system, is at the bottom of the ladder. At the top is biblical law (*de-oraita*), followed by rabbinic law (*de-rabbanan*), and below these are folklore and popular practice, which enjoy semi-halakhic status. Custom is part of the structure of law, which must be properly respected and observed. It is a regular pipeline for the transmission of halakhic tradition from one generation to the next, no less important than other channels. And

29 M. Scott, "The Saxon Europe," *Medieval Europe*, ch. 4 (1977).

even though the place of custom in halakhah is very limited (e.g., as regards punishments for infractions), it has great significance from an educational and cultural-traditional perspective, which is in itself a solid normative value within halakhah. Nevertheless, it is only custom, always dependent on the authority of the overall halakhah, without the authority to oppose or contradict it and without any weight of its own. Its existence is an honorable thing in itself, a desideratum but not a necessity: halakhah will survive even when custom is absent.[30] Such was the position of custom in Babylonia during the geonic period and in parts of Spain and North Africa until the fourteenth century.

R. Hai (b. Sherira) Gaon (939–1038) of Pumbedita encouraged strict adherence to local custom, and he spoke with great esteem and approbation of the customs observed by his forebears who had preceded him as Geonim, the customs observed at the talmudic academies, and especially the customs cherished by "all Israel." In addition to the talmudic literature and the post-talmudic sources, custom served as one of the basic pillars for R. Hai Gaon's halakhic rulings, especially when he could not establish the law on the basis of the Talmud.[31] However, in cases where he found custom in conflict with explicit or implicit halakhah, he urged that the custom be abolished. On the other hand, he was sometimes willing to support customs that deviated from those observed at the academies, for fear that an attempt on his part to abolish them might lead to contention. That was why, on occasion, he forced himself to condone a custom that, at first blush, appeared to be in conflict with a talmudic law. The rabbis of the Talmud showed great understanding even for deliberate deviations from the accepted norm. In any discussion of custom, they paid due consideration to the necessity for avoiding dissension. Needless to say, given such talmudic precedents, R. Hai attached great significance to this important consideration of communal welfare in all the cases brought before him. However, he categorically and uncompromisingly rejected any custom that clearly deviated from the explicit way of talmudic halakhah.

The picture was altogether different in Ashkenaz. First, extravagant homage was paid to custom in the words and writings of the early Ashkenazim. It was they who coined the phrase "the custom of our fathers is Torah,"[32] which constituted the credo of Orthodox Jewry in that part of the Jewish world. It was they who upheld the authority of custom even when it contradicted the talmudic sources and was demonstrably erroneous: "Although it seems that

30 Custom enjoyed a similar status in Roman law. See C.K. Alien's summary in his great work *Law in the Making*, 7th ed. (1964), pp. 80–86.

31 A detailed description of R. Hai Gaon's position may be found in Tzvi Groner's work "Rav Hai Gaon and His Halachic Methodology," Ph.D. dissertation (Jerusalem: Hebrew University 1974), pp. 135–187 (Heb.).

32 According to S. Abramson: "At present it seems that the first source is the statement of R. Isaac b. R. Judah" (*Inyanot be-Sifrut ha-Geonim*, p. 284).

you are correct...this is what we have seen of the custom of the ancients...do not budge from it" (*Ma'aseh ha-Ge'onim*, p. 14). Rashi agrees:

> [With regard to] the question about saying [in our liturgy] "*ha-Melekh ha-Misphat*" ["the king the justice"]; i.e., that we should rather say "*Melekh ha-Mishpat*," I have been asked the same question for many years, and my heart tells me that the cantors, in their haste, made the error of becoming accustomed to saying "*ha-Melekh ha-Misphat*," because they were thinking of "*ha-Melekh ha-Kadosh*" [i.e., "the holy King," which, unlike "*Ha-Melekh ha-Misphat*," is correct Hebrew], but lest we change ancient custom, we should rely on several Biblical verses that [did, indeed,] use such turns of phrase..." (Responsa of Rashi, ed. Israel Elfenbein, 1943, sec. 18).

Even when custom cannot be reconciled with halakhah and cannot be adequately explained, one ought to observe it as sacred:

> R. Yakar—may his memory be a blessing—wrote: I noted the following custom in Speyer on a Sabbath that actually was the Ninth of Av [when the fast is postponed until the next day], or was it the eighth of Av: At the final meal before [beginning] the fast, they eat no meat at all [even though it is still the Sabbath], but rather eggs and fruit; they sit at the table [and not on low stools or on the ground] because of the honor due to the Sabbath...I wondered about this, yet it is forbidden to question them for they [i.e., customs] are all precious. (*Shibbolei ha-Leket*, sec. 266).

R. Nathan, R. Yakar's brother, replied as follows to an inquiry from one R. Joshua (who apparently lived in Bohemia) about the permissibility of abolishing a particular marriage custom:

> It is customary in our parts that they draw up a *ketubah* on a Friday and sign it after the Sabbath, and sometimes they also form a *kinyan* with a *ketubah* written on a Friday. And he [R. Nathan] reprimanded: What need is there to question the custom of the holy communities from the saintly days of the sages of old in Mayence...who never appealed or protested—all of them precious and sweet? And praise be to the Guardian of Israel they are not doing anything wrong, because that is their custom, and they have proof and support [for what they do]. Who knows why it was their custom to begin their wedding feasts on the Sabbath? Perhaps it was because of severe poverty among the majority of the congregation... (ibid., p. 55, and cf. more detailed, important parallel in *Shibbolei ha-Leket*, Part 2, sec. 59).

R. Nathan reports:

> I heard [it reported] in the name of R. Isaac b. R. Judah may the Garden of Eden be his resting place, that when he was asked why it is our custom to read the *haftarah* on *Simhat Torah* from the first chapter of the Book of Joshua (contrary to the specifications in the Talmud, *Megilla* 31a) he replied that we follow custom, because custom cancels the law (*Sefer ha-Pardes*, p. 353).

Likewise:

> When R. Isaac b. R. Judah was asked about [the permissibility of a] tile roof for a Sukkah, he permitted it without reservations, because this is the custom of the people, and custom should not be changed (*Makhzor Vitry*, p. 413).

Compare this to the following reply given by R. Isaac b. R. Judah (according to *Shibbolei ha-Leket*, sec. 23) when he was asked for the source of the custom in which a *kohen* refrains from reciting the Birkath Kohanim while he is in mourning:

> On this matter our teacher [R. Isaac b. R. Judah] found no explicit support, but he said: "It is not for no [good reason] that they act thus, for any *kohen* who refrains from reciting the Priestly Blessing violates three positive commandments and yet this *kohen* sits idle and does nothing [thus apparently violating these commandments]." And he said: "It seems to me that the reason for this custom is as follows: That he who rises to bestow this blessing must be in a joyful mood [when he does so]." And the Master said that it is a *mitzvah* to observe the customs of earlier generations to the greatest possible extent, for we find in the Jerusalem Talmud that custom cancels halakhah and we have found the same [dictum] in our own Babylonian Talmud.

Similarly, the author of the cited section in *Sefer ha-Pardes* (Ehrenreich, p. 329) writes, after explaining the custom of taking three paces forward and [then three paces] backward at the beginning and at the end of the Amidah (giving an explanation that is both intrinsically difficult and without foundation in the Talmud):

> Hear, my son, the instruction of your father and do not forsake the teaching of your mother [Prov 1:8]. It is proper and right that you must follow all this, as is the custom of the leading figures [of your community], even if the support for it is weak. This applies all the more to the custom of the ancients [who went] before us. Scripture states: "Go your way by the footsteps of the flock and feed your young goats" [SoS 1:8]. All these customs were not adopted without reason but because it was seen that they were good customs. [Therefore] do not turn from them, neither to the right nor to the left."

In a similar vein, the early Ashkenazim had already written to their brethren in "Sepharad" [the Iberian peninsula], who apparently had attempted to influence them to adopt their own custom with regard to the text of the *birkat ha-erusin*: "You must realize that we will not adopt your custom, nor will we turn to the right or to the left from the custom of our ancient Geonim, the sages and pure of knowledge...."[33]

[33] The exchange of letters was cited by Simha Assaf from the work *Shibbolei ha-Leket* in his article "Halifat Mikhtavim bein Yehudei Ashkenaz u-Sepharad" and included in his book *Mekorot u-Mehkarim* (Jerusalem 1946), pp. 119–129. Assaf was not correct in his assumption that the first letter (ibid., pp. 126–127) was, indeed, a letter from the men of

Not only did the Ashkenazim honor customs that involved action, but they considered as custom even the act of abstaining from certain behavior. Thus, R. Eliyakim b. R. Joseph of Metz, father-in-law of R. Eliezer b. Nathan of Mayence (Raban), who was active in Mayence at the turn of the twelfth century, writes in an epistle of reproof to the scholars of Cologne:

> Concerning the building erected for your synagogue in Cologne, where they drew figures of lions and serpents on the northern wall: I wondered very much why they [the scholars of Cologne] should have done this, deviating from ancient custom in accordance with which our precursors never did such a thing in any of the places where they were exiled. Surely it is obvious to my teachers that the customs of the ancients are perfect Torah and a firm hook to grasp. Though their intention was [for the sake of] heaven, to beautify themselves in *mitzvot* before their Creator, we were warned in the Second Commandment against doing that... (*Raviah*, 1049, published in Jerusalem, 5736 [1975/76], pp. 9–10).[34]

The very fact that customs are handed down from generation to generation vouches for their authenticity. Regarding the aforementioned *ketubah* that was drawn up on a Friday and signed after the Sabbath, R. Nathan states in the complete text of his reply that has been preserved in *Shibbolei ha-Leket* (Part 2, sec. 59):

> Whosoever questions [the validity of] these *ketubot* would thereby invalidate the *ketubah* of his own wife, his own mother and his own grandmother. Therefore, we have no cause to worry about this.

For this reason, the above-mentioned sages of Mayence did not protest, "so as not to cast aspersions on the *ketubot* of their mothers."

It is considered axiomatic that earlier generations were always superior to those that followed them, and that the past, as a whole, was better than the present, becoming better the farther back we go.[35] It is considered unnecessary

"Sepharad" to those of "Ashkenaz," as he states in his title, and that the former wrote it in response to an earlier question that the sages of Ashkenaz had addressed to them, as is requested in the text of that reply. Both the title Assaf gave to his article and his views in this connection are incomplete.

34 The reply from the scholars of Cologne has not survived, but it seems that they did not see anything wrong in violating "negative" custom, even though it may have represented a historical standpoint (but see, for example, the synagogue of Dura Europos), and they did not view this innovation as an obstacle since they regarded it as permissible *per se*. R. Ephraim the Great in Ashkenaz likewise permitted it, and other communities also followed this practice. It may be worthwhile to consider the chronological proximity between the interest in the permissibility of paintings on the windows of the Cologne synagogue and the first appearance of stained-glass windows in European churches during the first half of the twelfth century, when the Gothic style first infiltrated into church architecture.

35 This is the meaning implicit in the ancient prayer "Restore our judges as at first, and our counselors as at the beginning." This interpretation has a firm basis in the words of the

to verify the claim that the sages of the past were greater than those of the present, and it is self-evident that the ancient customs bear the stamp of approval from those ancients; the binding force of these customs is as great as if they had been hewn from the talmudic sources and high in the order of sanctity. Customs of "[the house of] our teacher" are often cited in *Ma'aseh ha-Ge'onim* as models to emulate and, as indicated in the book itself, at the beginning of the section on "Blessings," the teacher's customs are methodically listed: "The custom of our teacher is Torah, and I must learn it." This statement is followed by a list of the customs of "our teacher" and those of R. Kalonymus. "Our teacher" conducted his life and that of his household according to the model he had seen among his own teachers, and not only he but also the other great scholars mentioned in *Ma'aseh ha-Ge'onim* did so. To quote R. Nathan ha-Makhiri: "I believe that R. Kalonymus the Elder did well...and that was his custom, which he heard from his grandfather, our great teacher R. Eliezer, may his resting place be in the Garden of Eden" (p. 22). R. Eliezer, too, surely did not make any innovations in this regard, but in all probability did as he had seen his own teachers do. This is the fixed assumption in all the rabbinic literature under consideration in this study: there is no glorious past that was not preceded by a past that was even more magnificent.

Because of these and other considerations, custom acquired a place of honor at the top rung of the halakhic ladder; it alone was above all doubt or debate, insured against the possibility of error. Error is a normal, almost routine fact in the dialectical give-and-take of written and traditional halakhah because the latter is "renewed" each day by its students, who constantly reveal new aspects of the sources according to their own scholastic level, the needs of their generation, their personal authority, and the conclusions hammered out in mutual argument among colleagues. The function of debate is to come closer to the truth, but it is well known that this objective is seldom attained, and the multiplicity of opinions generally tends to obscure the *middah* of truth even if categorical enactment wins the day. Custom is different: by its very definition it is infallible, not subject to debate or contradiction.

sages: "The hearts of the ancients were like the gate of the *ulam* (vestibule) [of the Temple] but those of the later generations were like the gate of the *hekhal* [less great] and ours are like the eye of a fine needle" (Eruvin 53a), and "If the ancients were like angels, then we are like men, and if they were like men, then we are like donkeys." This attitude is the basis of every conservative *Weltanschauung*; this distinction between the "ancients" and the "later generations" holds good to this very day. It was the basic concept that underlay the "sealing" of the Mishnah and the Talmud, preventing the sages of the Talmud from engaging in any dispute with the sages of the Mishnah and making it impossible for the post-talmudic sages to dispute that which had been set down in the Talmud. The gathering of the Children of Israel at Mount Sinai, which took place when the Jewish people began their life, was also the high point of its history. From that event on, the nation has moved away from Sinai not only in a chronological sense but spiritually as well. See the conclusion of Ta-Shema, "Hilkheta ke-Batrai," *Shenaton ha-Mishpat ha-Ivri* 6–7 (1979–80).

Moreover, custom is not only superior to halakhic innovation by virtue of its more solid base, but it is said to be even dearer to God than biblical law. R. Isaac ha-Levi, one of Rashi's teachers, writes with regard to the removal of the sinew from the thighs of animals that do not come under the classification of cattle (i.e., they are classed as *hayyot*, not *behemot*):

> Our rabbis made no distinction between *hayyah* and *behemah* except as regards the *helev* [suet] that is offered up on the altar, but the sinew and whatever derives from it is prohibited as in the case of a *behemah*...And [as for] the *shuman* [fat], Israel is holy and has accepted the prohibition against it [See *Hulin* 91a], and the prohibition against *shuman* is as strict as the Biblical prohibition.... Moreover, we have learned [*Eruvin* 21b]: 'My son, be careful about the words of the *soferim* even more than about the words of the Torah.' The assertion that the holy people of Israel have accepted the prohibition is considered as the words of the *soferim*; that is why it is necessary to be so stringent about this" (Responsa, *Rashi*, sec. 64).

Thus, the usual order is stood on its head and has become ambivalent: the punishment for violating a biblical (*de-oraitha*) law is more severe; nevertheless, custom is considered far more important than law.

The study of early Ashkenazi customs is difficult because of the paucity of available sources, the thousand-year gap in time, and, most of all, because of their remoteness from the halakhic tradition of Babylonia and their greater propinquity to the world of law and precedent in *Eretz Israel* and to the world of aggadah and liturgical poetry. It is becoming increasingly clear that the origin of many customs is to be found in the halakhic tradition of *Eretz Israel*, which in its day was normative in every respect. It apparently prevailed in Italy prior to the dissemination of the Babylonian Talmud and before the latter became the final authority at a date we cannot determine, when the halakhic tradition of *Eretz Israel* gradually gave way to that of Babylonia. In many areas however, primarily that of ritual, the old practices continued to persist as in the past, acquiring the force of *minhag* and, in the process, gaining authority superior to that of the theoretical halakhah: a position not open to doubt or debate. Undoubtedly what is being discussed here is a slow, continuous process, not a single event, in the wake of which the ancient halakhah of *Eretz Israel* was "kicked upstairs" as it were, to become sacred "custom"—side by side with the regular halakhah derived from the Babylonian Talmud. Nor is there any doubt that eleventh-century Ashkenazi literature reflects a very advanced stage of this process, when the outcome of that process was already a *fait-accompli*. The Babylonian Talmud did, indeed, stand at the center of halakhic thinking and of the yeshiva curriculum in Germany, but many practices continued to exist independently of this talmudic tradition because of their antiquity They were vestiges of another halakhic norm that had prevailed in the remote past and now enjoyed the enhanced authority of *minhag*—which in Ashkenaz protected those ritual details that found shelter beneath its umbrella. In several instances this conception of custom corresponds well—fortuitously or not—to that of the Jerusalem Talmud, as explained elsewhere;[36] it is possible then, that this special conception also is rooted in ancient traditions that had their origin in *Eretz Israel.*

And again one encounters an interesting similarity between a chain of events that clearly took place within Judaism, on the one hand, and a process in general history that unfolded on the outside, on the other. At this time, Germany had a judicial system based on the principle of local custom, in the most narrow geographical sense of the term—custom as defined by the local elders rather than on the basis of a broad, generalized structure of laws set down in writing and endowed with binding force. Of course, this is a reflection of the ignorance and illiteracy that pervaded most sectors of that society. Even more this reflects the basic tribal fragmentation of the German people and the great variations of local, family, and class practices that had taken hold among them. In any event, this legal structure served as a genuinely "national" element in Germany, so that students of law in Germany, from the Middle Ages to the nineteenth century, continued to argue profoundly for the role of custom and tradition as ideal guides to the legal structure. During the nineteenth century this "popular" conception was revived by leading German jurists, who introduced it into top-level academic discussion.[37]

RABBIS AND THEIR DISCIPLES

This tension between halakhah and practice, between the scholarly study of texts and the canonization of popular custom, between the recognized authority of the Babylonian Talmud and the principle of unwritten law—i.e., that "the custom of our fathers is Torah," which is to be given preference—is one of the most significant characteristics of eleventh-century rabbinic literature. It finds expression in the pedagogical system of the time as well as in the framework of teacher-disciple relationships, the strict discipline and supervision over the course of studies, and the narrowing of the intellectual freedom accorded to students.

Here, too, we lack detailed information about the practical conditions under which this structure operated. It is clear that the students were constantly in the immediate environment of their teacher, as indicated earlier—in his courtyard, his kitchen, his bedroom, etc. The following is an example of a teacher-disciple discussion on a problem of daily life:

> This is what happened: R. Shelomo did the following with a young man who got married. They made the wedding at the house of R. Shelomo and all the dishes that had been cooked for the feast were set out in a neighboring house.

[36] Cf. my comprehensive article on Ashkenazi custom between the tenth and twelfth centuries, mentioned above, n. 22.

[37] C.K. Alien, *Law in the Making*, pp. 87ff.

> However, [the Sabbath came and] they had forgotten to construct an *eruv* before the Sabbath. [As a result, they could not carry the dishes from the house of one to that of the other.] So they asked R. Shelomo [what they should do] and he told them: "Bring the owner of that other house [to me] and I will cancel my ownership of my own house in his favor." And the owner of the neighboring house came, and R. Shelomo did, indeed, cancel his ownership of his own house. Thereupon they asked: "Should he [the owner of the neighboring house] not also cancel his ownership in *your* favor?" [R. Shelomo] said: "If he did that, then what is his would be mine and what is mine would be his..." [and that would not solve the problem]. We then asked our teacher: "Why should *you* cancel your ownership? Let the [neighboring] householder cancel *his* ownership in your favor instead...." (*Siddur Rashbash*, p. 264, and parallel works).

In all these instances, which primarily involve sages of the generation of R. Isaac b. R. Judah and his disciples, the students attending their teacher speak as an anonymous body—a chorus without a soloist, as it were. They do not develop a true give-and-take discussion with their teacher. Rather, they seek to understand, by means of their own simple questions and the terse answers given by the teacher, how every detail of their teacher's behavior "accords with halakhah." One can readily see the full extent of the teacher's responsibility, how careful a teacher had to be in his every action, for whatever he did was automatically regarded as a final, authoritative model of halakhah. Moreover, given the small number of Jews at the time, the disciples, too, gained a guiding influence over the community even before they were authorized to issue halakhic rulings. The following is an excerpt from a responsum by Rabbenu Gershom:

> People were playing at nuts all afternoon one Sabbath until it was time for *minkhah* services. Some [of the players] won; some lost....When the matter came before the [leaders of the] community, they wanted to fine and penalize them. In answer to this they protested, arguing that "there had been a student in our presence who misled us, for we saw him playing, borrowing and returning, giving and taking like one of us...

The student to whom they referred was surely not one of the star disciples at his yeshiva, for Rabbenu Gershom comments: "[It was] That student who set aside the affairs of heaven when he should have been occupying himself with [things] eternal, and, instead, went and busied himself with inappropriate pursuits..." (Kupfer, *Teshuvot u-Pesakim*, Jerusalem 5734 F1973/741 p. 315).

The tension between the ambition to preserve all customs in exact detail, as accepted by tradition, and at the same time to safeguard the free investigation of halakhic sources, is aptly illustrated in the following account by one of the sons of Makhir. This excerpt recounts a halakhic discussion between this individual and his teacher about the kashrut of cheese from the milk of an animal that, when it was subsequently slaughtered, had been found to be *terefah*. The student discovered in *Halakhot Gedolot* (Venice ed., 135b) that if milk turns into cheese and afterward the animal from whose milk the cheese was made is slaughtered and found to be *terefah*, that cheese may not be eaten. On this basis, the student asked his teacher, should not all cheeses in the world be prohibited as food because of doubt, since surely some of the animals from whose milk the cheese is made will eventually be found to be *terefah*? This student then relates:

> My teacher rebuked me for probing so deeply into this matter....And then he answered me that nothing is presumed prohibited until it manifests the characteristics of a prohibition.

The next day his teacher corroborated his position with a proof taken from the *Halakhot Gedolot* itself, which establishes that the cheese is not forbidden unless it is clear to us beyond doubt that the animal was already *terefah* at the time it was milked—e.g., that it had already formed scar tissue from an injury at that stage. The student continues his story:

> I then asked him further: "According to your answer; i.e., that any animal is to be presumed kosher so long as no characteristic shows up that would render it prohibited, what are we to say about a case where the butcher removed the lung of an animal before [the lung] could be examined [to see whether it was damaged so as to make the animal *terefah*]?"

According to this teacher's view one should not, merely by reason of doubt, prohibit an animal whose lung had been lost before it could have been examined, for the animal must be presumed kosher until one finds a clear reason why it should be prohibited. Here the student, willy-nilly, touched upon the famous "lung dispute" in which Rashi stood alone against all of his teachers. They said that such an animal was prohibited, while he said that it was permitted. Rashi adduced one of his proofs from the precedent of this very question about cheese.[38]

In this argument, the student's position is identical to that of Rashi, though the student arrived at it as a result of having probed into the other matter with which he had been dealing. As reported by the student, the teacher gave this answer to his repeated query:

> He rebuked me severely for asking such a difficult question, but when [his anger] was appeased, he said [to me] in a whisper: "When something is permitted but there are others who prohibit it, you should not declare in their presence that it is permitted." And just as I myself was told this in a whisper, so I am passing it on to you in a whisper also.

The discussion between Rashi and his teachers about the "lung dispute," which has come down to us in part, is based on an analysis of talmudic material and is replete with proof texts, problems, and solutions, as is usually the case

38 A. (Victor) Aptowitzer, *Introductio ad Sefer Rabiah* (Jerusalem 1938), pp. 400–403.

in matters of Jewish law. In contrast to this, the procedure of the young scholars, who were trained in the presence of their teachers, was characterized by great circumspection during the eleventh century; their methods of study and scholastic development reflect stringent supervision. Students were rebuked by their teachers in order to keep them from probing too deeply into a particular matter; they were even "severely reprimanded" if they stubbornly continued to delve into a subject they had been told not to investigate. The teachers had no desire to give a student, who in their opinion was not yet qualified, the authority to hand down halakhic rulings lest this lead the student to act rashly, creating deviant paths and uprooting time-honored custom. At the same time, they did not want to hide from their disciples the truths derived from a full investigation of the sources. Therefore, they merely sought, by warning or discipline, to direct the student away from probing too deeply into a question until they considered him fit to do so. To be sure, those individuals who were preparing for rabbinic leadership and had an unquenchable thirst for study, men whose curiosity gave them no peace, persisted in their quest and were guided forward by their teachers with great care, very slowly and with "whisperings," to the knowledge they sought. Such a method of study was no longer prevalent during the twelfth century, the period of the Tosafists. On the contrary, study at the tosafist *yeshivot* required the widest possible scope of investigation and the presentation of all questions and answers for collegial discussion. By that time the way of "whisperings" had passed from the world.

LITURGICAL POETRY AND MYSTICISM

One of the principal aspects of worship that clearly had its origins in *Eretz Israel*, without any basis in the Babylonian Talmud and its traditions, is the *piyyut*.

The first of these sacred poems, which were standard accompaniment to the festival service, were created in *Eretz Israel*, which remained their source for several centuries. The *piyyutim* served a significant function in congregational worship, offering the cantor a set of alternative selections to be recited at the parts of the service for which they were intended.

From the viewpoint of halakhah, on the other hand, *piyyutim*—particularly those that were elaborate—presented a constant, intractable problem because they disrupted the order of prayer at junctures where such interruptions are expressly prohibited. Nevertheless, the recitation of *piyyutim* spread; they were read in all the congregations of Germany and France and eventually in Jewish communities throughout eastern Europe.

The halakhic problem posed by *piyyutim* was already addressed early in the eleventh century by Rabbenu Gershom. He mentions a *haver* who sought to forbid the recitation of *piyyutim*. Rabbenu Gershom argues for unrestricted permissiveness in this area; in his responsum he makes reference to a distinguished list of liturgical poets, among them scholars of the Italo-Ashkenaz culture who, at the same time, were preeminent in the study of Jewish law. In this, as in other areas, the Ashkenazim followed their own ancestral traditions, which reached back to Italy, where *piyyutim* of *Eretz Israel* and local provenance had flourished for many generations and had, in fact, brought forth quite a few poetic offshoots. The recitation of *piyyutim* became a hallmark of Ashkenazi prayer; apart from these *piyyutim*, there is no essential difference between the structure of Ashkenazi liturgy and that of other diaspora communities. Like the other liturgies, that of Ashkenaz is essentially "Babylonian."

In terms of the sources and motifs that nourish them, as well as in language, syntax, and general style, the *piyyutim* form a foreign body, as it were, in the liturgy. Sometimes they are so complicated as to be virtually unintelligible to the reader. This is true particularly of the wide selection of early *Eretz Israel piyyutim* that Ashkenazim recited in their worship, such as those of Yannai and R. Elazar ha-Kallir, Solomon the Babylonian, and the early Italian *payyetanim*, which require a running commentary and systematic listing of sources in order to be understood even at the most superficial level. Yet they were so popular that the great scholars of Ashkenaz themselves wrote *piyyutim* on the same order, with the same motifs and the same spirit, into which they invested considerable intellectual effort. Such men as Meshulam b. R. Moses Kalonymus, Simeon b. R. Isaac b. R. Abun, R. Elijah the Elder, and R. Joseph b. Samuel Tov Elem (Joseph b. Samuel Bonfils) are famous not only for the many *piyyutim* they composed but also for their halakhic rulings and the spiritual leadership they wielded among their contemporaries.

Already in the second half of the eleventh century, a literary activity began in Ashkenaz that spread widely during the two centuries that followed: the exegesis of the *piyyutim*. Among the sages who devoted their energies to this endeavor were R. Eliezer b. Nathan of Mayence, R. Elazar b. Isaac of Worms, and R. Abraham b. R. Ezriel of Bohemia. Contrary to scattered hints about Ashkenazi (or French) opposition to the recital of *piyyutim*, all the sages until the end of the twelfth century were ardent champions of the custom, using the language of threats and anathema against all opponents, including even those who merely wished to shift the *piyyutim* from the first three benedictions to the middle benedictions of the Shemoneh Esre, where the interpolation of *piyyutim* creates fewer halakhic problems in terms of the *halakhot* of prayer.

The constantly repeated defenses of the *piyyutim* imply that there must have been some opposition; but here, as in other areas, we note in the Ashkenazi-French literature a deliberate silencing, a sort of internal censorship, so that not so much as one line from the original writings of these opponents is known to us today.

Certain types of *piyyutim*, such as the *ophanim*, some of the *piyyutim* recited on the eve of Shavuoth, and the *piyyutim* for Rosh Hashanah and Yom Kippur, were devoted largely to descriptions of the world of mysticism as depicted in the *Merkavah* and in *midrashim* dealing with the *Merkavah* and angelology. These poems are replete with sublime angelology, including descriptions of the heavenly doxology recited by the angels, the seraphim, and the sacred *hayyot* before the Throne of Glory and the rivers of fire that surround the Throne. These mystical themes are close to the spirit of the *Shi'ur Komah* literature; they poeticize ancient texts from the *Hekhalot* literature that deal with the anthropomorphic dimensions of the Deity. Here, too, there was a set tradition to be followed. The works of Yannai and, occasionally, those of Kallir do not avoid this subject;[39] therefore, the Ashkenazi *payyetanim*, too, adopted the formula and improvised on the same theme. In no other circle of *payyetanim* do we find the same intensive involvement in these matters; this is a characteristic of Ashkenazi *piyyutim* and of the Ashkenazi mind as a whole.

The Ashkenazim had never been particularly given to philosophical investigation. Nevertheless, they had access to an early, anonymous, paraphrased translation of R. Saadia Gaon's *Emunoth ve-De'oth* (*Beliefs and Opinions*; originally written in Arabic and later translated into Hebrew by R. Judah Ibn Tibbon in 1186), which categorically opposes anthropomorphic portrayals of the Deity. Anthropomorphic characterizations of God that occur in the Bible are interpreted as referring not to the invisible Deity but only to His "Revealed Glory." The paraphrase was composed in a solemn, exalted style and its author was, therefore, willing to sacrifice accuracy. The translator succeeded in offering classical philosophical formulations as descriptions of a living Deity.[40]

The study of this book, to which they attributed great authority, caused the Ashkenazim to moderate their anthropomorphic position and to reformulate it during the twelfth century in the theological doctrine of *Hasidei Ashkenaz*. This remarkable doctrine rejected all anthropomorphic conceptions of the hidden God Himself, replacing them with an extreme corporealization of His environment, from the "Revealed Glory" down to the lowest angel. In the eleventh century *piyyut*, however, these signs of change are not yet evident. They are absent also from Rashi's commentary on the Talmud. Rashi does not seek to reinterpret or to rationalize the many *aggadot* that, according to their straightforward meaning, present God in anthropomorphic terms. Rashi limits himself to explaining the difficult terms and the syntax, as he does in other loci throughout his talmudic commentary.

But even the anti-anthropomorphist line of Saadia Gaon did not prevent many devout Ashkenazi Jews from adhering to the old line. Their position found a clear and remarkable expression in the *K'tav Tamim* of R. Moshe Taku, who was active in Germany or Bohemia during the first third of the thirteenth century. This book has survived only in the form of one incomplete

39 Z.M. Rabinowitz, *Halakhah and Aggadah in the Liturgical Poetry of Yannai* (Tel Aviv 1965), pp. 62–64 (Heb.).

40 Dan, *The Esoteric Theology*, pp. 22–24.

manuscript, undoubtedly because of attempts to suppress it. The author openly attacks the views held by most of the Ashkenazi sages of his day, who regarded the "Revealed Glory" as the subject of all anthropomorphic attributes in the Bible and in rabbinic literature. He accuses Saadia, Maimonides, R. Abraham Ibn Ezra, and even R. Judah he-Hasid of holding views rooted in foreign ideas and in a "know-it-all" philosophy and of improperly depriving us of the anthropomorphization of God in accordance with the straightforward meaning of the Scriptural text, which is one of the central signs of God's vitality, free will, and omnipotence. This book, one of the most magnificent and impressive works we have from the medieval period, reflects correctly (as far as we can tell) the principles of Ashkenazi mysticism as it existed during the eleventh century (and no doubt also earlier) and enables us to understand more authentically the historical significance of those majestic *Merkabah piyyutim* so dear to the early Ashkenazim.

KIDDUSH HA-SHEM AND *KIDDUSH HA-HAYYIM*
HALLOWING GOD'S NAME IN MARTYRDOM AND IN LIFE

The theology outlined above, which reflects a great deal of psychological intimacy with God in the form of both love and awe, is closely bound up with the shattering phenomenon of *Kiddush ha-Shem* (the hallowing of God's Name) in the form of martyrdom suffered by the communities of Ashkenaz—young and old, men, women, and children—during the terrible period of the First Crusade at the end of the eleventh century. We know the chronicles dating from that period, in which mass martyrdom is depicted so vividly that even the present-day reader can be moved to tears. It has already been noted[41] that there is a connection between this lofty ideal of martyrdom and certain conceptions of the Deity as discussed above. Several indications of this can be found even in the remnants of the eleventh-century literature and particularly in the historiography of the first half of the twelfth century.

In reading the accounts of this martyrdom, one is left with a feeling of profound awe rather than with horror. The full formal benediction recited before undergoing martyrdom and said with the awareness that "it is ordained in the decree of the King [of heaven]; therefore, let us fall into the hand of the Lord and come to see the Great Light" attests to the sanctification of life that preceded the sanctification of God's name by martyrdom. Those who were part of that generation could feel this, too, and it contributed to their sense of astonishment at the events, making the questions they addressed to heaven all the more agonizing. At the same time, this feeling gave rise to an explanation that sounds quite harsh: the decree does not come as a punishment for sins but

41 I. Baer, "The Religious-Social Tendency of 'Sefer Hasidim'" (Heb.), *Zion* 3 (1938), pp. 3–4.

as a trial intended to test a righteous generation that could be trusted to pass the test. It is compared to the binding of Isaac upon the altar, which also was a test administered to one (Abraham) who was judged capable of passing it. The difference, however, is that while Isaac was never actually sacrificed, the sacrifice of these martyrs—a thousand times greater—was, indeed, carried out with unparalleled cruelty.[42]

Side by side with these transcendental tendencies, which were deeply rooted in the life of the Jews of Ashkenaz, one must appreciate the solid material standing of these same generations, who enjoyed considerable economic prosperity and personal security. Their involvement in domestic and international trade carried Jews from Ashkenaz to far-flung corners of the world. Some of these traveling merchants were also rabbis and great talmudic scholars. The established economic position of many sages who, in addition to being prosperous businessmen, were decisors, *parnassim*, and leaders of the Jewish community, thus attaining considerable power, is typical of the Jews of Ashkenaz. For this reason there developed in Ashkenaz the tradition that rabbinic scholars, even those with no other profession, were not exempt from paying taxes imposed upon other Jews. Although this was in contradiction to a clear talmudic ruling, they shared the tax burden with everyone else.[43] No such cancellations of tax exemption outside the Ashkenaz community are known;[44] hence, they may be identified as yet another trait typical of Ashkenazi Jewry.

THE HISTORICAL IMAGE OF ASHKENAZI JEWRY: A SKETCH

The image of Ashkenazi Jewry, rabbis and plain folk alike, is uniquely varied and complex. It derives from the dual nature of the forces that governed them, the ideals that motivated them, and their own unique religious *Weltanschauung*. The dominant Babylonian influence is noted side by side with pronounced historic submission, conscious and unconscious, to the tradition of *Eretz Israel*; the conception of halakhah as the basic value alongside a practical and much more concrete commitment to precedent established by custom, and the profound dichotomy that resulted from these antitheses; metaphysical and mystical tendencies alongside material solidity and economic success—a ladder erected on earth, as it were, whose top reached into heaven. One notes

42 S. Spiegel, "Legend of Isaac's Slaying and Resurrection," in *Alexander Marx Jubilee* Volume, Hebrew Section (New York 1950), pp. 471–547. See also Y.H. Yerushalmi, *Zakhor* (New York 1980), pp. 37–39.

43 I. Ta-Shema, "Al Petor Talmidei Hakhamim mi-Missim bi-Yimei ha-Beinaim," in *Sefer ha-Yovel le-Ezra Z. Melamed* (Jerusalem 1982), pp. 312–323.

44 B. Septimus, "Kings, Angels or Beggars—Tax Law and Spirituality in a Hispano-Jewish Responsum," in *Studies in Medieval Jewish History and Literature* 2 (Cambridge: Harvard University Press, 1984).

a broad intellectual openness, on the one hand, and a strict discipline in following tradition and great care in teaching and education, on the other. Rabbinic literature is seen as absolutely authoritative in its basic substance but at the same time open to radical change through its textual variants. All these factors contributed to the complexity of the picture and fertilized the spiritual world of Ashkenaz.

In general, Ashkenazi creativity reflects the delicate balance between the opposing forces that strove within it, but sometimes we note the triumph of one tendency, one personality, or one defined period acting to upset the balance, suppressing the moderating elements. At these junctures we encounter extreme positions on both sides of the spectrum, formulated boldly and sharply by their spokesmen. Some of these extremes are quite startling because they are rarities outside the Ashkenazi camp. The dual nature of Ashkenazi culture, the oscillation between polar opposites moving toward a traditional consensus, led to the development of individualism—as opposed to stereotyped conventionality—as the basic quality of every scholar and, therefore, the basic quality of the religious-social leadership on all levels.

One of the contributing factors to this basic quality was the framework of elementary education that had flourished in Ashkenaz from time immemorial and that was based on the assumption that the primary mission of the Jew in this world was to study the Torah and to educate his children for Torah, *mitzvot* and the fear of heaven. As a result of this religious axiom, there was hardly a Jewish child—unless he was completely lacking in ability—who had not acquired at least some knowledge of Torah before he submitted to the yoke of earning a living. (One must remember that this was an era when ignorance and illiteracy were endemic among the vast majority of the non-Jewish populace.) Thus, the Ashkenazim who lived in urban communities were quite educated, a fact that helped accentuate individualism at the higher levels of scholarship and made for the adoption of strongly divergent positions.

This proclivity to extremes is evident also in the deep-seated Ashkenazi tendency to take a strict line in religious observance whenever possible. This tendency is clearly in evidence during the eleventh century; it gradually declines during the twelfth century, only to reappear during the middle of the thirteenth century. This adherence to the strict line was not primarily motivated by a desire to escape uncertainty (and the punishment for making the wrong choice)—though this factor, of course, exists as well—but rather by a desire to attain perfection in the service of God as an end in itself, distinct from the cold, logical-judicial consideration of the formal processes of halakhic decision. Such a tendency attributes intrinsic and paramount value precisely to the extreme position. It views the practical determination of the halakhah in any question as a legal compromise that is perhaps adequate as a halakhic minimum for the exigencies of practical life, but not as a response to the deeper requirement of the halakhah, which is to govern and sanctify every aspect of life. Hence the dictum "the follower of the strict line—may a blessing be upon him" became the most frequently used phrase in Ashkenazi literature throughout the generations. As far as we can tell, it is the Ashkenazim who first introduced it.

RASHI

There is no doubt that Rashi represents the best in Ashkenazi Jewry and the pinnacle of individual creativity in Ashkenaz. Immediately following him, and in clear relation to him and his work, came the achievement of the Tosafists. Theirs was an endeavor that, over a period of two centuries, occupied the best scholarly talents, who developed a new methodology of talmudic study, utilizing a variety of "modern" approaches (e.g., logic, jurisprudence, and scholasticism) that began to flourish, primarily in France, only decades later. This, however, is a collective achievement involving dozens, if not hundreds, of scholars coming from many *yeshivot*, great and small, studying together and writing their novel interpretations "in the presence of their teachers." Rashi's commentary on the Talmud, by contrast, is the individual product of the creative spirit enclosed within its own four cubits. Though Rashi made thorough use of the commentaries of his teachers and of the anonymous "Mayence commentaries," the structure, the final form, the editing, the style, the brilliant formulation, the choice of commentaries, and many of the interpretations themselves are his own, often explicitly opposed to what he had learned from his teachers. It is needless to say that the same is true of his commentary on the Bible, for which there is no precedent.

Since the time of its composition, Rashi's commentary has become the constant and perpetual companion text for any study of the Talmud, to the point where it has become an integral part of such study. Though it helped a great deal that Rashi adopted the style already described above—i.e., the *sub verbum*, which places the explanation into the framework of the text—the primary factor that has given this unique status to his commentary is Rashi's rare didactic sensitivity, which enabled him to determine exactly where to add the few words of elucidation that the student requires in order to move on safely through the text. Add to this Rashi's language: It is remarkably precise, terse, and well-defined, but at the same time it has an unusual artistic-literary quality and a sublime, peerless humility, consistently suppressing the author's ego, so that the voice seems to be speaking out of the text itself. It seems as if these very words had already been spoken in the days of the Amoraim and that the commentary before us is merely a channel through which these words are transmitted to us; a record that goes back to the ancients and whose fidelity is beyond question. It seems almost as if Rashi's novel interpretations, to which we alluded above and which disagree with those of his teacher, are stated against the commentator's own will. Rashi speaks quietly and modestly, confining himself to terse explanations, as if he had been compelled to do so by his sense of obligation to truth and by the internal logic of the original sources. With all this, one notes Rashi's deep involvement in the talmudic discourse, how effectively and yet how gently he imposes his conception of the text on the reader, from the quiet, almost silent *hakhi garsinan* ("this is the correct reading") to his open disagreements with his teachers. A study of the many debates that Tosafists conduct with Rashi's commentary on every page of the Talmud is sufficient to grasp the depth of Rashi's involvement with the text.

The depth of Rashi's penetration and involvement, on the one hand, and his almost anonymous modesty of technique and style, on the other, are much more important characteristics of his commentary on the Talmud than other components that, at first blush, may appear more prominent but that lack significance for the evaluation of Rashi's oeuvre. A simple illustration is Rashi's tendency toward lexicographic verbalism (a characteristic of eleventh-century scholarship), which can be discerned on almost every page. Today, when thousands of the vernacular equivalents included in Rashi's commentary are no more understood by the reader than the words they were intended to explain, the contemporary reader can omit them without difficulty, using some other lexicographic resource to fill in what is missing, and will lose nothing thereby.

It is one of Rashi's important achievements that his commentaries on the discussion in each talmudic tractate derive from a unified conception of the content of that tractate: the basic, universally accepted halakhic principles, the primary (and secondary) disputes among the Tannaim in the *Mishna*, *Baraitot*, and *Tosefta* and those of Amoraim in the Talmud, the interdependence of their principles and disagreements and the consistent way of resolving these disagreements and the problems emanating from them. Within the framework of each tractate Rashi adopts a clear, unified approach to these questions, for which he assumes responsibility to the reader from the beginning of the tractate to its end. All the discussions in the tractate are adapted to this fundamental conception, along with whatever compromises and difficulties this may necessitate. Rashi never explicitly states his basic approach in any one place; he does so only in a fragmentary, discrete manner. It becomes evident to the student only after long, continued, arduous study of the tractate and its commentators. As was noted earlier, the value of Rashi is greatest for a student reviewing the *sugya*, not for a first-time reader. What Rashi offers to the comprehending and experienced student is the reassurance that the student's understanding of the discussion is, indeed, correct and will not be refuted by what may yet come up in other parts of the tractate.

As a rule, Rashi's assumption of this responsibility does not extend beyond the limits of one tractate; however, it often takes into consideration parallel discussions in other tractates. This is the source of a phenomenon that astonished both the early commentators and more recent scholars. Rashi was careful about consistency within the framework of a single tractate, but not from one tractate to another—not even when he dealt with discussions that were virtually parallel and identical in both tractates. The same words, sentences, and even logical sequences are often explained differently from one tractate to the next. The accepted view is that in each tractate Rashi preserved the exegetical principles he had heard from his teacher for that particular tractate;[45] but this, of course, cannot be proven. At the same time, within the limits of each tractate, the reader will not discern any external signs of editing, emendation, additions, or changes in form style, or level, despite the fact that Rashi wrote his commentary over a period of many years and had not yet completed it when he died.

The outstanding quality of Rashi's commentary that makes it suitable for every student of reasonable attainment is remarkable, as is the fact that the benefits derived from the commentary rise in proportion to the competence of the student. The more competent he is, the better he will become able to distinguish, or at least believe he is able to distinguish, the allusions and oblique references in what is stated in Rashi and what is omitted there and plumb the "depths of Rashi's intention." This phenomenon has great practical significance even when the student is in error and has failed to capture Rashi's true intention, because it helps the student extract more from himself. This trait in Rashi enables the student to progress in his work with Rashi's help: no student ever outgrows Rashi's commentary. No matter to what heights he may soar, he will still find Rashi's commentary standing at his right hand, supporting him in his attempts to rise even higher—as high as his abilities will permit. Correspondingly, the reader's respect for the immeasurable greatness of Rashi and his commentary will also increase, along with the conviction that Rashi, indeed, saw everything, explained it all, and avoided problems everywhere, whether by explicit statement, by vague allusions, or even by silence. As is well known, an entire methodological literature has grown up along these lines.

Rashi's commentary on Pentateuch—to say nothing of his commentaries on the other books of the Bible—are not on this level, but they are even more popular than his commentary on the Talmud. His commentaries on Scripture hold a unique place of honor among the classics of the Jewish people. The same characteristics we discerned in the commentary on the Talmud may be noted in the commentaries on the Bible. If Rashi's commentary on the Talmud is based on the tradition of his teachers, his biblical commentary is based on the classic midrashic tradition—primarily that of the *Midrash Rabbah* and the *Tanhuma*—formulated in terse, clear, and precise terms, as responses to various didactic questions. Alongside this principal layer, Rashi added a layer of *peshat*—his own and that of others—based on Hebrew grammar and syntax, as

45 A. (Victor) Aptowitzer, "Le Toledot Perush Rashi la-Talmud" (Heb.), *Sefer Rashi* (Jerusalem 1956).

far as these were known in their infancy, or on the basis of alternate *midrashim*. In this work, Rashi's own individuality is completely suppressed, and he becomes the mouthpiece of the Midrash or of Hebrew grammar. Every verse in Rashi's commentary exudes great and moving warmth and feeling, full of love for God, for Torah, and for the land and people of Israel.

originally published in
Ashkenaz: The German Jewish Heritage,
ed. Gertrude Hirschler

CHAPTER 2

ON THE HISTORY OF THE JEWS IN TWELFTH AND THIRTEENTH-CENTURY POLAND*

THE PRESENT STATE OF RESEARCH

Jewish traders of Ashkenazi origin passed through Poland on their way to Russia on business as early as the first half of the eleventh century. A considerable amount of relevant material on this subject was assembled by F. Kupfer.[1] These itinerant Jews probably established some permanent settlements in various parts of Poland. Thus, we know of a Jewish presence in Cracow in the first half of the eleventh century. This presence included a regularly functioning religious court (*beit din*), empowered to issue religious rulings, to enforce its decisions, and to impose fines on Jews travelling through the city, in the spirit of—perhaps even inspired by—one of the *takanot* of Rabbenu Gershom Me'or ha-Golah. Our information touches upon a financial dispute; the problem, a complicated one, was briefly discussed by R. Judah ha-Kohen, author of *Sefer ha-Dinin* and a student of R. Gershom, who was active in Mayence during the first half of the eleventh century.[2] It is highly significant that most of our historical information about Jews in eleventh-century Poland derives from R. Judah's responsa. This is due to the regular communications on halakhic matters

* A highly abbreviated presentation of the following account was presented at the First International Congress for the Study of Polish Jewry, held at the Hebrew University, Jerusalem, in Jan. 1988. A Hebrew version of this article was published, in two parts, in *Zion* 53–54 (1988–89). The present revision includes many additional data and other general updates.

[1] F. Kupfer and T. Lewicki, *Zrodla hebrajskie do dziejow sloman i niektorych mnych Ludors srodkoaej i mchodmej Europy* (Warsaw 1956). I shall not deal here with sources already considered in the past, except where our understanding of those sources has been modified since the publication of Kupfer and Lewicki's work.

[2] I. Agus, *Urban Civilization in Pre-Crusade Europe* (New York 1968), pp. 93–97. This information is based on the manuscript version of a responsum of R. Meir b. Barukh of Rothenburg (Prague 1608), no. 912; see also A. Grossman, *The Early Sages of Ashkenaz* (Heb.) (Jerusalem 1981), p. 140 n' 123,185 n. 45. That the court had authority over visitors to the city is indicated twice in this complex episode: once in the community of Zimri, reported to be in "Russia," and once again in Cracow or its environs. Cf. the analysis of the story by Agus, *Urban Civilization*.

between him and Polish rabbis, who seem to have considered themselves his disciples. Combined with Polish Jews' observance of the *takanot* of R. Gershom, we thus have evidence of a strong historical and social affinity between these Jews and their co-religionists in Germany—most probably "the parent community of the early Jewish settlement in Poland."[3]

The Jewish traders who passed through Poland in the twelfth century included scholars and other individuals versed in religious learning. We have evidence to that effect from R. Eliezer b. Nathan (known as Raban), active in the first half of the twelfth century, and from R. Isaac b. R. Dorbelo, of the second half of the same century, one of the editors of the version of *Mahzor Vitry* in the printed edition. The latter writes: "Since we are not as well versed...as our predecessors, we should be circumspect, lest people accustom themselves to be lazy and rule leniently, as I have seen in the kingdom of Poland among the traders who travel the road."[4] R. Isaac b.Dorbelo and one of his contemporaries, R. Eliezer b. Isaac of Prague, are mentioned by Bernard D. Weinryb as the first two Jewish scholars to visit Russia "and possibly Poland" around the end of the twelfth century.[5] R. Eliezer, like his contemporary R. Isaac, was a disciple of Rabbenu Tam.[6]

We possess a letter written by R. Eliezer to R. Judah he-Hasid, vehemently protesting the latter's strictures, in an earlier letter to a Jewish community in eastern Europe, against payment of salaries to cantors. It was then customary "in most places in Poland, Russia,[7] and Hungary, where owing to poverty

3 As already pointed out by Agus, *Urban Civilization*.

4 Jews' College London, ms. Montefiore 134, *Sefer Ba'alei Asupot*, Hilkh. Pesah, § 352. Cf. Kupfer and Lewicki, *Zrodla hebrajskie*, 152; S.E. Stern, "Sefer Asupot" (Heb.), *Moriah* 15/5–6 (Spring 1987), pp. 5–10. On this important scholar and disciple of Rabbenu Tam, who lived in France and travelled around eastern Europe, see Kupfer and Lewicki, *Zrodla hebrajskie*, pp. 148–156; and more recently N. Danzig, "Excerpts from Geonic Responsa in Works of the Rishonim" (Heb.), *Proceedings of the 9th World Congress of Jewish Studies*, iii (Jerusalem 1986), pp. 71–78. Another scholar who apparently reached Russia was Raban's colleague R. Ephraim of Regensburg, referred to as the "teacher of R. Joel, who was there [in the kingdom of Russia] and saw with his own eyes that beer was brought to the priest to mix for idolatrous purposes" (Elazar b. Joel ha-Levi of Bonn, *Sefer Ravyah*, § 1050; V. Aptowitzer, *Mavo la-Ravyah* [Jerusalem 1938], p. 465). R. Joel's other teachers were R. Isaac b. Mordechai (Ribam), R. Moses b. Joel, and R. Samuel b. Natronai. Even though, as Aptowitzer pointed out, we have no direct knowledge of R. Ephraim's presence in Russia, this scholar is nevertheless acquainted with the customs of what he calls "the land of Yavan" (*Ravyah*, ii. 259). Finally, one of the Machiris was also in Russia; see Zedekiah b. Abraham Harofe, *Shibbolei ha-Leket*, n. 58.

5 D. Weinryb, *The Jews of Poland* (Philadelphia 1972), pp. 24ff.

6 E.E. Urbach, *The Tosafists*, 2nd ed. (Jerusalem 1980), pp. 212–215 (Heb.).

7 As defined by R. Benjamin of Tudela, "the land of Russia" denoted the entire region between Prague and Kiev: "These are the men of Russia, which is a great empire stretching

there are no Torah scholars, that they hire an intelligent man wherever they can and he serves them as leader in prayer and religious mentor and teacher of their children, and they assure his livelihood in return." That is to say: "To levy [payment or food] from those who entertain sons-in-law at their tables, who should give generously, because of the benefit of joy, food and drink...And appeals were made for them on Simhat Torah and Purim." R. Judah he-Hasid wrote to the Jews in one such place, instructing them to abolish both the hiring of paid cantors and the collection of taxes for that purpose, in the spirit of the old Ashkenazi pietist ideal that considered the function of the cantor as a sacrosanct post. R. Eliezer of Prague took exception to this position, appraising R. Judah of the grave danger that might arise if hired cantors were to relinquish their positions, heaven forbid, leaving their communities "without Torah, without prayer and without a religious authority." R. Eliezer ended his letter in a tone of deep concern: "Even if you retract, I am concerned lest your first views should have been heeded there and misfortune result."[8]

The following responsum was written when R. Judah he-Hasid was in the prime of his life, by an older scholar who did not mince words in his criticism of R. Judah:[9] "May He who forgives iniquity forgive your sin in perpetuity, that you may live and multiply." We may thus date the responsum to the last years of the twelfth century. Poland is explicitly mentioned, and the letter also provides definite evidence of the existence of Jewish communities at this early date, with some indications of their communal organization and level of religious observance. Later we shall learn some more of R. Judah he-Hasid's contacts with these first Polish communities and how he, rather than a recognized halakhic authority, achieved the profound influence in the region attested by R. Eliezer's letter.[10]

from the gate of Prague to the gate of Kieff, the large city, which is at the extremity of the empire. It is a land of mountains and forests...Thus far reaches the empire of Russia," *The Itinerary of Benjamin of Tudela*, ed. M.N. Adier [London 1907], pp. 80–81). In actual fact, the borders of Kievan Russia extended approximately from the environs of Lwow to the Kiev district. The northern border was not well defined, the Hebrew word "Russia" sometimes extending to Lithuania as well. The southern border was also not precisely drawn; at times it could reach the shores of the Black Sea. The political borders were not clearly delineated, but varied according to the power of the kingdom at any particular time. See below, end of the penultimate section. I am indebted to my friend Dr. Elhanan Reiner for this definition, as well as some other excellent advice on the structure of this article.

[8] *Or Zaru'a*, i, §113.

[9] Urbach, *The Tosafists*, pp. 212–215.

[10] The source is cited by Weinryb, *The Jews of Poland*, 24, but his annotation there is defective. The references he cites are concerned with other matters, and the correct—and only—reference for this responsum is omitted. Weinryb's statement that all the sources are preserved "in a late manuscript only" is quite wrong; as it happens, the ms. of *Or Zaru'a* is an early one, dating to the fourteenth century. Moreover, his arguments about the nature of

By the last quarter of the twelfth century there was a well-established Jewish community in Cracow, probably a direct descendant of the community whose existence was recorded some 150 years earlier. R. Joel ha-Levi (d. ca. 1200), father of "Ravyah," refers in a responsum to a person who was born in Cracow and travelled to his brother in Magdeburg. The man was born around 1175, at the latest, as he travelled to Magdeburg before 1200. Aptowitzer cited this responsum from an unpublished part of Ravyah's responsa.[11]

Our information about the Jewish community in Poland in the eleventh and twelfth centuries is fragmentary and does not provide a basis for a continuous historical account. It is generally believed that there were several "beginnings," not all of which took root. Continuous Jewish residence in Poland is usually dated from the mid-fifteenth century, though there are increasing indications of a continuous Jewish presence there from the end of the fourteenth century.[12] The sources seem to imply that in 1241, when the Mongolian invasion devastated Poland, the earlier Jewish presence, dating to the eleventh and twelfth centuries, disappeared. Later, from the second half of the thirteenth century and during the fourteenth century, there was no organized, rabbinically guided communal life and, therefore, no Polish scholars of this period figure in our literature. Graetz expressed amazement at this situation, as we have copious external evidence for the presence of Jews in thirteenth and fourteenth-century Poland. Suffice it to mention, for example, the detailed and important privilege granted in 1264 by Duke Bolestaw of Kalisz, which was re-validated in these centuries; decisions of the Church in Jewish matters; and coins struck by Jews. However, we lack evidence of the pulse of the Jewish heart there, because of the almost absolute silence of our internal sources, which contribute nothing of substance to our knowledge of Polish Jewish history of the time. As Graetz comments:

> Jewish history in the first three centuries of the sixth millennium [of the Jewish calendar, i.e. 1240–1540]...in the lands of eastern Europe...presents an amazing vision.... On the one hand, one learns from the various charters of privilege...from government records and decrees, from the writings of chroniclers...and from the evidence of travellers [and decisions of the Church] ...that by the beginning of the sixth millennium, and even earlier, Jewish settlement had made inroads not only in Poland, which was close to western

this letter, which he considers contrary to R. Judah he-Hasid's character and figure as it emerges in his writings and as portrayed by Gershom Scholem, are wrong.

11 Aptowitzer, *Mavo la-Ravyah*, p. 463. The text has now been published by D. Devlitzki, *Sefer Ravyah*, Responsa (Benei Berak 1989), p. 68.

12 E. Kupfer, "On the Cultural Features of Ashkenazic Jewry and Its Scholars in the Fourteenth and Fifteenth Centuries" (Heb.), *Tarbiz* 42 (1973), p. 130 n. no, and the addendum at the end of his article. The first figure in this group was apparently R. David Schweidnitz. See Y. Freiman, *Introduction to Leket Yosher* (Berlin 1903), p. 25.

> Europe, but also...in southern Russia.... Besides commerce, they also had a large part in industry, agriculture, trades, and all professions; but the pulse of the Jewish heart, the voice of the Torah, was still unheard in those lands ....And that is quite surprising, for the paucity of information and records of historical life persists until the mid-third century [end of the fifteenth century], and there is no trace of Torah study and *yeshivot* in the Jewish settlement of Lithuania and Poland—the lands which have supplied most Jewish communities, in all other Diaspora lands, with talmudic learning for the past three centuries.[13]

Graetz found the situation puzzling because of the "direct proportion" that has always existed between "the situation of the nation, wandering and tossed about among the nations in whose midst they lived...and the product of its spirit, the heights of its internal ethical and intellectual perfection."[14] This is clearly not the case in this chapter of Jewish history: the history of the Jews in Poland and Lithuania in the thirteenth and fourteenth centuries is, to all appearances, a success story from the point of view of economic and physical well-being—but lacks any substructure of Torah study and internal, spiritual-cultural creativity. This fact greatly puzzled the historian in Graetz. For him, the silence of the Jewish sources was clear, unequivocal evidence of a life devoid of scholarly creativity—evidence as reliable as any other material evidence. It did not occur to him to apply, here too, the well-known injunction against drawing conclusions *ex silentio*, as he was convinced that the silence in question was total, unlike other fortuitous silences of ancient sources. Later historians accepted Graetz's diagnosis. Some went even further, claiming to add this silence to other considerations that indicated, so they believed, that the Jews of Poland in the first stage, i.e., until the Mongolian invasion, had come from Russia or perhaps even beyond, and not from Germany, despite their halakhic connections to that country.

However, despite this seemingly universal agreement, the "fact" in question is dubious, as the silence on which it relies is far from complete. It is true that printed sources are silent in regard to the first periods of Jewish settlement in Poland; but the situation in manuscripts is quite different and, in fact, some of these have recently appeared in print. As we know, the number of Hebrew manuscripts now available is considerable and research can no longer rely on printed editions alone. True, even the manuscript sources are not too generous in relevant information; but they are certainly not silent. As we deepen our understanding of the nature of the available manuscript sources that have reached us from the Middle Ages, the reason for the relative dearth of Polish material—compared to other countries—becomes clearer. A major cause of

13 Z. Graetz, *Divrei Yemei Yisra'el*, trans. S.P. Rabinowitz (Warsaw 1898), pp. 183–184.

14 Ibid., p. 183.

this situation is that we lack photographic reproductions of Hebrew manuscripts still buried in various libraries or, in particular, in the possession of the Polish Church. In addition, most of the fragments in bindings of old books and archival envelopes in Poland have yet to see the light of day. Experience has taught us that most of our information about geographically defined areas reaches us through manuscripts originating in those areas. Other reasons will be mentioned below. All the information presented in this article has been garnered over the years, in the course of my browsing—for completely different purposes—through the treasure-house of microfilmed Hebrew manuscripts in the Jewish National and University Library of Jerusalem. I have no doubt that a systematic search would reveal even more. Nevertheless, despite the small quantity and random nature of the finds, we have sufficient material, I believe, to warrant a preliminary formulation of a quite different thesis about the nature of the Jewish community in thirteenth-century Poland—a thesis that will be much closer to undisputed facts than what we have today. This apparent silence of the sources, as well as the gaps between the early Jewish presence in Poland during the eleventh and thirteenth centuries, its continuation in the second half of the thirteenth century, and its final consolidation in the fifteenth century, have raised questions about the geographical origins of the first Jews to settle there.[15] It has been suggested that those early Jews were not an offshoot of the Jewish communities in Germany, but a branch of the ancient Jewish center of Kievan Russia. Eastern Jews—some of them learned in Torah—were living there as early as the twelfth century or before; their roots go back to the ancient Jewish presence in the various parts of Khazaria. The great historical controversy over this issue is well known and need not be discussed here.[16] In this article I shall assemble a variety of Hebrew sources that will tell

[15] See S. Ettinger, "Jewish Influence on the Religious Ferment in Eastern Europe at the End of the Fifteenth Century" (Heb.), in *Yitzhak F. Baer Jubilee Volume*, eds. S.W. Baron, B. Dinur, I. Halpern, and S. Ettinger (Jerusalem 1960), pp. 228–247: "The chapter of the judaizers in Russia enables us to view this [i. e. Polish and Lithuanian] Jewry while it was still driven by its rationalist tendencies." There were indeed "rationalist tendencies" as such, an issue that has received considerable support from E. Kupfer, in "On the Cultural Features of Ashkenazic Jewry," pp. 113ff.; however, Kupfer's article deals with the Jews of Germany and Bohemia and has nothing to say of the Jews of Kievan Russia or the Byzantine centers.

[16] See S. Ettinger, "Kievan Russia," in *The World History of the Jewish People*, xi: *The Dark Ages*, ed. C. Roth (Tel Aviv 1966), pp. 319–324. I would like to rectify a popular error—also marring Ettinger's account—that sees the existence of a R. Moses of Kiev, active around the middle of the twelfth century, who quotes Rabbenu Tam and was in contact with R. Samuel b. Ali, head of the academy in Baghdad, as proving that no extensive expulsions of Kievan Jews took place during that period. The truth is that R. Moses was known as "the Exile" from Kiev; moreover, he does not merely "quote" Rabbenu Tam, but actually studied under him in France; and his contacts with the Babylonian scholar were maintained from France and not from Kiev. This seemingly surprising fact emerges from the other, less well-known correspondence of Moses, the Exile of Kiev, and Samuel b. Ali of Baghdad, on the

us more about the existence of an admittedly sparse Jewish presence, including Jews well versed in Torah, in thirteenth-century Poland; about the continuous existence of this presence throughout the twelfth and thirteenth centuries; and, above all, about its Ashkenazi origins and its special, ongoing contacts with the circles of hasidei Ashkenaz in Germany. This is not to say that the "eastern" orientation should be entirely discounted—that is not my intention;[17] but I shall be able to show that the extent of the links between Russia-

issue of the prohibition on Passover of *hametz bemashehu* (mixtures containing minute quantities of leaven); see Aptowitzer, in his notes to *Sefer ha-Ravyah* ii, 77 n. 11, and in "Addenda and Corrigenda" 18 (repr. in his notes to part II, p. 73). It transpires, therefore, that Moses the Exile was apparently the only Kievan of the time who was learned in Torah—and we have now seen that his rabbinical activity, too, took place in France and not in his native land. However, we have other possible testimony to the existence in the twelfth century of a channel of transmission from Babylon through Kiev to Germany, namely, Moses Taku in his *Ketav Tamim*. He claims to trace certain ideas of R. Judah he-Hasid to Karaite literature that reached him from the East and rejects "the commentators" idea that [God] creates forms to speak with the prophets. That tradition has survived among the Karaites and the heretics, for thus we find it written in a commentary of theirs to the Pentateuch, which moreover contains calumnious remarks about students of the Mishnah and the Talmud, and we were told that "that crooked book came from Babylon to Russia and from Russia it was brought to Regensburg" (ms. Paris H711, fo. 28; facs. edn. [Jerusalem 1984], 55). According to A. Epstein, it was the traveller Petahiah of Regensburg who brought the book with him upon his return from the east (*Mi-Kadmoniyot ha-Yehudim* [Jerusalem 1957], pp. 240–241). The book thus reached R. Judah he-Hasid, who, in fact, edited and censored Petahiah's travelogue, as related by Petahiah himself: "In Nineveh there was an astrologer by the name of R. Solomon...R. Petahiah asked him when the Messiah would come, and he told him: I have already foretold his coming clearly from the stars. But R. Judah he-Hasid did not wish [me] to write [this], lest he be suspected of believing in R. Solomon's predictions." Incidentally, I have found the entire prophecy, two pages long, in an ancient manuscript, ms. Warsaw University i (Institute for Microfilmed Hebrew Manuscripts, mic. 32500)—the oldest extant ms. of the Sibuv. The fragment has now been published by S. Spitzer, in Alei Sefer, 15 (1988–89), pp. 133–134; and see my comment, ibid. 16 (1989–90), p. 187. There is yet another reference to Kiev in this early period, in *Sefer ha-Raban, Beitzah*, 172*: "It is my view...that [such fabrics] are not considered *kilayim* [mixtures], as are made in the land of Greece, and in Kiem I saw some of them without leather underneath...." For "Kiem" read "Kiev," as noted by S. Abramson, "Explanation of Words" (Heb.), in *Gevurot ha-Romah: Divrei Hakhamim le Moshe Haim Vailer*, ed. Z. Falk (Jerusalem 1987), p. 166. The period referred to pre-dates that of Moses the Exile by some fifty years.

17 The problem is, in fact, complicated by the unnoticed fact that Jewish communities in Ashkenaz itself maintained close spiritual-cultural and intellectual contacts with communities in Greece and Byzantium from the mid–tenth century and even earlier, not necessarily in connection with Poland, until the middle of the thirteenth century, as witnessed in the rabbinical literature of those three hundred years. The intensity, causes, and significance of those contacts have yet to be determined. I shall treat their history in a forthcoming article. It is not inconceivable that these two sources of influence—Germany and Russia-Kiev-Byzantium—drew from a major common source, at least from the eleventh century on.

Poland and Ashkenaz, particularly eastern Ashkenaz, was much greater than believed up to the present. Moreover, I believe that these links were essentially persistent and permanent, rather than a series of random occurrences.

R. JACOB SVARA OF CRACOW

R. Jacob Svara is the first rabbinical figure known by name from the Polish city of Cracow. He was active there in the first half of the thirteenth century. Although our knowledge of his personality and actions is growing steadily, he is still a largely obscure figure. Attention was first drawn to him by Kupfer.[18] While working at the Institute for Microfilmed Hebrew Manuscripts, he identified an unknown work of a disciple of the Tosafist R. Tobias of Vienne in France[19]—an abbreviated version of R. Moses of Coucy's *Sefer Mitzvot Gadol*, with halakhic rulings of the author's teacher R. Tobias interpolated.[20] The manuscript reads:

> It happened that a woman gave her son to a Jewish wet-nurse, and the wet-nurse was adjured, on behalf of the community, under biblical oath, a grave oath that cannot be annulled, that she would not retract her undertaking to breast-feed the child until it reach the age of 24 months. Upon doing this the mother married a certain *kohen* [person of priestly lineage], named R. Jacob Svara of Cracow, who resided in Poland, a great scholar versed in the entire Talmud, but the great authorities of the time disagreed with him, and were about to excommunicate him. Thereupon he sent responsa to the ends of west and south, and his words reached my teacher R. Tobias. And my teacher instructed, in so far as it is quite obvious that she would not renege, owing to the gravity of the oath, he could not be forced to divorce her, and even if he were not yet married to her, he could *à priori* marry her.[21]

The episode alluded to here concerns the fate of a woman widowed while still nursing her baby within 24 months of its birth. According to Jewish law (*Ket.* 60b), she may not remarry, for fear that she might neglect her baby. Ashkenazi Jewry took this prohibition very seriously throughout the centuries.[22] Such marriages were forbidden even when the couple took all feasible precautions to

[18] E. Kupfer, "From Far and Near" (Heb.), in *Dr. N. M. Gelber Memorial Book*, eds. I. Klausner, R. Mahler, and D. Sadan (Tel Aviv 1963), pp. 218–219.

[19] For a description of this book, see Urbach, *The Tosafists*, pp. 488–491, (Heb.) and cf. ibid. concerning R. Jacob Svara.

[20] Ms. Paris 329. A different version of the book (see Urbach, *The Tosafists*) renders a shorter and less specific account of the episode, which is reproduced verbatim, without mentioning the source, in *Piskei Rekanati*, § 240. It does not designate the protagonists by name and R. Tobias's ruling is quoted as "the *geonim* instructed."

[21] Ms. Vat. 176, fo. 51.

[22] The history of this prohibition in rabbinic literature, as well as the reason for the exceptional severity with which it was enforced by Ashkenazi authorities (of all generations),

ensure the infant's rights and welfare, and the rabbis insisted that, if a marriage had nevertheless been performed, it be dissolved by divorce; the couple would be allowed to remarry at the end of the 24-month term. The special feature of the case in question was that R. Jacob of Cracow was a *kohen*, and his "temporary" divorce would have separated him permanently from his new wife (as a *kohen* may not marry a divorcee). Nevertheless, the halakhic authorities of Ashkenaz insisted that he obey their injunction to divorce his wife and even threatened to excommunicate him should he refuse, despite the fact that he was considered—by them, too—as a "great scholar versed in the entire Talmud." In an endeavor to defend his position, R. Jacob sent letters "to the ends of west and south," and R. Tobias of Vienne supported his stand and completely upheld his actions.

The details of the case are unknown, and there is no surviving trace of the correspondence. No doubt the episode was censored by the contemporary Ashkenazi scholars, who completely expunged any expression of the more lenient view from their books. The few surviving responsa, and the few indirect discussions, give only the views of those who favored the prohibition. Nothing has reached us of R. Jacob's own opinion, as set out in his own language and sent "to the ends of the earth," which, in fact, reached the eyes of R. Isaac b. Moses, known as Or Zaru'a, himself ("And I read R. Jacob Kohen's letter and found nothing there that was worthy of response"); the same is true of R. Tobias's responsum permitting the marriage. The responsum of R. Isaac Or Zaru'a, who headed the camp opposing the rabbi of Cracow, was printed in his book;[23] it too censored. The first, informative part of his letter has been deleted. The text begins *in medias res* and in mid-sentence, clearly indicating that the previous page of the manuscript was torn out. This applies not only to the manuscript on which the printed edition was based, but also to other manuscripts of the work, including ms. Cincinnati 154. This manuscript contains the collection of responsa only and is independent of the other manuscripts, as it also includes new responsa found neither in the latter nor in the printed edition. The missing page is present in ms. Cincinnati, and it actually enables us to complete the end of the previous responsum, which is missing in the printed edition; but the beginning of our responsum is still missing, here

deserves separate discussion. Here, too, as in so many other cases, the root cause was a latent Palestinian tradition; but one must also consider the cruel reality of life in medieval Europe, which meant that a child handed over to a strange wet-nurse was generally doomed to die. See L. DeMausse, "The Evolution of Childhood," *History of Childhood Quarterly* i (1973), pp. 534–541. And cf. *Mishnah Sotah* 4: 3, which lists certain wives to whom the ordeal of the "bitter water" is not administered; one of them is a wife still nursing a previous husband's infant—as the marriage itself is not considered properly valid.

23 Pt. n, § 740.

too![24] Next to his own responsum, R. Isaac cited a ruling of R. Moses b. Hisdai of Regensburg, one of the leading scholars of the day, who also wrote in an extreme vein. The case is mentioned in other places, mainly by scholars who copied from the work of R. Tobias's disciple R. Isaac; all these accounts, however, are vague, obscure, and replete with incomprehensible hints in order to avoid voicing the permissive views.[25]

Prof. Urbach dated the episode to around 1245,[26] based on considerations to be clarified presently. However, R. Jacob was already known for his

[24] Such acts of censorship, and similar ones, were common practice in Ashkenaz even earlier. See my comment in *Kiryat Sefer* 56(1981), pp. 350–351.

[25] The reader should note that, had R. Tobias's disciple not mentioned his master's name, we would have been unable to attribute this almost unique lenient view to a specific scholar. Cf. R. Yomtov Ishbili's wording in his novellae to *Ket.* 60b: "But there are some of the last Tosafists, of blessed memory, who wrote that if the nursing mother took an oath on the matter....the matter is sufficiently public and it is permitted." R. Yom Tov wrote his book around 1300–20 and would certainly have been aware of the identity of the Tosafist in question. Similarly, R. Nissim, in his comments ad loc. writes "and the rabbi, of blessed memory, wrote...," deliberately or otherwise omitting the rabbi's name. It is interesting that R. Nissim himself, in his responsum, § 58, firmly prohibited the remarriage of a nursing mother, adding, "I have been approached on this matter on several occasions, and have prohibited it, particularly after the first case, concerning a prominent member of the Gerona community, and although the matter was extremely grave, I could not agree to grant permission under any circumstances, even though there was a willingness to impose restrictive conditions. Anyone who seeks a pretext to rule leniently in this matter is surely breaching the fence erected by the sages." So history repeats itself. Both R. Yom Tov and R. Nissim were following in the footsteps of their master, R. Solomon b. Aderet, who greatly admired the teachings of the French and German scholars (as did *his* master, Nachmanides); R. Solomon, in his responsum § 723, upheld the prohibition even for a case in which there were two wet-nurses! Cf. also the responsa of R. Moses Halawa, R. Solomon's disciple, in the last year of his life, and the pupil of his son R. Judah—these responsa were recently published in the collection of R. Moses Halawa's responsa, ed. M. Herschler (Jerusalem 1987), § 137, 142–143. French scholars, on the other hand, were inclined to take a more lenient approach, provided certain reinforcing conditions were observed; but we cannot go into detail here. The questioner in § 137 was R. Shealtiel Hen, and the wording of his question implies that R. Yehiel of Paris, the leading French authority of his time, concurred with R. Tobias of Vienne's permissive view. Another implication from that responsum is that there was also a lenient responsum of R. Solomon Aderet, unconnected, of course, to the episode of R. Jacob ha-Kohen; as yet, however, I have been unable to locate it in the printed editions. The episode is also referred to in the responsa of R. Meir of Rothenburg ([Lwow 1860], § 362 = [Prague 1608], § 864 = *Teshuvot Maimoniyot on Sefer Nashim*, § 24), but the story has been changed: "It happened that a *kohen* married a nursing mother...and they adjured the nursing mother... and this was done on the view of R. Jacob ha-Kohen of Krakow," as if he himself was not involved in the case; perhaps there were two distinct occasions, one involving himself and another, later one. Also preserved in R. Meir of Rothenburg's responsum are a few rare lines from R. Jacob's own words and the halakhic argument of his opponents.

[26] E.E. Urbach, *Arugat ha-Bosem*, iv (Jerusalem 1963), pp. 120–121.

scholarship some ten years previously, as R. Abraham b. Azriel, the author of *Arugat ha-Bosem*, who wrote his book in 1234, had heard an explanation of a line in a certain *piyyut* "in the name of R. Jacob of Poland, may he rest in peace," following a quote from a statement by R. Judah he-Hasid. Urbach quite rightly identified the two R. Jacobs, as is indeed beyond any doubt; the reference to him as deceased would then, obviously, be a late interpolation. In Urbach's view, R. Isaac Or Zaru'a wrote his responsum against R. Jacob of Cracow around the year 1245, because in that responsum he does not appeal to any of his great teachers but cites an "almost unknown" authority: "In our day the matter depends considerably on our master R. Aaron, for he alone survives in this generation, for in him is Torah, old age, and greatness, and he is worthy of zeal for the honor of the Lord and His Torah, and we shall all concur with him." This is quite plausible, argues Urbach, if the passage was written toward the end of the author's life, when his great teachers were no longer alive. I shall show later that the phrase "may he rest in peace" stands on its own merits, the whole episode having occurred before 1234, perhaps as much as ten years earlier. The failure to appeal to his teachers is not conclusive, for the author's most prominent teachers were dead already by the years 1220–25: Ravyah, R. Simha of Speyer, R. Judah he-Hasid, and R. Judah Sir Leon; hence there is, of course, no need to go as far back as 1245 to explain the text.

In 1973 Kupfer published a collection of "Responsa and Rulings" of French and German scholars from ms. Bodl. 692,[27] one of them being, "It happened that a certain woman sinned and had intercourse with her husband while menstrually unclean." R. Hezekiah b. Jacob of Magdeburg and his court strictly forbade the woman to maintain conjugal relations with her husband, and revoked her privileges under her *ketubah*, including her property rights. They sent letters to that effect to R. Aaron of Regensburg and R. Jacob b. Solomon of Courson. As transpires from the correspondence, at some time "the rabbi Jacob ha-Kohen" intervened in the discussion, suggesting that some compromise be reached between the parties concerning the monetary arrangements, rather than make the woman totally destitute. Finally, however, he "removed himself from the deliberations," and R. Jacob of Courson, therefore, held that his view was not binding "but merely advice." There is a similar reference in R. Hezekiah's letter, where the scholar in question is called "the rabbi Jacob son of Shalom." Kupfer conjectured that the person involved was the same R. Jacob Svara of Cracow, suggesting, moreover, that he was also the scholar mentioned in a responsum (§ 775) of R. Isaac Or Zaru'a addressed to "the generous R. Aaron" concerning the latter's prospective engagement. At the end of that responsum we read: "And concerning the fact that he has summoned you to appear before R. [Isaac],[28] think nothing of it, for there resides

27 E. Kupfer, *Teshuvot u-Pesakim* (Jerusalem 1973), p. 66.

28 Completion based on Hebrew Union College, ms. Cincinnati 154 (see above).

in your city the rabbi Jacob ha-Kohen, who is a qualified expert...." Kupfer smoothly assumes that the responsum was sent to Regensburg, as he tacitly identifies "the generous R. Aaron" with the celebrated sage of that name from Regensburg. That is not possible, however, for it is clear from the salutation at the beginning of the letter that the reference is to a different person, a respected layman ("a youth elevated above the common folk") and nothing more, who would like to cancel a marriage match concluded for his younger son ("that your son, from the day he reached maturity, did not agree to that match"). However, if the identification of R. Jacob ha-Kohen is correct—and I am inclined to agree—the responsum was most probably addressed to Cracow itself, R. Jacob's place of residence. In that case it is not necessary to assume that he moved from Cracow to Regensburg, or vice versa, in accordance with Kupfer's later correction.

Further progress was made in 1983, again thanks to Kupfer.[29] He was examining fragments of *tosafot* on a thirteenth or fourteenth-century parchment found in bindings of old books in Cracow—an interesting coincidence! —whose photographs had reached the Institute for Microfilmed Hebrew Manuscripts. Among these fragments was a marginal gloss to a passage from *tosafot* on tractate *Hulin*, which began, "And R. Jacob Kohen explained that the wording *le-bet halalo* was used because...." The fragments are identical to a manuscript (Vatican 159) of Ashkenazi *tosafot* on tractate *Hulin*—essentially the same as the presently printed *tosafot*—in which there are several references, both in the body of the text and in marginal glosses, to a scholar identified only by his initials, R.Y.K.[30] It now seems plausible that (at least some occurrences of) these initials should be interpreted as an abbreviation for "R. Jacob Kohen" rather than "R. Judah ha-Kohen" (of Friedburg) as suggested previously. Consequently, it is then very likely that here, too, the scholar involved was that same resident of Cracow, for as yet we know of no other early scholar of the same name. The plausibility is further enhanced by the fact that R. Jacob belonged to the geographical sphere of Saxony-Bohemia—a region whose scholars the editor of ms. Vatican 159, R. Elazar of Tuch,[31] was constantly quoting, as he had studied under them and worked with them.

29 E. Kupfer, "From the Archives of the Institute for Microfilmed Hebrew Manuscripts of the National and Hebrew University Library" (Heb.), *Kiryat Sefer* 59 (1984), pp. 959–960.

30 Described and defined by Urbach, *The Tosafists*, p. 666 and n. 28. He believed that the editor was R. Elazar of Metz.

31 Contrary to the commonly held view, as expressed by Urbach, *The Tosafists*, pp. 581–582, that R. Elazar was a French scholar (based on interpreting the Hebrew "Tuch" as Touques), it is quite clear that he was German. His relatives lived in Germany; his associates and

This identification, if considered sound, opens up another avenue of research and, for the first time, offers us a glimpse of the teachings of this forgotten scholar. The abbreviation R.Y.K. occurs quite frequently in the *Gilyonot Tosafot* from the school of R. Elazar of Tuch (see below), generally in halakhic debate with a scholar whose initials are R.M. Some of these marginal glosses, to several tractates of the Talmud, were recently published from manuscripts by R.M. Blau.[32] The editor has identified R.Y.K. throughout—rightly, I believe—as R. Judah ha-Kohen of Friedburg. Now ms. Vatican 159 also includes these glosses to tractate *Hulin*, incorporated into the main text of the *tosafot*, and they, too, feature the initials R.Y.K., presumably referring here, too, to R. Judah ha-Kohen of Friedburg. However, the fragment that Kupfer discovered explicitly designates R. Jacob ha-Kohen, perhaps with the express purpose of distinguishing him from the other R.Y.K.s in the book. I am not inclined, therefore, to decipher each occurrence of R.Y.K. in this group of marginal glosses as referring to R. Jacob. Nevertheless, the initials may well refer at times to one, at times to the other. The matter deserves further study.

In one of his many publications about medieval Bible exegetes, I.S. Lange referred to ms. Paris 260. This manuscript closely resembles the anthology *Moshav Zekenim*, published by R. S. Sasson (London 1959), which includes exegesis of the Torah by the Tosafists; the two texts, indeed, contain many parallel passages.[33] In his study, Lange pointed out several bibliographical and biographical details that are more complete in ms. Paris. In appendix v to the article, Lange cited a few examples pertaining to the book of Genesis only; in one of these the name R. Jacob S.B.R., which appears in Genesis 3: 4, replaces

close circle were from Magdeburg and the surroundings; and the few known facts and actions that can be connected with him took place there, as may also be seen from Urbach's own account. How did he ever become "head of the Academy of the land of France?" R. M. Blau argued correctly in this respect. Urbach's counter-argument that "this place [i. e. Tuchheim] is not mentioned in any source as a place where Jews lived" is no argument, for the same is true of the Normandian village of Touques—"we know nothing whatever of the history of its community" (Urbach, *The Tosafists*)—and there is no reason to prefer it over Tuchheim in Germany. Similarly, his statement that "R. Elazar's Frenchness is proven by all that is known of him" is inaccurate. On the contrary, it is his "Germanness" that emerges from all that is known of him, except when he studied under the French Tosafists for several years, after which he returned to Germany. The truth of the matter is also evident from his *gilyonot* (marginal glosses) on the *tosafot* to tractate *Bava Kama* (Blau made the above statements in his introduction to his edition of those glosses [New York 1977]), in which R. Elazar writes, 'The explanation that was proposed to me in France seems to me extremely far-fetched' (Blau, in his edn., p. 293).

32 On tractate *Shabbat* (New York 1978), at the end of an edition of *Sefer ha-Batim*, on tractate *Bava Kama*, in *Shitat ha-Kadmonim* (New York 1977).

33 I.S. Lange, "The Book 'Moshav Zekenim'" (Heb.), *Hama'yan*, Tammuz [s]732 (Summer 1972), p. 39. Cf. ibid., n. 26. Cf. *Moshav Zekenim* (London 1959).

the unqualified name R. Jacob at the end of the passage in the printed edition. Lange offers no comment, but this might appear to be a rare reference to R. Jacob Svara[34] of Cracow in connection to the explanation of a biblical verse. This intriguing possibility inspired me to examine the entire manuscript closely, but I found no other such reference. Nevertheless, I discovered that ms. Paris (= *Moshav Zekenim*) was culled from a variety of sources, among them the Ashkenazi work *Pa'aneah Raza* (first pub. Prague, 1607), from whose original version the appellation Jacob S.B.R. is taken. I then proceeded to examine early manuscripts of *Pa'aneah Raza*. The printed edition of that work is a highly abbreviated version of the original, as demonstrated mainly by the large, important ms. Oxford, Bodl. 3244 in Neubauer's Catalogue. There I found the following sentence: "The rabbi Jacob of C[racow?] explained in the name of R. Moses of Taku...,"[35] as well as the reverse, "R. Moses, who explained in the name of R. Jacob...."[36]

At the end of this manuscript there is a colophon by the author, from which we learn that it was written or, more precisely, edited by R. Isaac son of R. Judah ha-Levi. It is replete with uniquely Ashkenazi—and unfamiliar—material, including much from the school of R. Judah he-Hasid and his circle.[37] R. Isaac drew on several collections as his basic sources, which he lists as follows: "From my teachers, and from the words of R.Y.Z. and his novellae, and from the words of R. Jacob of Orleans and the commentary of our rabbi *Bekhor Shor* and some of what I found in the *Garden* [a well-known book] ...and some *peshatim* and *gematriyot* from the words of our rabbi Judah he-Hasid and from the words of the rabbi R. Eliezer...." Now material from all the sources that he mentions by name may be located in the text itself dozens of times, if not more, properly designated at the end of each quotation, except for the source that he calls "R.Y.Z. and his novellae." To the best of my ability, I have been able to pinpoint only about ten quotations from this source. On the other hand, the dominant figure in the book—on the personal level, rather than the literary—is a scholar referred to as R. Jacob. His name occurs hun-

34 The following passage appears in a manuscript collection of stories in the possession of the National and Hebrew University Library, Jerusalem (8vo 3182) (see below, n. 83): "There was a certain pious man by the name of S. B. R., and why was he known as S. B. W. R. [!] because he was a learned man (*ba'al sevarah*)...." This is the opening sentence of a fanciful folk-tale whose plot is placed in the time of the (talmudic) sages; nevertheless, one can derive from it (and from the other literary material in this collection) many realia pertaining to Germany of the thirteenth to fourteenth centuries. And see below, n. 83. And cf. A. Jellinek, *Beit ha-Midrash*, vi = J.D. Eisenstein, *Otzar Midrashim* (New York 1915), ii. 334 (§ i6): "A Story of Ben Savar."

35 "Va'era," fo. 52a; missing in the printed edn.

36 "Beshalakh," fo. 58a.

37 I hope to devote a special article to this work and its various manuscripts.

dreds of times as a source, though presumably not always referring to the same person. It is readily proved that some of the references are to Rabbenu Tam, others to R. Jacob of Orleans, and sometimes to other known Tosafists. Who is the R.Y.Z. who is cited in the colophon as a basic source but rarely mentioned in the text itself? Upon considering the problem, one immediately recalls a statement by the grandson of R. Samuel Schlettstadt, who, at the end of the fourteenth century, drew up for his own use a long list of abbreviations and acronyms for names of scholars culled from the Hebrew literature at his disposal,[38] based on his own learning experience; and there he wrote, "The R.Y.Z. in the *gilyonot* is R. Jacob Katz."[39] The signature R.Y.Z. is common in marginal *tosafot* in *Shitah Mekubetzet*, in the Ashkenazi glosses (*gilyonot*) to Alfasi's Code, and in glosses on *Sefer Mordekhai*, *Sefer Mitzvot Katan*, and others—a point we shall come back to later. Possibly, then, R. Isaac b. Judah was referring to this very scholar: R.Y.Z. = R. Jacob Katz = R. Jacob ha-Kohen, so that some of the designations "R. Jacob" would be referring to the scholar we are discussing here. Alongside R. Jacob's name, and associated with it, one commonly finds in the manuscript *Pa'aneah Raza* the names of two other scholars, R. Moses and R. Aaron. Everything suggested here in connection with *Pa'aneah Raza* is little more than conjecture, in need of corroboration and proof; I have chosen to include these suggestions in view of their importance, in the hope that time will bring further clarification.

R. Jacob of Cracow belonged to the circle of Judah he-Hasid's disciple-companions. This fact emerges from what is apparently the only manuscript of a book of *gematriyot* written by Judah he-Hasid's disciples, formerly in the possession of Avraham Epstein and later in the Jewish Community Library, Vienna. Together with most manuscripts in that collection, it was lost during the Holocaust and so far has not resurfaced. Epstein gave a brief description of the manuscript, from which it follows that one of the only three scholars mentioned there by name was "R. Jacob ha-Kohen the pious, of blessed memory."[40]

38 Published by I. Benjacob, "Shem ha-Gedolim," in *Devarim Atikim* (Leipzig 1844), pp. 7–10.

39 The enigma of the initials R. Y. Z. is encountered in a variety of contexts in rabbinic literature; the solution is, of course, not the same everywhere. See M. Kahana, "Commentaries on the Sifri Hidden in Manuscript" (Heb.), in *Studies in Memory of the Rishon Le-Zion R. Yitzhak Nissim*, ed. M. Benayahu (Jerusalem 1985), p. 102 n. 60.

40 See A.Z. Schwartz, *Die Hebräischen Handschriften der Nationalbibliothek in Wien* (Leipzig 1925), no. 234. One of my notebooks contains a comment that R. Jacob ha-Kohen is mentioned as one of R. Judah he-Hasid's teachers(!) in an old manuscript of a Torah commentary known to R.H.Y.D. Azulai, which he copied into one of his books (near the end of the book of Genesis). I was subsequently unable to locate the passage and concluded that my reference involved an error. The reference has now been located in the book *Penei David*

R. MOSES POLER

Another forgotten scholar who may be placed in thirteenth-century Poland is R. Moses Poler. He is mentioned in various manuscripts (and here and there in print as well) as Moses Poler, Moses Polak, Moses Polya, Moses Polier, Moses of Pol, and Moses of Polin (i.e., Poland). The sparse data relating to this scholar and his actions were first assembled by A. Marmorstein in a passing note in one of his articles.[41] In light of our increasing knowledge about this scholar, he deserves detailed discussion, which is of necessity preliminary at this stage. He is mentioned several times in an early commentary on the Torah, BL ms. 2853, whose author is anonymous but the time of writing is known—the turn of the thirteenth and fourteenth centuries,[42] and it is based on teachings of the Tosafists of that time. The same scholar is mentioned in a few other manuscripts,[43] and in a *gilayon* (or set of marginal glosses on the *tosafot*), cited by *Shitah Mekubetzet* on tractate *Ketubot*.[44] Unfortunately, Bezalel Ashkenazi

(Livorno 1792), afta. Cf. S. Emanuel, "The Lost Halakhic Books of the Tosafists" (Heb.), Ph. D. thesis (Hebrew University, Jerusalem 1993), p. 205 n. 10. My colleague Prof. Sid Z. Leiman has called my attention to the following passage in Elijah b. Moses de Vidas, *Reshit Hokhmah* (ed. pr. Venice 1579), *Sha'ar ha'Anavah*, ch. 3: "I heard it told of the hasid, R. Jacob Ashkenazi, of blessed memory, that he was a wonderfully learned scholar and wished to teach his lore to R. Judah he-Hasid. He first tested him in connection with anger, as they had a tradition that one should not transmit the lore save to a person who had been tested for anger and had not displayed anger, and they tested him, six times he suffered and on the seventh he could not resist etc." The story is also interesting in relation to R. Judah he-Hasid's personality. Prof. Moshe Idel has informed me that the hagiographical tales, particularly those about Hasidei Ashkenaz, scattered here and there in *Reshit Hokhmah*, were originally part of a lost historical work including an autobiography of R. Isaac of Acre, as well as hagiographical tales of famous Jews, mainly from the circles of Hasidei Ashkenaz, collected by R. Isaac during his lifetime. On this book, see A. Goldreich, "The Book *Me'irat Einayim* by R. Isaac of Akko" (Heb.), Ph. D. thesis (Hebrew University, Jerusalem 1984), pp. 408–409.

41 A. Marmorstein, "An Italian Scholar and *Posek*" (Heb.), *Devir* 2 (1924), p. 226.

42 Marmorstein devoted a special article to this manuscript; Urbach, however (*The Tosafists* 11, p. 486 n. 32), comments: "All Marmorstein's statements about this manuscript are unacceptable." Cf. the important work of M. Kahana, "Prolegomena to a New Edition of *Sifri* Numbers" (Heb.), Ph. D. thesis (Hebrew University, Jerusalem 1982), pp. 71–76; id., "Commentaries on the *Sifri*."

43 See previous note.

44 These references in *Shitah Mekubetzet* were already noted by Zunz, as pointed out by Marmorstein, "An Italian Scholar," loc. cit. They are of special interest, because this particular *Gilyon Tosafot* was edited by R. Elazar of Tuch himself, i.e., at the end of the thirteenth century. This is explicitly stated in *Shitah Mekubetzet* on *Ket.* 60b. He cites certain *kunteresim* (see below), which systematically criticize the *Gilyon Tosafot* here and elsewhere, as follows: "It is further written in another *Gilyon Tosafot* as follows....But the *kunteresim* write as follows: That is puzzling: what is the difference between this *gilayon* and the first

cited very sparingly from these marginal notes, both in *Ketubot* and in *Bava Kama*. At any rate, one of them reads as follows: "Our teacher R. Moses Polak posed a difficulty: If the Day of Atonement be postponed to Tuesday, the seventh day of the willow branch [i.e., Hoshana Rabbah, the seventh day of the Feast of Tabernacles] will fall on the Sabbath day! And our teacher R. Abraham explained: If [the Day of Atonement] fell on Sunday and should be postponed to Monday, it shall not be so postponed."[45] While in *Shitah Mekubetzet* on *Bava Metzia* we read: "In a marginal note to the *tosafot* it was written as follows: R. Moses Poler posed a difficulty: Why should he take the oath—after all, the borrower supports him!—or perhaps the text is concerned with a case in which the borrower is related to the owner. And my teacher R. Moses explained that this was a case in which there was some other transaction between them that required an oath."[46] The same case is mentioned in ms. Cambridge 781,[47] a most important manuscript, dealing with forbidden foods etc., by a disciple of R. Eliezer of Worms, yet to be described in the scholarly literature. The text on fo. 186a cites this brief exchange in the name of "the s[aintly] R. Moses Poler...and M.H.R.M. explained...," the latter being none other than the above-mentioned R. Moses. We have already found "R. –Jacob" deliberating in a similar vein with "R. Moses," in our discussion of *Pa'aneah Raza*. R. Bezalel Ashkenazi mentions him again in *Shitah Mekubetzet*, and again in *Gilyon Tosafot* in his commentary to the same tractate (50a). As we have pointed out, R. Bezalel made only scant use of this *gilayon*, and consequently we have very few quotations from the teachings of R. Moses Poler. At any rate, it is interesting that elsewhere R. Bezalel quotes from this *Gilyon Tosafot* as follows: "The difficulty posed in the *tosafot* of R. Samson, as to whether a defiling thought is considered speech [in connection with the sacrificial rite], how does he know...? And R.Y. said in the name of my teacher R. Aaron of Regensburg...." The eastern Ashkenazi provenance of this comment, as might be

gilayon, as the rabbi R. Elazar of Tuch wrote them both?" And the statement is also made directly by R. Bezalel Ashkenazi: "Know that the marginal glosses of the *tosafot* were formulated by R. Elazar of Tuch, the author of the *tosafot*" (fo. 32). The question of the *gilyonot* and the *kunteresim* is discussed in the new edition of Urbach's *The Tosafists,* n. 628. I disagree with his account on several points, but that is not relevant to the present issue. The *Gilyonot Tosafot* of R. Elazar of Tuch constitute the collected comments and deliberations of the last Tosafists, particularly the German contemporaries and compatriots of R. Elazar of Tuch, as well as his own comments (see n. 31 above) on the main corpus of the *tosafot*, which are mostly French, up to ca. the mid–thirteenth century. They, therefore, comprise an independent work of R. Elazar of Tuch himself, inserted in the margins of his monumental edition of the *tosafot*.

45 On *Ket.* 5a.

46 On *Ket.* 35b.

47 Fo. 186a.

expected from the nature of the previous *gilayon*, is clear here too. Our data, therefore, enable us to reconstruct the context with some confidence. R. Elazar of Tuch died before 1291; he was a nephew of R. Hezekiah of Magdeburg[48] and a disciple of R. Isaac Or Zaru'a. Hence R. Moses was active in the first half of the thirteenth century or a little later, in mid-century.

The same R. Moses is mentioned again in ms. Oxford 696—an Ashkenazi collection of rulings on matters of ritual slaughter, written in the region of Regensburg (whose leaders and rabbis the author mentions) around the middle of the thirteenth century. The passage of relevance here, which is headed with the Hebrew letters "*HG*" abbreviating the word *hagahah* (gloss), and ends with the phrase 'thus far the gloss', is part of the main text, like other 'glosses' in this work. It reads as follows: "Gl[oss] found in a responsum of Rashi: our statement concerning a lobe of the lung...But if the meat does not protrude beyond the adhesion, [the meat is] ritually unfit, because it has adhered breadthwise—a tradition transmitted by R. Moses Poler. And if the tubercle is adhering to the ribs, it is ritually unfit—in the name of R. Abraham Hiadik. Thus far the gloss." The author reports two halakhic traditions, one in the name of R. Abraham Hiadik, a leading authority on Jewish law and customs in eastern Ashkenaz in the first half of the thirteenth century, and the other in the name of our R. Moses Poler. Immediately after the gloss, the text states: "As to what Rashi wrote concerning the little rose-lobe, wherever there is an adhesion the animal is ritually unfit—I received a tradition from my teacher, R. Isaiah di Trani, that this is the case only if it adheres to a lobe...." R. Isaiah di Trani, a colleague of R. Isaac Or Zaru'a, died around 1230–40.[49] Our author is writing, therefore, around the third quarter of the thirteenth century.

A further reference to R. Moses Poler may be found, once more, in ms. Oxford 2344 of *Pa'aneah Raza*, which, as we have already stated, is an Ashkenazi commentary on the Torah from the first half of the fourteenth century, including a great variety of eastern Ashkenazi material. Part of the work has been published in print, under the same title, in several editions; but the bulk of it still remains in manuscript—and ms. Oxford is one of the most important manuscripts. Indeed, I have already referred to it here for other purposes. At one point in the book we read: "R. [Moses] Poliera posed a further difficulty, from what we say in [chapter 7 of tractate *Hulin*]: If an unclean fish be found among clean fish, one should throw it away and the remainder is permitted...But this raises the difficulty whether the same reason would not suffice to

48 Urbach, *The Tosafists*, pp. 581–585.

49 See my article "R. Isaiah di Trani the Elder and his Contacts with Byzantium and Palestine" (Heb.), *Shalem* 4 (1984), p. 411. On R. Abraham Hiadik, see S. Spitzer, "The *Minhagim* of R. Abraham Hiadik" (Heb.), *Kovetz Al Yad* 9 (1980), pp. 151–215.

declare all of the fish unfit.... And the difficulty was solved for him by our teacher R. Solomon..." (fo. 87a). In style, the passage is very similar to that of the discussion cited by R. Bezalel Ashkenazi in *Shitah Mekubetzet* (see above), between R. Moses and his colleague R. Abraham. On fo. 94a we read: "And R. Moses Polier posed the difficulty: Granted that the phylactery worn on the head is not considered an interposition; it should nevertheless be considered as superfluous [priestly] vestments...And our teacher R. Solomon explained..." This selfsame passage is cited in the aforementioned BL ms. 2853. Yet another passage in *Pa'aneah Raza* (fo. 89a) reads as follows: "R. Moses Poliera posed a difficulty: Why should one desecrate the Sabbath by cooking [for an invalid], which is a prohibition punishable by stoning, while one can do the same by telling a non-Jew And our teacher R. Haim explained...And our teacher R. Solomon explained...." And a fourth reference: "R. Moses Polier posed a difficulty...Why does the Talmud ask in tractate *Bekhorot*.... One who makes a slit in the ear of a first-born animal, is his son after him fined or not?...And our teacher R. Solomon explained that this question was asked on behalf of the rabbis..." Thus, though we do not know just who this R. Moses Poler was, we are acquainted with his colleagues: R. Solomon, R. Abraham, R. Haim, and R. Moses—a group of scholars studying and discussing points of law together, in a yeshiva excelling in Torah and wisdom. However, the yeshiva need not be in Poland; it is not inconceivable that our R. Moses came from Poland to study with his colleagues in Germany.

Another reference to R. Moses Poler may be identified in ms. Pans, Alliance 166, which contains a brief, four-page work commenting on Maimonides' Laws of Ritual Slaughter.[50] The work has an appendix entitled "Examinations of Our Master Moses Palier, of blessed memory" (fos. 107–9), very probably the same R. Moses Poler we have been discussing. In my first search of the card-index at the Institute for Microfilmed Hebrew Manuscripts, this particular work escaped my attention because of the distortion of the name (spelled here without a *vav*). However, a study of the work confirms the identification without any doubt. The author refers in his brief commentary to R. Moses Taku ("some authorities [test the adhesion in the lung] by rubbing it with the hand; R. Moses Tatu (*sic*) did this"); to R. Jacob b. Nachman of Magdeburg ("This was instituted by R. Jacob b. Nachman of Magdeburg [in connection with adhesions in the lung]: It happened that a tubercle was found...and the scholar R. Jacob b. R. Nachman permitted it to be eaten and said..."); to "our teacher R. Ezekiel" ("I heard from our teacher R. Ezekiel that if the two membranes of the lung have been examined..."); to R Isaac

50 I am indebted to my friend and colleague Dr. Simha Emanuel, who drew my attention to this passage after he had unearthed this work as part of his Ph.D. thesis, "The Lost Halakhic Books of the Tosafists," pp. 256–257.

("Thus said R. Isaac: I have not heard any prohibition from our rabbis in this connection..."); and to R. Eliezer of Bohemia ("and so I have heard that R. Eliezer of Bohemia permits..."). All these scholars belong to the group of Polish scholars, as listed below. This person Moses, then, in the brief span of four pages, mentions a fairly large number of local scholars, of the same period and circles discussed here; perhaps he was also personally acquainted with them. Moreover, apart from these particular scholars (and a few earlier Tosafists), the author mentions no one else, with one exception: "And I, the writer, have it on the authority of my teacher R. Shabtai, of blessed memory...that he told me in the name of R. Oshaia of Tran, of blessed memory, who proved from the wording of R. Shabtai, who said..." Now I have already demonstrated this link of tradition between R. Moses Poler and R. Isaiah di Trani—and on this very same issue—on the basis of another, independent source. It thus transpires that the link was by way of R. Isaiah di Trani's pupil R. Shabtai, who is also known to us from direct contemporary evidence[51] and may thus be assumed to have studied Torah in his youth, like his illustrious master, in the Torah centers of Germany.[52]

Ms. Paris, Alliance 166 was written in the year 1627 by "Benjamin son of...Abraham Motal of blessed memory"—none other than the anthologist of the great halakhic collection known as *Tumat Yesharim* (Venice 1622), which contains a rich selection of works by both early and late authorities. The same Benjamin Motal's ms. Paris is also a collection of various works on ritual slaughter and related areas, organized as a kind of commentary on Maimonides' Laws of Ritual Slaughter. Moses Poler's brief work is appended to the end of the collection. Anthologies of this kind on ritual slaughter and the like were very popular among Yemenite scholars of all generations, and they copied this

[51] See my article "R. Isaiah di Trani," *Shalem* 4 (1984), p. 414. Incidentally, the source currently before us provides conclusive proof—if such were still needed—for the identification of R. Isaiah b. Immanuel, mentioned in Nathan Kalkish's book *Even Sapir*, with the celebrated Isaiah di Trani, author of *Sefer ha-Makhria*, as I argued in my article. We may thus reject the arguments of S. Hasidah, who, without any basis, challenged the identification in his edition of *Shibbolei ha-Leket* by R. Zedekiah b. Abraham the Physician (Jerusalem 1988), p. 70 n. 36. Hasidah actually mentions the very passage from Kalkish's work and rejects the identification of the R. Isaiah b. Immanuel referred to there with R. Isaiah di Trani. However, the association of the disciple Shabtai with both figures clearly corroborates my argument. The sparse material cited in relation to the "unknown" scholar Isaiah b. Immanuel should also be associated with R. Isaiah di Trani the Elder. For an argument against Hasidah on another count, pointing out the fundamental error responsible for his misconception, see S.Z. Havlin in his "Survey of New Books and Studies" (Heb.), *Alei Sefer* 15 (1988–89), pp. 157–158.

[52] The rabbi Shabtai mentioned by R. Isaiah di Trani is, of course, a different person, apparently known to us from another source. Cf. the Italian work published by S. Assaf, "From the Teachings of the First Scholars of Italy" (Heb.), *Sinai* 34 (1964), pp. 15–40.

collection, too, together with Moses Poler's brief treatise (distorting the text considerably; one Yemenite manuscript calls our Moses "Pleiral"). A search of the card-index at the Institute for Microfilmed Hebrew Manuscripts brought up two such Yemenite manuscripts: Bar-Ilan University 235 (Institute Mic. 36593); New York JTS Rab. 589 (Mic. 39280). Two further Yemenite manuscripts of this type are mentioned in the list of Yemenite manuscripts at the Ben-Zvi Institute.[53]

A closer look at the collection of commentaries preceding Moses Poler's work in the Yemenite manuscripts reveals some new data of interest to our topic. Among the many sources from which Motal put his collection together, besides such familiar works as *Arba'ah Turim*, *Kolbo*, and *Sefer ha-Tur*, the anthologist cites quite copiously from a commentary to tractate *Hulin* by a R. Dosa, known as *Ner Yisra'el*. Yosef Tobi suggested that this R. Dosa was the son of R. Sa'adya Gaon.[54] However, comparison of the parallel manuscripts indicates that the author in question was R. Dosa the Greek, a Byzantine scholar who lived in the second half of the fourteenth century, studied under Ashkenazi scholars, notably R. Sar-Shalom of Vienna, and wrote, among other things, a commentary on Rashi's commentary to the Torah (still in manuscript).[55] The author's identity is quite clear from the fragments of this commentary to tractate *Hulin*—a lost commentary of which nothing was known until now, particularly in connection with the interesting material it contains relating to the Ashkenazi scholars. A description of the personality and activities of this Byzantine scholar would be of considerable interest, but that is not our purpose here. His importance in our present context stems from the fact that, according to the structure of the system of copying and quotation in these Yemenite collections—which cannot be discussed in detail here—it seems almost certain that Moses "Palier's" "Laws of Examination" were also copied from R. Dosa's commentaries to tractate *Hulin*, not from the original. That is to say: It was R. Dosa the Greek, who studied in Ashkenazi academies under the leading Ashkenazi teachers in the second half of the fourteenth century,

53 Y. Tobi, *Kitvei ha-Yad ha-Teimaniyim bi-Makhon Ben-Zvi* (Jerusalem 1982), nos. 121, 379.

54 Ibid.

55 Bodl. ms. Neubauer. A few passages from this manuscript, in which Dosa quotes teachings of his teacher R. Sar-Shalom, were published by S. Spitzer in *Hilkhot u-Minhagei Maharash* (Jerusalem 1977), pp. 180–189, based on a previous publication by A. Neubauer in the Dutch journal *Israelitische Letterbode* 8 (1882–83). See Spitzer's comments in his introduction (p. 17 n. 25). And cf. further id., "Data on R. Dosa the Greek from His Work on the Torah" (Heb.), in *Studies in Memory of the Rishon LeZion* iv, ed. M. Benayahu (Jerusalem 1985), pp. 177–184.

who received and transmitted these traditions of Moses Poler from his teachers; the latter presumably knew this material from a more direct source, being removed only by about one hundred years from Poler himself. R. Dosa's lost book has thus yielded information about another lost book—that of Moses Poler.[56]

Most recently, a further search produced a quotation from R. Moses Poler's teachings in a book of R. Joseph di Sigora, a disciple of R. Joshua Soncino (brother-in-law of R. Moses Isserles, the Rema), in ms. Benayahu (Mic. 44725), fo. 30b. The quotation consists of a question and answer concerning a passage in the first chapter of tractate *Gittin*. Joshua Soncino lived and wrote in Turkey and brought much Ashkenazi material to the attention of Sefardi scholars.

OTHER TORAH SCHOLARS IN THIRTEENTH-CENTURY POLAND

I will now list other thirteenth-century scholars whose teachings have been cited and who are explicitly associated with Poland. My attention in this article focuses on rabbinical literature only; but it should be noted that contemporary rabbinical sources contain further material, as yet unexploited, bearing on the history of Polish communities in the thirteenth century, both in manuscript and in print. Thus, for example, one finds, in the responsa of R. Haim Or Zaru'a (son of R. Isaac Or Zaru'a),[57] a responsum concerning a coercive divorce involving members of the Ludmir community. The responsum, dating back to the last third of the thirteenth century, may be added to an item of information from the year 1171 about "R. Benjamin the generous of Ludmir," who happened to be in Cologne at the time and fell victim to some kind of accusation.[58] The responsum, in contrast to the case of R. Benjamin, attests to the existence of a regular community with properly appointed leaders and institutions, including official rabbis: R. Isaac and R. Manoah b. Jacob,[59] who were involved in imposing the divorce. Here, too, it is quite clear that the far-off community of Ludmir, in Volhynia province, depended on the halakhic rulings and teachings of German and Bohemian scholars. But concealed in R. Haim Or Zaru'a's responsum is yet another revelation: mention is made there of Jews in the nearby town of Chelm, where the recalcitrant husband was staying: "Finally we sent after the woman and the agent that she should be divorced here in Vladimir [Ludmir], and we urged him that he should divorce

56 I. Ta-Shma, "On Three Lost Hebrew Books from the Middle Ages" (Heb.), in *Saul Lieberman Memorial Volume* (Jerusalem 1993), pp. 214–224.

57 § 157.

58 A. Habermann, *Sefer Gezerot Ashkenaz ve-Tzarfat* (Jerusalem 1964), p. 128.

59 The father's name is lacking in the printed edition but appears in the manuscript of the responsum, at the end of the collection *Simanei Or Zaru'a*, ms. Vat. 148, fo. 155^1.

[her] himself, but he refused, and to the town of Chelm, too, we decreed that he should be sent for...." I believe this is the earliest testimony in our sources to a Jewish presence in that city.[60]

In this connection, Mr. Adi Schremer has called my attention to a passage in *Or Zaru'a*, "Hilkhot Terefot," 56d (bottom): "Similarly, R. Gershon...and our rabbi Sasson...and our rabbi Samuel...and R. Isaac ben Judah...and in Mayence and Polanit [Poland] it is permitted in accordance with their ruling..." We have yet another relevant source in a responsum of R. Judah ha-Kohen, author of *Sefer ha-Dinin* (mid-eleventh century), mentioned at the very beginning of this article: "A certain Jew brought goods from the Land of Polum" included in R. Meir b. Barukh of Rothenburg, *Responsa* (Prague 1610), § 885)—probably also a reference to Poland.

Let us proceed now with our list of Polish scholars.

R. Moses b. Hisdai. Also known as R. Moses Taku, R. Moses was one of the central members of hasidei Ashkenaz,[61] a man of extraordinary learning who produced a tremendous literary output of high quality in both legal and philosophical genres. He was active in Poland, for Nachmanides calls him "the great scholar R. Moses b. R. Hisdai of Poland, may he live a long life," stating in his name that "the wording of this talmudic teaching has been distorted by the students...."[62] As there are good grounds for the assumption that Nachmanides' novellae to the Talmud had already been written by 1240, it seems likely that R. Moses was still alive at that time. A considerable quantity of infor-

[60] Dr. David Assaf drew my attention to the rather surprising possibility that R. Joseph ha-Helmi, whom Judah b. Shemaryah met in R. Meir of Rothenburg's study-house, was a native of Chelm. See N. Goldfeld, "A Commentary on the Torah by Judah b. Shemaryah in a Geniza Manuscript" (Heb.), *Kovetz Al Yad* 10 (1982), p. 144. And cf. S. Eidelberg, "On the Antiquity of the Communities of Chelm and Ludmir" (Heb.), *Zion* 31 (1966), p. 116. At one time I thought to identify a reference to the city of Ostraha in *Or Zaru'a*, i. § 112. The responsum in question is concerned with a Jew named Mattathias who inadvertently killed somebody and was banished to another city, where he was received with respect. The printed edition reads, "Therefore this Mattathias, in so far as he declared that for that event [he was banished], even though the people of Trigom [*benei adam Trigom*] treated him with respect, it is deemed a true exile." However, in all the manuscripts that I have examined the text reads, "even though the people of Ostrigom [benai Ostrigom; the letters would look similar in a badly written text] treated him with respect...." The difficult word was obviously misunderstood by the printers, who mistakenly split it into two. However, my colleagues have pointed out to me that the reference is to the city of Esztergom in western Hungary, home of the oldest Jewish community in that country, known to have existed as early as the tenth century. In fact, R. Isaac Or Zaru'a himself visited Esztergom, as attested in his *Hilkhot Nidah*, p. 51a.

[61] For a summary of this chapter in his life, see Y. Dan, introduction to facs. edn. of the book *Ketav Tamim*, pp. 7–27.

[62] Nachmanides, *Novellae* to tractate *Git.* 7b.

mation about him was assembled by Urbach,[63] creating a picture of his literary, social, and religious activities. He was active around the cities of Regensburg—where he probably officiated as rabbi; Magdeburg, where he was asked to intervene and resolve a conflict; Tachau (Tachov) in Bohemia (or Dachau in Germany), probably his native town; and Wiener-Neustadt, near Vienna, mentioned (in a later period) as his place of burial. He was also asked to intervene in the above-mentioned episode of R. Jacob Svara of Cracow, concurring in his responsum[64] with the majority view of the scholars, who required R. Jacob to divorce his nursing wife, even though, as a *kohen*, he would never be able to remarry her. A description of R. Moses' character, as one of the greatest Torah scholars of his time—and one of the most extreme on the "right wing" of hasidei Ashkenaz—and a full account of the philosophical, literary, and chronological problems that his biography raises require a special study.

R. Mordechai of Poland and R. Isaac of Poland. R. Moses Zaitman, son of R. Judah he-Hasid, studied under scholars who had attended his father's discourses on the Torah portions of the week. Known by name among those scholars are R. Mordechai of Poland and R. Isaac of Poland.[65] As implied, these two belong to a broader circle of scholar-companions. The leading figure was undoubtedly "R. Isaa[c] [b. Ezekiel?] of Russia," who is referred to as such dozens of times. A comparison of parallels indicates that he is identical to R. Isaac of Moriat.[66] Some authorities have identified him with R. Isaac of Chernigov, near Kiev, who was also a disciple of R. Judah he-Hasid; this R. Isaac travelled through Europe, even reaching England, where he told R.

[63] Urbach, *The Tosafists*, pp. 420–426. The report that R. Moses Taku visited Palestine is extremely dubious, as my friend Dr. Elhanan Reiner has shown me. The source is a responsum of R. Bezalel Ashkenazi, § 2, where the respondent quotes from the book *Ketav Tamim*: "Upon our arrival in Palestine…," citing several laws concerning agricultural matters that apply only to the Holy Land. However, R. Moses Taku's name is not mentioned at all, and there is no doubt that the scholar concerned is some other person who wrote a similarly named book; indeed, the very same passage is quoted verbatim in two manuscripts as the beginning of a letter by Isaac Hilo, a Spanish scholar of the thirteenth century, after his journey to Palestine. It is common knowledge that the letter describing a journey to Palestine, purportedly written by Isaac Hilo, is a forgery (see G. Scholem, "The Book *Shevilei Yerushalayim* Attributed to R. Isaac Hilo Is a Forgery" [(Heb.], *Me'asef Zion* 6 [1934], pp. 39–53; and see my article "Matters of Eretz-Israel" [Heb.], *Shalem* 1 [1974], pp. 82–83, and the argument that evolved on the affair in the subsequent two volumes of the journal). However, there was also a genuine letter, but it has not survived—except for its first lines, which match the quotation from *Ketav Tamim* word for word. At any rate, further research is needed.

[64] *Or Zaru'a*, i, § 740.

[65] I.S. Lange, *Perushei Rabbi Yehudah he-Hasid la Torah* (Jerusalem 1975), Terumah 19: 18; Beshalakh 14: 2.

[66] Ibid., index, s.v. For his father's name, Ezekiel, see below, text around n. 73. Cf. Kupfer, *Teshuvot u-Pesakim*, p. 162 n. 14.

Moses b. ha-Nesi'ah that the Hebrew verb *yabem* (to marry one's brother's widow) meant "sexual intercourse" in Russian. However, there is no support for this identification, and to my mind the identification with R. Isaac of Moriat must stand. Since R. Judah he-Hasid died in 1217, the members of this circle were active in the first half of the thirteenth century.

For the moment we can say nothing further, or more detailed, about these figures. Nevertheless, two further passages might be mentioned. One occurs in ms. Gaster 730 (London Or. 9931), fos. 121a, 123b, where there are a few statements in the name of one "R. Isaac Poler," whom I am inclined to identify with R. Isaac of Russia (and even if the two are distinct, we may at any rate add a further scholar to our list). The other passages appear in a commentary on the prayers by R. Eliezer of Worms, in manuscript, fo. 21a:

> "He will order His angels to guard you." And whence do we know that he commands an individual angel?—from the verse "The angel of the Lord camps around those who fear him." ...And he answered him: The verse "The angel of the Lord camps..." refers to the Prince of the Countenance, who stands in the camp and commands the angels under him...[67]

In ms. Paris 772,[68] however, we read, "...asked my teacher R. Y. b. R. Mordechai...." At first sight this would seem to refer to the celebrated R. Isaac b. Mordechai (known as Ribam), one of the greatest Tosafists of the generation before R. Judah he-Hasid, a resident of Regensburg, who was surely consulted by R. Judah on occasion. However, R. Eliezer of Worms could not have studied under Ribam; moreover, R. Judah could hardly have consulted him, for chronological reasons: R. Judah himself was still young when the latter was quite an old man. Urbach was, therefore, fully justified in not listing R. Isaac b. Mordechai as one of R. Eliezer of Worms' teachers, passing over Aptowitzer's statement to that effect in silence.[69] One should, therefore, prefer the simple reading "R. Mordechai," as is indeed the case in other manuscripts of the commentary that I have examined.

An interesting passage is included in a commentary to *Sefer Yetzirah*, attributed to R. Sa'adya (a Franco-German scholar of the twelfth century): "He made them by weight"—*kaf* and *lamed* occur halfway through the alphabet....

67 Text from ms. Moscow 614, fo. 21a.

68 Ed. and pub. M. Herschler (Jerusalem 1992), p. 87.

69 Urbach, *The Tosafists*, pp. 389 and 199: "Ribam was a man of halakhah and we do not know that he was active in any other area, except, perhaps, for a hint that he showed some interest in esoteric lore, as he asked R. Judah he-Hasid a question in angelology," citing the source before us now. This is not quite accurate, for Ribam—if the reference is, indeed, to him—was asked by Judah he-Hasid and not the opposite. Urbach's comment also contributes a major consideration in favor of our conviction that the person involved was not Ribam. Cf. Aptowitzer, *Ravyah,* introduction, 317 n. ya.

"And He exchanged them all for one"—that is to say, when He made the alphabet. He placed the *alef* at the beginning of the alphabet with all twenty-two letters...and from them derived the alphabet *alef-tav bet-shin* etc. ...And R. Mordechai received [a tradition] that the middle of *alef-lamed bet-mem* was prior to that."[70] This is not the proper place to discuss the commentary itself, which is a French work from the mid-thirteenth century, as Prof. Moshe Idel has assured me, though the bulk of its material belongs to the beginning of that century. At any rate, it is clear that in the first quarter of the thirteenth century (or slightly before that) there was a scholar named R. Mordechai in the circle of mystics; perhaps this is indeed our R. Mordechai.

R. Mordechai and R. Isaac of Poland are also mentioned in ms. Cambridge 53 (Cat. Schiller-Szinessy), fos. 163–64.

R. Simeon "Polner" and R. Pinehas of Poland. Another pair of scholars, active in the third quarter of the thirteenth century, is mentioned in the sermons of R. Haim Or Zaru'a: "I heard from the *h[aver]* R. Simeon Polner, may God protect and preserve him, a good mnemonic for Counting the Omer, so as not to forget..."; and also: "I heard from the *h[aver]* R. Phineas that in the land of Poland...."[71]

R. Aaron and R. Ezekiel. The aforementioned responsum of R. Isaac Or Zaru'a concerning R. Jacob ha-Kohen and his marriage with a nursing woman (ii, § 740) is worded as an open letter and manifesto addressed to all rabbis of the region, but one of the latter is designated in particular by name and specifically urged to act:

> Therefore, rabbis of all places, gather together and assemble and force him to divorce her, so that the words of the learned shall not come to nought; in our day the matter depends particularly on our teacher R. Aaron, for he alone remains in this generation, for in him is Torah and great age, and he is worthy of exercising zeal in honor of the Lord and in honor of His Torah, and we shall all sign after him.

As we have pointed out, the first part of the manuscript page was censored at some time in the Middle Ages and we have no way of identifying the particular addressee. It transpires from the heading, as stated, that it was an open letter, but it is obvious that R. Aaron, and another scholar, named R. Ezekiel (see below), were among those actually named in the salutation. At the end of the letter, after a repeated call to take a stand and act in concert, R. Isaac Or Zaru'a ends his responsum as follows: "To you, our masters R. Aaron and his yeshiva, and R. Ezekiel, [greetings of] life and peace." It is quite obvious that

70 *Sefer Yetzirah* (Przemysl 1885), end of ch. 2. Cited from BL ms. 754, fo. 124a. This passage and others are omitted in the printed edition.

71 *Derashot me-Har Or Zaru'a* (Jerusalem 1974), pp. 73, 84.

these two scholars, like the other anonymous scholars alluded to in the letter, were local residents, for the responsum is worded as follows: "Therefore, gentlemen, do not shirk your duty and divorce her from him in any way you can, for you surely know that this breach will spread to all places." It is very doubtful whether the person in question is the celebrated R. Aaron of Regensburg, for the special tone of respect in this responsum is absent in other responsa of R. Isaac Or Zaru'a and his companions sent to the rabbi of Regensburg. I would assume that he and his companion R. Ezekiel were Polish scholars from around Cracow; we may be able to identify them in time. Special attention should be paid to the most unusual honorifics heaped upon R. Aaron, far exceeding the usual verbiage then in vogue. Incidentally, it was presumably to this scholar that R. Avigdor Kohen-Zedek of Vienna was alluding in his responsum, as cited in *Sefer Mordekhai* on tractate *Shabbat*, ch. 11 (end):

> R. Aaron asked R. Avigdor Kohen-Zedek, instruct us, our rabbi: concerning a cure by a spell, whether it may be pronounced on the Sabbath, if this involves a danger of pounding spices? And thus he replied: Chief of leaders, most honored among the thirty, prince of fifty, *holy of holies*, builder of ruins and restorer of paths and many more mighty deeds, well versed in the channels of knowledge and wisdom, and nothing he proposes is impossible for him, *most eminent of the generation*, R. Aaron [...], may his memory be for a blessing, for his words are a cure and a remedy. In Sanhedrin, chapter 'Helek': It is permitted to rub the stomach with oil and feel it, it is permitted to pronounce spells against snakes and scorpions on the Sabbath, etc. ....And, moreover, our master and Rabbi Simha [of Speyer] had a disorder of the eyes, and he ordered that spells be pronounced for him even on the Sabbath. Peace be upon you, I, the worm, Avigdor Kohen.[72]

Now, in the printed edition of *Sefer Mordekhai*, *Shabbat*, § 385, we read: "And once our R. Simha's eyes were unwell, and a certain woman taught the rabbi, R. Avigdor Kohen, a spell, and he pronounced this spell on the Sabbath twice a day on the eye, once in the morning and once in the evening." The exceptional laudatory terms used in the salutations indicate quite clearly that we are concerned here with the same person.

As to R. Ezekiel—I know nothing. Nevertheless, I have found a reference in a book named *Minhag Tov*,[73] written around the year 1275 by an Ashkenazi Jew resident, apparently, in Italy, to a scholar by the name of R. Isaac b. R. Ezekiel of Russia. It is quite intriguing that the name of R. Aaron of Regens-

72 According to Bodl. ms. Neubauer 666, ad loc.

73 Printed by M.Z. Weiss, "The Book *Minhag Tov* (Based on ms. Kaufmann)" (Heb.), *Hatzofeh le-Hokhmat Yisra'el* 13 (1929), pp. 217–245; and see my "Havdalah Made on Bread" (Heb.), in *R. I. Nissim Memorial Volume*, ed. M. Benayahu (Jerusalem 1985), p. 145.

burg, too, mentioned above several times, occurs in this book, and the reference is most probably to the same circle or one of its offshoots.

R. Isaac of Breslau. This scholar is mentioned in R. Abraham b. Azriel of Bohemia's *Arugat ha-Bosem.* Urbach wrote in his introduction to the book: "The author heard an explanation of a passage in the *Mekhilta* from R. Isaac of Vratislau, that is, Breslau. This scholar was the first Jew in that city to be mentioned in Hebrew literature. In many respects, it was a Polish city."[74]

R. Israel of the land of Poland. This scholar's interpretation of a verse in Exodus (4: 2) is cited in an anonymous collection of exegeses in ms. Strasbourg 44.[75] This Ashkenazi collection, written in the fifteenth century, consists, for the most part, of commentary by R. Judah he-Hasid as reported by his son R. Moses Zaitman. The manuscript was one of Lange's prime sources for his edition of R. Judah's Torah exegesis.[76] Alongside these comments, it includes a selection of further Ashkenazi sources: from commentaries by R. Eliezer of Worms and R. Meir of Rothenburg, as well as from two unknown books: *Mahaneh Elohim* and *Kupat ha-Rokhelim.* Our passage ends with the words: "Received from Israel, may the Lord protect and preserve him, from the land of Poland, but I added a little to his words." By all indications, the collection was edited at the turn of the thirteenth and fourteenth centuries, and R. Israel lived in the last quarter of the thirteenth century.

Eliezer of Lublin. A scholar named Eliezer of Lu[b?]lin is mentioned at the end of R. Meir of Rothenburg's work *Sefer Tashbets* as it appears in the *Rothschild Miscellany.*[77] In fact, many of the numerous works included in that manuscript contain various additions. In the text of *Sefer Tashbetz*, § 489, we read: "R. Eliezer of Lulin, may he rest in peace, used to pronounce the blessing whenever he begin to study." And compare my comments in the description of the *Rothschild Miscellany* introducing the facsimile edition, where I proved that the manuscript from which this passage was copied into the *Miscellany* was written in 1300.[78]

74 Urbach, *Arugat ha-Bosem*, p. 120.

75 The entire commentary was published by J. Gellis, *Tosafot ha-Shalem* (Jerusalem 1987), p. 96.

76 See above n. 65.

77 Currently in the Israel Museum, cat. no. 180/51. Possibly the correct reading should be "of Poland" (me-Polin) rather than "of Lu[b]lin" (me-Lu[b]lin). R. S. Schneersohn, who is currently editing *Sefer Tashbetz*, has pointed out to me that in the printed edition §133 and in many manuscripts this decision is attributed to R. Elazar of Metz.

78 I. Ta-Shma, *The Rothschild Miscellany: A Scholarly Commentary* (London 1989), pp. 53–55.

Asher b. R. Sinai. An interesting item of information about a Polish scholar who died young, before being ordained a rabbi, is reported by R. Jacob b. Asher in his celebrated legal code *Arba'ah Turim.* A youth named Asher, son of R. Sinai, was studying in R. Asher b. Yehiel's yeshiva at Toledo; on his way home "to Russia," he died in Sicily. According to R. Asher,

> he told them his name, and that he had studied here with us, and showed them *tosafot* [to "a few tractates that our teacher, the aforementioned rabbi, had composed"; i.e., *Tosefot ha-Rosh*] that we know he took with him from here.... And we attest, and it is known to all members of our group, that since the day he came here no one else has come here to study whose name is Asher, save that same R. Asher son of R. Sinai, and he was from the land of Russia and came here with a certain youth named R. Jonathan.[79]

In another report of this "student," a companion defines him as "an important German [Heb.: Ashkenazi] student."[80] As we have already seen, the term "Russia"—at least for Benjamin of Tudela—defines the region between Prague and Kiev, that is, Poland. However, the reference may be to the territories of Silesia in western Poland, rather than the region of Kiev, as possibly indicated by the more complete, detailed account of the event rendered by R. Asher b. Yehiel himself: "There was also here a certain youth by the name of R. Reuben, and he was from the land of Bohemia, and he was an acquaintance of R. Asher, who had died, who was from the land of Russia." The event occurred somewhere between 1306—the year in which R. Asher's yeshiva was founded at Toledo—and c.1328, the year of his death.[81]

79 *Tur*, "Even ha-Ezer," end of ch. 118. The rare name Sinai is rather intriguing. It appears once more—again in connection to Kiev—in an old text published by N. Golb and O. Pritsak, *Khazarian Hebrew Manuscripts of the Tenth Century* (Ithaca, N.Y. 1982), p. 14: "Sinai b. Samuel."

80 Ibid.

81 Asher b. Yehiel, *Responsa*, ch. 51, § 2. Our traditional chronology holds that R. Asher died in the year 5081 of the Jewish calendar, i.e., 1320/1. A. Freimann, in his famous essay on R. Asher (*JJLG* 12 [1918], pp. 265–66), argued that he died in 5088 (1327/8), and on that basis Y. Baer (*History of the Jews in Christian Spain* [Heb.] [Jerusalem 1959], p. 185) fixed the date as 1327. The source of the traditional date is the book *Tzedah la-Derekh*, whose author, Menahem ibn Zerah, studied under R. Asher and his sons and should be a reliable authority. None of the proofs cited by Freimann for his later date is wholly valid, while there is clear evidence that 5081 was the last year for which there are reports of R. Asher's activities. See, e.g., his *Responsa*, ch. 8, § 11, cited by Freimann, as well as the new fragments published by Urbach in *Shenaton ha-Mishpat ha-Ivri* 2 (1975), p. 39. And cf. my article, "Philosophical Considerations in Deciding the Law in Spain" (Heb.), *Sefunot* 3 [18] (1985), pp. 106–107. Today I would nevertheless be inclined to support the 1327 dating.

POLISH SCHOLARS AND HASIDEI ASHKENAZ

A perusal of the list of Polish scholars indicates that in the first half of the thirteenth century the Jews of Poland maintained close contacts with R. Judah he-Hasid, who might be considered their spiritual leader and principal mentor. The situation recalls the intimate link between the Polish Jews and the Torah scholars of Germany in the first half of the eleventh century. Almost every Polish scholar of the thirteenth century who is mentioned (or cited) in our ancient sources is clearly a member of the circle of R. Judah he-Hasid himself or of his successors. This aptly explains R. Judah's rather surprising involvement in the appointment of cantors in the new communities of his disciples or close associates, as described at the beginning of this article. It also clarifies why R. Eliezer b. Isaac of Prague was so concerned that R. Judah's letter to the Polish Jews would cause irreversible harm. The whole surprising picture almost automatically raises the question of Judah he-Hasid's departure from the city of his birth and upbringing, Speyer, to Regensburg. The move apparently took place about thirty years before his death, and we know nothing of its cause or exact date, just as we possess almost no other information about R. Judah he-Hasid's personal biography; we do not even know under what masters of esoteric or exoteric lore he studied. But the move to Regensburg was undoubtedly significant: he would not have departed his birthplace, his family's native town—the celebrated city of Speyer, cradle of Jewish mysticism in all of Germany, the seat of his greatest predecessors in learning and piety—and gone to live in the far-off city of Regensburg without some very cogent reason. True, Regensburg was also renowned for its Torah and learning; prominent scholars had lived there as early as the late eleventh century and certainly in the twelfth century, when it was the home of such famous personalities as R. Isaac b. Abraham, R. Isaac b. Mordechai, and their associates. However, the suggestion that R. Judaḥ he-Hasid uprooted himself from his hometown because of economic and physical difficulties in 1196–97 and moved to Regensburg, where living conditions were more comfortable,[82] clashes with what we know of the man's character from his many letters.

In this connection, we have an interesting observation. A collection of tales from Germany, written in the sixteenth century,[83] contains a few dozen

[82] *Germania Judaica* 1 (Tübingen 1963), p. 293. This account is based on A. Epstein, "Das talmudische Lexikon *Yihusei tannaim ve'amoraim* aus Speier," *M. GWJ* 39 (1895), p. 449 n. 5. However, Ashkenazi tradition itself considers the move as an "exile" and punishment for incautious treatment of the mystical literature entrusted to him. I agree wholeheartedly with Ivan Marcus's approach in the introduction to his edition of ms. Parma of *Sefer Hasidim* (Jerusalem 1985), p. 19 n. 45.

[83] N. Brill described the collection at length and copied many passages from it. See N. Brill, "Beiträge zur jüdische Sagen- und Spruchkunde im Mittelalter," *Jahrbücher für Jüdische Geschichte und Literatur* 9 (1889), pp. 1–71. He and other scholars learned from this

old folk-tales about R. Judah he-Hasid and his miracle-working. It turns out that these miracles all took place in Regensburg; not one of them is reported from the Rhine cities. Moreover, some of the tales feature various prominent personalities of Speyer Jewry, community leaders and rabbis, relatives of R. Judah who came to visit him or happened to come to his Regensburg home, where all these events occurred. Although the tales in the collection are all imaginary, their narrative frames tell us something of life and *realia* at the time. This is particularly true with regard to names of places and contemporary people. R. Judah, having completed his studies in his home city and established a reputation for himself, moved in middle age to Regensburg, where most of the major events in his life took place. It was there, along the eastern border of Germany, that he exerted his main influence and it was from there that his fame spread. Interestingly enough, all appeals to him for guidance in Jewish law and ethics, as well as all the quotations in these fields, come from the same geographical region,[84] though the material that has survived is far from exhaustive and much of what exists still awaits publication. Thus, for example, one of the main speakers in an early German book of *minhagim* from the thirteenth century, ascribed to the eastern part of the country, is R. Jacob b. Nachman of Magdeburg.[85] The text reads: "R. Jacob taught in the name of R. Judah he-Hasid and R. Baruch and R. Abraham"[86] (in connection with how long the baking of *matzah* on Passover should take). The phrasing is very similar to that of R. Ephraim b. Meir: "And I decided to send to my masters R. Baruch, and R. Abraham, and the Hasid R. Judah, to hear what they might instruct me on this matter."[87] All three were members of the Regensburg *beit din*.

The last quarter of the twelfth century was the period of the German *Drang nach Osten*, eastward into Poland. And, as we have seen, all the scholars whose names are identified with Poland in the sources for this period belong to R. Judah he-Hasid's circle of companions and admirers. It is not inconceivable, therefore, that groups of hasidei Ashkenaz moved in an organized—or unorganized—manner to the new, "Germanized" territories. It is also possible that this organized movement provided one of the main motives for R. Judah's

text various details of R. Judah he-Hasid's family connections and some relevant matters of *realia*. The manuscript is now in the Jewish National and Hebrew University Library, Jerusalem, 8vo 3182.

84 With the exception of the passage in *Sefer Tashbetz*, § 219.

85 Concerning this scholar, see Urbach, *Arugat ha-Bosem*, pp. 125–126. R. Jacob was the father of the celebrated halakhic authority R. Hezekiah of Magdeburg, as Urbach wrote there (and accordingly I do not understand why Urbach himself wrote R. Hezekiah's name in his *The Tosafists*, p. 564, as R. Hezekiah b. Jacob b. Meir).

86 Bodl. ms. Neubauer 1150 (Institute for Microfilmed Hebrew Manuscripts, mic. 16610); also ms. Vat. 45 (mic. 162), fo. 88.

87 *Sefer Hasidim*, ed. Wistinetzki, p. 390.

own move to Regensburg: a desire to be as near as possible to his disciples at the new scene of events. The fact that so many of the "Polish" references have been located in the *gilyonot* literature, whose editor was active around Magdeburg, in Germany, and that some of the chief figures in that literature lived in the same area, supports this conjecture. Moreover, the link with hasidei Ashkenaz also helps to explain the background to the literary silence of which we spoke at the beginning of this article. These scholars, who held a unique position in regard to the study and teaching of Torah,[88] confined their pronouncements to brief *ad hoc* sayings, mainly as comments on biblical passages or short, laconic exchanges of views in other areas of halakhah and aggadah, as well as *gematriyah* and *notarikon*.

The direct, intimate ties between early Polish Jewry and hasidei Ashkenaz in those early generations may provide an apt explanation—as suggested by my friend Prof. Moshe Idel—for a most puzzling phenomenon that is unique to kabbalistic literature in Poland at a later time, when Lurianic kabbalah began to spread in the seventeenth century. Kabbalistic literature in Poland is replete with elements of *notarikon* and *gematriyah*, which generally make their appearance interspersed in kabbalistic texts. They are quite extraneous to kabbalah proper, quite foreign to the original works of Lurianic kabbalah, whether by the mystics of Safed or by their disciples. This phenomenon is so unique to Polish Kabbalists that one can immediately attribute the source of any kabbalistic material of this sort to Poland or to Polish writers. Now it is common knowledge that one of the most salient characteristics of the writings of R. Judah he-Hasid, his disciples, and their successors, for many generations, is an almost obsessive preoccupation with *gematriyah*. The close historical link of the early Polish scholars with these circles, as it emerges from our account, may provide a clue to a correct evaluation of the phenomenon in its second, later guise, when scholars of the school actually settled in Poland. Thus, one also perceives a considerable—and surprising—internal continuity of Jewish life in Poland in all periods.

To summarize: Early Jewish settlement in Poland, as we have seen, was intimately bound up with—and most probably an offshoot of—*hasidut* Ashkenaz from its very beginnings. Little wonder, therefore, that those early Polish Jewish scholars modelled their method of study and style of instruction on those of the mainstream German Jewish pietists: brief, mainly oral, ephemeral, *ad hoc* comments, questions, and answers; short-breathed discussions and makeshift arguments between teacher and disciple. These teachings were almost never written down in a systematic literary fashion, but rather transmitted as traditions and occasionally preserved by someone who saw fit to

88 I. Ta-Shma, "The Precept of Torah Study as a Religious and Social Problem in *Sefer Hasidim*" (Heb.), *Shenaton Bar-Ilan* 14–15 (1977), pp. 98–113.

include some of what he had heard, personally or otherwise, in a "book." For that reason, the early history of rabbinical literature in Poland, i.e., the early history of the major channel of Jewish cultural expression, is still buried under a heap of as yet unidentified manuscripts, most of them anonymous collectanea and miscellanea. Only a scrupulous, methodical comparison of these manuscripts may produce a more coherent description of that "pulse of the Jewish heart" whose absence so troubled Graetz's historical consciousness.

(Translated by David Louvish)

Originally published in
Jews in Modern Poland,
Polin Studies in Polish Jewry, vol. 10,
ed. Gershon David Hundert.
London and Portland, Or. 1997.

CHAPTER 3

LA CULTURA RELIGIOSA — THE CHAIN OF TRADITION

SOUTH-ITALIAN RABBINIC TRADITION IN THE TWELFTH AND THIRTEENTH CENTURIES

Medieval rabbinic literature in Italy has scarcely been treated in modern Jewish scholarship as a subject in itself. Indeed, lack of interest in early Jewish scholarship in Italy is much older than recent times. Already R. Menahem ha-Meiri, the late–thirteenth-century Provencal luminary, in his distinguished chronographical introduction to tractate *Avot*, omitted the "Italian chapter" from his review, and Prof. I. Twersky dedicated a large section of a lecture on "The Contribution of Italian Sages to Rabbinic Literature" to some possible explanations of this strange phenomenon. According to Twersky, and that was actually the central theme of his lecture: "Ha-Meiri did not perceive any conceptual, literary, or methodological unity and continuity"[1] in the Italian rabbinic literature. That is why he omitted Italy as a distinct cultural unit. Italy did not produce a "school" that could be described as an entity in itself.

I completely disagree with this view. As a matter of fact, the whole question does not exist, because R. Menahem ha-Meiri knew practically nothing about Italian Jewish scholarship, except R. Nathan b. Yehiel of Rome—the only Italian scholar mentioned by the Meiri—and his monumental *Sefer he-Arukh* could not very well stand and fill the Italian rubric all by itself. Twersky says that "there is no reason to assume that ha-Meiri, extremely erudite and generally comprehensive, was totally unaware of these developments"[2] but there is no need for us to assume anything, it being an established fact that nowhere in his huge literary edifice does ha-Meiri mention any of the Italian sages or books mentioned by Twersky (except the *Arukh*) or not mentioned by him. How could ha-Meiri "perceive"—or not perceive—"any conceptual, literary, or methodological unity and continuity" in a body of literature that he never saw? It was not only ha-Meiri who was unaware of the Italian heritage.

[1] I. Twersky, "The Contribution of Italian Sages to Rabbinic Literature," *Italica Judaica* 1 (1983).

[2] Ibid.

As far as I know, no other Provencal rabbi, before ha-Meiri or at his time, mentions an Italian book or scholar, except the *Arukh*, and some rare citations of R. Isaac b. Melchizedek, taken from secondary sources. And the same applies to the great Nachmanides, to the Rashba, and all his colleagues. The Italian rabbinic literature was completely unknown to Spanish and Provencal tradition, and it would have been a great surprise had the Meiri included a chapter on Italy in his work. It is the same lack of knowledge, now as in the past, that is behind the Italian lacuna in modern histories of medieval rabbinic literature, although we now know a lot more than was known in the past.

A full historical survey remains a *desideratum*, and I certainly do not intend to care for it here. But I would like to sketch a historical outline of that literature that will describe the basic underlying historical process during the eleventh to thirteenth centuries, dominating its inner development.

As is well known, northern Italy was a major geographic center from which the first permanent Jewish settlements in Germany drew a great influx of immigrants. This chapter in our history has been described by my good friend and colleague, Prof. A. Grossman, who showed in his book on the early Ashkenazi sages[3] that R. Meshulam b. Kalonymous (whose grandfather R. Moses was the first Jew to come over from Lucca to Mayence toward the second quarter of the tenth century) was actually living in Italy all or most of his life; it was his son R. Kalonymous III who was the first emigrant in the true historic sense of the word, toward the end of the tenth century. Besides the general considerations drawn up by Prof. Grossman, his view can now be corroborated by new evidence.

R. Kalonymous and his son Meshulam were the first Italo-Ashkenazi rabbis to have written responsa, quite a number of which are preserved and extant today, mainly in the collection of Geonic responsa *Teshuvut Geonim Kadmonim*.[4] The manuscript serving for the edition is now in Berlin (Or. Qu. 685) and contains, besides the 112 Geonic responsa and the 38 by R. Kalonymous and R. Meshulam, *Mishpetei Shevuot* and *Sefer ha-Mekakh* by R. Hai Gaon, both in an anonymous Hebrew translation, different from the printed translation done by R. Isaac b. R. Reuven of Barcelona in the year 1078. The manuscript contains also the famous *Iggeret R. Sherira Gaon*, and the commentary of R. Hai Gaon to *Seder Toharot*, besides some other small tidbits that do not concern us here. The manuscript is of Ashkenazi origin, very old and of great importance. Prof. Epstein dedicated an exhaustive study to it, first printed in German and now available in a Hebrew translation,[5] in which he corrected hundreds of false readings by Cassel. In his introduction to *Perush R. Hai le-*

3 A. Grossman, *The Early Sages of Ashkenaz* (Jerusalem 1981), pp. 29–78.

4 *Teshuvot Geonim Kadmonim*, ed. David Cassel (Berlin 1848).

5 *The Geonic Commentary on the Order Toharot Attributed to Rav Hai Gaon*, ed. J. Epstein (Jerusalem 1982) (Heb.).

Seder Toharot, he proved the German provenance and nature of the manuscript, and went on to say that it was probably copied from an earlier manuscript written in the Rhein area in the first half of the eleventh century.

I have always felt some curiosity about this manuscript because of a peculiarity that I could not explain to myself satisfactorily. The Geonic responsa represented in the collection are all, but five, attributed to different Geonim, all of whom are prior in time to R. Hai Gaon. A few are by R. Hai, signed together with his father, Sherira, that is—before the death of R. Sherira and R. Hai's ascendance to the Geonate. On the other hand, the manuscript has R. Hai's two big halakhic monographs, *Sefer ha-Mekakh* and *Mishpetei Shevuot*, in a Hebrew translation, different from the extant Spanish translation. This seemed to me to be somewhat extra-ordinary, as R. Hai's responsa usually occupy large parts of most other Geonic collections, and especially so since this manuscript has on it traces of an early numeration of the separate sub-collections that were put together to form the present manuscript, as first pointed out by Prof. Epstein, who counted ten different sub-collections here, and still so few R. Hai responsa in it. I, therefore, thought that perhaps the manuscript, or its urtext, was completed before the year 1006, when R. Hai proceeded to the Geonate.

Mishpetei Shevuot and *Sefer ha-Mekakh* were written before that, as shown by Prof. Assaf,[6] and translated into Hebrew (in Italy or Germany!) at a very early date, long before the Spanish translation was done. This would be very surprising, of course, but it could be true. I, therefore, asked Dr. Edna Engel, of the Institute of Hebrew Paleography at the Hebrew National and University Library, to consider the Berlin manuscript from a paleographic perspective and to compare it to the rich collection of dated and classified manuscripts at her disposal. To my astonishment she reached much the same conclusions. She fixed its maximal date at the period of the earliest dated Ashkenazi manuscript known to us, 1074, and probably before that to around the year 1000, stressing its unique mix of Italian and German paleographic components. She also saw a close formal paleographic similarity between the Berlin manuscript and the large Geniza fragment, published by L. Ginzberg[7] containing another early collection of responsa by R. Meshullam, and ms. Bodleian 544, containing another anonymous Hebrew translation of R. Hai's *Sefer ha-Mekakh*, out of which Prof. S. Abramson published a few chapters in the Rabbi Joseph B. Soloveitchik Jubilee Volume.[8]

6 S. Assaf, "Le-Heker Sefarav ha-Hilkhatiyim Shel R. Hai Gaon," *Hazofeh Quartalis Hebraica* 7 (Budapest 1923), pp. 277–287.

7 L. Ginzberg, *Genizah Studies in Memory of Doctor Solomon Schechter*, II (New York 1929), pp. 270–279.

8 S. Abramson, "Five Sections of R. Hai Gaon's *Sefer ha-Mekakh*," in *Rabbi Joseph B. Soloveitchik Jubilee*, II, eds. S. Israeli et al. (Jerusalem and New York 1984), pp. 1312–1379.

This manuscript was described by A. Neubauer, in his Bodleian catalogue, as being of the thirteenth century, but there is an earlier colophon to the manuscript that Neubauer overlooked. The two colophons and their possible readings and meaning were discussed by Prof. M. Beit-Arie in the supplemental volume to the Neubauer Bodleian catalogue, put out by the Institute of Microfilmed Hebrew manuscript in Jerusalem and printed in Oxford (1995).

All this seems to single out the Berlin manuscript as one of the earliest German manuscripts in our possession, written possibly around the year 1000, when R. Meshullam himself was still alive. It also stresses the Italian-Byzantine character of the Berlin manuscript and the three other manuscripts interconnected with it.

A few years (perhaps one generation) later, at the turn of the eleventh century, Rabbenu Gershom Me'or ha-Golah opened his academy in Mayence—the first of its type in Europe and active for almost a century, until the First Crusade hit the Rheinland. Many great luminaries headed the academy during the eleventh century, among them R. Jacob b. Yakar and R. Isaac b. Judah, Rashi's teachers. Rabbenu Gershom was not of Italian stock, notwithstanding the remote possibility mentioned by a sixteenth-century Italian Jewish chronographer, that he came from Ancona. See my article, together with Prof. D. Flusser, in the Archive Juive, 1975. Rabbenu Gershom came from Metz, in France, and at the center of his curriculum he placed the intensive study of the Babylonian Talmud.

During its century of activity the academy created a major change in the halakhic attitude and outlook of its many students. It can be easily shown, for example, that Rashi's commentary on the Talmud based, as it is, on his German teachers' early work, differs meaningfully from the still earlier Italian-Kalonymide tradition.

This process of "Babylonization" of the halakhah and its original reinterpretation and literary decoding surely had its opponents in Germany, mainly the more conservative sectors of its society, but the process could not be stopped. I have dwelt on this subject in great detail in my Hebrew book on early Franco-German ritual and custom,[9] and I shall not take up space here to argue the point. The Ashkenazi communities on the Rhein tried very hard to harmonize their homeland Italian customs and traditions—a lot of which derived from Byzantine-Palestinian halakhic tradition—with the conflicting, or dissenting, Babylonian texts with great intellectual ability and agility, but with little convincing success. Their efforts are duly mirrored and registered in the eleventh-century book *Ma'ase ha-Geonim* and its literary parallels. These sources also bear witness to the intensive efforts to collect, verify, and register for posterity the Italian tradition and practice, to its minutest detail and from wherever it could be gotten.

9 I. Ta-Shma, *Early Franco-German Ritual and Custom* (Jerusalem 1992) (Heb.).

The net result of all this was the gradual establishment of what became later known as *Minhag Ashkenaz*, its main characteristic being the upgrading of rejected Palestinian halakhah to the newly sanctified status of *minhag*, thereby preserving its sacred existence as such, despite its disagreement with the Babylonian Talmud.

This process of "Babylonization," which was a natural result of the intensive activity of the newly established academy in Mayence, quickly found its way back to homeland Italy, where the rich literary output of the German academies became very widespread, mainly at the central academy in Rome, where R. Nathan b. Yehiel was active at the time, composing his famous talmudic dictionary *Sefer he-Arukh*. This great rabbinic personality—son to an old and well-rooted Italian family of rabbis and halakhists and himself a leading figure in his community—adopted the new teaching, citing it side by side with traditional Italian exegetical tradition, already tinted with more than a touch of Babylonian-Geonic literature, as he found it integrated and represented in Rabbenu Hananel's commentary to the Talmud. Rabbenu Hananel was of an Italian descent, probably born in Bari, but he came over to Qairouan with his father, R. Hushiel, when he was still a young man. In Qairouan he completed his studies under Rabbenu Nissim Gaon, and there he adopted a deep layer of Geonic tradition and influence.

Rabbenu Hananel's classic commentary to the Talmud was not known in Franco-Germany before the beginning of the twelfth century, that is some fifty years after its author's death. Therefore, it had no influence on Rabbenu Gershom Me'or ha-Golah's academy, neither in his lifetime nor later in the century under the spiritual leadership of his great disciples. Yet from an overall historical point of view, Rabbenu Hananel contributed as well in Italy—where he was intensively studied in the second half of the eleventh century—to an amplification of the same "Babylonization" process, begun by Rabbenu Gershom Me'or ha-Golah in Germany and transmitted to Italy through his disciples, colleagues, and followers. Cultural ties between the Jews of the Rheinland and their compatriots in Italy were never severed throughout the eleventh and twelfth centuries. We know that early Mayence commentaries to various *midrashim* were initiated and made possible by a lively traffic of Greek-speaking Jews from (southern?) Italy to Germany, who brought with them oral and written auxiliary linguistic material that enabled this initiative.[10]

It is also interesting to note that most of what is known to us today from Rabbenu Gershom's attributed Talmud commentary—which had become superfluous and practically obsolete with the appearance of Rashi's superb commentary—has been preserved mainly by secondary Italian authors, as noted

[10] I. Ta-Shma, "An Unpublished Franco-German Commentary on *Bereshit* and *Vayikra Rabba, Mekhilta*, and *Sifrei*" (Heb.), *Tarbiz* 55 (1985–86), pp. 61–75.

by Avraham Epstein in his basic article on Rabbenu Gershom's commentary, printed over one hundred years ago![11] Even the direct manuscript material is mostly of Italian origin.

It is furthermore interesting to note, that Rabbenu Hananel's commentary on the Talmud was warmly accepted and immediately adopted in France and Germany as soon as it arrived there, at the beginning of the twelfth century, while the *Halakhot Rabbati* by R. Isaac Alfasi, the famous Rif, was practically avoided there until the second quarter of the thirteenth century. This occurred despite the great affinity between the two books, both being of Qairouan origin and scholarship, and despite the fact that, to a large extent, the Rif was actually dependent on Rabbenu Hananel's commentary (Rabbenu Hananel being considered generally his very teacher). Rabbenu Hananel's recognized Italian origin and background promoted its widespread acceptance in Germany, in contrast to the Rif, who represented pure Spanish tradition and was, therefore, considered foreign and uninteresting. Only toward the beginning of the thirteenth century, at the height of the Tosafist period, when the process of Babylonization was already a *fait-accompli* in France and Germany, was the Rif accepted and granted a proper hearing. This subject has been described in full in my article on the acceptance of Rabbenu Hananel, Rif and *Halakhot Gedolot* and France and Germany.[12]

We have, therefore, Rabbenu Hananel playing a double role—and to a certain extent a conflicting role—on two different geographical arenas: as an arbitrator of Babylonian-Geonic Talmudism in Italy and as a carrier of Palestinian-Italian traditions in Franco-Germany. This is a focal point in every assessment of the historical importance of his Talmud commentaries throughout the high Middle Ages, and his place as an outstanding bridge over the wide gap that existed between early eastern and western Talmud interpretation. This aspect of Rabbenu Hananel's work has been developed in my book on rabbinic literature in Provence.[13]

The "Babylonization" of central European halakhah had its substantial beginning in Germany at the turn of the eleventh century and moved on from there to Italy. But the gradual break from earlier Palestinian influence was progressing in Italy at a considerably slower pace than in Germany, and all through the twelfth century we can still discern Palestinian traces, a whole Palestinian

[11] A. Epstein, *Der Gerschom Me'or ha-Golah zugeschreibene Talmud-Commentar*, Moritz Steinschneider Jubilee Volume (Leipzig 1896), pp. 115–143.

[12] I. Ta-Shma, "The Spread of the Writings of R. Isaac Alfasi (Rif) and Rabbenu Hananel, and of the *Halakhot Gedolot*, in France and Ashkenaz in the 11th and 12th Centuries" (Heb.), *Kiryat Sefer* 55 (1980), pp. 191–201.

[13] I. Ta-Shma, *R. Zerahia ha-Levy "Ba'al ha-Maor" u-Bnei Chugo: le-Toldot ha-Sifrut ha-Rabbanit be-Provence* (Jerusalem 1992).

stratum one may say, in the quite rare halakhic material that reached us from twelfth-century Italy. I have discussed a few interesting examples in my aforementioned book on early Franco-German ritual.[14] However, the main agent of German influence in Italy who really changed the over-all orientation of halakhah in Italy, detaching it from its historical Byzantine-Palestinian tradition toward a clear Franco-German submission, was R. Isaiah di Trani the Elder, by his own life-long endeavor and through the literary activity of his devoted follower R. Zedekiah b. Avraham Anav, the author of the *Shibbolei ha-Leket.*

The figure of R. Isaiah has attracted much scholarly attention, but this side of his personality and activity does not seem to have merited equal attention. R. Isaiah was of Italian pedigree, studied in Speyer, Germany under the renowned R. Simha of Speyer, and went back to Italy. But all his known public activity is connected directly with the historical Byzantine territory, including Southern Italy, Greece, and Macedonia. He travelled a lot in these areas—including two visits to *Eretz Israel;* one at the beginning of his activity and the other toward the end of his life—to inspect and control the religious norms and standards of behavior within the Jewish communities there. He corresponded intensively with their sages, striving hard to correct many of their religious practices that to him seemed to be contrary to halakhah, but to us reflect old Palestinian traditions. R. Isaiah's early studies in Germany, under R. Simha of Speyer, are very properly outlined in R. Wertheimer's introduction to his edition of R. Isaiah's responsa.[15] R. Isaiah's historical connections with the Jewish communities in the Byzantine are entirely missing from S. Bowman's book on the history of the Jews in Byzantium,[16] but are fully detailed, and explained, in my article on R. Isaiah.[17]

New information on R. Isaiah di Trani's early sojourn in Germany is now available from a unique manuscript in the Günzberg collection in Moscow, lately microfilmed for the Institute of Microfilmed Hebrew Mss. in the National Library in Jerusalem. The manuscript contains R. Isaiah's Bible commentary: a short, choice collection that had been known to exist in two different manuscripts, printed twice in the past and lately in an annotated, critical edition by Rabbi C. Chavel.[18] The printed edition, which is quite short, derives from R. Zedekiah Anav's self-prepared copy and is accompanied in both manuscripts by his signed glosses and they, too, were printed in the edition.

[14] n. 9.

[15] *The Responsa of R. Isaiah The Elder*, ed. A. Wertheimer (Jerusalem 1967), pp. 17–86 (Heb.).

[16] S. Bowman, *The Jews of Byzantium — 1204–1453* (New York 1985).

[17] I. Ta-Shma, "A New Chronography on the Thirteenth-Century Tosafists" (Heb.), *Shalem* 3 (1981), pp. 319–324.

[18] C. Chavel, *Isaiah di Trani Bible Commentary* (Jerusalem: Mossad Harav Kook, 1972).

The new Ginzberg manuscript is much larger, though still not entirely complete, and it reflects the florilegium that was in the possession of R. Avigdor Katz, the famous Viennese rabbi, himself a disciple of R. Simha of Speyer, and a great admirer—and maybe a pupil too—of R. Isaiah di Trani. His glosses accompany his manuscript, much the same as R. Zedekiah's glosses accompany the first set of manuscripts. A detailed description of the manuscript is given in my article on *Nimukei Humash*.[19]

This side of R. Isaiah di Trani's personality, and the great influence it had on many of his contemporaries, created an interesting literary phenomenon, misunderstood and, therefore, not appreciated by students of rabbinic literature. As is well known, the famous Italian book *Shibbolei ha-Leket*, by R. Zedekiah b. Avraham, has come to us in three different versions: the so-called "short" edition, which was the first to see the light of day, printed in Venice in 1546; the *Shibbolei ha-Leket Completum*, which was edited and published by S. Buber in the year 1887; and the book of *Tanya*, which was already printed in the year 1517—that is before the short *Shibbolei ha-Leket*—and was thought by most scholars and rabbis to have been plagiarized by its anonymous author from the *Shibbolei ha-Leket Completum*. It is quite obvious that *Sefer Tanya* is heavily dependent on the *Shibbolei ha-Leket*, the anonymous author having borrowed whole sections from it verbatim, mostly without accreditation, thereby turning some of R. Zedekiah's family relatives into his own!

Much has been written on this subject, but the riddle of *Sefer Tanya* was finally disentangled only a few years ago, by my good friend, the late Dr. Zvi Feintuch.[20] Feintuch proved that its author was actually the thirteenth-century R. Yehiel b. Yekutiel, the famous scribe who copied the Leiden manuscript of the Talmud Yerushalmi, and who also wrote *Hilkhot Shekhita* (still in manuscript and published by Feintuch himself) and the well-known Italian ethical thesis *Ma'alot ha-Midot*. He proved also that the many paragraphs in the book wherein he cites Zedekiah's personal relatives as his own are all spurious, being missing in the nine existing manuscripts, while two others are cited with a different degree of familial relation that could be true, the author being of the same family, Anav, as R. Zedekiah, who wrote *Shibbolei ha-Leket*. He proved also that the book *Tanya* was originally composed as a companion to the Italian-rite prayer book, most of its manuscripts copies being written as glossaries to the Italian prayer book. Feintuch concludes his excellent paper with the following sentence: "Now that the identity of the author of *Sefer Tanya* is known, and we indeed know that he was a student, and relative, of R. Judah b. Bin-

[19] I. Ta-Shma, "*Nimukei Humash* by R. Isaiah di Trani," *Kiryat Sefer* 64 (1992–93), pp. 751–753.

[20] Z. Feintuch, "Tanya Rabati," in *Versions and Traditions in the Talmud*, ed. D. Sperber (Ramat-Gan 1985), pp. 65–76.

yamin, and that he wrote other halakhic books, and that he is exempted from all suspicion, we can start an examination of what he had actually done in his *Sefer Tanya* without bias."[21]

As a matter of fact, the answer to that question is very simple, and already implicit in Feintuch's analysis itself. R. Yehiel simply turned the *Shibbolei ha-Leket* from an academic book, organized according to a rational principle of thematic order, into a cursive companion to the Italian-rite prayer book, changing its order to suit the prayer book, and summarizing its contents in an abridged form. The reason why Feintuch himself did not end up his paper with that simple, and true, solution—although all the ingredients necessary for it were pointed out in his paper and were actually his own original findings—was the relatively many pieces of information added by R. Yehiel that contribute to a feeling that R. Yehiel saw himself, in a way, as an author, not a mere editor. But the truth is that Feintuch's paper, right and correct all the way through, has missed a crucial question: What version of *Shibbolei ha-Leket* was R. Yehiel editing or, rather, processing?

An interesting aspect of the *Shibbolei ha-Leket* literary complexity is the nature of the *Shibbolei ha-Leket ha-Katzar*—the short *Shibbolei ha-Leket*, mentioned before. The author of that book was sharply attacked by rabbis and scholars for doing his best to obliterate his plagiarism, by changing and concealing everything in the original that could give a hint as to who its author was. It is impossible for me to deal with this in the necessary detail, but progress has been achieved lately, by R. Simha Chassida, in his introduction to his edition of the second part of *Shibbolei ha-Leket*, which was published in a stencilized form by R. Chassida's grandfather many years ago.[22] The short *Shibbolei ha-Leket* was never carefully compared to the complete version; this was done for the first time by R. Chassida the younger. He noticed that there were important additions in the short version, citing R. Judah b. Binyamin, adding thereby to the many quotations from that rabbi in the *Shibbolei ha-Leket Completum*. He also noticed—what Buber had noticed much before him—that many of these additions quote Maimonides, who is scarcely—and probably not at all—mentioned in the complete version of the book. Chassida, therefore, warns the reader to be more careful regarding the identity of the anonymous editor of the short version, since he too was undoubtedly a disciple of R. Judah b. Benyamin, very much like R. Zedekiah himself.

I can say with full certainty that the short *Shibbolei ha-Leket* is an earlier version of the book written by R. Zedekiah himself. What is more, it is not the only earlier version of the book known to us. In an article published in 1984, I described briefly another early version, ms. Oxford, the Bodleian Library,

21 Ibid., p. 76.

22 *Sefer Shibbolei ha-Leket*, ed. S. Chassida (Jerusalem 1988), Introduction, pp. 51–56.

659, which also includes quite a lot of material that was not included in the last version.[23]

The question, therefore, is: What exact version did R. Yehiel use when he transformed the book to accompany the prayer book of the Italian rite? If he had in front of him the long and the short version, not to mention manuscript Bodleian 659, there is no need to attribute any private additions of his own into the companion, thereby solving completely the riddle of *Sefer Tanya* on the basis of Feintuch's work.

The real question to be asked is: Is there a perceivable inner development along the line of the progressive original versions of the *Shibbolei ha-Leket* and if so, what is it? The answer to that question is a positive one. The versions seem to progress from a distinctive Italian tradition to an ever increasing Ashkenazi influence that is undoubtedly the outcome of R. Isaiah di Trani's work.

I shall end with a mention of still another Italian manuscript belonging to some other scion of the Anav family: a halakhic compendium on various chapters of the law, like prayer, Shabbat and holidays, etc., which is still very much Italian and on which the German influence is slight. The ms. München was described by Steinschneider as an anonymous *sefer dinim*. The author was also a disciple of R. Judah b. Binyamin, but his principal teacher was R. Jekutiel b. Moses Anav. This precious manuscript preserves many interesting Italian traditions and usages.

originally published in
*L'Ebraismo dell'ltalia VIeridionale Peninsulare
dale origini al 1541 Societa, Economia, Cultura,
IX Congresso internazionale dell'Associazione Italiana per lo studio del Giudaismo*
Potenzi-Venosa, 1992.
eds. C.D. Fonseca, M. Luzzati, G. Tamani, and C. Colafemmina.

23 I. Ta-Shma, "On the Beginning of the *Piyyut*" (Heb.), *Tarbiz* 53 (1984), p. 287.

CHAPTER 4

THE LIBRARY OF THE FRENCH SAGES

In a former article, I tried to formulate three basic principles necessary, and adequate, for a working description of the early Ashkenazi library.[1] These are: totality, eclectic use, and an active-aggressive adaptation.

Almost every book written in Hebrew and known to be extant at the time was included in their library. That is not to say, of course, that all such books could be found conveniently gathered in one place, and certainly not in all places. What is meant here is that all the Hebrew books known to exist at that time could be gotten, and within reasonably easy reach, in the central communities of medieval Germany. This is the principle of totality, described and exemplified in minute detail in my article.

This intellectual yearning to read and master everything committed to writing in Hebrew does not indicate a parallel wish to absorb and internalize the abundance of information and opinion acquired through this comprehensive reading. Far from it. Further mental processing and practical (or even theoretical) use of this book lore was highly eclectic, and subordinated to critical examination of its contents, in the light of accepted local tradition. Indeed, what these sages really strove for was a better understanding of their difficult texts and versatile traditions, whether holy—like the Bible, Talmud, and various mystical books—or profane—like books on medicine, astronomy, magic etc. Therefore, they tried, with astonishing success, to lay hands upon anything that might improve their understanding or furnish further support for their ancient traditions, but they unanimously rejected anything and everything that spoke otherwise. This is the principle of eclecticism.

The third principle, that of active-aggressive adaptation, describes the rooted Ashkenazi usage of active interference in the books and the conscious rewriting of words, sentences, and whole paragraphs—not to mention omissions and additions—in whatever book they might be reading. Such textual changes, many of a radical nature, were instituted by the sages whenever they

1 I. Ta-Shma, "The Library of the Ashkenazi Sages in the Eleventh to Twelfth Centuries," *Kiryat Sefer* 60 (1984), pp. 298–309.

sensed danger or, at least believed they saw some gross mistake, in a book. In my article I put together many concrete examples that were known to me at the time. Later, I added some others in a short article published in the same periodical.[2] Additional material has since been brought forth by other scholars and still more is on its way.

These three characteristic features should be taken and understood as one whole, mutually complementing each other. The deeply rooted conservatism, so characteristic of the early and high Middle Ages, was counteracted to some extent in eleventh-century German Jewish scholarly circles by a great urge to learn and constantly improve the understanding of their old traditions and classical texts, in order to conserve their content and safeguard their religious message. Therefore, much of what was considered harmful toward this end was actively treated; either omitted, re-written, or otherwise emended, and non-helpful or neutral material simply ignored and forgotten. This is the reason why so many Hebrew classics have an independent Ashkenazi literary "version," untestified in any other manuscript tradition, creating the "optical mistake" of an alternative source-reading, as explained and exemplified in my aforementioned article.

It is impossible for me to enter this subject again now, but keeping this short summary in mind, we can now go on to understand the deep changes that matured in the period of the Tosafists, during the great Franco-Jewish renaissance of the twelfth century. In short terms—as we have not near enough time here to cover the subject more fully—we may say that all three principles, laid out above and valid for the eleventh century, were overturned, and their opposites now ruled the scene. Some more elaboration is certainly called for here. One of the most impressive facts in connection with the huge tosafist literature is its absolute disregard for earlier Franco-German literary tradition. The voluminous *tosafot* literature, composed in France and Germany by six successive generations of Talmudists during a period of about two hundred years and covering the whole stretch of the twelfth and thirteenth centuries, does not mention the rich eleventh-century rabbinic literature, anywhere and anytime, except for Rashi.

One may of course argue that Rashi's work served them as an excellent sorted compilation of the best of eleventh-century halakhic and commentative tradition, but as our knowledge of eleventh-century learning is progressing, we understand more and more that that was not the case. On the contrary, the Tosafists' disregard *in itself* contributed much to the disappearance of the earlier scholarship, as new copies of it were no more in demand and the old copies perished naturally.

2 Ibid., 61, Addenda.

The new approach developed and propagated by the Tosafists called for an independent and innovative attitude toward the study of the Talmud based upon a critical reading of the text and the comparison of its legal issues with other talmudical stances, from far and from near, that might have some logical relevance to it. Such comparison gave rise to a multitude of questions that evoked an endless series of novellae that were actually new interpretations to the old laws. This change was, of course, in accord with the general developments in twelfth-century renascent France and, as my friend Haim Soloveitchik says in some of his articles, the Tosafists actually re-wrote anew the old Talmud, giving entirely new meaning to most of its laws.

Such an avant-garde attitude to the Talmud could make very little use of the traditional material coming down from the eleventh century, and it was simply abandoned. The Tosafists also ignored the flourishing rabbinic literature written at their time in Provence by first-rate talmudic scholars, among them renowned figures such as Ra'avad and R. Zerahya Ba'al ha-Maor of Lunel. Many Provencal rabbis stood under the deep influence of the French Tosafists, and a lot of Provencal literature is dependent, directly or indirectly, on the Tosafists. On the other hand, the complete ignoring of their work by the Tosafists, and the absence of their literature from the tosafist library, until the very end of the period is a classic proof of the Tosafists' self-assurance and self-esteem as absolute halakhic leaders of their times.

The same trend can be followed in the thirteenth century, from which period a very qualitative library has come down to us by illustrious Spanish Talmudists, among them R. Me'ir Abulafia, R. Jonah Gerondi, Nahmanides. Next to nothing is represented in the tosafist literature as we know it today, there being only very meagre evidence that they ever saw it. That is not to say, of course, that an individual Tosafist, here and there, did not see or even study Provencal and Spanish books—a few, such as R. Moses of Coucy, are actually known to have done so. But tosafist literature as a whole (as a unified literary phenomenon) certainly did ignore the bulk of this external body of literature. Even a luminary as outstanding as Maimonides is very rarely mentioned in their work; the few quotations can be found in a short article by J. Dienstag.[3]

I would go even further than that: It seems that the French Tosafists did not show great interest even in the parallel work of their contemporaneous colleagues in Germany, and many German citations in the French *tosafot* came to be there through French correspondence and mediation. But this was not the case with the German Tosafists, who made regular use of their French colleagues' work. One could actually go even further than that, and claim that the Tosafists of the thirteenth century did not mention *any tosafot* literature, even

[3] J. Dienstag, "The Attitude of the Tosafists to Maimonides" (Heb.), *Shmuel Mirsky Jubilee Book* (New York 1958), pp. 350–380.

of fellow contemporary tosafist schools. They, of course, made regular recourse to earlier, "classic" *tosafot*—as can be seen from individual, unedited, *tosafot* sheets, printed lately from manuscripts. But this point too demands further elaboration.

I must add here something that should have been said right at the beginning. By the term "tosafist literature" I mean not only the *tosafot* to the Talmud alone, but also the large tosafist literature on the Pentateuch exegesis. Though scarcely used, or even known, by many historians, this literature is by no means small, and certainly not smaller in volume than the *tosafot* to the Talmud. Only a small part of it has been through the press, but well over two hundred such manuscripts exist today, exceeding by far the number of manuscripts of talmudic *tosafot*. Prof. Urbach did not deal with this material in his classic book on the Tosafists, and it, therefore, still lies untouched in over a hundred microfilm reels in the Institute of Microfilmed Hebrew Mss., although it is replete with rich material of important historical and ideological interest. I want to emphasize that when considering my subject I took into account this branch of their literature too, and my conclusions are, therefore, valid for the whole range of *tosafot* literature. So much for what happened in the twelfth century to "totality," the first of our three principles.

As for the second principle, that of eclecticism, there is, of course, no need to elaborate much. The mere idea of a native, communal, or local tradition, was foreign to the Tosafists, who fought vigorously for the standardization of talmudic law as the basic law norm for all, and against many old and traditional *minhagim* (that is local customs and usages) that could not be accounted for in talmudic literature. The Talmud became the one and only source for Jewish law, and whatever could not be traced back to its authority did not count. Back to the Talmud meant, to the Tosafists, back to its manyfold interpretative system, which was quite open and versatile in their hands, and a tendency toward restrictive eclecticism in their circle was, therefore, unthinkable. Their library was indeed much more restricted than their fathers', as explained, but they were far more "modern" and open-minded than their predecessors to new ideas and understandings of the old traditions. This being the case, they had, of course, no need to alter the ancient texts; these texts either did not carry important meaning to them, or—if they did carry such meaning—the Tosafists were quite tolerant toward it, and could, therefore, live with it and leave it as it was. Therefore, all three principles that were correct, and valid, for the eleventh century, were overturned and rendered invalid for the tosafist period in twelfth- to thirteenth-century France.

The complete reversal of the three distinctive attributes of the eleventh-century library is, of course, symptomatic to—and an integral part of—the twelfth-century intellectual revolution, usually called the Twelfth-Century Renaissance, but is not the only difference evident between the libraries of the two centuries. There is also a marked quantitative difference between them.

The twelfth century saw many more copies extant for each individual book than had the eleventh. Proof of this is to be found in the relatively large number of European Hebrew manuscripts—between thirty and fifty—originating most probably from the twelfth century, mostly from its last third. Dated manuscripts from the twelfth century do not exist, but some are datable and others are paleographically believed to be such. From the eleventh century we do not have even one dated, or datable Hebrew manuscript from France or Germany. There are better purely physical chances for the conservation of the twelfth-century manuscripts, eleventh-century manuscripts having undergone an extra century of grinding; but this alone is quite unsatisfactory as a full explanation to the complete absence of all eleventh-century manuscripts and certainly so in comparison with Latin manuscript statistics for the same periods.

We mentioned before the disregard of eleventh-century wisdom by twelfth-century Tosafists. That was undoubtedly another important reason for its disappearance, as it was not being committed to further copying by later generations. But the main reason is, undoubtedly, the paucity of copies extant in true time, that is, in the eleventh century proper.

Higher talmudic education was not wide-spread in eleventh-century Germany, not to mention France, where it scarcely existed. German rabbis of that early century carefully watched the gradual—and well-controlled—progress of their student, from plain fluency and skill in the texts, through deeper and ever more penetrating studies, to the final stages of independent decision-taking. Disciplinary and intellectual supervision was very exacting at that early age and stage of Talmud study in Germany, meant to safeguard the old traditions and be ware of premature and novel halakhic pathways.[4] That being the case, and the number of high school pupils being small, there was no need for copious libraries, which were very expensive to create and consulted by a mere few. The spread of academies in the Tosafist period, in many cities and towns of Germany and France (including southern France), and the opening of their gates to all talented and willing youth, revolutionized the intellectual atmosphere and necessitated the production of an ever-growing number of manuscripts, in an increasing number of centers, large and small, where new *yeshivot* were started.

There is another factor that must be touched upon and that is the problem of internal censorship. It seems that the twelfth century was a direct continuation of the eleventh, censorship being an important tool of spiritual and religious guidance in the hands of the rabbis. This subject—in contra-distinction to the entirely different subject of Gentile censorship, or internal censorship done in anticipation of such external, Gentile, censorship—has not been raised yet, as far as I know, with the one exception of the Maimonidean controversy.

[4] I. Ta-Shma, "Law, Custom, and Tradition in Eleventh-Century Ashkenaz" (Heb.), *Sidra* 3 (1987), pp. 137–141.

As a matter of hard fact, censorship was also conveniently used to tune down irregular halakhic opinions, mostly minority opinions voiced by respected rabbis but rejected by their vast majority, and considered dangerous to the traditional conduct of the communities.

The point can be easily illustrated by the famous controversy on the permissibility of saying the *piyyutim* in the obligatory sectors of our prayers. We know that this controversy seethed continuously, within the limited historical borders of Franco-Germany, for nearly three hundred years, with a minority calling for its complete cessation or, at least, removal to other loci in the prayers, and the vast majority of rabbis advocating the popular practice in its traditional framework, notwithstanding the inherent halakhic difficulties. The fact is, that to this day we have not found in the vast literature even three original lines as phrased by "minority sages." We have quite a lot of "minority" quotations, transmitted to us through the services of their opponents, in order to refute their case. But nothing original has reached us, although the argument has been going on for almost three hundred years. The majority was always very militant in its efforts to enforce its views on this subject, and they saw to it that no further copies be made of their opponents' part in the correspondence when it was given to scribes for further copying and distribution.

An example of this phenomenon can be noted in the early thirteenth-century controversy over the permissibility of a wet-nursing widow to marry again within the 24 months of her obligatory wet-nursing. Most German rabbis were extremely against it, not willing to accept any sort of financial arrangement to ensure the baby's natural right, sticking absolutely by the talmudic injunction against such marriage. The controversy concerned an important Polish rabbi who personally married such a woman and, being a *kohen*, could not afford to divorce her, even temporarily until the 24 months passed, because he would then not be allowed to re-marry her. For some reason, which cannot be explained here, the issue held great religious importance in German halakhic tradition, and majority opinion was extremely rigid and outspoken, demanding his divorce from her, notwithstanding its final consequence. Nevertheless, a few rabbis, among them the French R. Tuvia of Vienne, quite a well-known rabbinic figure, permitted their marriage and certified it *à priori*. We know from the existing fragmentary correspondence that letters were sent "to the four corners of the world," but for all this, nothing has reached us from the original pen of the permitters. Moreover, long quotations from their letters, which were included in a letter by their bitterest opponent, R. Isaac Or Zaru'a, were afterward torn out of his book, and to this day this page is missing from all Or Zaru'a manuscripts and has never been found. This affair was described in full detail in my article on the early settlement of the Jews in Poland.[5] Other

5 I. Ta-Shma, "The Early Settlement of the Jews in Poland," *Zion* 53 (1988), pp. 353–356.

examples of merciless censorship in eleventh- to thirteenth-century Franco-Germany can be found in some of my other articles, and the whole issue can be safely taken as a unique spiritual trait of Ashkenazi librarianship.

Originally published in
Patrimoines: Rashi 1040–1990, Hommage à Ephraïm E. Urbach, IVe Congrès européen des Études juives textes,
ed. Gabrielle Sed-Rajna. Paris, 1990.

CHAPTER 5

HALAKHAH AND REALITY

THE TOSAFIST EXPERIENCE*

The revolutionary *tosafot* phenomenon, widespread over most of France (and parts of Germany) in the twelfth to thirteenth centuries, undoubtedly marked a major breakthrough in the development of Jewish law in the Middle Ages. A balanced appreciation of its historical import is, however, more difficult to achieve. This article will give a short survey of the Tosafist achievement and the major scholarly views on the historical significance of the reformatory tendencies recognizable in their work. It will also present a new approach that will be helpful to the better understanding of the phenomenon itself and to its historical appreciation as an internal, cultural development of eleventh-century, traditional Ashkenazi Torah study rather than as a novel, renascent twelfth-century phenomenon.

I.

No one accustomed to studying the *tosafot* should have any difficulty in summarizing their main methodological innovations. Rashi was concerned with molding an authoritative interpretation and unified conception of the talmudic *sugyot* from the abundance of possibilities and readings at his disposal. The Tosafists, however, wished to go beyond these limits, and surveyed as many reasonable alternatives as could be derived from the text of the *sugya* on logical or linguistic grounds, whether these had been weighed previously and rejected by Rashi (or his predecessors) or whether they were their own creative innovations. To this end, the Tosafists resorted to the same techniques as had been used by the Amoraim themselves: *ukimta*, *le-shitatayhu*, etc., and in particular the power of *sevara* (logical and legal reasoning); thus they were, so to speak, continuing—after a gap of several centuries—the ancient tradition of Amoraic study. They invested the old, hackneyed term *hiddush* (innovation) with new,

* This is a verbatim script of my plenary lecture in the Colloquium—only footnotes have been added here. This lecture constitutes the opening section of the second part of my long essay: "Law, Custom and Tradition in Eleventh-Century Germany," *Sidra* 3 (1987), pp. 85–61 (Heb.)—which limits its discussion to the eleventh century—and should be understood as its immediate continuance.

dynamic meaning, converting it into the peak of accomplishment and major goal of every Torah student: In their hands, logical and legal scrutiny and criticism of the text by the study group, under the guidance of their master, became the major criterion for selecting the preferred interpretation and halakhic outcome.[1]

The *Tosafot* school created a radically new conception that saw the entire Talmud, in fact, the whole of rabbinic-halakhic literature, as a uniform corpus, each part of which necessarily agreeing with all other parts; there can be no contradiction in its concepts or among its principles, arguments, and conclusions. This universality must apply to the whole Talmud, with a few exceptions of a technical and editorial nature (such as the phenomenon of "inverted *sugyot*" and the like). The frequent apparent contradictions between parallel *sugyot* in the Babylonian and Jerusalem Talmud are to be understood as *mahalokot* (conflicts of opinion) like those common all over the Babylonian Talmud itself, and the same applies to the many discrepancies between the biblical *masorah* and the readings of many biblical words according to the tradition of the Babylonian Talmud, which represent "conflicts of opinion" between the masorete and the talmudic scholar. Each party in such a conflict is understood to be fully aware of his opponent's view and capable of answering any criticism raised against his position.

This thesis may possibly be tenable within the limits of one single *sugya* and its parallels, and, with some difficulty, over one chapter or even one tractate of the Talmud; to uphold it for the length of the entire Talmud, however, is well nigh impossible, and Rashi consistently refrained from so doing. This "idyllic" conception, of course, extended the range within which the harmonistic principle remained valid and applicable as the fundamental element of proper *talmud Torah*, that is to say: The obligation to reconcile, in any possible legal-logical or philological manner, the host of discrepancies uncovered by such a meticulous comparison of the enormous talmudic corpus. And since this harmonistic reconciliation depends on *sevara* and may always be achieved in more than one way, each with the same relative advantages and disadvantages, the Tosafists perforce had to recognize the principle of interpretative pluralism: the possibility that the same *sugya* might have different, but equally legitimate, interpretations, existing side by side. A necessary implication of this situation was that the alternative interpretations were also, putatively, equally valid. Backing up any one of them *de facto*, to the practical exclusion of all others, was the authority of the headmaster, in whose study house and "before" whom, i.e., with whose approval, the interpretation in question had been pro-

[1] The nature of the Tosafist enterprise has been explained in its many aspects in E.E. Urbach's classic *The Tosafists*, especially in its more recent, updated and broader 1980 edition. Of course, there is much more to say about this golden period of medieval rabbinic literature.

posed. In any case, in the next generation, the whole body of interpretations, whether accepted or rejected, would again be available to students of the law, for them to sift through and select. This "fluid" state of halakhic debate is reflected, of course, on each and every page of the Talmud, and in this respect, too, the Tosafists were simply continuing a standard talmudic method, on the implicit assumption that the finalization of the Talmud did not affect their right to go on using the method.

In this way, the Tosafists founded a new school of Talmud study, not merely of new exegetical techniques. Their system became a veritable fashion, mainly in France but also in Germany, during the twelfth to thirteenth centuries, attracting the sharpest young intellectual minds of the time. In this way the "closed" system of study, popular in the eleventh century, came to an end.[2] It was not only that the student was now given absolute freedom to examine the text, delve into it to his heart's desire, and draw his own conclusions. It was not only that the veil of supervision and semi-secrecy was lifted from the student's personal progress. The students were actually expected first and foremost to broaden their intellectual horizons and exhaust all possible halakhic implications implicit in the text. Halakhic *hiddush*, innovation, became the supreme peak of achievement in the study of the Talmud and a student unable to "add to his learning" (*le-hosif*: R. Tam in *Sefer ha-Yashar*)[3] was not entitled to issue halakhic rulings to the community.

The original supervisory framework was apparently maintained, in so far as the student would commit his *tosafot* to writing "before" the head of the yeshiva, as stated in all the original, unedited *tosafot*, until the mid-thirteenth

[2] I. Ta-Shma, "Law, Custom and Tradition in Eleventh-Century Germany" (Heb.), *Sidra* 3, pp. 137–141.

[3] This meaning of the verb *le-hosif* lies beneath the term *tosafot*, which means "to add external halakhic considerations to the talmudic source-material." See the *responsum* of R. Avraham b. Isaac of Narbonne (ed. Kafih, #61), discussing the permissibility of Torah study before the morning prayer. He says:

ומי שאומר מזמורים בין של שבת בין של תחנונים בין קודם תפילה, בין לאחר התפילה
אין לנובב עליו, מפני שהוא כקורא בתורה וכשאמרו (ע"ז, ז', ע"ב) "יתפלל אדם ואח"כ ישאל צרכיו,
או ישאל בשומע תפילה", הם דברי צרכיו מפרנסתי ומזונותיו ומחולין, ומה שאתה כותב לאחר ההלכות,
אם אתה מאת בעצמך, שאינך נותן דעתך להוסיף על מה שאתה כותב,
וגם אינך נותן דעתך לפשפש ולחקור אותי

Kafih's perplexity is straightened out in the manuscript reading of the last sentence:

ומה שאתה כותב וגם אינך נותן דעתך לפשפש ולחקור מותר

The two versions should, of course, be integrated, meaning that there is no injunction against writing straight-forward *halakhot* before prayer, but one should not "add" to them, that is: go deeper into their profundities, until he has finished his prayers. The term is used here—in the second quarter of the twelfth century—in connection to the *halakhot* of Rif (or possibly R. Judah ha-Barzeloni).

century. This term indicates the teacher's approval of the argumentation and conclusions recorded in writing "before" him; it is this element of approbation that confers authority upon the entire literary genre. Nevertheless, the situation was now radically different: the halakhic discourse was now open to all, the entire body of literary sources was at the student's disposal for free inspection and criticism, and would actually expand ever more, in the course of the lively incessant debates that went on and on in the *yeshivot*. The principal goal of this mode of study was to bring out the entire halakhic potential of the *sugya*, and the final stamp of approval was necessary only to bestow the authority of a distinguished and celebrated personality—the head of the Yeshiva—on the collective, anonymous deliberations of his many pupils. This procedure and style is an ever-green characteristic of any institution of higher learning in whose precincts both teachers and students enjoy academic freedom, and the situation was similar also in the emergent academic environment of the late twelfth-century French universities.

What went on in many of the new tosafist *yeshivot* was nothing short of a halakhic revolution; others were less radical, inclined to preserve no less than to improve and progress. All of them, however, relied on the Talmud as a sole and overriding authority; first and last point of departure for all halakhic debates and decisions. The Talmud thus underwent a considerable metamorphosis, from a theoretical book, mainly important as a medium for observance of the precept "recite it day and night"—as was the case in eleventh-century Germany—to a practical and exclusive guidebook for religious and everyday life in accordance with halakhah. The key to this metamorphosis was the "translation" of its theoretical deliberation and study into detailed halakhic conclusions. The time-honored institution of current *minhag* (that is custom or usage), which was the accepted religious guidepost in the eleventh century, lost its central position. Another result of this situation was the removal of the heavy barrier that, in the eleventh century, had separated exegetical activities from the practical business of determining Jewish law.

II.

First and foremost among the French Tosafists was Rashi's grandson R. Jacob Tam. It was he who set the limits of the system and broadcast it abroad; he, in fact, represents the farthest extremes of its innovative potential. R. Tam proposed many daring halakhic rulings and introduced a great number of changes to what was then accepted usage. However, opinions differ among scholars as to the historical significance of his vigorous activity. Prof. E.E. Urbach devoted a whole chapter to R. Tam in his first edition of *The Tosafists*.[4] After giving

4 Jerusalem, 1956. In his second edition Urbach did not take into consideration the criticism aimed at this chapter—to be discussed in a minute—and stuck to his original phrases, and quite rightly so, as we shall soon see.

some fine examples of R. Tam's lenient rulings, Urbach sharply criticized the views of a celebrated nineteenth-century scholar, Isaac Hirsch Weiss, saying:

> On the basis of these lenient rulings and others like them, Weiss purports to erect a whole structure, making out that R. Tam was actually a reform rabbi. According to him, "R. Tam arose like a lion and abolished many harsh rulings issued by his predecessors…For he understood in his heart that it was not a good thing to make the yoke of Torah and commandments weigh heavily upon the people and invent restrictions." Clearly, he [Weiss] was writing here as a typical Maskil. The desire to attack the rabbis of his own time warped his judgment and caused this important scholar to disregard the sources. After all, it is common knowledge that R. Tam promulgated preventive regulations and took a most stringent attitude even with regard to seemingly minor customs…He issued decrees and stringent rulings even in matters for which he could find no firm halakhic basis. Therefore, believes Urbach, any contention as to systematically lenient decisions as such—is untenable. [R. Tam's] lenient and stringent decisions both rested on arguments which cannot always be adequately understood today, but their purpose was to preserve the integrity and welfare of the (Jewish) communities in the context of a life of Torah and faith…He maintains this concern for the needs of his generation in his exegesis of Rabbinic literature, straying far from the Sages' original intentions…Thus, he interprets the Amora's words in keeping with the conditions of his own time. Such concerns inspired him to find distinctions whose practical implication was the abolition of laws that could not possibly be observed under contemporary circumstances.

The late Prof. C.H. Ben-Sasson, in his review of Urbach's book,[5] referred to this passage in a sharply rebuking tone:

> The question arises: Is there really such a great divergence of opinion between Urbach and Weiss, as might be implied by Urbach's argument, or is Urbach actually at pains to distance himself from Weiss because they are both actually saying rather similar things, the basic difference between them being that Weiss, a 19th century man, has the hero of his account concerned for the heavy yoke imposed upon the people by the observance of the commandments; whereas Urbach, a man of the 20th century, has him knowingly alter the Halakhah for the good of the community and in order to maintain the authority of the Torah.

Ben-Sasson, for his part, advances a new outlook, the implication of which is that the changes made, in Urbach's interpretation "knowingly" and deliberately, actually had unconscious motivation. Such changes were dictated by the necessities of life, and R. Tam and his associates took them up in the sincere belief that they were merely continuing and "explicating" the heritage of the past. The halakhic give and take pervading the *tosafot* is, therefore, sincere,

[5] C.H. Ben-Sasson, "Hanhagata shel Torah," *Bekhinot* 9 (1956), pp. 39–52.

true, and absolutely unbiased, not to be seen as a hollow intellectual exercise, of purely formal significance. As a result, writes Ben-Sasson: "Such turns of speech as a 'desire' for change, 'admission' of change, 'attempts' to adapt halakhah, and so on, run counter to the immanent nature of the changes in halakhah as due to its own inner strength."

Like Urbach, Ben-Sasson too believed that the necessities of life dictated the development of halakhah in the Middle Ages in the first place; in his view, in fact: "the power of 'needs', of 'reality' and of 'the universal custom' is much greater than might be implied by Urbach's wording." In contrast to Urbach, however, Ben-Sasson holds that R. Tam was unaware of the significance of what he was doing, but acted out of an inner conviction that he had, indeed, been privileged to penetrate the true meaning of the *sugyot* in question and to bring their hitherto concealed lenient undercurrents into the open.

However, this solution is no improvement whatsoever over Urbach's. On the contrary, it is significantly weaker. It does, indeed, call our attention and warn us to treat R. Tam's halakhic deliberations more seriously, rather than see them as hollow machinations. However, this at a considerable cost, as it assumes that R. Tam was a naive person, missing the full significance of his vigorous involvement in the everyday life of the Jew. Ben-Sasson's question as to the real difference between Urbach's and Weiss' theses merits attention; but this is no less true with regard to the difference between Ben-Sasson's own thesis and that of Urbach. As long as one admits that it was the exigencies of life that moved R. Tam to reexamine the talmudic sources and, as it were, rewrite them by the use of *pilpul*, the argument is, once again, not whether R. Tam was aware of what he was doing, but to what degree he was aware. Just as Urbach would undoubtedly admit that R. Tam's casuistry is not a mere show of intellectual prowess, but authentic words of Torah, meaningful and significant in and of themselves, Ben-Sasson would certainly admit that R. Tam was not entirely blind to what he was doing, and certainly had some idea of the importance of his activities and their implications for Jewish life. One should beware of such "totalistic" solutions, no less than one should avoid the other extreme, as posited by S. Albeck,[6] that: "certain principles commonly known to scholars of those times, were universally seen as logic, pure and simple, and therefore the Tosafists, too, being children of their times, also understood talmudic halakhah in accordance with the then accepted rules of logic and justice."

III.

The problem dealt with here is as comprehensive as life itself. Just how far R. Tam was willing to go in his legal decisions to meet the exigencies of life may be gauged from an article by S. Shiloh that assembled dozens of relevant exam-

6 S. Albeck, "Rabbenu Tam's Attitude to the Problems of His Time" (Heb.), *Zion* 19 (1954), pp. 104–141.

ples, all from the realm of commercial and economic affairs. The detailed examination of this aspect of the problem leads Shiloh to draw the following conclusions:[7]

> When so many halakhic rulings, pertaining to different topics, point in one general direction, and this direction accords well with R. Tam's environment, the question arises: Do such rulings not betray a purposeful effort, indicative of considerations which are not purely halakhic? In view of such amazing consistency in laying down the Law, there would seem to be no escape from the conclusion that it must mean something....With all our understanding of the problematic nature of attempts to explain the halakhic rulings of great scholars in general, and of R. Tam in particular, as founded on a specific place and time,...there is no escaping the conclusion that there really was an accumulated body of halakhic rulings of amazing consistency in a certain direction.

Shiloh, therefore, advocates accepting Albeck's extreme position, as indicated above, perhaps, as he says, "with a pinch of salt."

However, there is another side to this coin, not raised thus far by modern scholarship, as far as I know, and that is the extraordinary inner congruity between R. Tam's new, original readings of the talmudic sources and the true, "objective" sense of the text as any sincere Torah student would judge it today. In most cases the student will objectively prefer the text as read by R. Tam as against his predecessors', including Rashi, in the immediate realization that it permits an easier and more convenient understanding of the *sugya*. In other words: As remarkable as is the "practical-environmental" tendency revealed in R. Tam's halakhic conclusions, no less striking is the real, objective, interpretative cogency and consistency of the halakhic argumentation through which R. Tam reached his conclusions—that same argumentation that, it has been claimed, is superfluous, artificial, almost "intrinsically counterfeit," since, after all, his final goal was known to him in advance! And this is really the heart of the problem.

IV.

A different kind of solution to our problem was proposed by Prof. J. Katz,[8] who disputed the very idea that life's necessities, or any other non-professional considerations, dictated the rulings of medieval decisors:

> If conditions of existence had any power to break down the barriers of prohibitions, surely many of the major elements of Halakhah that limited the Jew's Lebensraum during the Middle Ages would have been uprooted. They im-

[7] S. Shiloh, "Idud ha-Miskhar veha-Kalkala be-Pesikat Rabbenu Tam," *Sinai* 100 (1987), pp. 882–896.

[8] J. Katz, *Introduction to Halakhah and Kabbala* (Jerusalem 1986), pp. 2–3 (Heb.).

> posed restrictions on what he could eat and drink, forbade him to engage in economic activities a good many days each year, and these restrictions remained firmly entrenched despite the pressures of existence. One cannot but ask, therefore, where were the limits of Halakhah's flexibility, which of the restrictive precepts were easily pushed aside, which of them maintained their resistance even under conditions of pressure, and so on?

Accordingly, Katz suggested that the prime mover in the history of halakhah, at least during the Middle Ages, was practical, popular *minhag*, as exercised *de facto* by members of the particular community or communities in question. In his view, it was not the so-called "innovative," lenient rulings of R. Tam (and his associates) that created the shift in halakhah. They only put the official seal of scholarly, authoritative approval on the change in question, after it had already come into being and spread through the community gradually, until R. Tam could, in most cases, truthfully pronounce it valid by definition, under the category of *minhag avoteinu Torah* ("The custom of our fathers is law"). Acting as primary influences on the Tosafists, then, were not the necessities of life themselves, but the slow, gradual changes that occurred in their wake; such changes gained popular acceptance to the extent that it became necessary to obtain explicit halakhic authority for them, *ex post facto*. As Prof. Katz put it:

> The task of the authoritative halakhic scholar was to regulate and supervise, to ensure that the transformations should not bring about an uncontrollable violation of the traditional bounds, but that the changes occurring in tradition should be legitimated, so that continuity be maintained despite developments. At any rate, the medium of this process of "persistence-and-change" is practical Halakhah, as sustained and observed by the community. The community adheres to the patterns of tradition, but it is the community who is also influenced by the visible and invisible transformations that leave their stamp on the patterns of Halakhah. It is the community that senses the urgency and the challenges from without...and it is it that, more or less unconsciously, identifies with values which, if objectionable to certain halakhic patterns, may cause the rejection, or alteration, of these *halakhot*.

We might liken the situation to that of a blind man feeling his way with a staff. The staff goes ahead, and in this sense it is the leader; but it is the blind man who dictates the staff's direction, and the staff obeys his wishes and not vice versa. Within the general direction stipulated by the blind man, the staff guides the latter's footsteps, lest he stumble along the path he has chosen. It is the masses—the blind man in our parable—that dictate the direction to be taken by the sages, who play the role of the staff, warning the people against dangers along the way and guiding them with the requisite caution to prevent them from falling into lurking pitfalls.

V.

Yet another approach, different from all those just described, will be discussed below. But before I do that, let me refer to some historical aspects of tosafist literature.

Many scholars have alluded to the basic similarity between the tosafist system of casuistry and the dialectic system that emerged in the late eleventh century in France, and reached its peak toward the middle of that century. A perfect instance is the figure of Abelard. This was aptly expressed by Prof. Urbach in the first edition of his *The Tosafists*:

> A similar development took place in spiritual life in general. At the end of the eleventh century contradictions were discerned in various works and books on the theological and legal sciences. The art of dialectics, coupled with the weighing of different explanations and arguments, began to flourish, but it could not achieve anything new. The "traditionalist period," i.e., the work of collecting and interpreting the material, had ended, and a period of harmonization began. The dialectic method, as applied to the theological, legal and philosophical sciences, aimed at proving that the numerous contradictions in the views and tradition of the ancients could be resolved.

Urbach goes on to describe Abelard's personality, the similarity between his activities and those of R. Tam, as well as the crucial difference between them: Abelard, proud and haughty, contemptuous of his masters and associates alike; as against R. Tam, whose arguments always concentrated on the essence of the matter, whose concern was to get at the truth, maintaining all the while respect for his masters and his associates, always ready to admit to the truth. Finally, writes Urbach:

> We have already stated that the Christian environment influenced the Jews, and their scholars as well, and R. Tam is known to have been in contact with members of the ruling classes. Nevertheless, the Jews consciously distanced themselves from [the Christians] and from the reprehensible, and negative aspects of their lives.

In the second edition of his book, Prof. Urbach repeats the passage with some amplification, but ends with the following words:

> There was no need to learn the methods of the Talmud, which R. Tam continued and developed, from the scholastics, nor from the glossators.

And he adds in a footnote:

> I say this emphatically contra what has been written by S. Albeck[9]... and even more contra what has been written by J. Faur[10]...[who] is quite dogmatic

[9] n. 6.

[10] J. Faur, "The Legal Thinking of the *Tosafot*—An Historical Approach," *Dinei Israel* 4 (1975), pp. 43–72 (English Section).

...Interestingly enough, it did not occur to him at all to ask, whether those glossators had not learned...something from the Jews.

Urbach then goes on, however, to end with the statement that: "I am not implying thereby that the scholastics were necessarily influenced by the Tosafists."

Truth to tell, there is really no disagreement between Urbach and Faur. Faur, too, in his interesting paper did not claim that the Tosafists had learned from their Christian environment; he merely stated that similar historical circumstances naturally create similar responses. This is, after all, Prof. Urbach's position too, as expressed excellently—and illustrated in detail—in the new chapter added to the second edition of his book (chapter fourteen), a major addition to the thirteen chapters of the first edition.

There is, however, a basic assumption underlying the above views: the similarity between the activities of the Christian academics, legal scholars, and theologians, and those of the Tosafists. Urbach, Faur, and many other scholars not quoted here assume this similarity to have begun at the turn of the eleventh to twelfth centuries, as summarized by Urbach:

> Let me first say a few words about the development of the glosses to Justinian's Codex and the Canon Law. The ancient glosses, composed between the years 600 and 1070, are mainly linguistic and grammatical (parallel in a sense to the commentaries of the *Geonim*). The juristic glosses of the Bolognese, Imerius and his disciples Bulgarus and Martinus [i.e., the end of the 11th century and the first half of the 12th century], consist mainly of references to parallels or conflicting sources. They were inscribed in the margins of the codex or between the lines. The work of the glossators began at the end of the 12th century and came to an end with Accursius (1263)...The first compilation of Canon Law upon which glosses were written...was composed in 1142...Scholars disagree on whether the renaissance of legal science in late 11th century Europe, which began in Bologna and moved to France, was influenced by theology, or whether it drew from the school of jurists that was active in Pavia, the seat of the Imperial Court...Nevertheless, even the protagonists of the last opinion admit that the glossators could not possibly have learned everything from their predecessors.

VI.

A much earlier point of contact between the Jewish and non-Jewish intellectual worlds, which will also help us better understand the early rabbinic background to the *tosafot* and the inner contacts between the two, has now come to light in a recent study by Prof. Radding.[11] He presented a detailed study of a forgotten dispute concerning the proper attitude toward the interpretation

[11] C. Radding, *The Origins of Medieval Jurisprudence: Pavia and Bologna, 850–150* (New Haven 1988).

of legal texts, between *antiqui* and *moderni* in the above-mentioned juristic school of Pavia in the eleventh century. Radding's research reveals a striking similarity between the conceptions held by these ancient jurists, natives of Lombardy in northern Italy, and the commentators on the Talmud in early- and mid–eleventh-century Germany—Rashi's masters. One finds that indeed, as Urbach claimed, these early juristic glosses are "mainly linguistic and grammatical," but they are not "parallel in a sense to the commentaries of the Geonim," as he contends, but rather to the commentaries of Mayence and Worms, written in the first half of the eleventh century by Rashi's masters.

This parallelism, which to my mind goes much deeper than the similarities detected for the twelfth century, is yet another indication of the internal, organic evolution of the tosafist method from the earlier stages current in eleventh-century Mayence. This development is similar to the way in which twelfth-century glossators constitute a further step in the internal evolution of the lore of the Pavese jurists of the early eleventh century. The truth of this last assertion emerges in considerable detail from Radding's study, which we shall now proceed to briefly summarize.

Radding's main interest lies in the development of mental attitudes in the Middle Ages; his study of the Pavese jurists in the eleventh century is a sequel to his previous studies of the status of different scholarly disciplines in the Early Middle Ages.[12] He has thus been able to assess correctly the innovative nature of the Pavese jurists' accomplishments, though previous legal historians, who approached the topic from a vantage point after the Bologna period, considered their contribution trivial and uninteresting. Radding stresses this point in his introductory chapter, and it has implications for our present topic, too. As he says: "I had no doubt that the appearance of these attitudes [of literal interpretation] toward texts in the first half of the eleventh century was significant. Not only did early medieval lawyers invariably reason as did the *antiqui*, so did early medieval scholars in all fields."

The *antiqui* believed in a strictly literal reading of the text of Lombard law as they found it, whereas the *moderni* defended more flexible interpretations, farther removed from the legislators' immediate wording. This dispute is one of the first recorded juristic debates of the Middle Ages, and it is evident from the sources that even the jurists of the mid-eleventh century were aware of the essential importance of the shift toward "modernism." These eleventh-century jurists, of both schools, taught law to students, albeit not in any educational institution but on an individual basis, as in Paris a century later. This distinction is of particular importance if one wishes to understand the rapid development of the profession, culminating in the maturation of the real analytical methods

[12] C. Radding, *A World Made by Man: Cognition and Society 400–200* (Chapel Hill 1985).

within two generations. It was the result of intense personal rivalry between the individual masters, who were constantly proposing legal conundrums in the hope of baffling one another, for the mere pleasure of winning an argument.

The desire for a pure, literal interpretation of the text was rooted in the ancient Lombard system, according to which each particular law was to be read independently, divorced from whatever went before or after. This approach was intimately related to the evolutionary history of the Lombard code of law, which is essentially a collection of *ad hoc* royal capitularies, issued by various kings in response to specific cases or queries addressed to them and recorded in order with their dates. Nevertheless, the *antiqui* made an important contribution to Lombard law, by virtue of the extraordinary care that they lavished on each word of the text, the many questions they raised (i.e., on matters such as what categories of persons or special conditions and circumstances are affected by a law), and the way in which they derived the solution to their problem by meticulous linguistic examination, grammatical or syntactical, of the text. These jurists' strict adherence to the language of the text, their refusal to permit any flexibility on that count, frequently forced them to declare that certain laws in the code were utterly contradictory, in which case the later law "broke" (i.e., superseded) the earlier one. The *moderni* were sharply critical of this approach, but "in the early eleventh century the effort to correlate texts on similar topics was an important step toward seeing the body of Lombard law as an intellectual whole, and toward the ultimate victory of the juristic mentality over the grammatical, a vestige of the Early Middle Ages."

In this context Radding lays particular emphasis on the numerous textual emendations proposed by the *antiqui*, on the sole basis of logic and reasoning, unsupported by manuscript evidence. Naturally, textual emendations based on other books were quite common in the Middle Ages, and it was generally known that manuscripts might contain numerous errors, it being necessary to compare several manuscripts in order to achieve a reliable text. Here, however, we are concerned with emendations inspired by "legal logic" (by legal and/or logical necessity alone) rather than by a corrupt word, faulty syntax, or alternative reading. This is but one more example of how legal-professional criteria were beginning to prevail over deeply entrenched linguistic-grammatical considerations, even among the *antiqui* as early as the first half of the eleventh century. To cite Radding: "After several centuries in which this kind of textual criticism was not to be found in any discipline, its appearance among the jurists of early eleventh-century Pavia is noteworthy."

The *antiqui*'s tireless scrutiny of the texts in order to extract answers to their various circumstantial and legal questions (such as: Does the use of the masculine gender imply that the law in question is not applicable to a woman, or is it just a question of linguistic usage?) exposed areas of uncertainty in the law books, greatly facilitating the work of the next generation of jurists, who were able to apply themselves to the search for other methods of solution. And whereas the *antiqui* were so engrossed in questions of language that they became entangled in individual sentences, their successors were able to move forward in their attempt to examine the meaning of individual laws against more general legal conceptions and not only with reference to the specific situations before them. But once the later jurists had mastered such purely legal criteria, their attitude to the work of the previous one or two generations became one of contempt—they no longer referred to them or cited their works, considering them of little worth compared to their own.

I am, of course, not expert on Lombard law, and I cannot pronounce an opinion on the validity of these theses on Lombard legal history, but I can surely say that they shed much light upon the early stages of Talmud study in mid–eleventh-century Germany. It should be remembered that both the *antiqui* and the *moderni* were active during the eleventh century, before 1070, so both preceded the earliest glossators of the school of Imerius and his disciples at the turn of the eleventh to twelfth centuries. Both systems surveyed here—the conservative, grammatically minded approach, versus the "modern" trend toward greater flexibility and conceptual criticism—were prevalent during the time of Rashi's masters, the heads of the *yeshivot* of Mayence and Worms.

We must also bear in mind the basic fact that all Jewish centers in eleventh-century Germany have their historical roots in northern Italy, in the city of Lucca not far from Pavia, from whence the Jews immigrated to the Rhine districts toward the end of the tenth century.[13] Although we have no direct record of their teachings in their own words, the main features are clearly visible through Rashi's commentary: the same archaic inclination to verbalism, exaggerated attention to details, narrow local conceptions, and, above all, utter fidelity to the text, a similar propensity to emend texts, sometimes on the basis of a critical comparison with manuscripts and/or later *sugyot* and parallel passages from other sources, but mainly guided by logical considerations alone. A comparison of the commentary attributed to R. Gershom *Me'or ha-Golah*, wherever extant, to Rashi's commentary clearly reveals the same distinction seen between the Pavian *antiqui* and the *moderni*, despite the very different subject-matter. Another striking point of resemblance is that even the earliest Tosafists almost completely ignore everything done in the eleventh century; to the extent that they do make any mention of eleventh-century scholars and their teachings, the references are minimal.

The import of this view of European legal history, as Radding points out in the concluding chapter of his book, is its strong emphasis on internal, legal-"professional" processes as the prime movers, and the minor role it allocates to the impetus provided by economic and other factors external to the realm of

13 A. Grossman, *The Early Sages of Ashkenaz* (Jerusalem 1981), Ch. 1.

law. On the other hand, Radding rejects extreme views of the opposite category, according to which there was *ipso facto* nothing new in the European adoption of Roman law, because it was, after all, just the natural continuation of a slow, gradual process, during which Lombard law was constantly absorbing sporadic and fragmentary material from Roman law. Radding rejects this conception, arguing that no comparison can be made between sporadic adoption of random laws, dictated on various occasions by special circumstances, and systematic absorption of Roman law as a legal entity with its own abstract concepts and fundamental principles. In Radding's view, the historical facts as described in his book imply a third kind of process, not just a compromise between the two processes outlined above, but an independent, self-contained evolution. And although the first roots of that evolution are certainly to be sought in economic and social changes taking place outside the legal system, these changes were not directly responsible for the necessary legal solutions; rather, they brought about a revolution in ways of thinking, and it was this revolution that in turn opened up new horizons of legal thought and led to the requisite legal innovations. Thus it follows that the external cause was perhaps the first cause, but nevertheless a remote, indirect cause of the transformation; whereas the internal development, emerging from the depths of legal theory itself, was the immediate and important cause.

VII.

We can now go back to the first theme, with which we began our discussion, namely, halakhah versus historical reality, and reconsider the whole issue in the light of Radding's findings.

The different views and assessments of the halakhic revolution effected by the twelfth-century French scholars, headed by R. Tam, may be briefly summarized as follows. Prof. Urbach believes that changing economic realities exerted a direct influence on the rabbis, who did their best to find the halakhic techniques necessary to permit the changes. Prof. Ben Sasson thinks that the rabbis were led to their decisions unconsciously, giving in to modern needs and demands by using the old, orthodox techniques in good traditional faith, almost unknowing and unaware of what they were actually doing. Prof. Katz, in contrast to both Urbach and Ben-Sasson, believes that not one revolutionary change may actually be attributed to the rabbis; the changes in question were simply adopted, *de facto*, by the community, gradually and naturally. Jewish society itself was always the bearer of halakhic evolution, accepting or rejecting the various options by virtue of a natural intuition. The rabbis were honored with the secondary role of supplying the theoretical back-up for what was popularly accepted, and the power to veto certain things that seemed to them entirely unacceptable on a halakhic basis.

We now realize that one can speak of yet another avenue of approach, penetrating even much deeper than Katz's theory: It was the changing conditions of life, across a broad front, that brought about a fundamental change in the ways of *thinking* of the Tosafists—more than a change in the technique of decision—as they did among the Pavese jurists described above. This overall transformation, which was rooted in a general widening of horizons and possibilities, paved the way for the internal, legal-theoretical breakthrough thanks to which the talmudic vista was broadened and a sophisticated technique of harmonistic casuistry evolved as a legitimate and intrinsically valuable tool of study. It was this tool that provided the key to the specific, innovative decisions that had to be made. The Tosafists believed that their lenient attitudes were based on a genuine, thorough, and justifiable examination of halakhah, comparable to the halakhic efforts of previous generations, and relying directly on the sources as we have them today and in their spirit. But it was precisely this realization—that their broad-ranging, vigorous casuistry, *per se*, was legitimate and in complete harmony with halakhic method and talmudic tradition—that was produced by the re-emergent conditions of life in all areas of material and spiritual culture in Europe, at the end of the eleventh century and in particular in the twelfth and thirteenth centuries. This is no mere compromise between the two conventional—externalist and internalist—conceptions, but a third, independent way, similar to that proposed by Radding in his specific area of interest. Only this third alternative is capable of combining the two conceptions, each of which is correct in its own way, into an integral whole.

Originally published in
Revue des Études juives
and subsequently in
Rashi et la culture juive en France du Nord au moyen age,
ed. G. Dahan, G. Nahon, E. Nicolas. Paris–Louvain, 1997.

CHAPTER 6

HALAKHAH, REALITY, AND THE CONCEPT OF HISTORICAL CHANGE

The issue to be taken up in this paper is the historical function of the element of history, that is, the passage of time and its changing realities, as a valid and lawful factor in deciding the halakhah. The pending series of questions is large, intricate, and tricky. To start with: Should the far-reaching adaptations of medieval halakhah to reality be ascribed to inner, methodical developments of a purely professional-intellectual, juristic nature or, rather, to an instinctive, vitalistic, and dramatic response by the rabbis to external coercion, which took on the form of a battle for survival in a rapidly changing world? And, if we do accept the second alternative as being nearer to the truth, does that necessarily mean that that was also the understanding at the time? How did the rabbis themselves understand the process? Were they, or were they not, aware of what they were actually effecting?

The rift between theoretical halakhic norms and the practical challenges of life, the pressure exerted by the basic desire to survive the hardships of life and adapt to its ever-changing conditions, has never been as markedly evident and as patently manifest as in France of the later parts of the eleventh, and all through the twelfth century. The enormous changes that characterize the period, generally considered to be the first European Renaissance, which covered almost every aspect of life: demography, economy, culture, religion, human relationships *etalia*, necessitated massive changes in the traditional halakhic attitude toward many day-to-day matters on a large scale never experienced before. As is well known, the French Tosafists, headed by the great and authoritative figures of Rabbenu Tam, Ri of Dampierre, Shimshon of Sens, and others, caused a major revolution in this respect, re-working the Talmud and adapting it to the newly nascent needs, opening new vistas for halakhic invention and directing public and individual life in a much more flexible, lenient, and sophisticated manner. The Tosafists themselves mention sometimes, as second in importance, practical considerations of various types, among them the change in the historical realities between the period of the Talmud and their own times, but the revolutionary dimension of their collective work goes far beyond the incidental mention of an historical consideration here and there. This is all, of course, common knowledge. Many pertinent examples and quotations can be found in the second edition of Prof. Urbach's *The Tosafists* and there is no need to go into further detail.[1] On the other hand, I would like to review in very short terms the main scholarly approaches and attitudes to the matter, dwelling mainly on Prof. Katz's theory, to which I may possibly add something myself.[2]

What we have before us here is a clear, exemplary case of the profound and far-reaching influence changing temporal circumstances might have on the rigid, unchanging, and eternal halakhah. And it has given rise to an interesting and lively debate among some of our distinguished scholars, on how it should be understood and correctly explained by modern scholarly standards, taking into account its authentic medieval background. Was abstract halakhah considered at the time to be subordinate to earthly, material realities, in a sort of a liberal extension of the famous halakhic maxim "*vechai bahem*"? Were the Tosafists, in their own way, early religious reformers or were they acting innocently, carrying on the talmudic *pilpul* from the point where the later Amoraim have left it hundreds of years back, in a true endeavor to clarify the many questions still pending thereon? Were they looking in advance for preferred solutions, or did they come upon them one by one, by an authentic academic procedure of re-reading and re-interpreting the Talmud?

As one can easily see, none of these alternatives, taken by itself, is satisfactory to the knowledgeable and experienced ear, and they all leave much to be required. Nevertheless, all of them were advocated by one or another of the main speakers on the subject: Isaac Hirsch Weiss, who took Rabbenu Tam to be an outright orthodox reformer (with the stress on the word "orthodox"); the late Prof. Urbach, who emphasized the prevalent line of stringencies current in Rabbenu Tam's work, and, therefore, depicted him as the responsible leader of his period, whose life-work was dedicated to upkeep the main institutions of Jewish life in the face of changing realities; Prof. Ben-Sasson, who saw in Rabbenu Tam the model type of an outstanding and genial scholar, arriving at his decisions by an entirely innocent and unintending study, and being, as a matter of fact, wholly unconscious of the revolutionary aspect of what he was doing. These scholars and a few others who developed some minor variations on these main themes were all quoted and analyzed in my book on halakhah in the Middle Ages,[3] and I shall, therefore, say no more here. I shall nevertheless express my wonder that not one of these noted scholars

1 E.E. Urbach, *The Tosafjsts* (Jerusalem 1980) (Heb.).

2 J. Katz, *Introduction to Halakhah and Kabbalah* (Jerusalem 1986), pp. 2–3 (Heb.). See chapter 5 for a full explanation of Prof. Katz's theory.

3 I. Ta-Shma, *Ritual, Custom and Reality in Franco-Germany, 1000–1350* (Jerusalem 1996), pp. 19–35 (Heb.).

offered an opinion on the quality of Rabbenu Tam's talmudic discussions, and the extent to which they constituted, at their time, a substantial contribution to a better understanding of the relevant talmudic *sugyot*. After all, in trying to assess the inner self-conviction and bona fide nature of Rabbenu Tam's work, the question of his actual contribution—at the time—to an improved understanding of the relevant *sugyot* seems to be crucial. It might be an uneasy question to answer, but undoubtedly crucial, and certainly worthwhile.

An important step forward has been taken by Prof. J. Katz, who minimized the Tosafists' contribution—and for that matter, the contribution of medieval rabbinic authorities in general—to the development of halakhah. Prof. Katz emphasized, in many of his articles, the other side of the historical coin: If halakhah could, indeed, be subordinated by any of the above-mentioned alternative techniques to the material demands of life, why then were not many other disturbing prohibitions and halakhic impediments, some of which were undoubtedly much more of a social burden, lifted by the same techniques? Was not the absolute prohibition imposed upon having a glass of wine with a Gentile more of a burden than, let us say, the restrictions put upon using his services as a cook on Shabbat? Were not the severe laws governing Gentile proximity to Jewish wine, laws that were never alleviated in Franco-Germany, much more damaging to the pocket—and to social convenience—than the talmudic restriction upon Gentile cheese, which was practically abolished by Rabbenu Tam? Please note: Where Urbach raised the relatively minor question of the occasional—perhaps somewhat more than occasional—cases of stringent rulings by Rabbenu Tam, Katz pointed to the far more important fact of Rabbenu Tam's total forbearance in "reforming" the multitude of true obstacles impeding normal Jewish life. He thereby stressed the need to answer the question of *what* was changed in the Middle Ages and what was not, rather than *how* the change was achieved.

Prof. Katz, therefore, proposed the idea that new halakhic norms were basically adopted, or rejected, not by the rabbinic body, but by the traditional God-fearing communities, in accordance with their natural, spontaneous, "genetic"– if one may borrow a modern and somewhat irrelevant term—perception, as to what was adaptable and what was not so, within the traditional framework of Jewish life. The rabbinical authorities functioned as *post-factum* critics, only after a norm had already taken a strong and public hold in the community, strong enough to have their attention drawn to it. The rabbis generally conformed with public sentiment and the mere fact that a norm was widespread served as a contributory factor to its academic reception. Sometimes the rabbis conformed unanimously; sometimes they differed among themselves. However, they always furnished the necessary halakhic background and clarification, and sometimes added some necessary correctives. A useful parable here is the classical case of the blind man and his stick. The stick clears the way before the blind man and directs him on his way, but it does not dictate to him where he should go or what direction he should take. The blind man decides on where he wants to go and what direction to take, and the stick controls the road before him and corrects his steps, thus saving him from the many hazards and pitfalls strewn along the road that he—and he alone—has chosen to take. In a like manner, the Jewish social body, dispersed in hundreds of small and large communities, is the blind man, who, notwithstanding his overall ignorance of the exact mathematics and workings of Jewish halakhah, is still naturally "aware" of what is acceptable by traditional standards, and adopts *de facto* such new norms that can help make life easier. After having set themselves on their chosen route, their steps were carefully watched and controlled by their rabbinic leaders, who generally approved of what was commonly accepted, applying the necessary academic deliberation, the missing *de jure* factor, sometimes offering technical or other helpful correctives.

Katz's social theory could be resolved by simply adducing proof that halakhic norms considered to be tosafist (mainly Rabbenu Tam's) "novelties" were actually widespread before their first appearance in rabbinic literature. At first sight this is a mission impossible: Outside rabbinic literature what do we know —or what can we aspire to know—about what was or was not widespread many centuries before? Nevertheless, Prof. Katz himself has dedicated a small and edifying book trying to do exactly this,[4] and I myself offered further examples in my book on early Ashkenazi lore and ritual,[5] and in articles published in the past or published in my book on halakhah in the Middle Ages.[6]

Although I certainly favor Katz's social attitude, which I consider preferable to the entire variety of intellectual attitudes taken by Urbach, Ben-Sasson, Albeck and many others, there are still two major reservations that I must take.

Katz's theory does give an excellent description of the groundwork of halakhic development within Franco-German society, but it will not hold water when applied to Spanish realities. The social attitude is applicable to eleventh-century Franco-German Jewish society, because of its rooted adherence to oral, customary (partly Palestinian) law, rather than to the "written" Babylonian talmudic law, and it is, therefore, adequately applicable to the twelfth-century generations, who were at the time fighting their way out of these traditional oral influences, gradually positing the Babylonian Talmud as their exclusive halakhic guide, as explained *in extenso* in the detailed introduction to my above-mentioned book, *Early Franco-German Ritual and Custom.*[7] Such adherence to practical norms, rather than to abstract theoretical principles, is an imperative condition for the "social" attitude to take effect, and we must

4 J. Katz, *The Sabbath Gentile* (Jerusalem 1983) (Heb.).

5 I. Ta-Shma, *Early Franco-German Ritual and Custom* (Jerusalem 1992) (Heb.).

6 n. 3.

7 n. 5.

always keep in mind that these so-called "novelties" were revolutionary only in regard to the Babylonian Talmud. On the other end, Spanish halakhah was, from its early beginnings under Moslem rule, totally dependent on the Babylonian Talmud and on the Babylonian Geonim, with whom they corresponded for centuries, and who completely governed their religious life and behavior. Under the Babylonian-Spanish regime, the great rabbinic luminaries had always had the first and last say, and whatever developed there in the realm of halakhah was of an academic nature and origin. The two alternative processes, described by Urbach and Katz respectively, thus stand to be prototypes of two distinct types of halakhic development in Medieval Europe, both equally valid, but for two distinct geographical units.

Let us now move a step further, and examine whether it is possible for us to discern variant forms within the social attitude itself, as it took shape in the eleventh and in the twelfth centuries. Major halakhic developments, some of them quite revolutionary, took place in France and Germany a long time before the tosafist period, although the phenomenon did not reach its historical peak until that period, which was far richer in novelties—in every realm of life—than the earlier eleventh century, not to mention still earlier periods. The lay community—and not its elite groups—was always the carrier of all conservative and novel religious norms and practices, and from Katz's "social" point of view the developmental processes were always the same, before as in the later twelfth and thirteenth centuries (and probably back to Second Temple periods, which do not interest us here). The question now to be asked is whether we can identify variant reasoning within earlier and later stages of the system.

Let us consider for example the relationship between Jews and Gentiles as decided by talmudic halakhah and as experienced, understood, and explained by eleventh-century popular and rabbinic scholarship. It is an outstanding fact that practically each and every Mishna—the relevant talmudic discussions included—in the first three chapters of tractate *Avoda-Zara* had already lost all relevance in the daily life of Franco-German Jewry in the eleventh century (and actually much before). I have elsewhere treated the subject of Gentile-Jewish commerce on Sundays and the various apologies offered by the Franco-German rabbis of the eleventh and twelfth centuries. But the question of forbidden commerce is just one in a long series of prohibitions and limitations laid by talmudic halakhah on Gentile-Jewish relationships, none of which was *de facto* kept: the sale of domestic beasts, arms, and houses; visiting any town that worshipped a local deity and handling their sacred garb and utensils; letting women spend time in Gentile company, eating their bread and cooking, etc. etc. The contents of the third chapter, dealing mainly with the different forms of images prohibited under the laws of idolatry and the legal manner by which they may be recycled, has also lost any concrete meaning, and the trade in Christian holy objects of most, if not all, sorts was common practice in eleventh to twelfth-century Franco-Germany.

May I add in passing that, in my opinion, this is the true reason why some of the leading eleventh-century Ashkenazi sages never taught—and probably never studied at all—tractate *Avoda-Zara*. This strange rarity has been noticed by scholars, but never properly explained.[8] It seems clear to me that tractate *Avoda-Zara* has been skipped over by these early sages, because the practical religious behavior current in Ashkenaz, by old and much respected oral tradition, concerning the enormously vital subjects included in its first three (out of five) chapters, was entirely different from the pure, theoretical demands as formalized therein, and there was no point in dedicating time to explicate this mostly "irrelevant" tractate. In my book I indicated a few striking examples illustrating the important didactic principle current at the time, according to which a teacher must avoid at all costs handling halakhic texts and discussions that might lead to premature questions and doubts by the untrained student concerning accepted halakhic norms and standards. Generally speaking, the phenomenon resembles the contrary example of the Geonic avoidance of teaching in public tractate *Nedarim*, as part of their effort to dissuade people from practicing *hatarat nedarim*, a procedure strongly attacked by the Karaites.

It is, therefore, interesting to notice the different technique used by these early Franco-German sages in order to rationalize their dissenting practices. The main double argument quoted was:

1. The new order of Jewish life in the Diaspora, the total economic dependence of Jewish existence on regular commercial relationships with the neighboring Gentiles, and the perils inherent in arousing their hostility and ire against us.
2. The different character of Christian religious life in medieval Europe in comparison to the Pagan realities that were at the background of the various talmudic prohibitions. Most Gentiles were not worshipping their gods as true believers should, but rather followed mechanically what their forefathers did.

This double argument is quoted ever so often in Franco-German rabbinic literature before the tosafist period, with secondary variants and in versatile literary garb, and it served our early sages well enough to explain away with it a major part of tractate *Avoda-Zara*. Twelfth-century Tosafists, headed by Rabbenu Tam, changed the tactics entirely, and worked out entirely different academic solutions to each of the many contradictions between the tractate and public behavior so as to fit the individual *sugyot* involved. For example, whereas Rashi and his teachers were content to allow commercial dealings with Christians on Sundays because the historical situation had radically changed from talmudic times, Rabbenu Tam taught and advanced pilpulistic proof to the effect that neutral commercial dealings with Gentiles on Sundays were

[8] A. Grossman, *The Early Sages of Ashkenaz* (Jerusalem 1988), pp. 231–232 (Heb.).

never prohibited in the Talmud, where only trade with ritual offerings was censored.

The principal difference between the old and the new does not lie just in the preference of *ad hoc* and specific solutions to a categorical approach, but rather in the edifying fact that whereas the older, more "conservative" attitude justified glaring aberrations from the written law by pointing to historical changes in the surrounding reality, the new and "modern" tosafist approach preferred to justify the same by changing the reading—or, rather, the understanding—of the relevant *sugyot*. The social attitude is evident in both cases. The practices advocated were all initially adopted by the people and only later discussed by the rabbinic leaders, as explained, but the tactics used by the different "schools"—the early rabbinic generations of the eleventh century, and the twelfth- to thirteenth-century Tosafists—were quite different, although all amounted, finally, more or less to the same thing.

This leads to my second reservation. Katz's analysis minimizes the intellectual dimension inherent in the developmental processes of medieval halakhah, assigning to it marginal importance, if any at all, in his scheme of events, which credits the lower social ranks for the initiative, and the real acceptance of the reformed norms and attributes to the scholars the modest *post-factum* role of quasi-automatic *de jure* approval, with some possible correctives added. This may very well be true, but nevertheless one can hardly deny the parallel development in talmudic thinking that took place at the same time, to which I have tried to call attention and for which Katz cannot assign a historical importance, being superfluous as far as "revolutionary" development of halakhah was concerned. And while Urbach, Ben-Sasson, Albeck, and others completely ignore the social factor in their analyses, Katz does not ignore the intellectualistic factor in his analysis, but he does not assign to it any clearly defined historical function and, therefore, leaves the issue "open."

It is interesting to note that Katz contradicted himself clearly on this point on two different occasions while discussing two different subjects, as I showed in a short note in *Tarbiz*.[9] On one occasion Katz openly claimed that the lengthy and detailed halakhic explanations and discussions that crowd medieval (and of course later) rabbinic literature are fruitless from the point of view of the modern historian, who has his own "external" outlook on the historical development of the subject at hand and is, therefore, in a much better position to appreciate the truth of the matter than the Rishonim, who invented their deductions *ex nihilo*, "from within," and, therefore, fathered so many conflicting ideas. As a matter of fact, it was I who had the privilege of having provoked that argument from Prof. Katz in a printed response to some criticism

[9] I. Ta-Shma, "Response to Criticism by J. Katz" (Heb.), *Tarbiz* 60 (1991), pp. 673–675.

of mine on a minor point in his book on *Goy Shel Shabbat*.[10] But it was Prof. Katz himself who wrote the following, in a sweeping criticism on earlier scholars, printed in the methodological introduction to the volume of his collected works.[11]

> But all the labour invested by scholars in that [sort of research] and its like, did not bear fruits other than mere rabbinical biographies, never a history of Halakhah itself...at most do we learn about themes and motives [that occupied their attention] and about halakhic decisions that touch upon matters of public interest...[but] how have these sages reached their decisions and how did they reason them out in terms of Halakhah proper—in this scholars never found interest, and it stands to reason that they did not attach much meaning, or historical importance to it. Sometimes we hear clear and amazing expressions on this subject. In the "Semicha" dispute between Rabbi Jacob Berav and Rabbi Joseph Karo, both parties justified their stand by halakhic reasoning, but Graetz went out to tour after the "true" motives of the disputants, and was not ready to take into account the halakhic reasons given by them, not even as secondary factors, because in this field—according to Graetz—"reigns a disordered confusion of opinions, according to which one can be pro or con anything."

I have, of course, pointed out this discrepancy in my response to Katz's note,[12] but at the time I could not fathom how could such a major methodological discrepancy find its way into Prof. Katz's regularly clear and consistent thought. It now seems clear to me that it has its roots in the undecided and "open" role ascribed by Prof. Katz to the creative intellectual element in the field of medieval halakhic development and reform. As we saw, the intellectual element is pushed into a very narrow corner by his excellent, and undoubtedly correct, analysis, while at the same time the major and parallel developments within this very element cannot be denied and, therefore, clearly call for some historical function to be assigned to them. It, therefore, looks as though a combination of both factors was active in bringing about the tosafist halakhic revolution, while any one of the two could suffice.

Finally, I would like to call attention to another possible avenue of approach, entirely different from Katz's, nearer to the intellectualistic type of approach, but free from their weaknesses. The basic idea is that the very same complexities of life in the newly awakened and "reborn" France of the twelfth century, which necessitated the many religious adaptations and gave rise to the great tosafist enterprise, also opened wider intellectual horizons before the talented elite, causing, thereby, a true and real intellectual revolution, wholly

10 J. Katz, "Response to Criticism by I. Ta-Shma," ibid., pp. 667–672.

11 n. 2.

12 n. 9.

independent of the immediate material needs aroused by the new world. The new economic conditions created in the wake of the demographic multiplication, the dramatic amelioration of agriculture and the intensive urbanization all along the twelfth century, the mere new dimensions of economic creativity, made possible –or, rather, enforced—a new apprehension of the true nature of economic activity and a better understanding of the meaning of its various rubrics and termini. The same is true for almost all other fields of human interest. The required changes and the halakhic solutions leading to them were, indeed, tied together by a Gordian knot, but not as cause and effect, rather as two mutually independent effects of the same cause.

There is, therefore, no need to posit a will or suppose an active initiative on the side of the rabbinic authorities, to take definite steps in any given direction; rather, they were intellectually impelled to re-read the talmudic material in a new "modern" way, by the wider intellectual perspectives now open to them. Such an insight of the historical process nicely explains the striking fact, alluded to before, that most of Rabbenu Tam's novel expositions of talmudic subjects are by far more sophisticated and intellectually satisfying than those of any of his predecessors. It also explains nicely the principle difference between early–eleventh-century halakhic apologetics and twelfth-century tosaphistic work, cited before. What is more important, such an understanding lends a stronger feeling of authenticity to the huge tosaphistic endeavor without taking away any of its inner value, and at the same time keeping it well within its medieval setting.

I took the idea on loan from Prof. Radding's stimulating book, where it was used to explain medieval developments in Canon and Roman law, about which I cannot express an opinion.[13] Personally I favor Katz's social approach, but if I were to consider the alternative approach, I would certainly prefer this variant, which is actually more than a mere variant, nearer to be a third avenue of approach, on its own merit.

Radding's work met with critical opposition by some historians of law,[14] while others praised his work greatly.[15] Both praise his jurisprudential analysis—which is the main point of interest for us here—but Chodorow finds fault with his periodization and moves the date of the "moderni" texts to the beginning of the twelfth century rather than the middle of the eleventh as Radding would have it. I can, of course, contribute nothing to the learned argument between the two, but I may add in passing that moving the "moderni" to the twelfth century will improve the analogy to our sources.

[13] C. Radding, *The Origins of Medieval Jurisprudence: Pavia and Bologna, 850–1150* (New Haven 1988). See also *A World Made by Men: Cognition and Society, 400–1200* (Chapel Hill 1985).

[14] S. Chodorow, *Speculum* 65 (1990), pp. 743–745.

[15] C. Wickham, *English Historical Review* 106 (1991), pp. 685–686.

CHAPTER 7

BETWEEN EAST AND WEST

R. ASHER B. YEHIEL AND HIS SON R. JACOB

R. Asher b. Yehiel ("The Rosh") is one of the more thoroughly studied personalities in our medieval rabbinic gallery. In the year 1916, A. Freimann—then under twenty years of age!—published a detailed life of R. Asher,[1] and four years later he produced a separate long article on the "Ascherides,"[2] altogether a masterpiece of scientific work that was recently translated into Hebrew with only minor emendations added to it.[3] Two great scholars of our time summed up major areas of R. Asher's activity. Prof. I. Baer sketched an appreciation of R. Asher's social and religious deeds and his personal status in Spain,[4] and Prof. Urbach included a description of R. Asher's literary work as a Tosafist in his book, *The Tosafists.*[5] Urbach went on to publish a detailed article—in fact, a small book by itself[6]—wherein he brought to light a large number of new responsa culled from many manuscripts. Some of these responsa are arranged in an arbitrary order, entirely different from our classified, printed edition. As is well known, the printed edition is arranged under a system of some one hundred and eight *kelalim*, that is to say, a defined set of topics wherein all responsa touching on aspects of the same halakhic subject are arranged in numerical order under the same heading. On the basis of these new manuscripts, Urbach was able to supply a wide range of addenda and corrigenda to the printed text, mainly by being able to reunite and put together disjointed members of original responsa that were broken by the editor and

[1] A.C. Freimann, "Rabbi Ascher b. Yechiel," *Jahrbuch der Jüdisch-Literarischen Gesellschaft* 12 (1918), pp. 237–317.

[2] Idem, "Die Ascheriden," ibid. 12 (1920), pp. 142–254.

[3] Idem, *Ha-Rosh* (Jerusalem 1986).

[4] I. Baer, *Toledot ha-Yehudim bi-Sefarad ha-Nosrit* (Tel-Aviv 1959), pp. 174–176, 185–190.

[5] E.E. Urbach, *The Tosafists* (Jerusalem 1980), pp. 586–599 (Heb.).

[6] Idem, "She'elot u-Teshuvot ha-Rosh bi-Defus u-bi-Kitvei Yad," *Shenaton ha-Mishpat ha-Ivri* 2 (1975), pp. 1–153.

scattered throughout the edition according to their changing subject matter. Urbach was also able to fill in missing parts that were omitted or, rather, rejected by the editor. By doing this and by adding dates and proper names of persons and localities that were also omitted by the editor, as a consequence of his splitting the multi-paragraphed responsa into separate entries, Urbach granted a renewed historical vigor to the venerable book and opened it to a new study, which is yet to be done. To top it all off, the full collection of responsa, including the new material, was indexed by the Institute for Research in Jewish Law, Hebrew University Law School, in four comprehensive volumes,[7] wherein they were thoroughly analyzed as to almost every possible literary, historical, and judicial aspect, including a full index to literary sources and a complete onomasticon. Note also should be made of D. Zafrani's doctoral thesis on *Sefer Piske ha-Rosh*—R. Asher's main claim to posterity—with useful indices of its own.[8] And, of course, there are the many articles on various specialized points of the subject, some of which will be mentioned as we go along. Ranking first among them is Poznanski's chapter on R. Asher's biblical exegesis, included as it is in two tosafist collections known as *Hadar Zekenim* and *Da'at Zekenim*.

Thanks to these tremendous efforts, we can now proceed to a more detailed and precise study of R. Asher's responsa and examine the collection in its entirety, setting it in its proper context, and determining its impact.[9] A salient

[7] M. Elon, ed., *Mafteah ha-She'elot ve-ha-Teshuvot shel Hakhmei Sefarad u-Sefon Africa* (Jerusalem 1981), pp. 231–238, 242–248, 276.

[8] Cf. D. Zafrani, "Darkhei ha-Hora'ah shel ha-Rosh" (Ph.D. dissertation, Tel-Aviv University 1980), Index.

[9] Many biographical details in Freimann's work can now be corrected, but that is outside of the scope of this article. In one instance—which is of some importance to the following—Freimann believes that R. Asher was born ca. 1250, because in his *Halakhot Ketanot, Tefillin*, #14, he says that he was taught the laws of laying tefillin from his brother, Judah, and, therefore, he must have been younger than thirteen in 1263, when his father died. But in his article, p. 7, Urbach copies a better version of a question put to the Rosh (*kelal* 108:9) and his answer to: "My teacher R. Joseph. What my teacher has asked about Reuven...and the case has been laid before my master and teacher your father-in-law and that was his responsum..." The correspondence between "my teacher your father-in-law" and his addressee is conveniently printed in Maharam of Rotenberg's collected responsa (*Mekitzei Nirdamim*, #145), under the heading: "And R. Hezekiah sent this case to R. Yehiel of Paris" (the former letter in this series is printed ibid. #143!). The Rosh is quoting this very responsum for the benefit of R. Yehiel of Paris' son-in-law, R. Joseph (b. Abraham), who is known to us from various sources: Cf. Y. Bialer, *Min ha-Genazim*, vol. 1 (1967), pp. 43–44, and *Sefer Mordekhai ha-Shalem*, on tractate *Beitzah* (Jerusalem 1983), pp. 17–18. It is, therefore, clear that R. Asher in his early youth learned in Paris under R. Yehiel, probably around the year 1264, the year of R. Yehiel's death. Therefore, he must have been born a few years before 1250. He might have already been in Paris with his brother, Judah, on his bar mitzvah—away from home and parents. Freimann himself confirms his stay in France while still

fact is its almost purely Spanish character. Around ninety percent of its material was composed in Spain, responding to Spanish addresses, and only a scarce ten percent is of German (or French) provenance. This solid statistical fact could already be conjectured on the basis of the printed edition, but the new manuscript material renders it beyond doubt. About a third of the material in the printed edition could be ascribed to Spain on clear historical grounds, but the rest is neutral and does not offer clues as to its origin. Under "clear historical clues" I include such elements as names and addresses; citings of minhag *ha-arets ha-zot* (מנהג הארץ הזאת; by the way, בארצנו is always Germany); memoirs of past experience in Germany and Provence; discussions of unique local customs and topics, like concubinage and polygamy; mention of rabbinic personalities known to us to have been Spanish; Arabic words; fourteenth-century dates quoted or implied; and mention of *Piske ha-Rosh*, which we know was composed in Spain. To these, one may add such responsa as *kelal* 2:4, which is part of a letter written to R. Abba Mari in the year 1305, included in its entirety in *Minhat Kena'ot*, and the many responsa sent by the Rosh to his son Yehiel, who lived separately for some time in Barcelona, as already noticed by Freimann. German material is identified by mention of German cities and incidents (*be-yom hereg rav*) or by its being a part of a wider net of correspondence, encompassing a number of pupils of Maharam Rotenberg, dealing with the same question and opting for mutual confirmation of their halakhic stands. I would also be ready to consider German addressees as an adequate indication for German provenance, although R. Hezekiah's query (for example, *kelal* 52:5) was sent from Germany (or France) to Spain, as can clearly be seen from the last sentence of R. Asher's responsum:

וכן עשינו מעשה באשכנז בשעת הגזירות, היתרנו נשים עפ" עדות בעלי תשובה, וכתבתי על זה תשובה גדולה

As most of its material—about two-thirds—is neutral, one could conveniently argue that it did represent mostly German material, which is less prone to identification, lacking, as it does, the rich and ramified Spanish coloring that helps us recognize it. But now that the rich manuscript material described by Prof. Urbach is open to us, it becomes perfectly clear that the more than one thousand responsa included in the printed edition represent no more, and probably less, than half that number of original, unbroken, mainly Spanish responsa that can be accurately reconstructed to their original form. What is more important, we now know that a lot of truly "separate" responsa were originally part of a series sent to one person in a single answer to a group of questions. The concatenation of broken paragraphs into original wholes and the further linking together of these unified wholes into original groupings

very young by different reasoning. The exact date of R. Yehiel's death, 1264, has been demonstrated by my pupil and friend, Mr. Simcha Immanuel, whose article on the subject will soon go to press.

clear up a lot of mess and reduce drastically the number of neutral, unidentifiable responsa, thereby greatly increasing the identifiable share of Spanish material in the book. The new supplement of proper names and localities also adds to the geographical clarification, and the same is true for the entirely new responsa, all of which point to Spain and almost never to Germany.

To appreciate the implication of this properly, let us consider briefly the main facts of R. Asher's biography. Born in Germany probably around the years 1245–1250, he studied under R. Meir of Rotenberg, becoming his favorite pupil and eventually inheriting his leadership position in Germany, especially after R. Meir's imprisonment and death around the year 1290. R. Asher left Germany in 1303 with his large household (including many pupils) on his historic emigration to Spain, where he arrived after a lengthy trip through France, Provence, and Catalonia in the year 1305. There he finally settled in Toledo and was successfully absorbed by the Jewish community, with the enthusiastic support of the Rashba. He was intensely active as Rosh Yeshivah and rabbi, later becoming chief rabbi under the formal recognition and auspices of the king, until the end of his life in the year 1328.

The question now is simply this: How is it that the hundreds of his responsa reflect, almost entirely, the last twenty-three years of his long life? R. Asher left Germany when he was around fifty-seven years old and had been the leader of the Jewish communities there for nearly fifteen years, and yet reflections of this long period are almost nonexistent. How are we to account for this extraordinary phenomenon? To be sure, halakhic correspondence with R. Asher is included, or at least mentioned, in the large collection of responsa by Maharam of Rotenberg; but all these, and many other responsa, were apparently not transmitted to Spain with the family or were simply ignored by them afterward and, therefore, fell into oblivion. But why? And why did the Spanish responsa enjoy a different fate? Had R. Asher possibly altered his orientation upon reaching Spain and decided to ignore his heavy Ashkenazic experience and heritage? The answer to that last question is, of course, a most definite "no."

Another outstanding feature of R. Asher's responsa is their purely Ashkenazic orientation, to the exclusion of almost anything that is reminiscent of Spanish halakhic origin and lore. Let me repeat. For the last seventeen years of his long life, R. Asher lived in Spain, acting as chief rabbinic authority for Castilian Jewry, and yet he only seldom mentions a Spanish halakhic authority (with the exception of the great local Toledan, R. Meir Abulafia). Nor does he frequently mention Nachmanides or the Rashba, that great luminary who actually paved the way for his happy landing in Spain. Citations from Nachmanides and Rashba are rare, and once he even denies Nachmanides' authorship of an opinion that he would not accept. To one of Rashba's decisions, which was quoted by his correspondent, the Rosh reacted in these words:[10]

10 This is an important point toward a clarification of the complex relationship that

פליאה נשגבה היא, מנין הרגלים? לא יכולתי למצוא טעם וראיה לדבריו ,לא מגמרא בבלית ולא גמרא ירושלמית, ולא מן התוספות. והאומר דברים תמוהים כאלו ראוי לו ליתן סעד לדבריו, אולי יודו או יוכיחו לו שלא כוון יפה, כי אין אלו אלא דברי נבואות, ואין לשמוע לו עד שיביא ראיות נכוחות למבין...

Rif and, therefore, Maimonides are, of course, constantly cited, but they were already fully recognized and accepted as first-rank *poskim* in Germany since the middle of the thirteenth century and their works were most fervently advocated and consulted by Maharam of Rotenberg himself, who even generalized a rule to the effect that Maimonides is always to be followed except where the Tosafists oppose him.[11] The historical process that brought about this inter-

existed between the Rosh and the Rashba, and was far more intricate than the simplistic description current among the scholars (see *kelal* 2:14–15, and the latter's reply to it, #461–466). These letters describe one aspect—authentic, true, and intimately personal— of a multifaceted picture. Rashba certainly paved the way to a successful absorption of the Rosh in Toledo. The two rabbis knew each other personally, and there existed a deep and mutual appreciation between them. Rashba inherited from Nachmanides a profound admiration for German talmudic scholarship and the pietist way of life, and R. Asher was certainly the pupil par excellence of R. Meir of Rotenberg, and the faithful carrier of his traditions. On the other hand, his strict adherence to these German traditions and his near-total disregard of the rich Sefardic heritage in his hundreds of responsa written in Spain—added to his occasional expressions of the type quoted above—brought about a similar reaction by the Rashba and his pupils and followers. One of the most powerful phenomena of fourteenth-century rabbinic literature in Spain is the tacit rejection of R. Asher's work by the school of Rashba followers, among them the Ritva, Haim b. Samuel of Toledo, Crescas Vidal, Rabbenu Nissim and others, who simply ignore his work. The first to point out this plain fact—and with surprise—was Prof. J. Spiegel in a footnote to his article, "Shaar Reshit Hokhmah he-Arokh," in *Rabbi I. Nissim Memorial Volume*, vol. 3 (1985), pp. 211–212, but he did not notice the reciprocal effect and the literary parallelism, nor their historical significance. Embodied here is much more than local "isolationism" and intellectual seclusion; there is here, rather, a sense of covert disappointment with R. Asher's idiosyncratic style of absorption in his new homeland.

11 E. Ellinson, in his article "Le-Heqer ha-Pesiqah shel ha-Rosh," *Sinai* 93 (1983), p. 235, considers the occasional omission of a relevant reference to Maimonides as an additional proof of "R. Asher's German loyalty." This is clearly a mistake, as shown on different grounds by Dr. D. Zafrani in his article "Le-Darkhei ha-Pesikah shel ha-Rosh," *Sinai* 94 (1984), pp. 278–283. Ellinson's article calls for other corrections, too. On page 237, n. 11, he has it that R. Asher rejected R. Isaac of Corbeil's opinion (on the issue of *kitniyot*) in his book *Semak*, saying: "Cursed be they who are prone to decide the law according to what they find written in the codes of the great sages, without any comprehension of what is stated in the Midrash and Gemara..." But the Rosh used this harsh language against his correspondent, who misunderstood completely the meaning of the *Semaq*, and not against the *Semaq* himself! Ellinson erred, too, in saying that the Rosh, although holding fast to German tradition, sometimes did obey Sefardic halakhic habits out of respect to the halakhic norm "we load on him the stringencies of his new homeland." Ellinson reached that conclusion after having found five well-known German customs that were "missing" in R. Asher's responsa.

esting development was explained in detail in my article on the early inroads of Rabbenu Hananel and Rif into Franco-Germany during the twelfth and thirteenth centuries, and there is a lot more to say.[12] But outside of this narrow stretch of common ground, the Rosh seldom made in his responsa any use of the rich halakhic literature written by such excellent Spanish authors as R. Meir Abulafia, R. Yonah Gerondi, Nachmanides, Rashba, not to mention others like R. Aharon of Barcelona, his brother R. Pinhas, or the Ritba. He did quote them, or at least most of them, in his *Piske ha-Rosh*, but that is a different matter, serving, in fact, to sharpen our judgment as to what really happened to his responsa.

On the other hand, the Rosh made regular use of the long array of Franco-German books and scholars, quoting a lot from Maharam of Rotenberg, his most cherished teacher. He often delved into German reminiscences and was fond of occasionally citing a chat or a dispute he had in the past with Maharam or a case decided by him. He frequently juxtaposed German customs and habits with those prevalent in Castile, always denying the latter any measure of religious credibility. It is obvious that his spiritual world always remained deeply rooted in German tradition and style and, as is well known, he was ready to fight hard at times for the abolition of Spanish customs that were alien to his German orientation and education; albeit on other occasions he would decide not to fight a hopeless war but rather to keep his own way and let others behave as they would. R. Asher was involved in many a bitter controversy on this account, some of a deeply personal nature. I cannot recount here the relevant material, but I will mention my own article, in which I described one such incident:[13] The dramatic quarrel he had with R. Israel of Toledo, his good friend and colleague, wherein R. Asher brought to the fore with an extreme force of inner conviction his deeply rooted Ashkenazic values, attitudes, and principles, in crushing frontal opposition to R. Israel's Castilian viewpoint—and that a full seventeen years after leaving Germany.

But the prohibition on *kitniyot*, which R. Asher omitted, was much debated in Germany and France a long time before his time, and many sages there were against the custom—among them R. Yehiel of Paris, who was R. Asher's teacher (see my article on *kitniyot* in *Asufot* 3 [1989], pp. 347–355). Ellinson goes on to discuss the question of who was the first to prohibit the use of *kitniyot*—was he R. Isaac of Corbeil or was he Rabbenu Peretz, his disciple? But the prohibition was already known and disputed in Franco-Germany a hundred years before both of them. The other customs "missing" in the responsa are also all late and much debated. Zafrani's arguments are right throughout, except #A, where Ellinson is quite right in his answer. There is, of course, no doubt about R. Asher's complete and absolute subjection to the German tradition, with no exceptions.

12 I. Ta-Shema, "Kelitatam Shel Sifrei Rabbenu Hananel, R. Isaac Alfasi ve-*Halakhot Gedolot* beTsarfat u-be-Ashkenaz ba-Me'ot XI–XII," *Kiryat Sefer* 55 (1980), pp. 191–200.

13 Idem, "Shikkulim Philosofiim be-Hakhra'at ha-Halakhah," *Sefunot* 16 (1985), pp. 99–110.

Let us now return to our first question and formulate it in yet stronger terms. We know that he only rarely quoted Spanish material in his responsa and never gave up his homeland traditions. Why, then, are there so few German responsa included in R. Asher's collection in spite of the fact that he spent most of his adult life in Germany, including fifteen years as the leading rabbinic authority?

It is historical fact that nearly all Franco-German rabbis from the beginning of the eleventh century until the end of the thirteenth, excluding Maharam of Rotenberg, did not attach a permanent value to the many responsa they wrote or received. Not one of them, with the single exception of the early–eleventh-century R. Judah ha-Kohen of Mayence, author of *Sefer ha-Dinim*, left an organized collection of his own responsa, nor was such a collection kept by a devoted student. Even first-class halakhic figures, such as Rabbenu Gershom Me'or ha-Golah, Rashi and his three rabbis (as well as his famous grandsons), and the outstanding Rabbenu Tam—or, for that matter, Ri ha-Zaken, Rash of Sens, Ritba, and the many other major Tosafists—never took the trouble to gather their own responsa and hand them over to their pupils for the benefit of later generations. Modern scholarship has to go through the infinite task of carefully reading and collating many antique manuscripts in order to identify whole or fragmentary responsa quoted in secondary and tertiary literary sources. We do not yet possess a satisfactory edition for any of these great sages—not even for Rabbenu Tam, whose rich responsa literature is still mostly unknown to us. The same is true for Ri, Rash of Sens, Risba, and all other major Tosafists. The first to note this curious fact, though unable to explain it to his own satisfaction was Haim Soloveitchik,[14] but he singles out Tosafist France for this phenomenon and thinks that German scholars did, indeed, attend to their responsa, as we do find some small collections of responsa attached to some of their books. As for myself, I cannot see any difference between the two countries. Some German rabbis, such as Ra'avan, R. Isaac Or Zaru'a, and, of course, the indefatigable Ravia, did, indeed, include select responsa written by themselves or by other sages as part of their *opera magna*. So did the Frenchman Rabbenu Tam. By the second half of the thirteenth century it had become truly the fashion to form large compilations of such material, like the well-known literary storehouses of the *Mordekhai*, *Teshuvot Maimoniot*, and the *Teshuvot u-Pesakim* published by E. Kupfer.[15] Such collectanea were, indeed, very common in thirteenth-century France and Germany, where they formed a well-defined literary genre all by themselves, a genre many medievalists now consider to be wholly typical and characteristic of that century.[16]

[14] H. Soloveitchik, *Kalkalah, Halakhah ve-Dimui Atzmi* (Jerusalem 1985), pp. 83–84.

[15] E. Kupfer, ed., *Teshuvot u-Pesakim* (Jerusalem 1973).

[16] N. Hathaway, "Compilation: From Plagiarism to Compiling," *Viator* 20 (1989).

We are once again confronted with one of the many interesting quasi-incidental conformities or parallelisms between German Gentile and Jewish social and cultural phenomena, which derive from different and indigenous motives but amount, in fact, to the same end result.[17] I have dwelt on this intriguing point in much further detail in the introduction to my book on early German ritual. As I noted, although French and German rabbis did form their own private collections of choice responsa, until the end of the twelfth century they never went further than that to collect their own or their teacher's responsa or even to keep a systematic record of them. The striking fact remains that before the fourteenth century we have nothing nearing a collection of responsa for any of the Franco-German sages except Maharam. The reasons for that will be dealt with later on. Maharam was the first German rabbi to pay attention to the subject and he seems to be the first German rabbi who did keep regular records and copies of his responsa. He collected responsa written also by earlier Ashkenazic rabbinic authorities, mainly his teachers in Germany, and many of these were later incorporated into his own responsa by his pupils, who organized his archive into a book-form collection.[18] It is worthwhile to note, *en passant*, that among the twenty-plus manuscripts of Maharam's responsa registered and described by Mr. Immanuel in his thesis, there is but one that is of Spanish origin. I take this as adequate proof that R. Asher did not have with him even a basic corpus of Maharam's responsa when he reached Spain, but I will not argue the point. This is probably the reason for the near-total disappearance of R. Asher's Ashkenazic responsa, which were never collected by him or by his pupils and were, therefore, not transported to Spain as part of the family heritage. But this is not the full answer.

Let us now proceed a little further and ask the question: Who, then, collected R. Asher's Spanish responsa? It was probably not he himself, since he did not care to do so in Germany and had not changed his views about it upon reaching Spain. More probably, his pupils and other Spanish followers and colleagues who studied with him, who were members of his Bet Din, and who admired him greatly did that for him, according to the long-standing Hispano-Jewish literary tradition. This is probably true of the many manuscript collections of the regular type. But the sorted type (later to be printed), which was radically edited, arranged according to topics, and broken into specialized subjects, needs further elaboration.

We now know, thanks to Prof. Urbach's work, that the printed edition reflects a small group of manuscripts. The vast majority (including manuscripts that were not seen by Urbach) are not divided into *kelalim* and are similar to

[17] I. Ta-Shema, "Halakhah, Minhag u-Masoret be-Yahadut Ashkenaz ba-Me'ot XI–XII," in *Minhag Ashkenaz ha-Kadmon* (Jerusalem 1992), Introduction, pp. 10–13.

[18] S. Immanuel, "Kovtzei Teshuvot Maharam me-Rotenberg" (M.A. thesis, Jerusalem, Hebrew University 1987).

other responsa collections of the Rishonim period, in print or in manuscript form, which are not classified according to content but rather follow a more or less random pattern. As a matter of fact, the pattern evident in the printed edition is unique, and I do not know of any other medieval collection that is arranged in strict topical order, not to mention being artificially fragmented to fit such a pattern. The printed version, which was heavily processed into its present format, is the work of R. Jacob Ba'al ha-Turim, R. Asher's son and spiritual heir, the leading authority of fourteenth-century Spain. R. Jacob prepared this special volume of responsa as a major preparatory step—one of a few—toward the publishing of his monumental *Sefer ha-Turim*, and as a main halakhic backup for it.

R. Jacob's fingerprints can still be traced in the volume, and Prof. Urbach himself noted that fact, ascribing to him the more restricted task of editing the small group of responsa sent by the Rosh to his other son, Yehiel. Prof. Urbach followed an incidental remark by R. Jacob recording his treatment of R. Yehiel's material, but other clues teach us that he did the overall editing of the printed version. For example, I would call attention to *kelal* 27, which deals with *Hilkhot Avelut*, the first paragraph of which is actually a sort of "*hanhagot ha-Rosh*," recounting his behavior on the sad occasion of the death of one of his sons a week before *Rosh ha-Shanah*. The paragraph goes on to tell in great detail what he did and what he refrained from doing in each of these seven days, and it was written by one of his sons (*mah she-ira la-adoni avi* etc.), who also wrote paragraph 5 of the same *kelal* (*Halakhah le-ma'aseh hitir adoni avi le-ekhad she-shiddekh na'arah* etc.). The inclusion of halakhic material that is utterly personal and was never issued as an answer to an outside question—and this by the author's own son speaking out of personal knowledge—definitely proves that the printed edition was arranged by this son. For a further example, see *kelal* 32:13–14.

Following an abridged and much fragmented letter of R. Asher to one of his sons, we find an additional note, starting with:

ועתה כשלמדנו יבמות דקדק א"א לשון השאילתות ופי' בענין אחר, וזה לשונו...

This note was added by the editor of this collection, who transformed the oral discourse into written form. Similar filial expressions are dispersed in other parts of the volume; for example, *kelal* 51:2, and the famous introductory note to *kelal* 4:10, on the German prayer. The contents of *kelal* 51:2 were copied in very similar terms into the *Tur* and were, therefore, edited in this way by R. Jacob himself. All this, added to the evidence adduced by Urbach for R. Jacob's involvement in the editing of at least restricted parts of the volume, is by itself enough to prove the point. But there are many more clues.

R. Jacob's literary activity was wide and ramified, and besides his major work, *Sefer ha-Turim*, he also compiled *Kitzur Piske ha-Rosh* to extract pure halakhah from his father's more elaborate *Piske ha-Rosh*. R. Asher's original *pesakim* represent a modified mixture of *pesak pilpul*, modeled after the *Halakhot Rabbati* by R. Isaac Alfasi, following its format and structure. R. Asher measures Alfasi's views against those of the Franco-German Tosafists. R. Jacob, whose heavy reliance upon his father's work and family traditions is very well known, summed up his father's *pesakim* in short, unsubstantiated phrases as one of a series of preparatory steps on the long way toward compiling his own *Sefer ha-Turim*. One can easily see the basic similarity existing between this and the elaborate editorial work accomplished on R. Asher's responsa, which was also intended to facilitate the use of the collection as a practical backup and reference book for *Sefer ha-Turim*. And we all know, of course, the enormous use made by R. Jacob of his father's *pesakim* and responsa. R. Jacob also installed in the collection short halakhic paragraphs or, rather, monographs taken verbatim from *Piske ha-Rosh*, such as *kelalim* 47–49, *Hilkhot Nidah* and *Netilat Yadayim*; *kelal* 47 taken from *Piske ha-Rosh* to *Niddah* (the end of the book), and *kelal* 49 taken from the same book to *Bekhorot* (the end). These two *kelalim* are obviously not responsa at all but part of *Piske ha-Rosh* (and maybe *Kitzur Piske ha-Rosh*. Note their location at the far end of *Piske ha-Rosh* to the two tractates, and they, too, carry evidence as to who was the editor of these responsa).

Contrary to Urbach's opinion, the arrangement according to *kelalim* is the original one and antedates an arrangement—any arrangement—according to a simple numeration. As a matter of fact, the *kelalim* can actually be traced back to a quotation in R. Jacob's own responsa. His responsum was printed in *Zikhron Yehudah* #62. This book is the only existing collection of responsa by R. Judah, the Rosh's son, brother of R. Jacob, and most of its material was assembled by his nephew, R. Asher b. Shlomo, who also penned most of its questions. The responsa of the Rosh are cited many times and always by *kelal* and paragraph number, and the same is true for R. Jacob's responsum, which is also included there. According to the book's preface, which was written by the editor, David Kassel, *Zikhron Yehudah* was printed from a private manuscript originating in North Africa and written by a Russian hand. In the epilogue to the book he says that the referential system to *kelalim* and paragraphs were added to the manuscript by the copyist. But he himself has it that the copyist was a complete ignoramus and, therefore, we must install somewhere along the line a later copyist who was learned enough to do that sort of work with a proper version, which was yet later to be ruined by another ignorant copyist. Apart from its intrinsic frailty, this whole theory cannot be true, for the simple reason that there is no indication of any other numeration in the book, which must have been there at one time if the responsa were not originally quoted by *kelalim*. It is clear that the first collections were kept in the arbitrary order they originally came in; each collection different from the others in its order (or, rather, disorder), as can still be seen from the existing manuscripts, which are not arranged according to *kelalim*. R. Jacob was the first to arrange the material and he chose to edit it thematically, according to classified *kelalim*.

It may be interesting to mention here another editorial work done by R. Jacob, unknown to scholarship as far as I can see and found in a Hamburg manuscript. This work is of a somewhat different nature from that done previously and consists of an abridged version of Rashi's commentary to a few Talmud tractates, adapted to accompany the *Piske ha-Rosh* to these tractates for the use of students in the Toledan Yeshivah, who studied these *pesakim* instead of the normal curricular focus, *Piske ha-Rif* (which had its own adapted Rashi version prepared for it many years earlier). A description of this manuscript and the history of the transition from the study of the Talmud proper to that of *Piske ha-Rif*, and from the latter to *Piske ha-Rosh*, and what happened to Rashi's commentary in the process of adaptation to its new roles are included in an article I've written.[19]

Having reached this point in our discussion, we can now proceed to the main theme of the paper. In order to assess better the diverse activities of R. Asher and his son Jacob, we must probe more deeply into the matter and place our facts in a wider historical setting. Consider again what I said about the general air of insouciance seemingly demonstrated by the twelfth and thirteenth-century Franco-German scholars toward their own responsa literature. That gave us an answer to our question as to why R. Asher's Ashkenazic responsa were not included in the collection, but the question now seems to loom larger: Why, indeed, did they all adopt such an unnatural attitude, and what made them differ so much in that respect from the long-established Geonic and Spanish tradition? They made abundant use of contemporary responsa, using each other's responsa freely, discussing them in detail, and striving to own copies of the more important ones as they happened to learn about them; yet not even one of them—during a period of nearly three centuries—ever set his mind to form his own, or his teacher's, full and authoritative collection until the days of Maharam of Rotenberg, at the very end of the Tosafist period. This is a bothersome question and it, too, calls for an historical answer. I like to reflect on this problem in terms of the total and inbred Franco-German opposition to centralized halakhic authority. The autonomous status of the old Jewish centers in eleventh-century France and Germany and their complete halakhic independence is very well known and described by many scholars, most recently in the articles and book on France by my good friend A. Grossman.[20]

[19] I. Ta-Shema, "Rashi-Rif ve-Rashi-Rosh," paper delivered at the Bar-Ilan University Rashi Conference. Published in *Rashi Studies*, ed. Z.A. Sternfeld (Bar-Ilan University 1993), pp. 209–220.

[20] A. Grossman, "Yahasam shel Hakhmei Ashkenaz ha-Rishonim el Shilton ha-Kahal," *Shenaton ha-Mishpat ha-Ivri* 1 (1975), pp. 176–198.

I have also treated the subject in a long essay,[21] calling attention to the fact that the three great codifiers of Jewish law, i.e., Rif, Maimonides, and R. Joseph Karo, were all of Spanish breed and education; and the fourth, R. Jacob Ba'al ha-Turim, although a native German and of old German stock, lived most of his life in Spain and did all his literary work there, under the umbrella of the royal court and authority. The early–eleventh-century German scholars and their followers—Rashi and the multitude of French and German sages of the twelfth and thirteenth centuries—never thought to produce a central, definitive law book that would put an end, once and for all, to the innumerable controversies over so many details of the law that were current in their countries. On the contrary, these differences of opinion and practice were of major importance to them, because many of them represented old communal, local, or familial customs and traditions, which were by definition much more important and sanctified than the plain, normative talmudic text. Contrary to the Geonic-Spanish view of controversy as representing, basically, a mistake—or at least a misunderstanding—that happened sometime in the past (or perhaps in the "present") and must, therefore, be corrected one way or another, the northern European attitude was to view controversy in principle as representing various legitimate practices that should all be kept alive together, side by side, in the different places where they were practiced. Ashkenazic *minhagim* books, from their early beginnings, always give many contradicting customs side by side, stating the geographical localities where they were practiced, but very seldom deciding between them. The principle of free, local-traditional halakhah was essential to their way of life and formed an impenetrable psychological and practical obstacle to centralized halakhah, Spanish style. And this, in very short terms, is also the deep historical reason why we never had an Ashkenazic chief rabbi—not even for restricted geographical areas or periods of time—until the early twentieth century. This is opposed to the Spanish and oriental tradition of Hakham Bashi, Rishon Le-Zion, and other similar titles.

Even the modest efforts of some Franco-German rabbis to achieve a minimal measure of extra-local authority in their books, like *Sefer Yere'im*, *Semag* and *Semak*, *Or Zaru'a*, *Sefer ha-Terumah*, do not really decide the halakhah in the normal Spanish hard-cut style, but in a rather hesitant and somewhat shaky manner. They cite first numerous contradicting opinions on the matter at hand, and only after doing this will they duly proceed to the actual business of reasonably deciding the halakhah. One can hardly imagine Maimonides going about his business in this way, nor the later R. Joseph Karo, although they do mention at times a differing opinion. The Rif does, indeed, quote redundant opinions in order to refute them, but he was basing his book on the *sugya* itself and could, therefore, not avoid polemicizing and rationalizing. But even he tried, in the main, to avoid such procedure and when he had to do so, he was

[21] I. Ta-Shema (see above, n. 17), p. 26.

always very firm and assertive—even aggressive—in his refutations, never hesitant or merely challenging.

Following this line of thought, one can see why the French and German rabbis did not assign standing importance to their responsa: they did not intend their responsa to carry authority further than the immediate case at hand. Needless to say, when they were consulted and their opinion explicitly asked for, they could naturally expect to be obeyed and followed, but they never thought that their opinions would be decisive to other learned scholars. These were just individual opinions handed out to colleagues who were interested in them and ready to follow their instructions. We must also remember the tiny differences in circumstance that always exist between so-called similar cases and that would usually carry major significance with the independent practicing halakhists in France and Germany, because of their natural tendency to argue a point and reach their own individual decisions. R. Jacob Ba'al ha-Turim was the first German rabbi who was ready to manifest centralized halakhic authority, thus reflecting clearly the deep historical change that overcame the second generation of emigrant German scholars in Spain.

R. Asher always remained a German scholar, very much like his great teacher, Maharam of Rotenberg. He always remembered Maharam's written and oral teachings, and forever preferred the traditions of his German homeland to local Spanish halakhic lore. Sometimes—as in his attempt to change the traditional date for the cessation of the rain liturgy—he would give in, unable to win his cause with the local Bet Din and wishing to avoid a lost quarrel and an unnecessary commotion; but many times he would really fight hard for his views, with varying degrees of success. But even where he failed in his efforts to impose German custom, he did not abandon it but privately kept it. On such occasions he would plainly express his disregard for the Spanish lore (see, for example, the *kelal* on the problem of whether the stork was an *of tahor*).[22] On

[22] There are many examples of that sort in the responsa, but they have not yet been gathered. They cover versatile aspects of life, including finance and business matters. Sometimes R. Asher would not decide upon a case, because the situation seemed to him bizarre:

> Since I first came to this country, I was opposed to old bills and promissory notes, which are in circulation here. I suspect fraud in such cases. Why should a man withhold archaic bills, drawn at a much earlier date? When such cases come before me, I inquire deeply into the matter, and if the explanations satisfy me, I shall go on and decide the law, otherwise, I shall tell the man: I do not annul your bill, but I shall not proceed with the case. Go to another judge. If I am convinced that there is actually some sort of fraud involved, I decree that no other judge may deal with the matter, and this I write, sign, and give to the claimant (*kelal* 68:20, 77:4).

Such bills were sometimes very old indeed: "They are prone in this country to draw bills aged sixty to seventy years" (*kelal* 77, end). R. Asher never met with such habits in Germany. He tried very hard—without much success—to stop the habit, because he could not handle it properly for lack of experience and halakhic tradition, and also because of the relevant lim-

the other hand, he was ready to accept certain halakhic innovations that he was not used to in Germany, and was ready—even eager—to utilize the surprising royal license to exact capital punishment, which was absolutely outside official German rabbinic practice and tradition. The Rosh was accorded full recognition as the top halakhic authority in Castile, although he was not living there spiritually and although he was constantly fighting to achieve a far-reaching social and religious change in the easygoing Hispano-Jewish way of life.

The same applies to his literary activity. His *tosafot*, which were written in Spain, are very much the usual type of German *tosafot*, and his *Piske ha-Rosh*, which were composed also in Spain, are not different, categorically, from the many other Franco-German *pesakim* books. They devote much of their space to the various differing opinions, consider them all, and gradually progress toward a final decision. The only change recognizable in these two works is the incorporation of classical Spanish commentaries and *poskim*, like Ibn Ghiyat, Ri Migash, R. Meir Abulafia, R. Yonah Gerondi, and Nachmanides.

This was never done in Germany or France before him, and not for a very long time after him. Spanish quotations in Franco-German rabbinic literature are so rare as to be practically nonexistent. R. Asher did quote in his books—and quite a lot—from these Spanish authorities, most probably in order to facilitate their becoming standard textbooks in his yeshiva[23] and, thereby, to promote the study of the Franco-German *tosafot* as the normal auxiliary to the Talmud. I fully agree with Prof. J. Faur,[24] who justly emphasized these Spanish additions, in contrast to Urbach's contention that there was nothing at all new in *Tosafot ha-Rosh* compared to the classical *tosafot* of Ri ha-Zaken and R. Samson of Sens. His promotional intentions, as explained previously, can be inferred *ipso facto* from the fact that there was so little Spanish material included in his responsa, as I have pointed out previously.

When the Rosh came over to Spain he did not have with him a copy of Maharam's (or his own) responsa, except for a small, choice collection. This was the characteristic German attitude of advocating local halakhic authority and tradition and strongly opposing centralist tendencies. And this, indeed, was the reason why most of his German responsa were lost. But his pupils—and especially his son and heir, Jacob—completely changed this traditional attitude, not only by methodically collecting and keeping track and copies of all

iting laws of *shemitah* (*kelal* 77:1). The phenomenon, though, is quite well known and was analyzed recently by Prof. J. Shatzmiller in his book *Shylock Reconsidered* (Berkeley 1990).

23 Quite a few literary sources testify to the same, among them the letter of R. Jacob—R. Asher's son—to one of the German rabbis who planned to emigrate to Spain: "Bring over all your books... except your *tosafot*, which will not be needed here, as no one here studies anything else but my father's *tosafot*." Cf. Urbach, *The Tosafists*, p. 587; J. Faur, "Novellae to *Seder Zeraim* by R. Mordechai Romano," *Sinai* 60 (1967), pp. 218–224.

24 J. Faur, "Tosafot ha-Rosh le-Pereq ha-Madir," *Sinai* 57 (1965), pp. 18–42.

R. Asher's responsa but also by converting them into a springboard toward a far more drastic goal: to create a central, authoritative, and full-range code of Jewish law that would determine the halakhah for the whole of Castile, something that was quite unthinkable, even impossible, in France and Germany, but very fitting in the new homeland with its centralized political system of government.

Some illuminating points of similarity between *Sefer ha-Turim* and the contemporaneous Spanish monumental code of laws, the Siete Partidas, were brought to light by Prof. Urbach,[25] who called our attention to the important historical backdrop of contemporaneous Spanish jurisprudence for the better understanding of the *Tur* and its place in Jewish codification.[26] There is no need for me here to quote the interesting list of similarities, but I want to say this: It is not only the similar organization, system, and basic concepts that call for such a comparison. Far more important is the principle itself of dealing unified, central, and codified authority to the various communities, which was very much un-German and had a lot to do with the radically different legal and internal Jewish situation in Spain. In Spain, one finds far less knowledge of Torah and more limited occupation with it as compared to Germany. In addition, the marginal importance attached there to extra-talmudic customs, the far-reaching differences in the ritual and in the social environment between the two countries, and the general disbelief in the authenticity of local Spanish traditions—these and other weighty considerations urged R. Jacob to create a new, German-oriented code for the Jewish communities. The centralized governmental system, coupled with the strictly centralized character of the Jewish autonomy in Spain dependent upon it, gave him the power to do so, but he certainly had to cross a heavy psychological barrier before he could actually proceed to offer centralized and authoritative law to the public. As Urbach showed in his article, R. Jacob went about his work very gradually, basing himself fully on his father's accepted authority and writings. He devoted—as we now know—much time to a preparatory adaptation and suitable editing of these writings and he avoided making a clear-cut decision according to the Spanish tradition. He listed, instead, various differing opinions and arguments before finally deciding the issue. All this helped much to ease the way, but there is no doubt that a major barrier had been crossed, something that his father would not venture to do because he was close to German tradition. It is exactly the classic break between the first and second generations of immigrants that we can watch here, and both are embodied in the same book, the responsa of R. Asher.

25 E.E. Urbach, "Darkhei Pesikah: *Sefer ha-Turim*," *PAAJR* 46–47 (1980), pp. 1–14.

26 Urbach does not actually posit a direct influence of the Spanish *Partidas* on the *Tur*, but rather wishes to point out that similar historical conditions bring about similar sociological, juridical, and literary phenomena.

I would like to end by pointing out, for the sake of clarity, that R. Jacob's work was by no means the only reasonable way open before a halakhist of his type and circle. His brother, Judah, for example, was apparently opposed to it. It is surprising, at first sight, to notice how infrequently Rosh responsa—not to mention R. Jacob's work—is cited by him. The point was, indeed, mentioned in passing by David Kassel, but he offers no explanation for it. The answer lies in #54 of the collection, in which R. Judah defiantly rejects a decision taken by the Toledan community—of which he himself was rabbi!—to accept Maimonides as sole and absolute arbiter, except where the Rosh decides against him. R. Judah viewed this decision as a personal insult to himself, even proposing to step down from his rabbinate if he were so requested. But what is most interesting in his letter to the community are the pertinent reasons that he gives for his objection. One, he says, should never blindly follow a book—any book—even though most of it is unequivocally known to be true and reliable. Every book has its faults and mistakes, which, although they may be minor in quantity, are still major from a qualitative point of view and might carry a blind follower into great religious harm. Each *pesak* should, therefore, be considered by the judge on its own merits and decided upon by live argument. This assessment seems to include *Sefer ha-Turim*. R. Judah was still treading the traditional German course, which was boldly abandoned by R. Jacob in favor of the new world of which he, more than his other brothers, became an integral part.

Originally published in
Studies in Medieval Jewish History and Literature, III
Isadore Twersky and Jay M. Harris, eds.
Cambridge, Mass., 2000

CHAPTER 8

CHILDREN IN MEDIEVAL GERMANIC JEWRY

A PERSPECTIVE ON ARIES FROM JEWISH SOURCES

The last thirty years have witnessed a lively and steadily growing interest in the history of childhood. The point of departure for this surge of interest was undoubtedly the appearance in 1960 of Phillipe Aries' *Enfant et vie familiale sous l'ancien regime*, a work that has retained near canonical status in the profession,[1] but that has also been challenged by subsequent historians on numerous points.[2] What has characterized this new field of research from the outset is its interdisciplinary nature: its use of historical, social, psychological, biological, and medical tools and data. Armed with these new resources, historians have re-read many well-known medieval texts with the resulting discovery of much interesting evidence hitherto neglected by conservative and inattentive scholars. Besides helping to further the area of the history of childhood—the practical and openly declared goal of a major part of this research—these scholarly efforts have also lent considerable impetus to historical inquiry into the enigmatic medieval mentality, opening up entirely new vistas.

It is, therefore, somewhat surprising that few efforts have been made up to now to re-examine medieval and Renaissance Hebrew literature with a view of extracting relevant information and evaluating its contribution to the history of childhood. Considerable research was done—mainly in the late nineteenth and first half of the twentieth centuries, before any serious attention was given to our subject—on the history of Jewish education, which, though verging on the subject of childhood, is quite a different matter and actually has very little direct bearing upon it. The study of medieval Jewish education, which began at the average age of four to six, is concerned mainly with the curriculum and the teacher, and touches upon the child only insofar as he was seated before his teacher and his books. The history of childhood, on the other hand, takes a global interest in the totality of the adult-child relationship, with emphasis on

1 Philippe Aries, *L'enfant et la vie familiale sous l'ancien regime* (Paris 1960).

2 A particularly powerful challenge was articulated by Lloyd deMause in his impressive article, "The Evolution of Childhood," *The History of Childhood Quarterly* 1 (1973), pp. 503–575. The critiques of Aries will be outlined briefly in the article.

early life and the more developed stages of childhood within the family unit and the larger communal framework.

In this paper I shall examine the thesis presented by Aries from the perspective of Hebrew legal and non-legal sources. More specifically, I shall question whether the sources emanating from medieval Ashkenazic Jewry support Aries' thesis that the idea of a separate phase of human development, known as childhood, did not exist in the Middle Ages to an extent children were not considered entirely "human," and as a result various practices associated with medieval parenting, such as beatings, farming out children to wet-nurses, and even infanticide were logical corollaries.

Two major critiques of this thesis have already been articulated. On the one hand, some have argued that there is strong evidence for an appreciation of childhood on its own terms in the Middle Ages, and that Aries has turned a blind eye to the evidence of love for children. From an altogether different beginning point, scholars such as Lloyd deMause have argued that exploitation, cruelty, and brutality constituted the backbone of child-rearing practices in the Middle Ages. As a psycho-historian, deMause does not perceive this brutality as an epiphenomenon, resulting from the image of the child as a young adult. Instead, he argues, the brutality is at the very heart of the parent-child relationship, with profound social implications. The importance of our inquiry into the Hebrew sources is its possible contribution to a better understanding not only of Jewish family life and function—itself a much neglected subject—but also of the history of childhood in general.

Special mention must be made of the pioneering work of Ephraim Kanarfogel, who, in an excellent article, follows the group of scholars who attack Aries by arguing that children were treated with better understanding and more love in the Middle Ages (and Renaissance) than Aries would have us believe.[3] Kanarfogel claims that his "study will demonstrate that if the questions that Aries raised are asked about Jewish society in Western Europe in the Middle Ages, the answers will not always be the same as those of Aries"—with which statement I readily agree. Kanarfogel adduces interesting evidence for "an appreciation of childhood for its own sake among medieval European Jewry," and he is, of course, well aware that there is much more evidence to that effect. But it should be borne in mind that this is true not only on the basis of Jewish sources, but also on the testimony of European sources in general, as has been amply demonstrated by many scholars, cited by Kanarfogel himself. Moreover, the undoubted truth of this argument in no way detracts from the cogency of the evidence produced in support of the other side of the coin, that children were treated in a curious and frigid manner, which Aries has depicted so sharply and convincingly. Both descriptions are valid and probably coexisted within

[3] Ephraim Kanarfogel, "Attitudes toward Childhood and Children in Medieval Jewish Society," *Approaches to Judaism in Medieval Times* 2 (1985), pp. 1–34.

the same society and the same families. The novel element of Aries' view relates to the strange, unfamiliar, frigid aspect of the parent-child relationship; love for children is, of course, common knowledge and taken for granted, even though Aries seems to have ignored it altogether.

On the other hand, notwithstanding Kanarfogel's evidence, it would seem that much of the information to be gleaned from Jewish sources tends to corroborate Aries' description. In fact, it can be shown that many of the central attitudes toward children described by Aries existed within the framework of the medieval Jewish family, although, as we shall soon see, they fulfilled fundamentally different social roles. In Kanarfogel's article I could find one example of this type.[4] He points out that the terms for small child, young child, adolescent, etc., were often interchanged in Jewish as in medieval French literature. Kanarfogel admits that "this interchangeability does show, to some extent, that the ages and stages of childhood were not as fixed then as they are today." But there is far more to be said in this respect.

It is a plain fact that children were far more assured of their personal safety in the Franco-German Jewish family than in the homes of their Gentile neighbors. We know of no Jewish child who was ever sold willingly into slavery, delivered to foreign servitude, or offered as an oblation to an outside institution. Neither were Jewish children sent away to study under advanced scholars until coming of age.[5] Jewish children were exposed—as were other children, and perhaps more so—to the dangers of abduction, captivity, and forced apostasy, but they were never surrendered willingly by their parents, although the latter were legally permitted to do so. Cases of infanticide of any variety were so rare in Jewish society as to be hardly detectable in the voluminous corpus of medieval Hebrew literature. Nevertheless, a few such cases are recorded. One of them, in *Sefer Hasidim* (#173), tells of a widow who indirectly caused the death of her children—of whom there were at least two—by a magic spell, because her prospective new husband refused to marry a woman with children.[6] Presumably, moreover, the bleak stories of child-devouring witches recounted in *Sefer Hasidim* indicate unexplained disappearances or straightforward infanticide, but, of course, one cannot be sure.

Another ancient type of silent infanticide is apparently accidental smothering of children in their sleep, known as crib death, which has long been suspected of possibly masking intentional and semi-intentional cases. The subject has been treated by many scholarly students of infanticide, who seem to eye

[4] Ibid., p. 25, n. 43.

[5] *Sefer Hasidim*, #554. *Sefer Hasidim* is a book of exempla emanating from a group of pietists (known as *Hasidei Ashkenaz*) in mid–twelfth-century Germany. References to some of the secondary literature are provided below. I have followed the second edition of Jehuda Wistinezki (Frankfurt 1924).

[6] We shall have occasion to refer to this story below.

this poorly understood but widely known phenomenon with deep suspicion. It is interesting to note that the earliest rabbinical testimony for crib death comes from the second half of the thirteenth century, from a responsum by R. Meir of Rotenberg, and only very few other cases are mentioned in fourteenth-century rabbinic literature.[7] These rare incidents, however, are exceptions to the rule.

The protection afforded the child in the Jewish tradition has, indeed, been mentioned in passing by some scholars. William Langer has emphasized the influence of ancient Jewish traditions on the firm, though inefficient, official Christian stand against all forms of infanticide and cruel estrangement of children.[8] Another interesting point has been made by Magdalene Schultz, who suggests that this very difference of attitudes toward small children—harsh neglect on the Gentile side compared to caring responsibility on the Jewish—produced guilt feelings that had to be warded off "through projection upon the minority in relation to which one feels inferior in this respect," therefore affecting mainly small children, as demonstrated so well by the sanguinary history of the blood libel.[9] I cannot form an opinion of any value on the psychological plausibility of this theory, but we can safely accept the basic assumption of both Langer and Schultz as to the substantially different treatment accorded small children in Jewish and Gentile families, though neither of them has systematically analyzed the subject on the basis of contemporaneous source material.[10]

There is a twofold reason for this difference between Jewish and the Gentile attitudes in regard to children under one's control. First and foremost, one has the unequivocal halakhic concept of *pikuakh nefesh*, which permeates every nook and cranny of Jewish existence and is the major and absolute consideration governing each and every circumstance, with the three exceptions of adultery, idolatry, and homicide. To be precise, under no conditions is a Jew allowed to commit one of these three transgressions. He is instructed to give up his life rather than agree—even under duress—to rape his fellow man's wife, act against his own God, or take someone else's life. The Jews of Germany stretched this principle to its extreme; not content to let themselves be killed

[7] This has been amply demonstrated by E.E. Urbach, who has collected all the relevant material and added interesting insights on the subject of Jewish infanticide in his "On Manslaughter and Crib Death" (Heb.), *Asupot* 1(1987), pp. 319–332.

[8] William Langer, "Infanticide: A Historical Survey," *History of Childhood Quarterly* 1 (1973), pp. 353–365.

[9] Magdalene Schultz, "The Blood Libel—A Motif in the History of Childhood," *Proceedings of the Ninth World Congress of Jewish Studies* Div.B–1 (Jerusalem 1986), pp. 55–60.

[10] In fact, the subject has not been analyzed by anyone, nor has its importance in our context been properly understood. As already indicated, it is not my intention to undertake such analysis here, though I shall presently produce some interesting supportive evidence.

by their oppressors, rather than superficially and temporarily adopt Christianity, they went much further, slaying their wives and children with their own hands lest they fail the difficult test and surrender their faith rather than their lives. This is one of the most tragic and famous chapters of Ashkenazi experience.[11] It is also, incidentally, a rare manifestation of Jewish infanticide—if it can really be called that. With these three exceptions, preservation of Jewish life was the ultimate desideratum of Jewish law, and responsibility for its destruction, even second-degree responsibility, was the gravest possible crime. This very deep-rooted sense of the sanctity of Jewish life is the major reason for the specifically Jewish attitude toward children within the family, as children themselves are unaware of the dangers of life and unable to care for themselves.

The contrast between the traditional Jewish approach to life, which derives from the religious stratum of the personality and is related to the primary idea of the holy, and the pagan attitude, which derives from the social stratum and is related to the sophisticated idea of utility, has been described, explained, and copiously demonstrated by Moshe Weinfeld in an outstanding article dealing with Jewish attitudes toward abortion.[12] My point will be clarified by a few sentences from the English summary of Weinfeld's Hebrew article:

> In comparison with the Jewish-Hellenistic and Christian view concerning abortion, the Biblical and Rabbinic outlook in this matter is more lenient and more tolerant.... The difference between the Jewish and Hellenistic views of abortion seems to lie in their different attitude towards the life of an individual as a value. Abortion in the pagan world is mainly a sin against state and society (loss of manpower and the strength of the community), whereas the Jewish legislator cares about the religious-moral meaning of murder: the term murder applies to a living creature and not to a foetus that is part of its mother's body. The view of the pagans concerning infanticide may be learned from their attitude towards exposure of children. Contrary to the rigid approach towards abortion, we encounter complete lawlessness in respect to exposure and especially the exposure of crippled children. This shows that the motive force concerning abortion and infanticide was mainly social-political and not religious-moral, as it was amongst the Jews and later among the Christians.[13]

Before I proceed to the second reason for the protection of the Jewish child, there is one more aspect of Jewish child-rearing that derived from the traditional principle of *pikuakh nefesh* that must be addressed. There is a long-standing and strictly observed injunction among the Ashkenazim against mar-

[11] It has been studied at length by Haim Soloveitchik in an as yet unpublished article.

[12] Moshe Weinfeld, "The Genuine Jewish Attitudes towards Abortion" (Heb.), *Zion* 42 (1977), pp. 129–142.

[13] Ibid., from the English summary. For further interesting material, see I. Jakobovits, "Jewish Views on Infanticide," in *Infanticide and the Value of Life*, ed. Marvin Kohl (London 1978), pp. 23–31.

rying a widowed mother who is still nursing her child for a period commonly agreed to be 24 months. The reason is the fear that the new husband might force the mother to neglect her child, since breast-feeding was an onerous task (it was then considered the mother's duty to feed the baby whenever it cried and could not be pacified, day and night). As nursing was the sole technique of effectively feeding a baby, concern for such an orphaned child is readily understood. The matter is discussed at length in the Talmud (*Ketubbot* 60a-b) and Shmuel, the great first-generation *Amora*, rules that such a marriage is forbidden even if the baby dies within the 24-month period, lest the mother kill the child intentionally to clear the way for an expected marriage. The Talmud rejects this seemingly repulsive idea, adding that the incident quoted by Shmuel as evidence for such inhuman behavior concerned an insane woman, whereas normal, healthy women do not strangle their sons. The Jerusalem Talmud (*Sotah* 4:3) accepts Shmuel's position, though without mentioning his name, and rules against such marriages. Another important difference between the two Talmuds concerns the acceptability of various safeguards against possible neglect on the part of the mother, such as arranging for an alternative prepaid wet-nurse. The Babylonian Talmud seems to sanction such legal solutions, provided they are really reliable, but the Jerusalem Talmud makes no mention of them and on the whole treats the matter with excessive stringency. Other early Palestinian sources stress the prohibition even more explicitly, mentioning the fear of deliberate murder.[14]

There is no need here to enter into a full analysis of the talmudic material. Medieval Ashkenazi Jewry adhered fanatically to this injunction, inclining heavily to the Jerusalem Talmud and absolutely rejecting any alternative arrangements suggested by the couple. Indeed, following the relevant discussion in the Babylonian Talmud, it was further ruled that all such marriages must be terminated by a formal divorce, and the couple re-wed after the 24-month period by a full-fledged marriage ceremony.

A case in point—a *cause celebre* at the time—occurred in the city of Cracow, Poland, some time during the first quarter of the thirteenth century, i.e., in the earliest stages of Jewish settlement in that country. A certain scholar, R. Jacob Ha-Kohen, wedded a nursing widow within the forbidden 24 months, contrary to all accepted rules and norms. However, he took extraordinary measures to safeguard the baby's interests. He contacted two different wet-nurses, paid them in advance and enjoined them under pledge and an oath in God's name not to forsake their post. The most interesting point is R. Jacob himself was a great rabbinic scholar and authority, recognized as such by first-rank German rabbis such as R. Isaac Or Zaru'a (who actually headed R. Jacob's opponents).

14 *Sefer ha-Hillukim she-Beyn Bene mizrakh u-Vene Eretz Israel* (Jerusalem 1983), p. 95 and *Sefer ha-Ma'asim li-vene Eretz Israel*, as cited by B.M. Levin in *Tarbiz* 1 (1930), p. 94 (Heb.).

We do not know too much about the whole affair, and none of the Polish rabbis involved is known to us by name. All we know is that R. Isaac Or Zaru'a and his colleagues in Germany took an intransigent stand and employed very strong language, threatening to excommunicate R. Jacob if he did not immediately divorce his wife—a very unusual procedure when dealing with a colleague. But R. Jacob was a *kohen*, and according to Jewish law, if he divorced his wife he would not be able to remarry after the 24-month period nor, indeed, at any other time! This did not deter the German rabbis, however. R. Isaac Or Zaru'a expresses in his letter a profound concern that if R. Jacob were allowed to keep his wife, the ban on such marriages would be completely violated, to the detriment of many other orphaned children, for people would remember R. Jacob's precedent but not his pledges, details of which would be unknown or forgotten in remote localities and at distant times.

The desperate R. Jacob appealed to numerous rabbinic authorities, in various and far-off countries, to help him in his anguish and to approve of his halakhic position. We also know that R. Tobias of Vienne, a well-known French tosafist, actually approved of the marriage and ruled that it was permissible *à priori*, given the special provisions made by R. Jacob. All these letters—and there were certainly many of them—are now lost, and there can be little doubt that they were censored by the Ashkenazi rabbis, who forbade them even to be copied.[15]

Comparing the situation described here with the general practice of wet-nursing, which was extremely common in twelfth- and thirteenth-century France and Germany and was tantamount to getting rid of the baby for good, one clearly perceives the fundamental difference between the two cultures and, at the same time, fully understands the significance of this notable rabbinic controversy. On a personal note, when I first encountered the material relating to this affair, I was utterly unable to understand the obstinacy of R. Isaac Or Zaru'a and his group, especially under the unusual circumstances associated with the case from the start. True, German Jewry is known to have been under relatively strong Palestinian influence from the Early Middle Ages on, as I myself have pointed out on other occasions.[16] And this is a clear instance of a Palestinian tradition exerting its hidden power on the German rabbis. There is

[15] The unusual affair was described by Ephraim Kupfer in his "From Far and Near," in *N.M. Gelber Jubilee Volume*, eds. Y. Klausner et al. (Tel Aviv 1963), p. 218 (Heb.) and later by E.E. Urbach in his introduction to *Arugat Ha-Bosem* (Jerusalem 1963) (Heb.). For a more detailed account, see my article, based upon manuscript material, "On the History of Polish Jewry in the Twelfth to Thirteenth Centuries" (Heb.), *Zion* 53 (1978), pp. 353–359. I must add here that far-reaching inner censorship was certainly not rare in medieval Ashkenazi literature, though the subject has never been discussed by modern scholars.

[16] Israel Ta-Shma, "Law, Custom and Tradition in Eleventh to Twelfth-Century German Jewry" (Heb.), *Sidra* 3 (1987), pp. 85–161.

no other example, however, of such strong feelings being expressed under similar circumstances. A true understanding of this strange case can be achieved only on the background of actual wet-nursing practices and their true significance in the Germany of those times.

In addition to the protection of *pikuakh nefesh*, the second reason why the child was protected has to do with the specifically Ashkenazi concept of the religious duty of *hinukh*, i.e., the obligation to educate children for full and informed participation in their traditional communal life. The primary mission of the Jew in this world was to study Torah and instruct his children in Torah, *mitzvot*, and the fear of heaven. By thus ensuring the continuity of absolutely orthodox, devout, meticulous, and pedantic halakhic practice and Torah study, the individual fulfilled his mission in the best possible way; his offspring would do the same in his turn, guaranteeing that the eternal chain would never be broken. Such was the responsibility that lay on a Jewish parent's shoulders. And one should always remember that normative Jewish practice consisted, to a considerable extent, of local customs, *minhagim*, which were not set out in any written book but were current in daily practice, and the younger generation was expected to learn them in the family and in the synagogue.[17]

These two major reasons—the absolute sanctity of life and the supreme educational responsibility of the parent—created a major difference between Jewish and Gentile families, saving the Jewish child from many of the hardships that befell his Christian counterpart. Analysis of the contemporary Hebrew sources, therefore, makes it possible to examine Aries' thesis regarding the frigidity of adult-childhood relations without the background of physical danger. And, in fact, there are many similarities between the Jewish and non-Jewish family on this score and, thus, these phenomena indeed developed from deeply rooted family practices, as Aries claims, and have little to do with other external factors and sectors of the social complex. It must be borne in mind that although there was very much in common between Franco-German Jewish practices and Gentile behavior—this is common knowledge today and was, in fact, admitted by our ancestors, too—Jews were kept apart from their neighbors by a not inconsiderable barrier, due to the existence of the unavoidable, omnipresent, ubiquitous halakhah, which completely dominated Jewish private and community life. Sometimes of little significance, the gap could at other times be of major and decisive importance. One simple example—which, incidentally, has a direct bearing on our subject—will help clarify my meaning. The ideal of extreme religious piety coupled with social sectarianism, so fundamental to the ideology of *Hasidei Ashkenaz*, had its striking parallel in the contemporaneous European monastic ideal. Yizhak Baer elaborated on this equation in a famous paper on *Sefer Hasidim*, demonstrating many of the less

[17] On this weighty and complex topic, see above, n. 16.

prominent aspects of the similarity.[18] It should be remembered, however, that *Hasidei Ashkenaz* did not, indeed, could not, adopt celibacy, a crucial element of monasticism, since halakhah postulates marriage and procreation as one of its central and most significant demands and the attitude of *Hasidei Ashkenaz* to family life as a religious duty was most enthusiastic, to say the least. Hence, they were absolutely convinced, in the face of the Christian *consensus omnium*, that religious piety did not involve abstinence from marital life; in consequence, they never withdrew from society into remote seclusion and molded their conception of the sexual impulse and its ambivalent nature in a different way. Thus, the Christian and Jewish brands of pietism reflect the deep religious spirit of the age and similar attitudes toward God and human society, and, indeed, have many features in common. But a clear realization of the differences and their underlying reasons is necessary to set proper limits and permits better delineation of the true frontier lines between the two cultures, which had so much in common and yet were so different.

Having stated this, we can now return to the issue of the attitudes expressed toward children. Even a partial survey of the medieval Hebrew material relating to Aries' thesis concerning the attitude toward children would be beyond the scope of this article, but I would like to present a few examples gleaned from the inexhaustible *Sefer Hasidim* in order to press my point.

The first issue one notices is the rarity of any direct reference to children in Hebrew literature from the eleventh to the thirteenth centuries, including *Sefer Hasidim*. Moreover, even when children are mentioned no age is given, the age terms—*na'ar*, *yeled*, *tinok*, *bahur* and the like—being vague, ambiguous, and inconsistent. Most important of all, nothing positive is ever said about them, nor are they ever described as engaged in some praiseworthy activity. What is described is merely their innocent—or, more often, noxious—presence, in situations that call for a halakhic or moral decision by the rabbi, which is the only reason they are mentioned at all. To the best of my knowledge, toys are never mentioned in early medieval Hebrew literature; children are always playing adult games or imitating the daily routine of adults. This is all typical of medieval literature, as observed and described by Aries. At first sight this would seem to present an insurmountable obstacle to research, but actually that is far from being the case. On the contrary, it implies that we now have at our disposal a set of candid snapshots, so to speak, taken *in situ* and without any distortions.

Small children—that is to say, children under the age of five to six years, which was considered early for standard schooling—were the direct responsibility of their mother; the father was usually not at home. According to *Sefer Hasidim*, fondling one's children and going out for a walk with them was a

[18] Y. Baer, "The Religious and Social Tendency of *Sefer Hasidim*" (Heb.), *Zion* 3 (1938), pp. 1–50.

major—if not the major—delight and recreation for the busy and usually absent father. *Sefer Hasidim* holds that the pious, who avoid such amusement even when their children are crying and their hearts go out to them, because they will not interrupt their holy studies for such mundane and egoistic ends, will not exchange divine love for fatherly love; such pious souls will, therefore, leave the crying child to his mother's care and will be fully rewarded in the world to come. The domestic scene of the father embracing and, especially, kissing his children, crops up here and there in *Sefer Hasidim*. Attraction to children and women, playing with friends and idle walk and talk are the main causes of *bitul torah*, neglect of the study of Torah (#815). Renouncing these pleasures is a taxing demand, certainly something hard to expect and difficult to achieve.

The crying baby was a notorious nuisance in antiquity. A baby was usually expected to be crying day and night, wreaking havoc on its parents' nerves, most probably because it was constantly in a state of semi-hunger, the outcome of ineffective and inordinate nursing and the total lack of alternate baby food. Incidentally, babies' physical development was nevertheless not hindered, as we learn from the laconic statement in *Sefer Hasidim* (#944): "Children are not strong enough to hold something in their hands until they are six months old"—a figure somewhat lower than contemporary averages. Another important factor was the already mentioned absence of toys, which were unknown at the time. Even dolls were apparently unknown in the Jewish home, probably because they contravened the injunction against three-dimensional human images. The prescribed remedy for a crying baby was to breast-feed it again, and when that did not help lullabies were sung—*Sefer Hasidim* warns against the use of Gentile melodies or even synagogal-liturgical songs! As a last resort one appealed to magic, which certain women knew how to perform, in order to counteract the effects of the evil spell that had evidently been cast by some witch, anonymous or otherwise, who was always held responsible for constant, incessant weeping (#174).

Children used to roam about with their noses filthy and dripping. This was the norm and to be expected: "Small children are customarily filthy around their noses"; there was nothing amiss in children appearing thus before guests and strangers visiting their homes. But small children accompanying their father when he was visiting another household were expected to have clean noses; otherwise the father was considered responsible and was even liable to be sued for damages (#104). However, the main significance of this piece of information lies in the field of medieval pediatrics, which needs separate treatment.

As stated, children were normally under their mother's care. An unusual case is described in *Sefer Hasidim* (#569). The text may be rendered approximately as follows:

> The wise man heard somebody say his Grace after Meals hurriedly. He said to him, when you ate you did not hurry, why are you in a hurry now? The man answered, when my little children are near me I always make haste, lest they ease nature on me. So the sage said to him, then remove them from you! But the man answered, I am not the ruler of the house and its inhabitants, and the maidservants do not heed me, and my wife governs the money and from her hand do I eat.

As we have already encountered the unclean child, we may well understand the father's distress. But this man was not master of the situation in his own house. The mother regularly sent her dirty children to nag their pious father while he was at his meals and leave her alone. And the poor man could do nothing about it, not even call in the maids for help! Though this story seems to draw a topsy-turvy picture of the situation, it nevertheless brings out very vividly the same principle of complete—though ineffective—maternal responsibility, temporarily let loose on the "good-for-nothing" father while he was at home.

A very amusing instruction advises a person who cannot help meditating on the Torah even when he is in the lavatory to take his small children there with him in order to distract his mind. But, the text adds, "if he is afraid lest they become accustomed to being near him and distracting his mind when he is studying Torah," then it is better that he should not take them with him, but perhaps try to think about other matters in the privy! (#771)

The fact that children were completely under their mother's care was no guarantee of their good conduct. Undisciplined children appear quite often in our sources, which tell us that unruly, even wild, behavior was normally expected from them. We learn again from *Sefer Hasidim* (600):

> A person was told, many people hang pretty decorations in their *sukkah*, why do you not do so? But he said: What is the use? The children will disconnect the fruits and the threads on the Sabbath, so I had better not be the cause of their sins.

The children would do so any time, of course, but the pious man was worried only on account of the Sabbath. It did not occur to him simply to forbid them, on pain of punishment, to touch the decorations, thus enabling him to beautify his *sukkah*, as befitted his piety—and as his pious friends though fit. For if he did, most probably only his wife could see to it that his instructions were observed, and she was always busy indoors. At any rate, no one seems to have believed that issuing the necessary instructions and ensuring that they were carried out was an essential part of education and child rearing.

A similar situation is described and pictured in vivid colors in another interesting passage (*Sefer Hasidim* #684):

> A boy stood on a table upon which his father was accustomed to put his books. But the table was not reserved for books only, as he would place food on it too when he wished to eat. Books were always on the table, but when

> he ate he put them elsewhere. So the boy stood on the table, and as he let himself down he cut his foot on a knife that was lying on the table. And the father said, I am to blame. Why did I allow him to tread on a table that usually has holy books on it?

The moral of this story for its readers is quite clear, as is its significance for our inquiry: neither father nor mother thought it necessary to prevent the child from climbing the furniture. The pious father understood—too late, admittedly—that holy books were a different matter, but that is all. A much more interesting point is that the father's conscience actually troubled him. It troubled him that he was responsible for his son's accident; but he understood his guilt as directed against the holy books, not against the child himself, whom he could easily have trained never to climb tables (provided, of course, that his wife cooperated). As already pointed out, these passages capture for us minute snapshots of domestic scenes, complete with soundtrack, recording the actual voices of the protagonists. The same scene could be encountered in any household; the unique feature in this case was the pious father's reaction in taking the blame upon himself and admitting that holy books demand special care. Ordinary fathers would never have such sentiments, even if they happened to have holy books regularly lying upon their tables.

Harsh disciplinary measures were considered a necessity in school, that is, before a teacher, but nowhere else. Elsewhere children were known—and expected—to act as they pleased, as long as they did not encroach upon someone else's rights. This was understood as part of their underdeveloped nature. The solution was to have them seated before a teacher as early and for as long a time as possible. However, this is beyond the scope of this article, as we are interested only in pre-school years.

Children's games, on the testimony of *Sefer Hasidim*, were all of a social type. Children old enough to walk and talk always played in the company of other children, mainly imitating adult activity or playing their games. There is no telling how younger infants occupied themselves when not crying; I have already stated that, to the best of my knowledge, toys, dolls, and puppets are never mentioned. Table games and open-air games alike are mentioned mostly in connection with adults, and it is clear that recreation of any variety was mainly an adult occupation, children imitating them in this respect as they did—and still do—in all other fields of behavior. Jewish boys played together with their Gentile coevals, and no one seemed to mind. For example (#1243):

> If children brought stone weights and scales that Gentile children had calibrated according to their father's, whose measures were considered more or less exact, and Jewish boys played with them and calibrated their stones accordingly....

The writer seems to be concerned with the stones, ignoring the children's behavior.

Children under schooling age were considered incapable of coping with academic material of any level. Even later, when they attended school, they were allowed to progress only very slowly and under strict supervision. As I have discussed this principle at length elsewhere, I shall not dwell on it here.[19] The reason for this distrust, which is an inheritance from time immemorial and still lingers today, is rooted in the ancient belief that wisdom literature conveys more than its superficial content and always conceals deeper matters between the lines. Neither do Nature or Holy Scriptures speak to us in an unambiguous, direct manner: a real and thorough understanding of their true inner meaning—which is always there—can be achieved only through able intermediaries, who interpret their message to us. Interpretation, mostly professional and often counter to the simple sense of the text, is unavoidable if we are to understand the sayings and teachings of old; otherwise, we might easily be misled into gross errors by the superficial meaning. I mention this in passing as a mere digression.[20]

Returning now to our main inquiry, it would be particularly interesting to see what individuals in the Middle Ages thought of the general abilities and inclinations of young children and how they assessed their talents, which they do not seem to have noticed at all. Unfortunately, direct evidence to that effect is most rare in medieval Hebrew literature. I shall now proceed to cite the sparse information I have been able to cull from *Sefer Hasidim*.

The *melamed*, who teaches the youngsters, is instructed to point to the sky with his finger, to show his pupils where God is:

> Later on the teacher should explain to the boy the existence of paradise and hell, because a child's intellect is like that of an adult in his sleep, believing everything to be true. In the same manner children believe everything you tell them is true, before bad friends accustom them [to wrong opinions]. (#820)

This naïvete, considered here to be the best short-cut to correct beliefs, is only one side of the child's immature personality. The other side may be found in his straightforward commonsense and healthy critical attitude:

> One should not reveal to children strange legends, lest they say there is nothing to them, they are not true, and since they are not true other things [that the children have been told] are also not true. (#811)

Being naive, the small child will easily accept the existence of God, paradise, and hell, but he will not give credit to apparent absurdities and will be quick

[19] See n. 16, pp. 136–140.

[20] Interesting material on this topic has been assembled by Jane Chance Nitzsche, *The Genius Figure in Antiquity and the Middle Ages* (New York 1975), esp. pp. 56–64. On the famous *Book of Nature* and its significance for a true understanding of *Sefer Hasidim*, see Haim Soloveichik, "Three Themes in *Sefer Hasidim*," *AJS Review* 1 (1976), pp. 311–325.

enough to reject prior information of the same type or quality, previously accepted on a *bona fide* basis and now recognized as false and rejected—quite a realistic assessment of juvenile reasoning.

The emphatically social nature of childhood was perfectly understood: *Sefer Hasidim* says that "small children, before they get married, cannot do without friends" (#1084) and, therefore, advises the father to ensure that the child has worthy friends. It also warns against permitting the child to eat in other homes, lest he adopt evil ways and come under the influence of bad friends.

In apparent disagreement with talmudic conceptions, *Sefer Hasidim* is of the opinion that young boys under the age of thirteen are responsible, under certain conditions, for their deeds, though they are not punishable or answerable to the law before reaching that age. After achieving maturity at the age of thirteen, they may be required to rectify some of their past misdeeds. This idea is worthy of a detailed scrutiny, which is beyond the scope of this chapter. Suffice it to quote *Sefer Hasidim* on this intriguing point:

> A person came before the rabbi and said to him, "I remember that when I was a child I used to steal from people and commit other sins." And he said, "Presumably I need not repent, because at the time I was not yet thirteen, and as I was still young why should I repent or repay my thefts?" But the rabbi said to him: "All the sins that you remember and everything that you stole you must repay.... But if a person was told by others that he used to steal when he was a child and he does not remember this himself, he need not repay [or repent]." (#216)

Religious responsibility depends on intelligence, whereas legal liability depends on age. Intelligent boys are answerable for their actions, as can be proved from the Bible (2Kings 22). People who recall negative personal involvement in events from their younger days are, therefore, fully responsible once they grow up for their misdeeds. The very fact that the events in question were recorded in their memory as negative or forbidden acts is proof positive that at the time they possessed sufficient understanding and were fully conscious of their wrongdoing.[21] That is why they are held responsible after reaching maturity.

I cannot enter here into an inquiry concerning the opinion of professional halakhists on this very moot point. Suffice it to say that we have here a very elegant "Aries motif," identifying the adult male with his younger version, the child, and postulating a purely quantitative difference between them regarding

[21] Or consider the following passage (#1774): "A person having a fruit tree in his garden should have a thornbush fence, so that children should not break through, climb the tree, and pluck its fruit on the Sabbath. The owner cannot say, "Let the wicked gorge themselves and die" [Babylonian Talmud, *Bava Kama* 69b], because they are still children" and, therefore, not responsible for themselves.

physical maturity and intellectual level. In other words, we once again have evidence of a very interesting point: despite the special physical treatment accorded the Jewish child, ultimately the child was not treated as a distinct entity as in the non-Jewish world, an adult-in-miniature. The edifice of parent-child interrelationships, though quite similar to that described by Aries, was built on a completely different infrastructure. The implication is that medieval concepts of childhood, as delineated and characterized by Aries, stemmed from medieval mental and social attitudes and were not connected with—certainly not a result of—the cruel treatment accorded to medieval children, as argued by some of Aries' detractors.

These conclusions must not be extrapolated to all of medieval Jewry. They represent one attempt to re-examine Jewish sources and focus only on medieval Germanic Jewry. New studies of other times and places will undoubtedly yield variations on the thesis presented above. The importance of other such studies, which carefully examine the legal and non-legal literature of the Jews and are sensitive to historiographic debates of medievalists, is, I hope, amply demonstrated in the above study.

Originally published in
Studies in Medieval and Renaissance History XII,
J. A. S. Evans and R. W. Unger, eds., 1991.

CHAPTER 9

THE LAW IN ACCORDANCE WITH THE LATER AUTHORITY *HILKHETA KE-VATRA'EI*

HISTORICAL OBSERVATIONS ON A LEGAL RULE

THE ASHKENAZIC UNDERSTANDING OF THE RULE

> This great veneration for the views of earlier authorities did not prevent Jewish law from establishing, over a period of time, a fundamental principle for determining the law—a principle that, on the surface, seems contrary to the principle of priority of the earlier over the latter, but which was essential in order to empower the authorities of later generations to make legal rulings responsive to contemporary problems and consonant with contemporary conditions. This important principle is that "the law is in accordance with the views of the later authorities" (*hilkheta ke-vatra'ei*), and it has existed since the geonic period.[1]

This is M. Elon's description of the substance and role of the rule "the law is in accordance with the later authority" (henceforth, "the law is like the later"). After some discussion, he concludes:

> Thus was established and accepted the fundamental principle of decision making in Jewish law—"The law is in accordance with the views of the later authorities." It should not be thought that this principle diminished in any way the respect that later generations accorded to the earlier generations. It was precisely this respect that induced the later authority responsible for declaring the law to ponder his own decision earnestly, fearfully, and humbly, because he was aware that he was dealing with a question already considered by the earlier authorities. Nevertheless, when he finally reached his conclusion, his view, and not the view of the earlier authorities, became the law.[2]

This extraordinary description of the rule "the law is like the later" is far from a unanimous, or even a majority view. Though currently popular, it is based on the opinion of only some of the later halakhic authorities. While, from a legal point of view, only the rule's final formulation is valid (an interesting case of halakhic self-reference), it is nonetheless illuminating to inquire into its

[1] M. Elon, *Jewish Law* (Philadelphia and Jerusalem 1994), vol. 1, p. 268.

[2] Ibid., p. 271.

early history and the meanings attributed to it in the past. Although a thorough investigation of the subject would require specialized historical expertise, even a schematic outline should suffice to stimulate reflection on the true significance of "the fundamental principle of decision-making in Jewish law" and help determine whether, indeed, it fits this description.

To the best of my knowledge, the earliest source that presents the rule in this spirit is R. Judah, the son of R. Asher b. Yehiel (the Rosh), in a responsum (*Zikhron Yehudah* #23) in which he sought to rule according to the decision of his father against the author of *Sefer ha-Terumot* on the grounds that his father was a later authority. His opponent disagreed, arguing that "the principle of 'the law is like the later' refers only to debates among Amoraim." R. Judah argued as follows: "My father, of blessed memory, asserted that "the principle that 'the law is like the later' applies also to later generations." He refers to the Rosh's commentary on *Sanhedrin* 4:6, in which the Rosh employs the principle "Jephthah in his generation is like Samuel in his" and not the principle "the law is like the later authority." R. Judah's brother R. Jacob, author of the *Turim*, concurs, saying "in the commentary on *Sanhedrin*, my father, my master, of blessed memory, wrote that the law is like the later holds even among contemporary scholars" (ibid.). This development of the Rosh's teaching is the first time that the principle "the law is like the later" is referred to in the halakhic literature as bestowing legal primacy on decisions of an authority who is later than others who have ruled on the subject, as Elon has argued. Rabbi Moses Alashkar quotes R. Joseph Colon (the Maharik) of the fifteenth century: [3]

> You have written that you were told by your teacher on the authority of the most honored R. Joseph Colon that the rule of "the law is like the later" applies to post-talmudic authorities (*poskim*) as well...and that R. Joseph Colon went as far as to assert that the rule applies to the opinion of a single later authority when it opposes the opinion of many others who preceded him, for example, the author of *Sefer Hamitzvot Hakatan*.

Alashkar attacks this view, ridiculing it:

> This view is groundless and does not even merit refutation. I wish I knew the period up to which he meant to say that "the law is like the later." If it was

[3] R. Moses Alashkar, *Responsa*, #54. For more on R. Joseph Colon's view, cf. #84 and #94, discussed below. Israel Yuval, in "Periodization and Self-Awareness in Ashkenaz" (Heb.), *Zion* 57 (1992), pp. 369–394, interprets the remarks by the Rosh, which his sons used as grounds for their argument, somewhat differently: "The position attributed to the Rosh, i.e., that he used the principle even in deciding disputes between post-talmudic authorities, is a later interpretation of his stance, as is evidenced by an examination of his actual words." This interpretation of the Rosh is groundless, for Yuval has failed to notice that what he calls "a later interpretation" is, in fact, the position taken by the Rosh's own sons, including R. Jacob, who studied with him for decades.

> intended only up to a certain generation, then the rule is qualified and cannot be applied generally; furthermore, there is no criterion for preferring one generation to another. Nor can we imagine that he did not wish to qualify his statement and that he intended to extend the scope of the rule forever. This would be preposterous, for our later generations resemble those of the earlier sages less than a man resembles an ape, and we could only wish for sense enough to understand their simplest teachings. All the more so for generations yet to come, since there is a gradual decline of intelligence.

He concludes:

> The Geonim who ruled that "the law is like the later" referred only to the later generations of the talmudic period that preceded them. They could hardly have been referring to future generations whose opinions they never heard and whose methods they were unfamiliar with, for only prophets can foresee the future.[4]

Indeed, from the time of R. Joseph Colon, Ashkenazic and Sephardic authorities differed explicitly and systematically over the scope and meaning of the rule "the law is like the later." R. Moses Isserles (Rema) of Cracow, the greatest of the later Ashkenazic authorities, clearly illustrates this when expressing his own position in the preface to *Darkei Moshe.* Explaining his motivation for writing, he gives as one of his reasons:

> Which is the essence and purpose...because it is known that the learned author of Beit Yosef had a natural inclination toward the great...Alfasi, Maimonides and Asheri...even though they are early, not later authorities ...but he does not heed the proclamation of the earliest authorities...instructing us to decide according to the later authorities and to disregard the earlier ones, even when a student rules against his teacher. And the later authorities, led by R. Joseph Colon and R. Israel Isserlein, always decided according to this...so he opposes the customs of those countries which usually rely on this rule straightforwardly.[5]

R. Israel Isserlein,[6] R. Joseph Colon,[7] R. Jacob Pollak, R. Shalom Shakhna and R. Moses Isserles are, indeed, staunch supporters of the view that the rule refers to authorities of the post-talmudic period, including themselves, and extends "to the end of all generations." For them, the rule that "the law is like the later" had, indeed, become what Elon calls "the fundamental principle of decision-making in Jewish law."[8] As we shall see, this strong interpretation

[4] Ibid., at the beginning of the responsum.

[5] Our translation. This passage is also cited in Elon, op. cit., vol. 3, p. 1354.

[6] R. I. Isserlein ruled, for example, that R. Meir of Rotenberg is a "later authority" with regard to R. Isaac of Duran. See *Terumat ha-Deshen*, part 1, #215.

[7] n. 3.

[8] n. 2.

originates in the fourteenth century. I can find no trace of it earlier, in either the Ashkenazic or the Sephardic authorities.

As to the Sephardic authorities, their tradition, represented by R. Joseph Karo,[9] R. M. Alashkar[10] and R. M. Alshekh,[11] clearly differed from that of the Ashkenazic *poskim*. They relied on the great early authorities, renowned for their wisdom, rather than on those of later periods. Maimonides states this doctrine in the introduction to his *Code*:

> Furthermore, if one of the Geonim taught that the law is so and so, and to another court of a later period it appears differently on the basis of the law as written in the Talmud—we are not bound to accept the earlier opinion, but the more convincing one, regardless whether it is that of the earlier or the later authority.[12]

The Ashkenazic authorities had a different policy. Elon[13] notes that R. Moses Isserles follows his teacher R. Shalom Shakhna, who refused his many students' request that he "become a *posek*," that is, commit his decisions to writing, saying:

> I know that they will not decide differently from what I would write, since the law is like the later, and I do not wish them to rely on me…for the judge should only consider what he beholds with his own eyes. Therefore, each one should judge for his own time at his own discretion.[14]

9 In his introduction to the *Shulhan Arukh*; see Elon, op. cit., vol. 3, pp. 1309ff., 1316ff.

10 n. 4.

11 R. M. Alshekh, *Responsa*, #39.

12 Maimonides, *Code*, ed. S.T. Rubinstein (Jerusalem 1956–57), p. 13. An additional Sephardic source in the same vein appears in R. Bezalel Ashkenazi's *Klalei ha-Talmud*, as reprinted by A. Marx in the Hebrew section of A. Marx, *Festschrift zum Siebzigsten Geburtstage*, ed. D. Hoffmans (Berlin 1914), p. 209, note 306:

> From Seder Olam, written by Nachmanides [Maimonides, notes Marx], it is known that the law is according to the later authorities to the extent that they reached a decision, whether they decided for the majority or the minority view, or between two opposing individual views. This does not mean that the later authorities dissented from the views held by the earlier authorities on any point whatever, God forbid.

The nature and content of Maimonides' *Seder Olam*, which is mainly known from quotes in R. Bezalel Ashkenazi's *Klalei ha-Talmud*, are not clear. There is little doubt, however, that the work accurately represents the views of the Sephardic authorities on this matter.

13 Elon, op. cit., vol. 3, pp. 1345ff.

14 R. Moses Isserles, *Responsa*, #25, Ziv, ed., p. 156b (our translation). This responsum by R. Israel, the son of R. Shalom Shakhna, is quoted in Elon, op. cit., vol. 3, p. 1347.

This passage touches on a historically significant point that is pertinent to the issues underlying our investigation. The reason for the appeal by R. Shalom Shakhna's students that he become a *posek* is given at the beginning of the passage: "He trained many students from one end of the world to the other and we all live by his teachings, which sustain us." This con-

As his son testifies later in the passage, R. Shalom Shakhna himself followed the policy of his own teacher, R. Jacob Pollak, on this matter: "and for the same reason his teacher, the illustrious R. Jacob Pollak, did not write any books. Nor did they copy and put on file any of the responsa that they sent to distant places, because they considered this overbearing assertiveness."[15]

Elon's description is, indeed, an accurate one of this Ashkenazic understanding of "the law is like the later," which originated in the fourteenth cen-

stituted yet another unsuccessful attempt to establish a central judicial authority for Ashkenazic Jewry. It failed for the same reasons the others failed, with one salient difference. For the history of these attempts, see E. Zimmer, *Jewish Synods in Germany during the Late Middle Ages* (New York 1978).

The main reason for the sterility of these efforts was the tradition of independence in the early Ashkenazic judiciary; of the non-intervention of one community in the affairs of another. This principle is already in evidence at the time of R. Joseph Bonfils, who lived in France in the early eleventh century. See A. Grossman, "The Attitude of Early Scholars of Ashkenaz toward the Authority of the *Kaha"l*" (Heb.), *Shenaton ha-Mishpat ha-Ivri* 2 (1975), pp. 180–181. Throughout its history, Ashkenazic Jewry never had a "Chief Rabbi," an individual with ultimate judicial authority (*posek yakhid*), or even a central authoritative rabbinical forum, except during the time of Rabbenu Tam.

On the other hand, the four major pillars of decision-making in Jewish law: Alfasi, Maimonides, Asheri, and R. Joseph Karo, flourished in lands where the communal social-political frameworks had always recognized the supreme authority of a central figure—a rabbinical authority who enjoyed royal recognition and official status. For a summary of the Sephardic legal literature, see H. Zimmels, *Codifications by the Jews of Spain (The Sephardi Heritage)* (New York 1971). Zimmels notes that all four of these outstanding figures had some connection with Sephardic lands, but he does not attribute any significance to this fact; he also fails to notice that even though their connections with "Spain" were incidental, the fact that they all lived where there were centralized political frameworks has clear historical relevance. Such centralization was a necessary condition for the creation of authoritative codes of Jewish law.

Against the background of the highly decentralized community organization that had existed since ancient times in the Ashkenazic countries (as well as in society in general), it is almost impossible to imagine the creation of a central, authoritative code of Jewish law. All that was created there during the twelfth and thirteenth centuries was a series of summaries of the legal works of the great commentators, such as Rashi and the Tosafists, compiled and arranged by their students, along with the students' analyses of their teachers' halakhic opinions. See my "The Characteristic Features of Halakhic Literature in Ashkenaz in the Thirteenth and Fourteenth Centuries" (Heb.), *Alei Sefer* 4 (1977), esp. pp. 20, 32–34.

The difference between earlier attempts at organizing a central authority and that of R. Shalom Shakhna's students is that, conscious of the problems inherent in assenting to his students' request, R. Shalom Shakhna himself sought to preserve the principle of freedom of judicial decision-making for future generations. It should also be noted that implied—though not articulated—in this passage is the beginning of a shift in the application of the rule "the law is like the later" from the last authority of the past (the traditional Ashkenazic interpretation) to the present authority. For more on this, see sec. 4 below.

15 R. Moses Isserles, loc. cit. (our translation); quoted in Elon, op. cit., vol. 3, p. 1347.

tury and has been dominant since. However, his account fails to acknowledge that the opinion of R. Joseph Karo and the Sephardic authorities, both before and after him, Maimonides included, is different. In their opinion, the rule does not apply to post-talmudic times at all.

Though I discuss the historical and theoretical origins of the dispute at some length, the divergence between the two traditions is not the main issue here. As we will see, there is no early evidence, and maybe even no late evidence, that the rule "the law is like the later" was meant to uphold contemporary decisions against a contradictory precedent. On the contrary, it tends to restrict rather than extend authority; it does not grant authority to the contemporary *posek*, but rather refers him to the authorities of the past with the stipulation that of the past authorities those of a later period must be preferred. That the current *posek* is also a "later authority"—in fact, the latest—is an entirely novel idea of Ashkenazic origin for which I can find no traditional sources, as I explain below. While the principle conferring authority upon the current *posek* is, indeed, genuine, it originates in the altogether different rule: "Jephthah in his generation is like Samuel in his generation." As we shall see, this has nothing whatever to do with the issue of "the law is like the later."[16]

THE RULES "THE LAW IS LIKE THE LATER" AND "THE LAW IS NOT ACCORDING TO A STUDENT IN THE PRESENCE OF HIS TEACHER"

This question of its applicability to later generations of halakhic authorities arose only after the rule "the law is like the later" had been in existence for a long time, evolving considerably over the years. There is no trace of it in the talmudic literature, and it is first mentioned in *Seder Tanaim ve-Amoraim* of the geonic period.[17] In the version published by R. Haim Joseph David Azoulay of *Shem ha-Gedolim*, the rule appears twice:

16 Cf. section 3 below. Elon, too, considers the rule "Jephthah in his generation is like Samuel in his" together with "the law is like the later," but does not discuss the relationship between the two rules (ibid., vol. 1, p. 266).

17 The many print and manuscript versions and numerous editions of *Seder Tanaim ve-Amoraim* is a serious problem requiring further study. The last critical edition is K. Cahane's (Frankfurt on Main 1935). The classic work on the subject is still A. Marks's paper in *Tiferet Yisrael* (Breslau 1911). For an updated comprehensive bibliography, see Y. Efrati, *Tekufat ha-Saboraim ve-Sifruta* (Petah Tikva 1973), pp. 14–32. In Efrati's opinion, *Seder Tanaim ve-Amoraim* came into being as a unified work (the version in *Makhzor Vitry*) only when *Makhzor Vitry* was compiled from the various early manuscript versions then available. I have not tried to determine which of the existing versions is preferable; indeed, I doubt it can be done. See S. Abramson, "Le-Toldot Nusah *Seder Tanaim ve-Amoraim*," in *Ezra Tzion Melamed Jubilee Volume* (Ramat-Gan 1982), pp. 215–248 (Heb.)

> Even though the sages defined rules such as "In a controversy between A and B the law is according to A"; if authoritative opinions of *later* Amoraim exist, the law is as they decide.[18]

And he continues:

> In instances in which two Tannaim or Amoraim hold different views and it is not stated whose opinion is upheld, if one is a student who contradicts his teacher, then the opinion of the student is not preferred over the opinion of his teacher. This is the rule up to the time of Rava. From his time onward, the law is like the later.[19]

In the *Makhzor Vitry* version, the first rule is the same; the second ends with the words:

> The opinion of the student is not accepted against the opinion of the teacher.[20]

In the version published by Samuel David Luzzatto (Shadal), neither of R. Azoulay's rules is given. Rather, the first rule is as follows:

> Even though the sages said "In a controversy between A and B the law is according to A," if there are existing authoritative opinions of our masters, the Amoraim, the law is according to them.[21]

This is a different matter altogether (if not simply an error). The second rule is identical to the version in *Makhzor Vitry*. Nevertheless, there is no disagreement here, for Luzzatto, a few lines later, in referring to the Amoraim, himself says:

> In an instance where early Amoraim such as Rav and Samuel hold different opinions, and there are also opinions of later Amoraim such as Abbaye and Rava or others, the law is according to the latter,[22] and if earlier and later authorities voice different opinions [in R. Azoulay's version these words are added: "for instance, their students, who added to the words of the earlier authorities"[23]], the law is like the later.

[18] R. H.J.D. Azoulay, *Shem ha-Gedolim*, Maarekhet Sfarim, *samekh, Seder Tanaim ve-Amoraim*, sec. 24.

[19] Ibid., sec. 25.

[20] *Makhzor Vitry*, p. 491.

[21] S.D. Luzzatto, *Kerem Hemed* (1839), vol. 4, p. 193.

[22] Cf. R. Meir of Rotenberg (Prague edition 1917) quoting *Halakhot Ketzubot*: "They [the Geonim] have communicated from the Academy — when it is found that two Amoraim disagree on a matter and there are later Amoraim who debate the same subject, the law is like the later, and we have a tradition that there were six generations of Amoraim." And see note 26 below.

[23] Azoulay, op. cit., sec. 51.

Aside from stylistic and editorial variations, the different versions do not conflict with each other. This indicates that, contrary to the common misconception, the statement "from Rava on, the law is like the later" is not a universally binding condition. It applies only to cases in which teacher and student disagree, and tells us that in these cases it is permissible to decide against early Amoraim, including Rav and Samuel, on the basis of the rule "the law is like the later."[24]

Furthermore, a closer look at section 25 in Azoulay's *Seder Tanaim ve-Amoraim* reveals that originally the condition "until Rava" did not apply to "the law is like the later," but to the other rule, "the law is not according to a student in the presence of his teacher." *Seder Tanaim ve-Amoraim* holds that this rule applies only "up to Rava"; from then on, "the law is like the later"—i.e., the student.[25]

Now the rule "the law is not according to a student in the presence of his teacher" is not found in the Talmud either; it originates in the geonic period.[26]

[24] This obviates Ginzberg's argument (in his *Geonica*, vol. 2, pp. 21–22) attributing great significance to the geonic responsum (ibid., p. 32) that states that the law is according to Rabba b. R. Huna (of the third generation) because he is "later" than Rav, even though they both preceded the generation of Abbaye and Rava. There is nothing new in this, since Rabba b. R. Huna was not a student of Rav (emendation to "Rabba b. Hana" is useless because the latter was Rav's contemporary and cannot be described as "later"). *Tosafot* (*Kidushin* 45b s.v. *hava uvda*) quoted by Ginzberg is also irrelevant, since it deals with R. Jose—a student of Rav.

See Elon, op. cit., vol. 1, p. 268, note 103, regarding the fact that Asheri (*Bava Metzia* 3:10; 4:19–21) expressed surprise at Alfasi's opinion on this matter. Elon argues that "Alfasi's statement, referred to by Asheri, indicates that this rule applies also to the period prior to Abbaye and Rava," implying that Asheri disagrees. This is incorrect. Asheri himself emphasized that "I could not comprehend the view of R. Alfasi...because only from the time of Abbaye and Rava do we decide according to the later, but before that the law is not decided according to a student against his teacher." Clearly, when a student-teacher controversy is not involved, Asheri agrees that the time of Abbaye and Rava does not serve as a boundary. Note that Alfasi rejected the time of Abbaye and Rava as a turning point, as his ruling in *Baba Batra* 34b, pericope *hahu arba*, shows.

I note these points only briefly, as my main concern is not with Asheri and *Tosafot* but with geonic opinions. The fact is, that in *Tosafot*, the rule is applied before the time of Abbaye and Rava even in a case involving a student-teacher dispute. See *Tosafot*, *Rosh Hashana* 34b s.v. *ledidi*: "Nevertheless since R. Abbahu disagrees [with R. Johanan his teacher!] we are inclined to rule according to him because he is later." Moreover, none of the passages quoted in the *Encyclopedia ha-Talmudit s.v. hilkheta ke-vatra'ei* (the law is like the later), in support of the view that the rule was applied before Abbaye and Rava, involves a student-teacher controversy. I have no knowledge of anyone disagreeing with this.

[25] Apparently S. Assaf holds the same view; see his "Darkei ha-Talmud u-Klalei Hahora'a be-Teshuvot ha-Geonim" in *Tekufat ha-Geonim ve-Sifruta*, ed. M. Margalioth (Jerusalem 1955), secs. 41–42.

[26] R. Hananel, *Sanhedrin* 22a.

To be sure, there are numerous talmudic references to a strict prohibition against a student's ruling in the presence of—or within a certain geographical distance of—his teacher, as well as references to a different prohibition against giving an opinion before one is properly qualified. The Talmud regards this as a commonly encountered problem with serious consequences.[27] It also deplores "dissent from the academy of one's teacher"[28]—an enigmatic expression—one of a number of behaviors showing disrespect toward teachers.[29]

None of this, however, implies that a qualified person is prohibited from ruling against the opinion of his teacher. On the contrary, some of the most renowned sages took issue with their teachers when they found their teachers' views unacceptable. The deciding rule here is "if profaning of the holy name is threatened, the respect due a teacher need not be accorded."[30] There is certainly no sign of a "decision rule" in the Talmud to the effect that "the law is not according to the student in the presence of his teacher." However, the Talmud does state that although "the law is according to a third authority who tips the scales," this rule does not apply to an authority deciding against his teacher.[31] Indeed, R. Hananel offers this interpretation of the rule, "the opinion of a third authority is not decisive,"[32] to make it compatible with the previous rule, but we cannot infer from this that the law is always decided in accord with the teacher's view rather than that of the student. The rule cited by R. Hananel has to do with whether, in a dispute between a teacher and another authority, the views of a student who is somewhere in between can be used to break the stalemate and create a majority. The opinion of the student is regarded as "dependent" on the opinion of his teacher, and cannot be counted toward a majority vote on a point on which they agree.[33] In the particular case in question, it is the opinion of R. Akiva that does not tip the scales in favor of either the opinion of R. Eliezer or that of R. Joshua, and R. Akiva is a student of both.[34] Clearly, in a dispute between two unrelated individuals, the law is not necessarily decided according to the teacher.

27 See, e.g., *Sanhedrin* 5b.

28 *Berakhot* 27b.

29 For details, see M. Aberbach, "The Relations between Master and Disciple in the Talmudic Age," in *Exploring the Talmud*, ed. H.Z. Dimitrovsky (New York 1976).

30 *Berakhot* 19b.

31 *Shabbat* 39b.

32 *Pesahim* 21a.

33 R. Eliezer b. Nathan (section 6) offers a novel interpretation of these passages and R. Hananel's remarks. It suggests that the student's opinion is particularly weighty because he is familiar with his teacher's opinions and their rationales. But this interpretation seems to conflict with the plain meaning of the texts.

34 On the possible existence of a version that reads "We do not learn the law from students," see S. Abramson, "Birurim," *Sinai* 58 (1966), pp. 183–185.

Be that as it may, the rule "the law is not according to the student in the presence of his teacher" was formulated by *Seder Tanaim ve-Amoraim*, which is, therefore, at liberty to qualify its account. It does just that by adding the limitation "until Rava," specifying that after Rava "the law is like the later"—even when it involves a student's ruling against his teacher. But when a student-teacher relationship is not involved, the law is like the later even before the generation of Abbaye and Rava. This is clear from perusal of the other places in *Seder Tanaim ve-Amoraim* where the rule is used; it is stated generally, without specifying a *terminus a quo*.[35] This observation appears to be verified by a statement of R. Hai Gaon cited in one of R. Joseph Colon's *Responsa*:

> And R. Hai Gaon wrote as follows: and now we examine the statement of R. Johanan, who is a later authority; do we, therefore, assume that he heard the statement of Rabbi [Judah the Prince]: "authorize expenses for maintenance" (*Ketubot* 69a), found it unacceptable, and rejected it, and since he is a later authority, we do not follow the opinion of Rabbi, or perhaps...[36]

R. Hai Gaon applies the rule "the law is like the later" quite casually, then, to one of the earliest Amoraim, and even uses it against R. Judah the Prince; neither he nor R. Joseph Colon have any problem with this. I should add here that though R. Johanan relates that he attended the lectures of R. Judah the Prince,[37] this does not make R. Johanan his student, because he was too young at the time, and—as he admits—could not follow the discussions at the academy.

For reasons I explain in section 4 below, there are serious doubts about whether R. Hai Gaon, indeed, made the statement attributed to him by R. Joseph Colon, and no additional source quotes or refers to the responsum in question. There is no doubt, however, that in substance, it reflects the opinion of R. Hai Gaon. The relevant material on this point has been collected by Groner,[38] who reports that there is no known instance in which R. Hai Gaon invoked the "student against his teacher" rule in deciding a controversy among later Amoraim. "The last authority to whom R. Hai Gaon applies this rule is R. Hisda." Groner also asserts: "but...for those earlier generations R. Hai Gaon did not invoke the rule 'the law is like the later.' He applies the rule only from

[35] This is not unusual in the halakhic literature. The author of *Yad Malakhi*, for example, wrote "I saw the new interpretation by Damesek Eliezer, which in his opinion also applies to the time of the Tannaim." Cf. R. A. Efrati's comment in his *Even Tzion* (Warsaw 1866), which includes "a comprehensive study of *Seder Tanaim ve-Amoraim*" (p. 31).

[36] R. Joseph Colon, *Responsa*, #94. This quote from R. Hai was apparently unknown to B.M. Lewin, who does not include it in *Otzar ha-Geonim*.

[37] *Hulin* 137b.

[38] Z. Groner, "Rav Hai Gaon ve-Darko ba-Halakhah" (Ph.D. dissertation, The Hebrew University 1974).

Rabba and R. Joseph on."[39] This is incorrect, even if we deny the authenticity of the responsum quoted by R. Joseph Colon—which Groner does not do. Here Groner is influenced by R. Yomtov of Seville (Ritba), who writes:

> The accepted rule that "the law is not according to a student in the presence of his teacher," applies only if they differ during the lifetime of the teacher, that is, if the teacher heard the dissenting view and did not change his opinion. However, if the student disagreed with his teacher after the latter's death this rule does not apply, otherwise we could not uphold the "like the later" rule, since every later authority is a student of an earlier authority—and the law is not according to the student against the teacher! And this is confirmed by R. Hai Gaon, may he rest in peace.[40]

On this analysis, all "later authorities" are in principle "the students of earlier authorities" and the distinction we made earlier is lost. But the Ritba is the only source attributing this view to R. Hai Gaon, and it is impossible that he held it, because he clearly states elsewhere that when the law is decided according to a teacher against a student it applies also to the students of the students,[41] who surely arrived at their opinions after the death of the first teacher, and not in his presence.

I am thus certain that Groner's conclusion—"Apparently, 'the law is like the later' [in his opinion, in later generations only] is applicable only when the student did not differ from his teacher in his lifetime"—is untenable. The doctrine of R. Hai Gaon is quite the reverse, since in almost every case he would state that the law is like the later, as explained above.

The Ritba's doctrine[42] is interesting in its own right, however, and constitutes proof that R. Hai Gaon does not hold the same opinion. It should be noted that, as he himself states, the Ritba's main concern is the apparent conflict between the two rules "the law is like the later" and "the law is not according to a student in the presence of his teacher," since a student is by definition "later" than his teacher. As we have already seen, the two rules do not contradict each other. On the contrary, *Seder Tanaim Veamoraim*, the main source of these rules, explicitly links them, stating that one applies up to the time of Abbaye and Rava, and the other thereafter. This seems to indicate that the Ritba based his formulation and interpretation of "the law is like the later" on a source other than *Seder Tanaim ve-Amoraim*.

Further scrutiny reveals that the Ritba's view is shared by the Rashba,[43]

39 Ibid., pp. 67–68.

40 *Otzar ha-Geonim*, *Nedarim* 75a.

41 See his remarks in Harkaby's *Teshuvot ha-Geonim*, sec. 358 (700, vol. 2, p. 43).

42 See the text near note 40.

43 *Hidushei haRashba*, *Shabbat* 141b.

Ran,[44] and *Nimukei Yosef*, quoting R. Aharon ha-Levi.[45] These views are summarized by R. Bezalel Ashkenazi in *Klalei ha-Talmud*.[46] This is also the view of Nachmanides, namely, that the law is not according to a student against his teacher even if the student is a "later" authority.[47] It is clear to me that these four fathers of the halakhah did not preserve the "like the later" rule in its original form as stated in *Seder Tanaim Veamoraim*,[48] but, rather, adopted Alfasi's interpretation of it. In Alfasi's opinion "the law is like the later" applies even before the time of Abbaye and Rava and even if a student disagrees with his teacher. In following Alfasi's interpretation, these authorities were compelled to resolve the apparent paradox that arises when the two rules—"the law is like the later" and "the law is not according to the student in the presence of his teacher"—are taken together.

It can be stated with certainty that this problematic interpretation was not adopted by R. Hai Gaon. In any case, whether one accepts Groner's conclusion that R. Hai Gaon does not apply the rule before Abbaye and Rava, or my view that he applies the rule partially (that is, not in teacher/student conflicts) before Abbaye and Rava, there is no contradiction between the two rules, which are fully compatible and even complementary. Hence, there is no need for the artificial solution attributed to R. Hai Gaon by the Ritba, or for any other such contrived compromise.

"JEPHTHAH IN HIS GENERATION IS LIKE SAMUEL IN HIS"

As is the case with all halakhic rules, the scope of "the law is like the later" is limited by its context. It stipulates that when a *posek* has to decide between conflicting opinions of earlier and later authorities, and there are no other relevant considerations or decision-making rules, such as majority-minority rulings, religious prohibitions, or monetary law, he is not merely permitted, but obliged, to prefer the later opinion. Thus, "the law is like the later" is in no way a principle delegating decision-making power or jurisdiction to the current *posek*. On the contrary, like all halakhic guidelines, the binding directive "like the later" deprives the *posek* of his freedom of independent decision-making. It certainly does not establish him as the "last of the later." At the same time, there is no doubt that even as early as the talmudic era, the responsibility for making final decisions had been delegated to the contemporary legal authority or court. Not by virtue of the rule "the law is like the later," which was un-

44 Rabbenu Nissim's commentary on Alfasi, the beginning of *Sukkah*.

45 R. Joseph Habiba's commentary on Alfasi ad loc.

46 R. Bezalel Ashkenazi, op. cit. (see note 12), no. 311, p. 204.

47 The opinion of Nachmanides is quoted by R. Solomon b. Aderet (Rashba); see note 43.

48 n. 24.

known at the time, but on the basis of a more fundamental principle: "Jephthah in his generation is like Samuel in his."[49]

In its original context, this principle is concerned not with resolving controversies, but with the delegation of power and authority to the courts as binding judicial institutions. The rationale for it is found in the Mishnah:

> And on another occasion two came and said, "We saw it at its proper time but on the following night it could not be seen," and Rabban Gamaliel accepted them. R. Dosa b. Hyrcanos said, "They are false witnesses, how can people testify that a woman has delivered if her belly is between her teeth on the following day?" R. Joshua said: "I agree with you." Rabban Gamaliel sent a message to him: "I command you to come to me with your walking stick and money on the day that according to your calculation is the Day of Atonement." R. Akiva went to him and saw that he was troubled....He went to R. Dosa b. Hyrcanos, who said to him, "If we were to argue against the court of Rabban Gamaliel, we would have to argue with the rulings of every court that has existed from the time of Moses...but any three persons who have arisen as a court over Israel are like the court of Moses."[50]

The Talmud explains: "even the least worthy person, if appointed to public office, is like the noblest of the noble." It is interesting to note the descending order here: "the court of Moses," "any three persons who have arisen as a court," "the least worthy person." As it indicates, the sages regarded all courts as equal with respect to judicial authority, in spite of their belief that mankind had degenerated from the days of Moses onward, a process reflected in the descending order of the courts noted by the Talmud. This dilemma did not go unnoticed by the sages, who stated their position concisely at the end of the pericope: "And you shall come to the priests and Levites and judges who shall be in those days."[51] Could someone go to a judge who did not live in his own time? Of course not. That is, "Do not say those of the past were better than these."[52] The Talmud thus explicitly rejects evaluation of contemporary courts by comparing them to courts of other eras, though it does not explain why such speculation is prohibited.

There is no direct connection between the delegation of power to courts and the rule "the law is like the later." As we saw, the latter has to do with the procedure for deciding points on which earlier *poskim* did not agree, and obligates the contemporary *posek* (note, however, that courts also fall into this category) to adopt the more recent ruling. The contemporary court cannot, however, include itself among the "later," and is not free to follow one of the earlier authorities, even if it prefers that opinion, since "earlier" and "later" refer only

49 *Rosh Hashana* 25b.

50 Mishnah, ibid., 2:8–9.

51 Deut 17:9.

52 Eccl 7:10.

to authorities of the talmudic era. Thus the thrust of "like the later" is that contemporary courts do not enjoy judicial autonomy as far as talmudic disputes are concerned.

The delegation of judicial power, on the other hand, places no restrictions or obligations on the court, but only on those under its jurisdiction. By its very nature it concerns the present—contemporary courts adjudicating current disputes—enabling courts to exercise authority when they deviate from halakhic precedent.

Delegation of authority to contemporary courts can be viewed, in a trivial sense, as covering all current disputes, including those over talmudic precedent where the "like the later" rule would be a relevant decision-making guideline. However, this does not suffice for the geonic rule "the law is like the later" to be automatically derived from it. From the principle of the delegation of judicial power it does not follow that future generations must also abide by the decisions of the court of the present generation, since they will have their own courts; hence, even if contemporary courts favor later authorities, the delegation principle alone cannot ensure that successive generations do not ignore them.

The principle "the judge who shall be in those days," and the rule "the law is like the later" are neither identical nor parallel, but at the same time, they are not contradictory. Their relationship may be described as complementary; they complement each other by limiting each other.[53]

53 The problems that arise from the delegation of jurisdiction to the courts are illustrated by the apparent contradiction between this principle and Mishnah *Eduyot* 1:5, which states that "one court cannot annul the ruling of another until it excels it in wisdom and numbers." Maimonides resolves this contradiction as follows:

> If a Great Court, using the proper procedure, decided on a law and another court after it has reason to contradict it, then the second court adjudicates as it sees fit, since it is written "to the judge who will be in those days." One is bound only by the court of his own generation.

But,

> A court that issued a decree or regulation or established a custom...and a later court wished to revoke it...cannot do so until it exceeds the first court in wisdom and in numbers (*Code*, Laws Concerning Rebels 2:1).

In his commentary, *Kesef Mishne*, ad loc., R. Joseph Karo notes that as a matter of historical fact, a categorical distinction was, indeed, invariably made between the Tannaitic and Amoraic periods, a situation that seems problematic given Maimonides' solution. Hard pressed, he explains:

> We can say that from the time of the redaction of the Mishnah, later generations undertook not to contradict their predecessors, and the same thing occurred after the redaction of the Talmud—from the time of its redaction, no one has been permitted to differ with it.

For rabbinical material on the subject (including "the law is like the later"), see A.Z. Ben Zimra, "The Court Cannot..." (Heb.), in *Kol Sinai* (1964).

The Amoraim recognized independent jurisdiction as an animating, regenerative principle in Jewish law. The decisions of the past, which they regarded as an era superior to their own, did not have the power to bind current judicial institutions, (though in practice they usually followed precedent), and their own rulings lacked the power to constrain future halakhic developments. A similar principle was applied to rulings of individual authorities, outside the courts, with the reservation that students were required to pay their teachers proper respect. Even within the area of individual rulings, autonomy in decision-making was recognized, as is reflected in the rule, "when the holy name is threatened, the respect due a teacher need not be accorded."

The Geonim added to the principles of their predecessors, asserting that by virtue of the power to resolve conflicts and even annul previous rulings that had been conferred on successive generations of "present" authorities, "the present" was endowed with permanent jurisdiction on questions relating to the past, though not the future.

The new element here is thus the retrospective or diachronic dimension added to the courts' prescribed authority. In principle, the Geonim declared, courts could decide according to their needs; they could exercise discretion.

The Geonim certainly did not dispute the talmudic authority-delegating rule "Jephthah in his generation is like Samuel in his," but added that a court seeking to decide a controversy between early authorities in a halakhically correct manner should always prefer the later authority among the contending views, because in that authority's own time the law was decided thus. This relative advantage of the later of the contending past decisions remains for the future, lending an element of "eternity" to each stage in talmudic decision-making. At the same time, though, the delegation principle ensures that future courts are free to make their own decisions.

The rule "the law is like the later," in this, its original form, is a purely formal-technical rule applying only to talmudic controversies. Its thrust is that every court, at the point in time when it is in session, has absolute and final authority to decide against all preceding courts—though in practice, as we said, courts would rule in most cases according to precedent—and this relative authority remains throughout future generations. There is nothing to suggest that, having formulated it, the Geonim applied it to contemporary courts. There is no question of a qualitative advantage of later rulings over earlier ones (such as their being "greater in wisdom"), thus querying whether the last Amora was aware of all the precedents misses the point entirely and is irrelevant to the issue as described here. All queries of this kind date from the post-talmudic period, after the rule had been "extended" to apply to this period as well. They arose as a result of the profound change that took place during this period in the interpretation and application of "the law is like the later."

THE TURNING POINT IN THE MIDDLE AGES

The Middle Ages saw a turning point in the history of "the law is like the later." Essentially, it had to do with the growing awareness on the part of the educated circles of twelfth-century Europe that despite the unquestioned superiority of the ancients in every sphere: wisdom, morals, knowledge of the esoteric, proximity to God, and so on, contemporary intellectual achievements also deserved recognition. They rejected the earlier assumption that everything had been known to the ancients and that anything ignored by the ancients could be dismissed as unworthy of consideration. The rationale offered by medieval thinkers for this revolutionary premise was the aphorism of the dwarf on the shoulders of a giant: granted, the ancients were all intellectual giants, with infinitely wide horizons, and scholars of the twelfth century were mere dwarfs in comparison; nevertheless, by assiduous learning, these scholars could access the heritage of the ancients and sit, as it were, on the shoulders of giants.

This aphorism, with its deep philosophical, religious and cultural, significance[54] was conceived by the philosopher Bernard of Chartres (d. 1126), one of the foremost scholastics and head of the celebrated school in his city. Preserved in the works of his student John of Salisbury (d. 1180),[55] it is typical of the peculiar genius, intellectual fertility, and intrinsic modesty that characterized the renaissance of the twelfth century.[56]

In Jewish writings the aphorism first appears in a responsum by R. Isaiah di Trani, author of *Tosafot Rid*, who died in 1250.[57]

> Regarding what you have written that I must not contradict the great authority of R. Isaac, may he rest in peace. Heaven forbid that I should do such a thing....I am nothing but a flea...yet I say that a statement that I cannot accept, I do not heed, even if it was uttered by Joshua the son of Nun, and I do not refrain from speaking my mind about it as far as my limited wisdom permits...and my witness is in heaven, that even when I think that I argue rightly against one of our early teachers, heaven forbid that my heart is vain to say that it was my wisdom that supported me, but I accept the metaphor that I learned from the wisdom of the philosophers. They asked the greatest philosopher among them: It is a given that the ancients were wiser and more knowledgeable than we are, but also, that we often dispute and contradict them, and we are right. How can this be? He replied as follows: Who can see farther, a giant or a dwarf? Surely the giant, because his eyes are higher than

54 See G. Sarton, "Note," *Isis* 24 (1935), pp. 107–109.

55 In his *Metalogicon*, ed. C.C.J. Webb, vol. 3, sec. 4, p. 136. The history and significance of the aphorism are rigorously treated in R. K. Merton, *On the Shoulders of Giants* (New York 1965).

56 The classic work on the subject is C. Haskins, *The Renaissance of the Twelfth Century* (Cambridge, Mass. 1927).

57 R. Isaiah di Trani, *Responsa*, #62.

> those of the dwarf. But if the giant carries the dwarf on his shoulders—who can see farther? Surely the dwarf, whose eyes are now above the eyes of the giant. We, too, are dwarfs riding on the shoulders of giants, because we have seen their wisdom and we transcend it. And it is by virtue of the power of their wisdom that we have learned all that we say, and not because we are greater than they were. My point is that we should not discuss the teachings of our early sages except when we see that they disagree with each other: one forbids what another permits—whom shall we rely on? We cannot measure them on a scale...and declare that since one is greater than the other his opinions should cancel out those of the other.

R. Isaiah di Trani's acknowledgment—"I learned from the wisdom of the philosophers"—is interesting indeed. In fact, his source is none other than John of Salisbury's treatise, written about fifty years earlier. The first[58] to use R. Isaiah di Trani's version of the aphorism was one of his students, R. Zedekiah b. R. Abraham Anav, in the introduction to his *Shibbolei ha-Leket.*[59]

The revolutionary dimension of the new intellectual climate symbolized so clearly by this aphorism is its recognition of the cumulative nature of learning; of the fact that a scholar's knowledge is not a self-contained entity, but a link in a chain. The more links added to it, the higher its quality. This awareness allowed medieval scholars to admit that the venerated ancients had sometimes been wrong—without detracting from their greatness and status as the true sources of wisdom or necessitating revision of the credo "from their wisdom is ours."

Before this watershed, revisions and corrections could be justified only on the basis of the principle "their ancestors left them room to draw their own boundaries,"[60] which conflicts with that of "whoso breaketh through a fence, a serpent shall bite him" (Eccl 10:8), which is said of those who deviate from earlier rulings (*Avoda Zara* 27b). This principle has nothing to do with the nature of knowledge; rather, it recognizes a charitable attitude on the part of the ancients (or divine providence) toward future generations, lest their creativity be blocked. As Rashi says, "If our descendants find nothing on which to improve, how can they achieve fame?"[61] The sages used this principle to assert: "A scholar who formulated a law [that is innovative – Rashi[62]] is not

[58] The Jewish versions of the aphorism are treated in D. Zlotnik, "The Commentary of R. Abraham Azoulay on the Mishnah" (Heb.), *PAAJR* 40 (1972), pp. 147–168 and "The Origins and History of the Aphorism of the 'Dwarf and the Giant'" (Heb.), *Sinai* 11 (1975), pp. 185–189.

[59] *Shibolei ha-Leket ha-Shalem* (Vima 1887; Jerusalem 1962), p. 18.

[60] *Hulin* 7a.

[61] Rashi ad loc. s.v. *makom hinihu.*

[62] Rashi ad loc. s.v. *mikan.* Cf. *Shita Mekubetzet* (Vilna ed., sec. 1).

ignored."[63] Without this extraordinary principle, which acknowledges the theoretical possibility of successive generations having something to add to the teachings of their forebears, the authorities would have had to suppress any new idea.[64]

The eleventh- and twelfth-century French-Ashkenazic commentators on the Bible provide a good illustration of this approach. In commenting on a verse in Ecclesiastes—"Say not 'How was it the former days were better than these?' for it is not out of wisdom that thou inquires concerning this"[65]—we find the following exchange. Rashi explains:

> Because the first generations were better and more pious than those of today; therefore, former days were better than these because it is impossible that these days should be like former days.[66]

The Rashbam comments:

> Do not ask, what deeds are done in the world now...that former days were better and more refined in their actions, because you do not ask this out of your inherent wisdom but because of your great stupidity because you should understand by yourself from the evidence of your own eyes that the world deteriorates everyday.[67]

63 *Hulin* 7a.

64 My presentation here is intentionally simplified to highlight the basic difference between the received view prior to the twelfth and thirteenth centuries and that which gained ground subsequently. In reality, the sages' attitude toward their predecessors is much more complex. It is marked by a differential evaluation of the various aspects of their accomplishments, though a parallel evaluative scale is used. Thus, for example, it did not go unnoticed by the great Amoraim that the quality of Talmud scholarship had been raised, not lowered, by their work, but they did not see this improvement as having any bearing on questions of authority or any moral significance. Consider the interesting conversation between R. Papa and Abbaye:

> R. Papa said to Abbaye, How is it that miracles were performed for the ancients but not for us? It is not due to their learning. During all the years of R. Judah, they studied only tort law, but we study all six branches of the law. And if R. Judah came to a passage about the laws of purity, he would say, This is a matter requiring deliberation for [our predecessors] Rav and Samuel, while we have twelve lectures on this subject at the academy. Nevertheless, when R. Judah took off one of his shoes [in preparation for a fast] the rains came, while we torment ourselves and cry out to heaven and no one listens to us. The other replied: The ancients suffered martyrdom willingly to sanctify the holy name...(*Berakhot* 20a).

Cf. the version in *Taanit* 24b, which attributes this to the misbehavior of the entire community rather than to the shortcomings of its leaders. To adequately understand the policy of "orthodoxy" adopted through the ages, thorough familiarity with these issues is required.

65 Eccl 7:10.

66 Rashi, *Rosh Hashana* 25b s.v. *al tomar*.

67 Even those who deny the attribution of the commentary on Ecclesiastes to the Rashbam agree that it "includes many of the Rashbam's explanatory remarks on Ecclesiastes, and

Another view of this deterioration is expressed by the twelfth-century scholar, R. Joseph Kara, in his commentary on the same verse:

> Do not ask what was in ancient days, which were before us. If one tells you so-and-so learned the Torah so well that there is no other like him since then, do not say "because there is no wise man in this generation like him, I do not go to learn the Torah from a scholar of these days." And so it is with regard to personal conduct. Upon being told that in ancient times so-and-so sowed and reaped a hundredfold, or a man reared a young cow and two sheep and of the abundance of milk they gave he ate butter,[68] or a man exerted himself little and earned much, do not ask "Why were previous generations so rewarded?" If you hear words like these do not say "Since the world is different I shall not toil any more." Do not say so, but as you conceive the world you should exert yourself in learning the Torah and toil for your sustenance.

A good example of this attitude is found in remarks in *Tosafot* on the passage in the Talmud that states that the judges of Caesarea erred in geometrical calculations pertaining to the ratio between a square and the circle that circumscribes it:

> It is perplexing—how could such men err...given that they did not measure, how did they formulate a rule without any data to base it on? And we have to state that the rule "a square inscribed in a circle—half," was masoretic; the rule is, indeed, accurate, but refers to area rather than circumference (*Sukkah* 8b s.v. *ribua*).

That is, they relied on a tradition and hence did not calculate it themselves. The tradition itself was accurate, but the judges of Caesarea erred in its interpretation.

In contrast to this traditional understanding, the new doctrine of knowledge as cumulative recognizes the possibility of ascent to greater heights, to a vantage point from which horizons are broader, allowing access to information that will, in turn, add to the stature of future generations. This insight marks a great step forward in the history of learning, though it does not even hint at the possibility of challenging the authority and wisdom of the ancients, let alone call for revolt. The crucial step in this direction would be taken only in the seventeenth century, with the Enlightenment's demand for a break from the binding heritage of traditional learning as preserved and handed down from ancient times. This would make possible discovery of the true order of the world through personal experience and observation of nature itself.[69]

the debate should focus...on one point only: whether the work in its present form was written solely by the Rashbam or includes also the commentaries of another scholar who emended some of the Rashbam's comments." See A. Grossman, "The Commentary on Ecclesiastes Attributed to the Rashbam" (Heb.), *Tarbiz* 45 (1976), p. 336.

68 Isaiah 7:21–22.

69 See R. A. Nisbet, *Tradition amid Revolt* (New York 1968).

Underlying the aphorism of the dwarf and the giant is the assumption, for the first time, that decisions of the "later authorities" are qualitatively superior to those of their predecessors. This made possible application of the rule to the post-talmudic period, transforming it from a decision-making tool useful only for adjudicating talmudic disputes into a fundamental legal principle. This breakthrough was achieved without detracting from the lofty status of the earlier authorities that to this day remains a cornerstone of the halakhic literature.

The novel epistemology expressed in the aphorism of the dwarf and the giant enabled the next historical development of the rule: inclusion of the *posek* and his contemporaries in the category of "the later." This could not have taken place without the elapse of a minimal period of time for the dissemination of the ideas underlying the aphorism and the internalization of their significance.[70] Thus, it could not have taken place before the fourteenth century.

Indeed, it took longer, and before the fifteenth century we have no example of the application of the rule "the law is like the later" to the post-talmudic period. The time-gap is recognizable from the noteworthy fact that there is no evidence the rule was ever applied to the long geonic period. This would have required an established chronology of the Geonim and their succession as a prerequisite for accepting a particular opinion. As a rule, the Geonim themselves did not identify their predecessors by name in their decisions, though they did so in exceptional cases. Nor was there a binding chronology of the post-geonic rabbinical authorities. The first to pursue questions of chronology, as far as I know, was R. Meir Hakohen, the fourteenth-century author of *Hagahot Maimoniot*, who emphasizes several times that R. Meir of Rotenberg is a "later authority" (relative to the Tosafists). It is, however, possible that the rule was applied earlier with respect to the post-talmudic authorities. See the cautious comments in a responsum by R. Abraham b. R. Isaac, the head of the Narbonne rabbinical court:

> And we rely on all he [the Rif] says, for he knew all that was said by preceding authorities, and differentiated the important points from the less important, as we say, the law is in accordance with the opinion of R. Ashi, because he is later (Kapah ed. [Jerusalem 1962], #35).

More importantly, one must remember that the aphorism of the dwarf and the giant was a product of Christian scholasticism and part of its general worldview. To the best of my knowledge, the aphorism and the ideological com-

[70] R. Isaiah di Trani did not embrace the new doctrine overnight. In his commentary on *Beitza*, he explains the statement, "Now we are skilled in astronomical calculations," as follows:

> This does not mean that we are wiser than the ancients because we can calculate the time of the new moon and they could not. The ancients, though far more skilled in calculation than we are, were not permitted to act except on the basis of seeing the new moon.

promise it entails were unknown in the fourteenth and fifteenth centuries among Islamic scholars, who also venerated "the glorious past."[71] Thus, they could not have influenced Jewish scholars in Islamic countries. This left its mark on Sephardic judicial decision-making up to the time of R. Joseph Karo, as we saw.

The new conception of the rule "the law is like the later" brought with it for the first time a demand that the decisions of the "earlier authorities" be made accessible to the "later authorities," since only in this way could the later authorities be visualized as riding on the shoulders of their predecessors. This demand—a basic element of "the law is like the later" for the late Ashkenazic authorities—is not mentioned at all in early sources, and first appears in the *Responsa* of R. Joseph Colon, who cites a responsum of R. Hai Gaon.[72] As I noted above,[73] even if R. Hai Gaon, indeed, held the opinion, the problem relates to the question of when chronology became an issue. The requirement that "later authorities" be familiar with the decisions of their predecessors is not mentioned by any authority before R. Joseph Colon and, indeed, given their method, was unnecessary.

Once this requirement was adopted, however, it served as the basis for R. Joseph Colon's stipulation that "the law is like the later" applied only

> where the opinions of the earlier authorities are written down in a well-known book [it can and, indeed, must then be presumed that they were known to the later *posek*], however, what is written in a responsum of a Gaon but not mentioned by a well-known book, even if there is a later authority who decided against the opinion of the Gaon, it can be argued that perhaps this later authority did not know this and had he known it he would have retracted his opinion.[74]

R. Moses Isserles concurs.[75]

CONCLUSION

The perception of the rule "the law is like the later" as a fundamental principle of Jewish law reflects neither its original substance nor the spirit in which it was understood through most of its history, but only the last stage in its evolution

[71] See S. Pines, "La Philosophy dans l'economie du genre humain selon Averroes: Une Reponse a Al-Farabi," in *Multiple Averroes* (Paris 1978). I am grateful to M. Idel for this reference.

[72] See above, notes 36ff.

[73] Notes 38ff.

[74] R. Joseph Colon, *Responsa*, #94 (see above, note 36).

[75] R. Moses Isserles on *Shulhan Arukh*, Hoshen Mishpat 25b; also cited by Elon, op. cit. (see note 1), vol. 1, p. 271.

according to the Ashkenazic tradition. The rule is basically just one of a number of guidelines, the majority of which were formulated in the geonic (or saboraic) period as part of the effort to regulate the normative use of the Talmud as an exclusive legal code. Like the other rules, it was meant to guide the *posek* or court in settling talmudic disputes. It most certainly should not be regarded as a law granting authority to the *posek*, or allowing his own inclusion in the category of "the later."

The principle of judicial independence, as applied to the rules for ongoing and exigent decision-making, was always a central element in halakhic practice, but it has never had anything to do with the rule "the law is like the later," which by definition limits rather than extends authority. The theoretical significance of the rule "the law is like the later," if it has any such significance, is to preserve for the future the relative authority of every stage of Amoraic ruling *vis-à-vis* rulings that preceded it. The Ashkenazic authorities of the fourteenth century apparently began to apply the "like the later" rule to the post-talmudic period when they started attributing to it a meaning more profound than that associated with other decision-making rules. Characteristically, such rules apply only to the Talmud, and are limiting in nature. An example is the rule "the law is according to the majority."

From the fifteenth and sixteenth centuries on, the Ashkenazic authorities began to apply "the law is like the later" to rulings of contemporary courts (though they did not admit this explicitly). This transformation came about as a result of changes that had taken place in the intellectual world of Christian Europe during the twelfth century (which Jewish scholars became aware of in the following century) with regard to the relationship between the wisdom of the ancients and contemporary scholarship. Its essence lay in the growing acceptance of the conception of wisdom as cumulatively acquired and developing from generation to generation. Poignantly encapsulated in the aphorism of the dwarf and the giant, this change was not internalized by the Islamic world, which accounts for the long period that was to elapse before the new interpretation of "the law is like the later" was accepted by Sephardic Jewish scholars.

POSTSCRIPT (1994)

On the basis of the arguments presented in this paper, Israel Yuval has recently attempted, in his "Periodization and Self-Awareness," *Zion* 57 (1992), to arrive at a significant historical conclusion. The question he undertook to answer was as follows: At what point did the Ashkenazic scholars begin to recognize a boundary marking the close of the era of the Early Authorities and the beginning of the modern period? On the basis of my article, Yuval concluded that for the Ashkenazic community, the dividing line must be drawn during the Black Death and the disasters that came in its wake, that is, in the mid-fourteenth century. He contends that though the Maharil was the first to actually employ "the law is like the later," followed by the Mahari Weill and R. Israel Isserlein, its dissemination can be attributed to its use by R. Joseph Colon. As noted above, Yuval's interpretation of R. Asher b. Yehiel's sons' comments on the subject is different from my own; see note 3 above.

But according to Yuval, even R. Joseph Colon extended the principle only to authorities who lived and worked in the period between R. Meir of Rotenberg and R. Jacob, author of the *Turim*, that is, until the mid-fourteenth century. It is only this circumscribed group of scholars that the Maharil and his colleagues, followed by R. Jacob Colon, described as "later," relative to the authorities who preceded them. They did not apply the term to scholars who lived in the period between the mid-fourteenth century and their own period.

Yuval's basic argument is that in spite of R. Joseph Colon's prodigious use of the principle, he nowhere applies it to any of the great Ashkenazic scholars, such as the Maharil, the Mahari Weill, the Maharam of Fulda and others of that stature, who were active between the time of the Maharam and his own time. However, what Yuval fails to understand is that these authorities and others like them are hardly mentioned at all in any of R. Joseph Colon's *Responsa*; R. Joseph Colon was simply not familiar with their writings. Although the Ashkenazic scholars, as a rule, made extensive use of the Maharik's *Responsa*, the simple fact is that R. Joseph Colon was Italian, and not Ashkenazic, and was completely unfamiliar with the writings of Ashkenazic authorities later than the Maharam. The Maharik's principle is intended to cover "later" authorities in general, as he states:

> And also R. Meir, who was a later authority—we follow him...and the reason is that the later authorities are more familiar with the explanations given by the earlier authorities than we are, yet in spite of this they still disagree with them...likewise, on the basis of the same principle, we, too, must follow the later authorities...it is our custom everywhere to follow the authorities who are later (*Responsa*, #181).

This approach was transmitted from R. Joseph Colon to R. M. Alashkar, and R. M. Alashkar's critical comments and ridicule target this very point. As for the Maharil and his colleagues, they could not have referred to any Ashkenazic scholar who lived after the middle of the fourteenth century, since the Maharil himself belonged to the first generation of scholars to emerge following the horrors of the Black Death and the other tribulations of that era.

According to Yuval, the principle that "the law is like the later" is applied only to Ashkenazic authorities in the period up to the middle of the fourteenth century, which is the historical boundary, the watershed, differentiating the periods in question. It is never applied to authorities who lived after the mid-fourteenth century, and certainly never to even later, or contemporary, authorities. Indeed, he argues that even R. Moses Isserles did not apply the principle to anyone other than the Mordechai circle, the Rosh, and the Tur; the Rema's criticism of R. Joseph Karo is that he "did not adopt this decision-making rule," let alone give absolute precedence to this group of authorities over the Rambam and R. Isaac Alfasi. Yet Yuval himself quotes the words of R. Moses Isserles, who states, "It is known that the learned author of the *Beit Yosef* [R. Joseph Karo] had a natural inclination toward the great...Alfasi, Maimonides, and Asheri...though they are early, not later authorities" (Yuval, op. cit.; cf. the text above near note 5). Thus the Rema himself describes the Rosh as early!

Yuval's position is so extreme that he asserts that even R. Jacob Pollak and R. Shalom Shakhna said nothing more on the subject, and did not entertain the possibility of applying the principle to contemporary authorities. However, I must confess that I cannot comprehend his arguments for this.

A totally novel interpretation of the subject is offered by A. Reiner in his "Developments in the Yeshivas of Poland and Ashkenaz in the Sixteenth and Seventeenth Centuries and the Controversy over Polemics" (Heb.), in *Jubilee Volume in Honor of H. Shmeruk* (Heb.), (Jerusalem 1993), p. 18. Further support for my position, generated in the discussion that arose following publication of my article, can be found in A.M. Rapeld, "The Scholars of Ashkenaz and Poland in the Fifteenth and Sixteenth Centuries on '*Hilkheta Ke-vatra'ei*'; Sources and Addenda" (Heb.), *Sidra* 8 (1993), pp. 119–140.

I find incomprehensible Yuval's claim that "It is puzzling why this idea took 300 years (!) to penetrate the world of Jewish law and make an impact." After all, the idea was first introduced into the Jewish world around the middle of the thirteenth century; as described in my article, its dissemination and evolution took about 150 years. Just what is it that Yuval finds so very puzzling about this?

There is no doubt that the changes in the way the principle "the law is like the later" was understood ultimately led to an increase in the decision-making power of contemporary authorities. This is true with respect to the way it was understood by all the Ashkenazic scholars, as is reflected in its treatment in the Shakh's "Klalei Horaat Isur ve-Heter," *Yore Deia* at the end of sec. 242; and as summarized in the *Encyclopedia ha-Talmudit*. The only questions are why, when, and how these changes took place, questions I hope to have shed light on here.

CHAPTER 10

EARLY MODERN TRENDS IN LATE WEST-EUROPEAN TALMUD COMMENTARY AND THEIR INFLUENCE ON POPULAR TALMUD STUDIES IN THE EIGHTEENTH AND NINETEENTH CENTURIES

I am not in the regular habit of "forewording" my lectures with unwarranted overtures and superfluous apologies, but as the issue before us is quite new, rather complicated, and covers much uncharted ground, and as I could consult but very little that has been written so far on the subject, I wish to apologize in advance for some unavoidable introductions, for a certain measure of frailty of composition, for posing more questions than I can satisfactorily answer, and for leaving much more to be expected than actually said.

The profound modernization of Talmud study throughout nineteenth-century Poland and Lithuania, in both its oral aspect (as practiced in the popular academies) and its written form, which is open to our evaluation and criticism in the outstandingly rich literature created in the academies and outside them, is the Orthodox parallelism to the quest for intellectual progress called for by the contemporary Haskalah movement, which was then achieving vigorous inroads into Polish-Lithuanian, Jewish society. It is, therefore, surprising that so little has been done to understand its nature and uncover the main historical stages that prepared and enabled its sudden appearance and rapid flourishing. In fact, research of the Haskalah movement has completely overlooked the unique influence of the movement on the very heart of Orthodox Judaism, because of the tacit and simplistic assumption that as the two stood in total historical contradiction to each other, there is nothing to look for in that quarter. General ignorance of rabbinical literature has also contributed to this neglect, which is by no means unique to the research of Haskalah, and covers many other fields of modern spiritual trends and influences.

A contemporary issue that exemplifies this point is the much acclaimed renaissance of Moroccan homeland culture, clearly evident in the large and highly influential Moroccan community in Israel in the last few years. This renaissance covers all aspects of social activity: political organization, education, music, folklore, language, scholarship, various forms of spiritual homesickness etc. and is much discussed in the Israeli press and within academic circles. However, its main and chronologically first expression in Israel—the radical revolution within Torah and yeshiva circles—has entirely escaped notice although it indirectly affected, and still affects, the highest political levels of the country. The break between modern Jewish scholars and modern Jewish Orthodoxy, beginning in the nineteenth century, is far-reaching and continues, unhealed, to this day. But that is beyond the realm of our present lecture.

Our study examines the later periods of rabbinic literature and will say nothing about the earlier periods of the Rishonim. Many characteristics attributed here to the later period will be found to be suitable, *mutatis mutandi*, to the Rishonim period as well, but that is wholly irrelevant and beside the point. Between the two periods there exists a wide gap, a historical break of about 150 years that was never bridged. The *tosafot* literature was accepted by later generations as an integral part of the Talmud, to be studied with it, page after page, as if it were its direct continuation—but its underlying creative method was never again adopted.

The phenomenon itself is wholly unprecedented. I may be mistaken, but I know of no other example of medieval scholarship, in any other field of human interest, that is still in active service and at the very heart of a modern curriculum, owing to its high and valid intellectual standard. On the other hand, it is very hard to comprehend how such material could be technically adopted and integrated while its intellectual implications were completely abandoned. But the fact remains that later generations devised new techniques for their academies, starting from scratch and forming a clear and total regression in relation to former Tosafist achievement, in full accordance with the general environmental decline of degenerating Europe of the fourteenth century. Only these later centuries, upward and toward the modern era, will engage our attention and occasional similarities with earlier procedures, however close they may seem, are, therefore, of no historical relevance.

Limiting our study, as we did, to the later periods of rabbinic literature, two terms need some clarification before we can safely proceed: "modernity" and the indivisible pair "Rishonim-Akhronim." We will define modernity as signifying the present state of the art as it is practiced in the central rabbinic academies of our time. The idiomatic use of the conceptual pair Rishonim-Akhronim is commonplace for Jewish scholars and Orthodox rabbinic writers, used freely in almost every possible context, although where exactly is the demarcation line between the two periods is still an unanswered question. Opinions range between the middle of the fourteenth century and the end of the fifteenth. An excellent view, and review, on some of the deeper historical implications of this seemingly technical and semantic subject[1]—although I do not

[1] I. Yuval, "Periodization and Self-Awareness in Ashkenaz" (Heb.), *Zion* 57 (1992), pp. 369–394.

agree with it—has been presented by Israel Yuval in a highly interesting article published in *Zion*...and I do not intend to discuss the problem further here.

Instead, I would rather address the fact, for which I cannot provide conventional proof but can bear personal witness from my long experience at the Institute for Microfilmed Hebrew Manuscripts, that wherever the historical demarcation line be put, anyone familiar enough with rabbinic literature will easily identify any unseen literary source as belonging to either the Rishonim or Akhronim period. We may probably not be able to go much further than that and fix with confidence the exact century within the periods, especially for the period of the Akhronim (unless, of course, we could find some bibliographical, or other, clues in the text itself). However, the dichotomy between the two historical periods as autonomous cultural entities, producers of separate and distinctly different literary outputs will be crystal clear to us.

What is more interesting to note in this context is the tremendous difficulty we would face if asked to explain in simple terms in what way the periods are different and how exactly our identifications were reached. There is clearly a characteristic and unmistakable literary stamp on both periods, but an analysis of it is very hard to accomplish.

Much more complex is the problem of mapping out an intellectual prosopography for any one of the central rabbinic figures in central and eastern Europe in the eighteenth and nineteenth centuries, so that he be uniquely discernible from his great colleagues and contemporaries. Is it at all possible to differentiate, in clear-cut and simple phrases, between Rabbi Yehezkel Landau and his book *Tzlakh* and Rabbi Arie Leib Heller and his book *Ktzot ha-Hoshen*, which is fundamentally different from Landau's *Tzlakh* and at the same time so similar? Certainly, both rabbis were *beki'im harifim*, *mefulpalim*, *ba'alei sevara yeshara*, etc., in short: *ge'onim*, according to the accepted nomenclature of these later generations. Is it true, therefore, that they—and for that matter most other great rabbis of their time—were of the same intellectual quality and stature, all belonging to the same rabbinic stereotype that never changes? Maybe.

The late Prof. Scholem challenged me, not long before his death, to outline a differential, academic analysis of Rabbi Jehonathan Eibeschitz's intellectual achievement as a rabbinic scholar that would characterize the uniqueness of his work in contradistinction to other rabbis' work, especially his enemy's, Rabbi Jacob Emdin's, work. For obvious reasons, he wanted Rabbi Jehonathan presented as an outstanding, individual, rabbinic figure so that a greater emphasis could be attached to his Sabbateanism, and the routine epithets *baki*, *harif*, *mefulpal*, etc., not to mention the degrading *ga'on*, were not strong or convincing enough for him. But is such a feat at all possible? Is there a discernible and, therefore, definable personal quality to the different top-grade produce of thirteenth to nineteenth-century rabbinic literature, a quality that, once detected, may enable us to trace a line of progress within this seemingly homogeneic literature, or are we merely goose-chasing?

The crux of the problem here is that we lack modern terminology that will adequately substitute for the old concepts: being capable of describing alternative, more specific, intellectual faculties and techniques other than general erudition (*beki'ut*), sharp-wittedness (*harifut*), casuistry (*pilpul*), profundity (*amkut*), logical thinking (*sevara*) etc. The talents expressed by these old terms go without saying for all scholars of the first magnitude, in all branches of science and the humanities, although their relative dosage might change between one scholar and the other. Former generations were content enough with such descriptions, but for modern research they will not do.

We shall revert to all this as we slowly progress, but let us now go back to our original point of departure: the Rishonim-Akhronim dichotomy, which is somewhat easier to handle but much more difficult to anchor within clear chronological boundaries. The problem here is that quite a number of "natural" demarcation lines present themselves as equally suitable and valid. Some of them are of a purely historical nature, such as the mid–fourteenth-century Black Death (1348), on the one hand, and the beginning of massive Jewish immigration and settlement in Poland at the very beginning of the sixteenth century, on the other hand. Some of them have a marked literary nature, such as early–fifteenth-century Maharil versus mid–fifteenth-century Mahari Colon and Israel Isserlein, or late–fifteenth-century Rabbi Jacob Pollak. All these serve as divisors in contemporary scholarship, according to the personal preferences or education of the individual scholar. But it seems to me, that instead of arbitrarily committing ourselves to any of these periodizations, we should rather consider the immediate theoretical context of the specific aspect under discussion and choose divisors that will categorically suit the purpose. For sociohistorical enquiries, the Black Death seems to be the more suitable; for the history of halakhah, Maharik would be better; and for the study of *minhagim*, Maharil or Rabbi Avraham Klosner would be best. Such flexibility is the key to future progress in the field, and shifting divisors should be allowed, or rather expected, even within the framework of a single work, in accordance with its shifting nuclei of attention.

For the immediate purpose before us, the period of the Akhronim is to open with Rabbi Samuel Eideles, the famous Maharsha, who flourished in Poland at the turn of the sixteenth and seventeenth centuries. This shifts the limits further than any mentioned before, but for the subject, early modern trends in late rabbinical Talmud commentary, Maharsha will serve the purpose best. His book, the first part of which was printed in the year 1612 in Lublin, was the first significant, pre-modern herald of what was to come. Were we to deal with modern trends in late responsa literature, I would take Mahari Colon as my starting point (some 150 years before Maharsha), but limiting our attention to Talmud commentary, we must fall back on Maharsha, as will become clear soon enough.

Having apologized right at the beginning for some unavoidable frailty in composition, I feel free now to leave aside the Maharsha for some time, and focus your attention on another great luminary, Rabbi Jacob Joshua Falk (born Cracow 1680, died Offenbach 1756). He was the author of the well-known book *Pnei Yehoshua*, the real turning-point of traditional Talmud commentary and study from its old pedestrian path to the vigorous and creative phenomenon familiar to all of us from its many versatile appearances in the present. This is one of the few assertions that can be proved finally and satisfactorily and it will, therefore, serve as a springboard for presenting my case. An overview of the total output of rabbinic literature created and printed in the field of Talmud exegesis in the post-Maharsha period will reveal the astonishing fact that up to the year 1739, when the first volume of *Pnei Yehoshua* saw the light of day—that is exactly 150 years after the *Hidushei Maharsha*—only about thirty Talmud commentaries had been printed. In contrast, a few hundred were printed between 1739 and 1810! This information is easily gathered from an article by Pinchas Jacob ha-Kohen and it certainly merits consideration.[2] The situation during these 150 years, mainly the transition from Talmud exegesis to practical deciding of the halakhah in the wake of Rabbi Joseph Karo's *Shulhan Arukh*, has been ably described by my friend Elchanan Reiner, in an outstanding article on the changes in Polish-German *yeshivot* during the sixteenth and seventeenth centuries.[3] However, his article is wholly retrospective and offers no explanation as to what happened toward the end of this period, which is outside the scope of his article, but the very heart of our present study. If you take a good look at any of the few novellae written prior to the *Pnei Yehoshua*, excluding *Hidushei Maharsha*, it will become clearly evident to you why they were so few. A shortcut can be taken by reading Prof. Dimitrovsky's articles describing some of these.[4]

I shall immediately say something about the way Rabbi Joshua Falk revolutionized the novellae literature, indicating *en passant* what was lacking before him. However, before I come to that, let me digress again and emphasize another irrefutable historical fact relating to the *Pnei Yehoshua*.

With the exception of *Hidushei ha-Rashba* to tractates *Berakhot*, *Gittin*, and *Hulin*, and Nahmanides' novellae to tractate *Bava Batra*, not one other book of the outstandingly rich Spanish library of Talmud commentaries—mainly: Nahmanides, Rashba, Ritva and their school—was known in Germany

2 P.J. ha-Kohen, *Otzar ha-Be'urim veha-Perushim* (London 1952) (Heb.).

3 E. Reiner, "The *Yeshivas* of Poland and Ashkenaz during the Sixteenth and Seventeenth Centuries—Historical Developments" (Heb.), *Studies in Jewish Culture in Honor of Chone Shmeruk* (Jerusalem 1993), pp. 9–80.

4 C.Z. Dimitrovsky, "On the Pilpulistic Method" (Heb.), *Salo Wittmaye Baron Jubilee,* vol. 3 (Jerusalem 1975), pp. 111–181 and "*Leket Yosef* and Sugyot ha-Talmud," *Alei Sefer* 4 (1977), pp. 70–116.

and Poland until the beginning of the fifteenth century (unless there happened to be a stray manuscript at their disposal). In the year 1715 the novellae to *Berakhot*, *Gittin*, *Hulin*, and *Bava Batra* were reprinted, for the first time, by the Amsterdam printer Attias. Two years later the Rashba novellae to tractate *Kidushin* was printed from manuscript in Constantinople, by the German Jewish emigrant printer Jonah Ashkenazi, who brought about a complete change in the literary horizons of his time by printing a sizeable part of the classic Spanish Talmud novellae, within a short period of twenty-five years.

By the year 1762—that is, in less than fifty years—about 90% of what is available to us now was made available and easily accessible to the scholars of the thirteenth century. That is not to say, of course, that the Ashkenazi academies were wholly ignorant of Spanish exegetic scholarship. Much of it was included—albeit in paraphrase and in a drastically abridged form—in a number of books that were current there, mainly the Ran (Rabbi Nissim) on the Rif to some tractates. They rarely, if at all, had an opportunity to study original chapters of the classic Spanish heritage in its pristine form, not to mention to study them in large groups and there is no need to explain here why that made such a big difference. This most important chapter in our spiritual history was clarified in great detail in an article I wrote to which I have very little to add.[5] I will take up the opportunity, however, to mention the edition of *Hidushei ha-Ran* to tractate *Shavu'ot*, printed at the end of Maharam Galanti's novellae, in Venice 1608, which escaped my knowledge at the time, but changes nothing as far as we are concerned here, as Rabbenu Nissim's work on the Rif was fairly known anyway among the Ashkenazim since the middle of the sixteenth century.

Rabbi Joshua Falk published his first volume in 1739, the second volume in 1752, the third in 1756 (the year of his death), and a last volume was printed after his death and does not concern us here. A quick comparison of dates will reveal at a glance what actually happened. Rabbi Falk's long creative years, from 1703 (when his life was miraculously saved from under the debris of his house, which toppled down and buried his wife, daughter, and mother-in-law, and he vowed, then and there, to abandon the accepted ways and methods of Talmud study and to commit himself to a true elucidation of the Talmud) to 1750 (when he finally resigned from public service) were also the crucial years in which the main body of classical Spanish Talmud scholarship saw the light of day; the two developments occurred, as a matter of fact, simultaneously. And, to be sure, the book *Pnei Yehoshua* is replete with references to the newly published books of the various Spanish Rishonim of the Nachmanides school, many of whose novellae he figured out himself, and was happy to find later on

5 I. Ta-Shma, "*Hiddushei ha-Rishonim*: Their Order of Publication" (Heb.), *Kiryat Sefer* 50, (1975), pp. 325–336.

in their newly printed books. This he says himself in his introduction to the book and many times throughout it.

These two irrefutable facts: the emergence of Talmud commentary as a large and ever-growing genre *per se* as a direct consequence of the appearance of the *Pnei Yehoshua* and the simultaneous publication of the lion's part of Talmud commentaries from the school of Nachmanides, added to the fact that the *Pnei Yehoshua*—and only he—is quoted by name and title by most later commentators practically to this very day, are by themselves reason and proof enough to establish him as the originator of modern Talmud commentary.

We must now turn our attention to the challenging questions: In what way was the *Pnei Yehoshua* different from his predecessors, and what was his unique contribution to Talmud commentary that created, or at least enabled, the great revolution that it did? The first question is very easy to answer: He simply refrained from following their pilpulistic methods—so wonderfully described by Dimitrovsky in his above-mentioned article.[6] The second question is far more essential and not so easy to answer. However, after long consideration, if I had to sum up in a nut-shell the quintessence of my answer, it would run thus: The *Pnei Yehoshua* highlighted, for the first time in rabbinic literature (including, for that matter, the period of the Rishonim), the great instructive potential inherent in a good question, targeted at the very center of the issue under debate, in contrasting comparison to the glaring ineptitude of a long array of alternative, weak answers.

By age old tradition, questions were always considered important mainly for clearing and preparing the way before the various possible answers, which were the true and final goal of every student: *shiv'im panim la-Torah*, all of which can, and actually do, co-exist together in perfect harmony. Answers signify the inner truth, or truths, of the matter, whereas questions demonstrate the straying, aimless blundering or, rather, the stupidity of the student that must be settled, one way or the other, before he can rest in peace and carry on. That iron pillar of traditional Talmud exegesis—to pacify the student at all cost—was shattered by the *Pnei Yehoshua*, who was the first among the Akhronim to aim straight at the heart of the issue under debate, thereby positing the question as his main intellectual implement and the answers as secondary in importance. On the whole, his questions are much nearer to the modern conception of criticism than to the traditional attitude of modest perplexity and therein lies their might and the overwhelming power of the book as a whole. It is an interesting fact, witnessed by all who are acquainted with his work, that the answers proposed are either tenuous and unsatisfactory, or, more rarely, highly innovative (which largely enhances the overall critical effect just now described). Later generations never ceased to seek better answers to his queries, bearing equivocal witness to the strange contrast between excellent *Frage-*

6 n. 4.

stellung and solutions of an inferior quality, which together characterize the book.

We must now go back to the Maharsha, whom we postulated as the first herald of what was to develop 150 years after him into modern Talmud commentary. What was said just now about Rabbi Joshua Falk seems, at a first glance, to apply equally well, perhaps somewhat better, to the Maharsha, who certainly excelled in asking the right questions, often leaving the reader in the dark regarding his answers with his cryptic "*ve-yesh le-yashev*," or with a shorthand solution that does not help much. Maharsha's remarks are certainly of a critical nature and later generations never ceased to offer better answers to his questions as well. Why then give primogeniture rights to the *Pnei Yehoshua* and not to his great forerunner?

The answer to this question is very simple: Maharsha rarely levels his queries at the very heart of the *sugya*. He adheres mostly to technicalities of a pedantic nature, raising true and well-calculated difficulties (some of them formal, others of a logical nature) inherent in the texture and up-build of the *sugya*, but rarely, and rather incidentally, touching on its very heart. Maharsha's work is of great and enduring importance to the routine study of the Talmud, but it never breaks ice, and once his questions find a satisfactory technical solution, they are forgotten. This very rarely happens to the *Pnei Yehoshua*. Maharsha's work marked a real revolution with regard to his predecessors in Germany and Austria, the sages of the by-now famous *pilpul Gornish*. But I cannot enter into this tricky chapter, which goes back well into the fifteenth century and is entirely outside the scope of this article. I will say only that Maharsha was the first among the Akhronim to discern properly between what was important and what was trivial and not worth its time in the business of Torah study, thus eliminating superfluous, sterile sophistications that so nicely characterized fifteenth-century German Gornish scholars, thus supplying the basic cornerstone for the later grand edifice of the *Pnei Yehoshua*.

To summarize what has been said: The Tosafist heritage of the twelfth and thirteenth centuries has been technically adopted by later generations and already attached to the Talmud as an integral part of it in the fourteenth century. At the same time, the creative, rather revolutionary didactic principles of the *tosafot* were totally abandoned, not to be followed again for many centuries to come. This break with the past brought about an unbridgeable gap between the periods and, beginning with the fourteenth century, scholars forged new techniques for their academies, starting from scratch and concentrating mainly on the many and various technical aspects of the *sugya*, constantly improving on it, but progressing very slowly with the advance of the centuries toward the modern era. The first conceivable move in this direction was made by the Maharsha, who taught how to discern between a technically correct, well-calculated, worthwhile question, and formal trivialities, which should be dismissed and not allowed to divert the student's attention. The great leap forward was done by Rabbi Joshua Falk, author of the classic book *Pnei Yehoshua*, who taught the difference between a technical difficulty and an essential query, targeted at the very heart of the *sugya*, and posing a veritable problem rather than a troublesome difficulty. He was the first to show the great instructive potential behind the question, but he was, at the same time, far less potent in proposing answers to his queries. That is why we find the *Pnei Yehoshua* quoted in so many later Talmud commentaries, chagrined by his well-leveled questions, but utterly dissatisfied with his or, for that matter, many others' solutions.

The next significant step was taken by early–nineteenth-century Rabbi Jacob Lurberboim of Lissa, who was one of the first to bring about a radical change in the answering mechanisms. His was an entirely new direction of solving a problem: not by customary machinations and sophisticated manipulations that rarely satisfy the student, but by a purely logical procedure of the *sugya*, determining its essence and boundaries and differentiating it from neighboring concepts that may seem identical but are nevertheless entirely different. This sort of solution is, of course, far better suited to deal with the critical type of attitude advanced by the *Pnei Yehoshua* and his talented camp of followers and it won the day in the Polish-Lithuanian academies of the nineteenth century. The method was much refined and improved upon toward the beginning of the twentieth century by Rabbi Haim Soloveitchik's analytical technique, which carried the process of conceptualization further, postulating a divisibly dual stratification for most halakhic conceptions. His method was itself further developed by improvisation and variation by his many epigons. But this outreaches the limits of this chapter.

CHAPTER 11

THE ACCEPTANCE OF MAIMONIDES' MISHNEH TORAH IN ITALY

The extraordinary spread of Maimonides' *Mishneh Torah* (henceforth: MT) throughout the medieval Jewish world was extremely swift and rapid, notwithstanding the enormous size of the work and the generally slow traffic of medieval men and goods. Its geographic apexes, to the east and to the west, were already achieved, for the most part, during Maimonides' lifetime. Early varied social and literary reactions, for and against, are known to us from east and west, many of them having been initiated during Maimonides' lifetime, and their late repercussions echoed for a long time after his death. Much has been written on this subject, mainly in connection with the wide research done on the long and bitter polemic directed against Maimonides' philosophical teachings. These ideational battles were seen by many scholars as the true motive behind much of the strong halakhic opposition to Maimonides, meant by his opponents as an effective tool, capable of "objectively" and clearly rupturing Maimonides' legendary "heroic" fame as a quasi-infallible talmudic scholar. It was Prof. I. Twersky, in his monumental book on Maimonides,[1] who seriously tried to balance the scales and give the halakhic opposition to Maimonides its own importance, *per se*, independent of outside considerations.

It is, nevertheless, surprising to see that the question of the historical attitude adopted by earlier generations toward MT, the extent and level of acceptance accorded to it, and the period of time required for the process to mature and take hold in different lands and geographical zones has never been seriously raised. Where and when did the book penetrate first? Who were its sponsors and opponents? What were the initial steps, or stages, in its adoption everywhere? Did the process have to do with concurrent local attitudes toward the philosophy and theology expressed in MT or in Maimonides' other works? As far as I can see, these elementary questions have not been analyzed for any given locality, and scholarly opinion on the subject is based on nothing more

1 I. Twersky, *Introduction to the "Mishne Torah" of Maimonides* (Cambridge, Mass. 1980).

than general historical observations and intuitive impressions, at least one century removed from the first appearance of MT on the historical arena.

I shall now try to outline the principal literary data necessary for a detailed construction of such an analysis relative to Italy, where the influence of Maimonidean halakhah is believed to have been greatly emphasized until the second half of the fifteenth century. At that time, in the words of my good friend Prof. R. Bonfil: "*Mishneh Torah* lost the pre-eminence that it had enjoyed until the middle of the fifteenth century."[2] According to Bonfil, at the center of the historical picture during the period of the Renaissance stood

> the question of the role of the Mishneh Torah in halakhic ruling. Maimonides' critical spirit drawing upon the world of philosophy, certainly left its impression in this area also. But if the weak points in his philosophical writings were easily picked up by his critics, in the realm of the Halakhah the picture was far more complex. Many and diverse forces—whose weight and influence have not yet been fully determined, despite the many studies that have been devoted to this subject—played a role here.

And here Bonfil quotes the only two existing articles on the subject,[3] both very far from exhausting their prospective goals. Bonfil's description is nicely balanced, as usual, and he is certainly justified in positing the increased Franco-German influence in Italy as a powerful rival to the regnant Maimonidean priority. He is also certainly correct in ascribing a concrete meaning to the increasing influence of the *Tur*, the important code of law written by R. Yaakov b. Asher, as an integral part of that same Franco-German conquering influence, in contrast to the simplistic view expressed by I. Sonne, who understood the increased efforts by late–fifteenth-century Italian printers to print the *Tur* as representing merely a commercial race to win the market by an innovation.[4] Reading further in Bonfil's book, one learns that, notwithstanding the decline in the prestige of MT, its relative power was still very much noticeable in Italy, in the major part of contemporary rabbinic literature, despite frequent halakhic disagreements and expressions of reservation and qualification by some of its important figures. To quote Bonfil again: "However, the study of MT has never lessened in Italy until our very own times, and it certainly did not happen in Italy during the period under discussion,"[5] i.e., the later part of the fifteenth century.

[2] R. Bonfil, *Rabbis and Jewish Communities in Renaissance Italy* (London 1993), pp. 255–257.

[3] I.Z. Cahana, "Ha-Pulmus Mi-seviv Keviat ha-Hakhraa ka-Rambam," *Sinai* 36 (1954), pp. 391–411, 530–537; 37 (1955), pp. 51–61, 157–164, 220–227, 381–385; 38 (1956), pp. 46–53, 114–117, 243–246; J. Dienstag, "Yahasam shel Baalei ha-Tosafot la-Rambam," in *Sh. K. Mirsky Jubilee Volume* (New York 1958), pp. 350–379.

[4] I. Sonne, "Excursions into History and Bibliography," in *A. Marx Jubilee Volume* (New York 1950), Hebrew section, pp. 209–235 (Heb.).

[5] Bonfil, op. cit., p. 256.

The question to be asked here is, of course, how far back is the Maimonidean tradition traceable in Italy? Was it really a rooted homeland tradition there, until it came under strong and massive Franco-German attack toward the middle of the fifteenth century?

Let us consider first Rabbi Isaiah di Trani, undoubtedly the foremost Italian rabbi of the early thirteenth century and one of the greatest ever active in Italy. Di Trani wrote comprehensive *tosafot* on most of the Talmud and re-edited—actually re-wrote—most of his novellae up to five times over, as he progressed in years and wisdom. He was still actively busy writing and re-writing around the year 1225. All five progressive editions existed simultaneously, side by side, and he himself directed the reader to study them all, as the case demanded. Besides *tosafot*, di Trani wrote a very large and comprehensive book of laws, in which he summarized the practical directives resulting from the Talmud, chapter by chapter and tractate by tractate, throughout the entire Talmud. In addition, he wrote *Sefer ha-Makhria* and detailed responsa to the many who asked his opinion on halakhic matters. Elsewhere[6] I am publishing a detailed essay on this great luminary, focusing mainly on his literary work, from which it will become clear that throughout his voluminous *Tosafot Rid*—certainly one of the largest rabbinic literary creations to have been written in the Middle Ages—Maimonides is mentioned not more than four times in all. Maimonides' name is completely absent from di Trani's book of *pesakim*[7] and volume of responsa, and in *Sefer ha-Makhria* he is mentioned three times. Di Trani's main rabbinic authorities are Alfasi, Rabbenu Hananel, Rashi, *Halakhot Gedolot*, a group of *baalei tosafot*—mainly German scholars who studied under Rabbenu Tam—and a small group of twelfth-century Italian scholars. But there is hardly any mention of Maimonides.

Di Trani studied in his youth under the famous R. Simha of Speyer, in company with R. Avigdor Katz, R. Isaac Or Zaru'a of Vienna, and R. Abraham b. Azriel of Boehm. I cannot discuss here the interesting career of MT in Germany and the various stages of its acceptance there, but it will serve our purpose well to mention that R. Azriel of Boehm quotes Maimonides sixty times and discusses his halakhic and philosophical sayings with the same acuteness reserved for all the other authorities that he quotes. To quote Urbach: "When reading his halakhic debates pro and con Maimonidean stands, one gets a sincere feeling of the great appreciation Abraham nurtured toward Maimon-

6 I. Ta-Shma, "Rabbi Isaiah di Trani u-Mifalo ha-Sifruti," in *Mehkerei Talmud* 3 [= *Prof. E. E. Urbach Memorial Volume*].

7 Somewhat surprisingly, the last volume of the critical edition of "Pesakim," on tractate Shevuot, published lately from manuscript, Jerusalem 1996, is quite replete with Maimonidean quotes. However, it alone cannot, and does not, change the overall "a-Maimonidean" effect.

ides."[8] Much the same can be said about R. Isaac Or Zaru'a and his well-known book of that name. But R. Isaiah di Trani, their colleague and lifelong admirer, behaved in an entirely different manner. This has nothing to do with possible reservations he might have had toward Maimonides' philosophical dogmas. Di Trani's commentary on the Pentateuch, which I have been fortunate to discover lately in the Günzberg collection, was written shortly after its author's return from Germany to Italy and still carries a heavy Ashkenazic flavor, and freely quotes long passages from Maimonides' *Moreh Nevukhim* without any qualification.[9]

Di Trani was not alone in behaving in this way. The same is true of his great disciple, R. Zedekiah Anav, author of the Hebrew Italian classic *Shibbolei ha-Leket*, the last version of which was composed around the years 1245–1260. This large, detailed halakhic catechism betrays a deep Franco-German influence and does not quote, or otherwise use, Maimonides even once. On the laws of *trefot* and *avelut*, where Maimonides is, indeed, mentioned once, I shall say something later on. The absence of Maimonides' name from the halakhic work of these two central rabbinic figures of the first half of the thirteenth century completely invalidates Maimonides' supposed status of preeminence in Italy, at least for that early period. But the same is true for the second half of the thirteenth century too.

To be sure, these two great rabbis are not the only ones to ignore Maimonides' MT. The same is true of two other important figures of the Anav family who bore halakhic responsibility in Italy at the time. First and foremost among them was R. Judah b. Benjamin Anav, a cousin of R. Zedekiah and one of his chief mentors. This rabbi wrote a comprehensive commentary on Alfasi to many tractates, with an expert eye on practical ends. Studying his commentary, one ends up with the same result: no mention whatever of Maimonides (again: excluding *trefot*). R. Judah died before 1280, probably some time after Zedekiah. The second figure is another member of the same family, who in the third quarter of the thirteenth century wrote an Italian customary law book, now in ms. München 232.[10] Beside these two, one should, of course, mention the *Tanya*, the popular thirteenth-century companion to Italian liturgy,[11] which mentions Maimonides very rarely, four times in all, two of which deal with laws of repentance, representing Maimonides' ideational world far more

[8] E.E. Urbach, *Sefer Arugat ha-Bosem*, IV (Jerusalem 1963), pp. 166–167.

[9] I. Ta-Shma, "Sefer *Nimukei Humash* le-Rabbi Isaiah di Trani," *Kiryat Sefer* 64 (1992–93), pp. 751–753.

[10] Idem, "Sefer Halakhot Italki Kadmon la-Rav Yehiel b. Yekutiel," *Kovetz Al Yad* 15 (1961), pp. 145–206.

[11] I.Tz. Feintuch, "Tanya Rabati," in *Versions and Traditions in the Talmud*, ed. Daniel Sperber (Ramat-Gan 1985), pp. 65–76 (Heb.).

than his halakhah. All through its hard halakhic core, the *Tanya* quotes Maimonides only twice and the central backbone of the book is, as usual in thirteenth-century Italy, the Franco-German tradition.

The profound effect that Franco-German law and custom had upon thirteenth-century Italian halakhah can be apprehended directly by a cursory examination of the list of books and authors quoted by R. Isaiah di Trani, R. Zedekiah, the *Tanya*, and the other Italian rabbis mentioned above. The resulting onomasticon is firmly based in the eleventh-century halakhic compendium *Maase ha-Geonim*, the early twelfth-century book of *Pardes*, the thirteenth-century *Sefer ha-Teruma* and *Sefer Yereim*, R. Simha of Speyer, R. Avigdor Katz and their circle, and others, forming together a well-defined literary group "Debei Rashi," and definitely pursuing the old Franco-German tradition. One should remember in this context that the early beginnings of German Jewry, some time in the mid-tenth century, have their roots in northern Italy, and that social and literary ties with the Italian homeland were still very much in evidence during the eleventh century and, to a somewhat lesser extent, during the twelfth.

There is just one exception to the rule. I call attention again to *Shibbolei ha-Leket*, but this time not to the standard Buber edition, the so-called "Shibbolei ha-Leket Completum," but to the first edition of the book, Venice 1546, which was published anonymously and is noticeably shorter than Buber's "complete" edition. The Venice edition was attributed by Buber—and by all later scholars—to someone who plagiarized the original work and radically changed it so as to cover his tracks. My article on *Shibbolei ha-Leket* pointed out the absurdity of anyone going to all the trouble of plagiarizing and distorting somebody else's work and then leaving out his name from the published abridgement in order to cover his anonymous tracks.[12] I also proved that the book was actually written by the same author, R. Zedekiah Anav, and is, therefore, in fact, simply an earlier version, one of several known to exist in print and manuscript.

The important point here is that, in this early version, Maimonides is, indeed, mentioned, and quite often. This, in fact, is one of the principal alterations between the early version and subsequent ones. This fact was already noted by Buber and further emphasized by S. Chassida,[13] both of them underlining it as the anonymous plagiarist's main "contribution" to his version. Chassida's important improvement upon Buber lies in his recognition that this anonymous person must have been a pupil of R. Judah b. Benjamin Anav, very much like R. Zedekiah himself, and could not, therefore, be taken for a simple urchin. But the truth is that the mysterious anonymous person was none other

12 I. Ta-Shma, "Sefer *Shibbolei ha-Leket* u-Kfilav," *Italia* 11 (1995), pp. 39–51.

13 S. Chassida, ed., *Shibbolei ha-Leket* (Jerusalem 1988), Introduction, pp. 51–56.

than R. Zedekiah himself, who did use Maimonides' MT in his early efforts to summarize Italian halakhah and custom, but afterward changed his mind.

Judging from what we have seen up to now, there is no getting away from the conclusion that, although MT was already known in Italy during the first quarter of the thirteenth century, it did not take root in that country and had very little influence on the study and deciding of halakhah there during most, if not all, of that century. This had nothing to do with Maimonides' theological and philosophical positions, which the same rabbis quoted freely. The real reason lay in the deep and dominant Franco-German tradition, which was quite self-sufficient and called for no substitutes, addenda, or corrigenda. This influence was upheld and strengthened by di Trani, who studied in Germany, brought back with him the tosafist way of studying the Talmud and deciding of halakhah, and taught his followers to do the same. It would, therefore, seem reasonable to surmise that the first draft of *Shibbolei ha-Leket* was written before R. Zedekiah came under the influence of di Trani. As is well known, R. Zedekiah was not a direct, face-to-face, personal pupil of di Trani and never actually sat before him as a student, as he never refers to him as "my teacher." He came under his influence at some later phase of his life and then became wholly dependent upon him. I believe, therefore, that the earlier version reflects a natural tendency by an up-to-date young author to use the newly arrived MT for his catechism. Later on, coming under R. Isaiah's profound influence, he withdrew Maimonides from his work and adhered strictly to the Franco-German tradition. Be it that way or another, this single exception, the "short" *Shibbolei ha-Leket*, cannot change the overall dominant picture of a vitally active and creative thirteenth-century Italian halakhic scholarship disregarding MT, which is almost totally absent.

A slight change in attitude is recognizable in the third quarter of that century. R. Isaiah di Trani the Second ("the Younger"), b. Elia, grandson to the first, generally known by the title of his magnum opus *Piske Riaz*, quotes Maimonides an average of three to four times for every part of his multivolume law book. This in itself is, of course, not much or in any way impressive—not to say convincing—and can hardly serve as testimony to Maimonides' increasing halakhic prestige, but it does signify a step forward, however small, in comparison to what was there before. In R. Isaiah the Second's other book, *Kuntres ha-Reayot*, a small part of which was lately discovered in a unique Jerusalem manuscript, theoretical discussions relevant to the *pesakim* are developed and the MT is integrated to a somewhat greater extent; but it still adds up to very little as, for example, in his *kuntres* to tractate *Bava Metzia*, in which MT is mentioned five times in all, starting on folio 100 of that large tractate.

A real interest in Maimonides' halakhic work is first detectable in Italy in the late nineties of the thirteenth century. At that time, "the sages of Rome, its princes and leaders, the mighty men of the land," initiated an effort to obtain a Hebrew translation of Maimonides' classic commentary to the Mishnah, which at that time existed only in its original Arabic version, incomprehensible to the Jews of Italy. Just one part of it, to the order *Zeraim*, was known at the time in a Hebrew translation by the famous Judah Alharizi, who had completed it one hundred years earlier, upon the order of R. Jonathan of Lunel. At the instigation of the elders of Rome, a certain R. Simha was sent on a mission to Spain, carrying with him introductory letters requesting the goodwill and assistance of the Jewish communities in Spain. The story of that mission is quite well known. R. Solomon b. Aderet, the famous Rashba of Barcelona, came to his aid and as not even an Arabic original could be found in Barcelona (Arabic not being current any more in that city), the Rashba begged other Jewish communities in Aragon that owned Arabic originals to see to its translation. It should be noted that in this manner Maimonides' classic commentary first came to be known in the western Jewish communities, more than a century after its composition. It was, therefore, due to Italian initiative, and Spanish financing and execution, that this great book was translated into Hebrew, and this certainly does mark a true interest in Maimonidean halakhah, although not yet in MT.

A true change in attitude is recognizable in Italy toward the end of the first quarter of the fourteenth century. The first Italian book to express a real and substantial halakhic influence derived from MT is the *Tadir* by R. Moses b. Jekuthiel de Rossi, who flourished in the first quarter of the fourteenth century. His book was devoted to a detailed description of the entire field of practical, everyday halakhah according to the Roman rite, in a fluent and down-to-earth manner. In this influential book—which at the time replaced the earlier and much honored book of *Tanya*—Maimonides' halakhic impact is already very clear, although the dominant tradition is still Franco-German. The same description will conveniently serve as true and entirely adequate for the well-known book of halakhic decisions composed by R. Menahem of Recanati, probably identical to the prominent kabbalist of the same name who lived in Italy, most probably in Rome, at the same time. MT plays an important role in Recanati's work, but the Franco-German tradition is dominant. These two books signify the beginning of the real and substantial acceptance of Maimonidean halakhah in Italy. But it was another, third, contemporaneous book, much less known today but most important and influential in its time, that made possible, and virtually caused, the major change in attitude toward Maimonides' MT.

The rabbinic figure who brought about this change was Judah Romano, who also flourished in the first quarter of the fourteenth century and whose main spiritual and literary efforts and fame lay in the field of philosophy, both Jewish and Gentile, while his more austere work in the field of halakhah sank into oblivion for centuries. Romano was much influenced by a group of well-known, moderate, Maimonidean followers, who were active in Italy toward the end of the thirteenth century, among them sages such as Zerahiah Hen

Grazian, Jacob Anatoli, and Hillel of Verona. The ranks of Torah study in fourteenth-century Italy were much depleted and Italian rabbinical literature of that period is very sparse and dull, but intellectual activity in the field of religious thought and Maimonidean philosophy was on a rather high level. Quite a number of the doctors who headed these moderate philosophical schools were capable also of normative halakhic and rabbinical leadership, and acted as practicing rabbis for their communities. Their devoted student, R. Judah Romano, was one of the foremost pupils of these philosophical schools; he was also well known for his rabbinical and talmudic ability and acted as untitled chief rabbi for the Jews of Italy during the first quarter of the fourteenth century.[14]

Romano wrote a commentary on MT, treating mainly the difficult, professional, and scientific "nomina barbara" in MT, words that were unknown or little understood by the laity, unversed in talmudic lore. Romano translated these words into the spoken Italian dialect of his time and explained their meaning in accordance with the classic commentaries of Rashi, *Sefer Arukh*, Rabbenu Hananel, and the like, thus facilitating and encouraging the regular study of MT by the common people. He also availed himself of the opportunity to explain some vague points of the halakhah at hand. The book was written in Hebrew and has been edited from manuscripts and translated into Italian by Dr. Sandra Debenedetti-Stow.[15] Surprising as this might appear to be, this book was the chief instrument for the Maimonidean halakhic breakthrough in Italy.

[14] On Romano, see G. Sermoneta, "La dottrina del'intelletto e la 'fede' filosofica di Jehudah e Immanu'el Romano," *Studi Medievali*, serie terza, 6, 11 (1965), pp. 3–78; id., "Jehudah b. Moseh b. Dani'el Romano, traducteur de Saint Thomas," in *Hommage a Georges Vajda*, eds. G. Nahon and Ch. Touati (Louvain 1980), pp. 235–262.

[15] Jehuda b. Moseh b. Daniel Romano, *La chiarificazione in volgare delle "espressioni difficili" ricorrenti nel Misneh Torah di Mose Maimonide*, S. Debeneddetti-Stow, ed., I–II (Rome 1990). There are many very curious mistakes throughout the book, which require some serious re-writing of its contents. The Italian translations include many strange decipherings of rabbinical Hebrew abbreviations, like ובה"פ, which is understood as ובהבנה פשוטה (see p. 41, #8) "secondo l'interpretazione comune" (e.g., p. 131—Barda, twice on the same page, and many others), or "in parole povere" (p. 152), instead of ובספר הערוך פירש. These many quotations should, of course, be added, recorded, and counted in the *Arukh*'s list. Strangely, on page 181, s.v. קטבלא, it is again translated "in parole povere," but the same locus is translated correctly in a different context (p. 41, n. 143, first line)! On the other hand, the Hebrew words כך פי' בה בערך, which mean: "that is how the *Arukh* explained it," are fancifully translated: "questo e il significato nell'ordine dei termini medici" (p. 127). See further on page 126: ניא שהמור הוא המוסק וא"ע יכחישם, which is translated: "è vi e chi dice che il mwr sia il mosco, ma lo stesso fato li smentisce"—probably because the abbreviation וא"ע was taken to mean something like ואת עצמו; whereas these letters stand, of course, for ואבן עזרא, and should be translated "but Ibn Ezra refutes them." Another gross mistake is the representation of the current ר"י as "R. Judah" (p. 41) or, even "better": "il nostro rabbino [R. Judah]" (p. 132 et al.), while these letters regularly stand for "R. Isaiah

The first quarter of the fourteenth-century marks, therefore, the historical beginning of the penetration of MT into Italy. The important halakhic litigation a century later, in fifteenth-century Renaissance Italy, concerning the alleged traditional seniority of MT in Italy relative to the newly arrived Franco-German influence to which my friend Bonfil has dedicated some interesting pages in his book, should be understood the other way around, as an attempt to stand up against the influence of the newly arrived, victorious MT, and thus re-establish the good, old, traditional Franco-German order, which reigned there until some hundred years earlier.

But the real historical import of our description lies elsewhere. In all other major Jewish centers in Europe, rabbis strongly opposed the blanket acceptance and adoption of Maimonides' halakhic code, for fear of a parallel adoption of his philosophical and theological positions, which were freely expressed in MT itself, as part and parcel of it. Only after a certain passage of time—generally three or four decades—and as a result of the unavoidable growing recognition of the tremendous accomplishment of MT was this work admitted into the first ranks of halakhic authority. But in Italy—and only in Italy—the process worked the other way around. At first, for almost seventy-five years, his philosophy was quite welcome, but his halakhah was discarded as superfluous and unnecessary in view of the well-established Franco-German tradition. Only with the passage of time and as a result of a growing recognition of the true magnitude of Maimonides' philosophy and theology, did the rabbis change their attitude toward acceptance of his gigantic halakhic creation. An exceptional phenomenon, indeed.

[the younger]" and are to be found in his *Piskei Riaz*, ad locum. There are many other stray errors, some of them unbelievable, like עוף שנחבט מעניין כי יחבוט "of senehvat e interessante" (p. 135) [!], instead of: "is like"; ...הקנים המתוקים וגומ' וידמה למלח (p. 154) is translated: "è [la frase] finisce con wa-idme le-melah" etc., instead of: "et cetera and it is like salt" etc. The Italian translation on page 155 is completely erroneous. See further the amusing translation on p. 162: קימונייא אמר רב יהודה שלוף דרין "dice R. Jehudah che e il lof spremuto." There is no need to record other examples here. I must add that Debenedetti's doctoral thesis, "Le glosse italiane al Misneh Thorah di R. Jehudah Romano," Gerusalemme 1986, "sotto la guida del prof. J.B. Sermoneta," which preceded the printed edition, contains very few direct translations and, therefore, does not reflect these shortcomings.

Originally published in
Italia. Studi e ricerche sulla storia, la cultura e la Letteratura degli Ebrei d'Italia, XIII–XV. Robert Bonfil, ed. Jerusalem

CHAPTER 12

THE PENETRATION OF ASHKENAZI CUSTOM-LAW AND FOLKLORE INTO THE ZOHAR

THE PHENOMENON AND ITS HISTORICAL ORIGIN

Although the Zohar is, unquestionably, one of the most celebrated literary perplexities of the Jewish Middle Ages, there are still some things that can be assumed in relation to its historical identity with a reasonable measure of certainty. These include, for example, its composition around the year 1280, its Castilian provenance, and even the personal name of its author Rabbi Moses de Leon, which is widely accepted as a near certainty, although I, personally, do not think so. The historical and literary evidence for all this is very well known and there is no need for us to recall and re-examine it here. In a series of articles and, of late, in a small book,[1] I presented evidence to the effect that beyond a characteristically Spanish halakhic and liturgical infrastructure, there exists in the Zohar a wide layer of Ashkenazic customs and folklore, cognizance of which is clearly traceable throughout the zoharic literature. This has since been widely acknowledged by scholars of kabbalah and there is, therefore, no need to discuss or illustrate the point here, but I shall return to it later, in a different context.

The question we must confront now is the possible historical meaning that might, or should, be attached to this Ashkenazi influence. Should such influence surprise us at all in the first place? Actually, was it not to be expected, given the excellent Spanish acquaintance with the Franco-German tosafist literature toward the end of the thirteenth century (a period that actually represents the very end of the long Tosafist era itself)? How should one appreciate this Ashkenazi influence on the Zohar? The mystical message and kabbalistic innovations of the Zohar—which are, after all, its main objective and intended goal—are apparently free of such influences as far as we can see and it is, therefore, only its "silent" background material that stands witness to this external influence. So what does it mean, if anything at all? In order to provide a sat-

[1] I. Ta-Shma, *Ha-Nigle she-Banistar: The Halachic Residue in the 'Zohar'* (Tel Aviv 2001).

isfactory answer to our question, we must first outline the relatively short history of the cultural and literary connections between Jewish Spain and Franco-Germany prior to the fourteenth century.

There is an essential difference between Spanish cultural penetration into Franco-Germany and its counter-process. Hispano-Jewish literature was known, studied, and criticized in France and in Germany as early as the end of eleventh century. But Franco-German rabbinic literature of all sorts was not known, or at least not spread, in Muslim—and afterward Christian—Spain until the first quarter of the thirteenth century, and even then only in a limited measure. This chronological gap was due mainly to the unsettled period between the year 1141—which marks the end of the Muslim term in Spanish rabbinic literature—and ca. 1200, which marks the renaissance of Jewish rabbinic culture under Christian rule. We are not interested here in the history of Spanish penetration into France and Germany, which is entirely outside the scope of this lecture, but we shall try to put some order and logic into the belated Franco-German inroad into Spain.

During the twelfth century we do not know of any cultural contacts between Spain and Franco-Germany. The first rabbinic authority to have used substantial Franco-German literature of any kind—with the single exception of R. Abraham Ibn Ezra, who traveled all over the continent and is, therefore, unrepresentative of his homeland Spanish culture—is R. Meir ha-Levi Abulafia (d. 1244). This great rabbi, descendant to an old and noble Spanish family, flourished in Toledo and was active there as head of the Jewish community and was a renowned *rosh yeshiva* during the first half of the thirteenth century. Being one of the most important leaders of the large Castilian communities, and a great rabbinic scholar, he took a major part in many of the central spiritual controversies of his time. His biography, great social and cultural achievements, and public involvement are all duly registered and analyzed in Prof. Septimus' excellent book.[2]

In his monumental book *Yad Rama*, on tractates *Sanhedrin* and *Bava Batra*, Abulafia quotes—for the first time in Spain, as far as I know—Rashi and *tosafot*, including *Tosafot Riva* by R. Isaac b. Asher the Elder, who wrote his *tosafot* in Speyer around 1120 and is, in fact, the first known Tosafist. Abulafia also quotes, by name and anonymously, Rashbam and Rabbenu Tam, whose work on the Talmud was known to him. He was involved also in a somewhat disappointing correspondence with some contemporary French Tosafists, whose aid he requested, in vain, during his energetic activity in the first Maimonidean controversy, ca. 1203. He never mentions anyone as "my teacher" —a most extraordinary phenomenon in medieval rabbinic ethos—and, therefore, we have no idea who his guiding teachers were and what first brought him into the

[2] B. Septimus, *Hispano-Jewish Culture in Transition* (Cambridge, Mass. and London 1982).

Franco-German literary ken. His novellae, which covered all the studied tractates and functioned as a widespread companion to their study, contributed much to the avant-garde knowledge and diffusion of Franco-German rabbinic literature in Spain.

At the same time, another famous rabbi contributed much to the introduction of Franco-German halakhah, custom, folklore, and tradition into Castilia: R. Abraham b. Nathan, the author of *Sefer ha-Manhig*. Abulafia's coeval, he was a pupil of R. Isaac the Elder of Dampierre, the most celebrated Tosafist of all times and nephew of Rabbenu Tam. Abraham b. Nathan was of Provencal origin, born in Avignon. He studied under the famous Provencal rabbis and later under Ri of Dampierre in France. He traveled much and for many years throughout the Jewish communities of France, Germany, Provence, and Spain in order to acquaint himself with their diverse halakhic traditions and religious customs. He diligently registered all he saw in his book *Manhig Olam*, which he dedicated to the great rabbis and leaders of Toledo, after having settled there in the year 1204. R. Meir ha-Levi Abulafia familiarized his generation with the Franco-German tosafist literary and academic achievement, but it was R. Abraham b. Nathan who first introduced into Spain a knowledge of the rich and versatile popular Franco-German liturgical heritage and practice, while serving there as rabbi and *dayan*.

These two personalities, Meir Abulafia and Abraham b. Nathan, were instrumental as early conduits for Franco-German rabbinic culture and lore. At that early stage, the first half of the thirteenth century, Spanish religious life was heavily dominated by the newly arrived Maimonides' *Mishneh Torah*, which won the day, becoming the major guide for the revitalized Jewish communities of Christian Spain. We can still catch some of the excited atmosphere in Jewish circles and the hearty reception accorded to Maimonides' codex through R. Jonah ibn Bahlul's unique book in praise of the codex. This Toledan rabbi flourished contemporaneously with R. Meir ha-Levi Abulafia and was described by Prof. Septimus in his article "Kings, Angels or Beggars."[3] In his most inspired book—still in manuscript—Jonah Ibn Bahlul considers the advent of Maimonides' *Mishneh Torah* in Spain an open act of divine grace. He describes in great detail the halakhic revolution evoked by it, and registers a long list of mistaken halakhah, commonly maintained by Castilian rabbis prior to the publication of Maimonides' codex and later corrected in accordance with it. The Franco-German contribution by the two rabbinic authorities mentioned above should, therefore, be evaluated against this historical backdrop. They were, indeed, two prime conduits of Franco-German rabbinic knowledge, but hardly more than just that. This is especially true of R. Meir

[3] B. Septimus, "Kings, Angels or Beggars," in *Studies in Medieval Jewish History and Literature* 2 (Cambridge, Mass. and London 1984), pp. 309–335.

Abulafia, who was strongly rooted in classic Hispano-rabbinic traditions. The newly acquired Franco-German rabbinic literature served him mainly as mere addenda and corrigenda.

As emphasized before, we confront a historical lacuna of some sixty years, between 1141 and 1200, during which period there was apparently no rabbinic creativity in Spain. As far as we know, *Yad Rama* and *Sefer ha-Manhig* were the first to mention, take into consideration, and treat Franco-German material in Spain during the first third of the thirteenth century. But there was still no essentially active Franco-German influence upon Spanish Torah study and practical halakhah, let alone upon the social structure and ethical behavior of the Jewish communities and their ideological propensities, which remained traditionally Spanish as ever before.

The true and substantial change was brought about by the joint efforts of two other giant Spanish rabbinic figures, both of Catalonian-Provencal origin and both active around the middle of the thirteenth century: R. Jonah Gerondi and Nachmanides, R. Moses b. Nachman. R. Jonah Gerondi, born in Perpignian, flourished in Gerona and later in life in Toledo, while his younger cousin Nachmanides was active in Gerona and Barcelona. Both accomplished their life assignment one generation after R. Meir Abulafia: Abulafia died in 1244, R. Jonah died in 1261 and Nachmanides in 1270. Nachmanides' principal teacher was the well-known Provencal rabbi and kabbalist Judah b. Yakar, who studied under the famous Tosafist Ri ha-Zaken of Dampierre, mentioned above as the teacher of R. Abraham b. Nathan. Nachmanides' second teacher, R. Nathan of Trinkentil, was also a devout French disciple. Much greater and direct Franco-German influence was brought to bear on R. Jonah Gerondi. He studied for many years at the prominent tosafist yeshiva of Evreaux, which was simultaneously a singular German-Pietist center of influence in France and a celebrated tosafist yeshiva in its own right. R. Jonah Gerondi was thoroughly transformed by the German-Pietist ideals and when he returned to his homeland, he took it upon himself, with the all-important support of his cousin Nachmanides, to transform Jewish social, ethical, and spiritual norms and standards of leadership, from their lenient, secular, greedy, courtier, open-minded style, to the far more strictly ethical and religious Franco-German standards.

Together they contrived a full-scale social and religious revolution in Spain, effecting a radical change in the social and spiritual climate, especially in the structure of the aristocratic Jewish leadership group, elevating the rabbinic elite to the prime status of communal and central leadership, replete with royal recognition and support. I cannot enter here into precise historical details and there is actually no need for me to do so, since the whole political background and final achievement were minutely described and analyzed by Prof. Septimus in his above-mentioned book.[4] What is relevant to our discussion here is the

[4] n. 2.

high place of honor that was now granted, for the first time in Spain, to the Franco-German talmudic tradition, custom, and style of study. It was a well-planned and well-conducted campaign for a central, positive, and leading role to be granted to the Franco-German rabbinic and talmudic standards and to their representative figures.

Let me call attention to one interesting point that should not pass unnoticed. Four of the five rabbinic personalities who were influential in transplanting Franco-German social and religious standards into Jewish Spain, namely Abraham b. Nathan, Judah b. Yakar, Nachmanides, and R. Jonah Gerondi, were of Catalonian-Provencal provenance; only R. Meir Abulafia was a local Spanish luminary.

Now, it is clear that, at least one hundred years before, much of the French and Ashkenazi synagogue and festival ritual was known—and probably here and there practiced—in Barcelona, as can be seen clearly in R. Judah ha-Barzeloni's *Sefer ha-Ittim*, which was written there around 1125. R. Judah ha-Barzeloni attacks in harsh and clear-cut phrases many of these customs and synagogue behavior, being himself a devout follower of the Spanish Rif, the great R. Isaac Alfasi, and representing a strong and exclusively Spanish influence emanating from the great and distant Torah center of Muslim Lucena. But his opposition surely proves a knowledge—although under heavy attack—of Franco-German liturgical practices current in Barcelona as early as the first quarter of the twelfth century. A century later, after the great communal reshuffle in the wake of the Reconquista wars, when Jewish communities from the south were vigorously re-establishing themselves in the northern parts of the country, the time became ripe for the Catalonian-Provencal way of life—led by rabbinic figures of the first order of magnitude who had studied under French Tosafists—to be absorbed by their newly established neighboring Spanish communities. The historico-geographical arrow is, therefore: Germany > France > Provence > Catalonia > Castilia (Provence being the chief mediator in the process).

Having reached this point in my outline, I shall now try to probe somewhat more deeply into the matter. I bound together R. Jonah Gerondi and Nachmanides as equal partners and co-workers, acting in concordance toward the ultimate goal of achieving a decisive Franco-German shift within the Jewish communities of Spain, but there was, nevertheless, a marked difference between them. R. Jonah Gerondi was far more extreme in his social outlook and severe in his religious demands. He was, in fact, representing absolute German Pietism, with its tough social and religious principles, and was dedicated to a self-imposed, life-long missionary career as a public preacher, advocating pietist social ideals combined with a standing call for individual and communal repentance. R. Jonah carried out his mission among the multitude, preaching in the synagogue and in diverse public communal meetings, propagating reformative communal regulations and advocating a strict control on individual and public behavior. In his work, he was aided greatly by the French R. Moses of Coucy, the author of the well-known book *Sefer Mitzvot Gadol*, who left France in the year 1236—in consequence of a visionary apparition that urged him to do so—for a difficult and very demanding journey throughout Spain. His aim was to preach, all over the country, for a general repentance movement in expectation of the final redemption, reckoned by him to take place in the year 1240—only four years removed—marking the beginning of the calendrical Jewish sixth millennium. R. Jonah's life story, his German orientation, his literary heritage, and his outstanding social and religious achievement in Spain were described in a detailed monographic article, and I refer the interested reader to that article for substantiation and further information.[5] I also refer the reader to another article[6] in which I uncover a previously unknown letter by R. Moses of Coucy written to his homeland France, one in which he describes an unbelievably enthusiastic public response to his efforts, beside other outstanding data of historical significance.

Nachmanides, on the other hand, represents the acme of Jewish scholarship and secular intellectualism of his time. He fought the revolutionary battle higher up the social ladder, among the learned, the *talmidei hakhamim*, whom he brought together under his tutelage as head of the central yeshiva of his time in Barcelona, where the future generation of elite rabbinic leadership was educated. He, too, was an ardent admirer of the Franco-German culture, with a much stronger emphasis on the intellectual French tosafist achievement than on the down-to-earth German social-religious, hasidic pietism.

It was exactly that double-headed activity that ensured such dramatic success to their joint efforts, being motivated by two distinct spiritual urges and aimed at two distinct social layers, but united by the same basic religious and social points of view, led by R. Jonah Gerondi with his keen social awareness and Nachmanides with his outstanding intellectual supremacy and correct political contacts.

The last stages in the long and slow process of the Franco-German infiltration, penetration, and final domination of Jewish Spain, which reached its peak around the year 1325, a century after its hesitant beginnings, occurred some twenty-five years after Rabbenu Jonah's activity with the physical emigration of thousands of Jewish households escaping the terrible hardships imposed on them by Rudolph I of Germany. Many of these refugees, whose number grew constantly, reached Spain. Among them was R. Asher b. Yehiel, the famous Rosh, chief rabbinic figure in Germany after the arrest of Maharam

[5] I. Ta-Shma, "Ashkenazi Hasidism in Spain: Rabbi Jonah Gerondi—The Man and His Work" (Heb.), *Exile and Diaspora* [= *Prof. Chaim Beinart Jubilee Volume*] (Jerusalem 1988), pp. 165–194.

[6] Idem, "Igerret u-Drashat Hitor'rut le-Ba'al ha-Semag O le-Rabbenu Yonah," *Moriah* 19 (1994), pp. 7–12.

of Rotenburg in 1286 and his consequent death in prison a few years later. When, together with his large family and many students and followers, the Rosh reached Toledo in 1305, he found a large, active, and identified Ashkenazi community there, including a large number of *talmidei hakhamim* and halakhic decisors. The large Ashkenazic community had branches in many other cities, all of them transformed over night by the arrival of R. Asher into an organized camp, under his spiritual guidance and leadership. From now on, we encounter in Spain not only a Franco-German spiritual influence and semi-domination, but a physical presence that divided the country into two well-defined camps, and whose influence and impact would be recognizable in Spain until the very end of Jewish history there.

Before concluding this part of my historical description, let me add one other important observation. The general outline of the Franco-German influence and impact on Jewish life and rabbinical literature in Spain is closely paralleled by the very similar historical trend recognizable within the contemporary Spanish Church, in its various theological and popular phases. I am, of course, no authority on the subject, but a detailed presentation can be found in Prof. Yom Tov Assis' chapter on "Trends in Religious Life in the Crown of Aragon."[7] A summary of the Jewish Franco-German cultural infiltration into Spain, based upon my earlier articles on the subject quoted there, is included in Prof. Assis' article on "The Judeo-Arabic Tradition in Christian Spain."[8]

Prof. Idel has drawn our attention in the past to the interesting historical fact that the Zohar was composed exactly within a narrow chronological "window,"[9] extending between the death of Nachmanides and the flourishing of his great pupil R. Shlomo b. Aderet, the famous Rashba, who opposed the Zohar and was probably personally responsible for its disappearance from the public arena in Spain for a long period after him. The relative eclipse of rabbinic acumen and authority during that short period made possible the appearance, diffusion, and acceptance of an anonymous kabbalistic work such as the Zohar, positing the until then clandestine kabbalah as a central topic of public study, while lacking the auspices or approbation of any worthy talmudic authority. To this important observation I would now add that what we have before us is, in fact, a "double window." Beside the necessary academic opportunity, this double window represents a short period between the first wave of Franco-German penetration and influence in Spain, which ended with the death of R. Jonah and Nachmanides, and the second wave of material, physical, and decisive demographic penetration and influence, headed by R. Asher b. Yehiel, which sealed the process and divided Spain into two well-defined and self-

[7] Y.T. Assis, *The Golden Age of Aragonese Jewry* (Oxford 1966), pp. 29–307.

[8] Idem, "The Judeo-Arabic Tradition in Christian Spain," in *The Jews of Medieval Islam,* D. Frank, ed. (Leiden, New York, Koln 1995), pp. 111–124.

[9] I. Idel, *Kabbalah: New Perspectives* (New Haven and London 1988).

identified camps. The large and deep-rooted Franco-German literary and customary residue found in the Zohar, with which I opened the chapter, was made possible only after the academic Franco-German revolution evoked by R. Jonah and Nachmanides, and is itself a major witness to it. The determined opposition of R. Asher b. Yehiel and the German rabbinic intelligentsia to any alternative, spiritual, public engagement beside Talmud and halakhah would have cancelled, from its very beginning, any attempt to go public with a book such as the Zohar.

My window exactly parallels Idel's window, as far as historical dates are concerned, but it seems to add another dimension to it. The question is now, of course, the extent to which the Zohar's Franco-German halakhic, customary and folkloric background is indicative of its spiritual origins as being deeply rooted inside the inner group of R. Jonah or Nachmanides pupils. It is easy to prove that talmudic versions quoted or alluded to in the Zohar are of Spanish provenance, as are the principal halakhic issues and the overall liturgical structure dominant in the Zohar. The large Franco-German residue covers mainly the fields of minor (or secondary) halakhah, custom, folklore, and superstition. It is, therefore, possible, and is actually to be expected, that wide knowledge of Franco-German lore was, at that time, quite diffused outside the inner circles of these two great luminaries. Therefore, the Zohar could be written anywhere in Spain, completely detached from the direct influence of these two rabbis.

What does come to our help at this point is another interesting discovery, examined and detailed in my small book on the Zohar.[10] A clear tendency is often discernible in the zoharic halakhah to follow unique halakhic decisions and Talmud commentaries held by R. Jonah Gerondi. This tendency has been noted by the late Rabbi Re'uven Margaliot in his book *Sha'arei Zohar*.[11] He promised there to dedicate a special paper to these parallels, but never did, perhaps afraid lest scholars draw the natural and inevitable conclusion from it that the Zohar was written after R. Jonah, while what he meant to show was that the zoharic material was actually ancient and known to Rabbenu Jonah. One must remember that a major part of R. Jonah's halakhic work was lost and much of what remained came to us through the intermediacy of his pupils, some of them anonymous, known to posterity as "Talmidei Rabbenu Jonah." Direct comparisons to the Zohar are, therefore, quite rare, but enough to draw attention to the phenomenon. R. Jonah's individual halakhic orientation as a decisor is Franco-German to a considerably larger extent than Nachmanides, whose dependence on the Franco-German school is more academic and theoretical, while in deciding practical halakhah in concrete situations he is usually observed to be under Spanish traditional influences. Examples to that effect

10 n. 1.

11 R. Margaliot, *Sha'arei Zohar* (Jerusalem 1978).

have been weighed in my book, but I must admit that they are not, as yet, enough to demonstrate the point beyond doubt.

It is, indeed, to be wondered how the Zohar could be critically researched for over a hundred years without trying to analyze its halakhic and liturgical content and background, even though evidence of direct mathematical nature and certainty cannot be easily produced. The Zohar is replete with halakhic and customary material, deposited there intentionally or inadvertently, and much of it has been, indeed, carefully gathered by many halakhists and kabbalists in the past, interested in the material purely for its religious significance. There is, of course, no reason why this rich material should not be reviewed for its historical and literary significance too. The same is true for philology and especially for talmudic philology. Many tacit talmudic citations can be found throughout the Zohar and though they are rarely quoted verbatim, it is still possible to trace the version that the author had in mind. If that sort of detective work would have been accomplished for the entire book, we could then have a better idea of its geographical backdrop. The Franco-German Talmud versions had been aggressively changed during the eleventh and twelfth centuries, by the leading rabbis there, and a methodological follow-up of zoharic overt and/or covert Talmud versions should produce interesting testimony on its cultural background.

I opened this chapter with the mention of the large residue of Ashkenazi customs and lore in the Zohar and then went on to discuss the question of what might be the historical lesson to be deduced from it. I did not quote any specific example, as I referred the reader to my book on the Zohar, which discusses quite a number of such examples. However, I wish to focus on one or two such examples that were not included in my book. As is well known, the Zohar in the Idra Rabba attaches great importance, not to say downright holiness, to the human beard (and hair in general), considering it a part of the full anthropomorphic figure of the Godhead and, therefore, a natural "Jewish" asset and an integral part of the Jewish personal image. Generations of kabbalists, before ha-Ari and after him, therefore, avoided almost entirely touching their beard and side-locks, attributing to them extraordinary taboo qualities.

Now it is absolutely clear that, according to strict halakhah, there is no problem whatsoever in cutting off one's beard (and side-locks), as long as one does not use a simple one-bladed razor, using instead a pair of ordinary scissors or shaving cream. There were always rabbis who restricted, even forbade, shaving with a pair of scissors, because of its functional similarity to a razor—*ke'ein ta'ar*—lest by confusion a razor, too, be thought permissible. There were others who forbade cutting off the beard and side-locks because of an independent prohibition of shaving one's head in a complete round circle or because they wanted to cut a clear and easily discernible distinction between the Jew and his Gentile neighbors. The question of whether individual Jews actually carried beards in the Middle Ages has no clear-cut answer; some of them probably did while others did not. In the Muslim East, beards were fashionable and highly respected, but in the Christian West the majority shaved off their beards while letting their hair grow long, and many Jews followed suit. In medieval Jewish Europe, the beard became a common sign of its bearer being a *talmid hakham*, a rabbinic student, a practicing rabbi or head of a yeshiva. The subject has been dealt with lately by Elimekech Hurwitz and Eric Zimmer and the information can be obtained from their two learned works.[12]

The interesting point is that nowhere in pre-zoharic rabbinic literature, excepting the literature of *Hasidei Ashkenaz*, is the beard conceived of as an intrinsic sign of "Jewishness" other than signifying a will to be different and apart from the Gentile environment. But according to certain anthropomorphic sects in German Pietism, the Godhead itself looks like a "beautiful old Jewish *talmid hakham*,"[13] that is, completely bearded with abundant side-locks, and whoever takes off his beard, even by a pair of scissors, will, therefore, suffer heavily for it, as R. Zalman, the son of R. Judah he-Hasid, quotes his father as saying to a rich and disobedient member of his community (*Sefer Hagan*). According to an unpublished manuscript by an early German Pietist, attributed to R. Judah he-Hasid himself, one who shaves off his beard with a scissors or grows his hair long and wears Gentile attire is forbidden to be called up to the *Sefer Torah*, because he has put on an outward appearance of a Gentile and lost his Jewish identity. *Sefer Hasidim* forbids taking off one's beard in order to safeguard against highway murderers, even though he permits one to change apparel and otherwise masquerade when traveling dangerous routes. There can be almost no doubt in my mind that this German pietistic attitude and the Zohar belong together.

Another relevant example comes to mind, reading the zoharic instruction (*Bamidbar*, *Naso*, p. 294) that every priest who does not love his congregation or is not loved by them is not permitted to lift his hands for the priestly benediction because of the great danger involved in it, for him and for them, the benediction turning into an ill-fated malediction. Now, there is no known rabbinical source for this unique opinion, but one is easily reminded of the words of R. Judah he-Hasid, quoted by his pupil R. Isaac Or Zaru'a (responsum 114, Part 1, p. 21), that a cantor must be on friendly terms with each and every individual of his community. If he hates one of his congregation, he cannot act for him and sometimes could even constitute a danger to him.

12 E. Horowitz, "On the Significance of the Beard in Jewish Communities in the East and Europe in the Middle Ages and Early Modern Times," *Pe'amim* 59 (1994), pp. 124–148. See also E. Zimmer, *Society and Its Customs* (Jerusalem 1996), pp. 17–71 (Heb.).

13 *"Ki ha-Kadosh Barukh Hu dome le-zaken yafe yehudi ve-talmid hakham"*—see *Arugat Ha-Bosem*, 4, p. 77.

CHAPTER 13

THE "OPEN" BOOK IN MEDIEVAL HEBREW LITERATURE

THE PROBLEM OF AUTHORIZED EDITIONS

The medieval Hebrew book, as refracted through the prism of the many diverse manuscripts now available for our inspection, often seems perplexingly left *in mediis rebus* and intrinsically incomplete, with the author confusingly hesitant, undecided, sometimes even self-contradictory, with regard to central issues in his work. As is well understood now, many of these textual difficulties arise from the objective, technical limitations of the medieval handwritten book and its trade. They do not originate with the author, and are mostly extraneous and incidental. Although we are by no means in a position to provide a comprehensive list of the obstacles and hindrances encountered in the writing and dissemination of medieval handwritten books, we shall mention in passing a few simple examples of these phenomena. However, we shall concentrate our attention more on subjective factors and on deeper, internal problems involved in authoring a medieval Hebrew book. These problems, although strongly connected to the realities of the medieval book trade, nevertheless originated with the author himself and were entirely independent of later external events.

A long and intensive review of the medieval Hebrew book indicates that quite often books were not meant by their authors to serve as final statements, but rather as presentations of an interim state of knowledge or opinion, somewhat like our computerized databases, which are constantly updated and which give the user a summary of the data known at the time of the latest updating. In a similar way, the medieval book was sometimes conceived of as no more than a solid basis for possible future alterations by the author himself. There were many reasons—some philosophical and psychological, others purely technical—for this profound phenomenon, which can give rise to serious problems as to finality, authorship, and authority of a given text of a work.

There was, of course, constant concern over simple errors of copying, which were frequent and widespread because scribes, especially in medieval Jewish Europe, were usually recruited from the lower, less educated echelons of society. Scribal errata vary from one manuscript to another, occur in the most unexpected—and unsuspected—places, tend to proliferate, and there is no known way of totally avoiding them. When the exact original wording, sometimes even spelling, was of great importance to the author, a single master codex (or sometimes two) was carefully made and deposited at a central locale, to which all future copies could be referred for verification. Classical examples of this strategy are the Aleppo Bible codex, Maimonides' *Mishneh Torah*, whose *Mustercodex* (if not actually its master codex) was kept by Maimonides himself and by his descendants for many generations, and R. Meir Abulafia's *Masoret Seyag la-Torah*, on the biblical *Masorah*, whose mastercopy, plus two *Mustercodices* of actual Torah scrolls written in accordance with it, were placed in Burgos.[1] But the problem of miscopying is wholly external and outside the author's responsibility and need not trouble us here.

Another problem that will not be dealt with here is the problem of the book that appears *prima facie* to be "open" but was not meant originally to be so: it has actually been "opened up" by its readers, not by the author himself. The books of *She'iltot* by R. Aha of Shabha and the *Halakhot Gedolot* of R. Simeon Kayara are excellent examples of this phenomenon, being prone, by their very nature, to the assimilation of additional halakhic material of a similar kind and to an ongoing process of editing.[2] The *Seder Rav Amram Gaon*, the classical Jewish prayer book, was so reworked and even rewritten in the Middle Ages in accordance with the different local rites and customs, that it is almost impossible for us to discover its original wording today. This type of textual variation is completely independent of the author and is, therefore, outside the scope of our present interest.

Publication of original books in the Middle Ages, as in earlier periods, was achieved by releasing the manuscript to be copied by a professional copyist or by a private individual for his own use. Further changes, corrections, and additions, not to mention point-blank retractions were, in most cases, out of the question, as the author had no effective way of contacting his audience and informing them of the changes. The decision that a book was, indeed, ripe for publication was, therefore, of paramount importance; it was, perhaps, the most important decision the author had to make. On the other hand, one must remember that in most places, and certainly in the Franco-German sphere, the Jewish communities were rather small, mainly sedentary, and very decentralized. Distribution of further copies of a work was not the author's duty nor had he the means to undertake it. The book was disseminated by the readers themselves, who had an interest in acquiring a copy and who actually paid the high

[1] See I. Ta-Shma, "Rabbi Meir ha-Levi ve-Yetsirato ha-Sifrutit," *Kiryat Sefer* 45 (1970), pp. 119–126.

[2] See R. Brody, *The Textual History of the She'iltot* (Heb.) (New York and Jerusalem 1991); N. Danzig, "Teshuvot ha-Ge'onim be-Keta min ha-Genizah ve-Yakhasan le-*Halakhot Gedolot*," *Proceedings of the American Academy for Jewish Research* 54 (1988), pp. 13–57 (Hebrew section).

prices for the parchment and the reproduction. From the psychological point of view, the author generally had in mind a small and quite restricted community of potential readers with whom he could hope to keep in contact with relative ease for as long as he lived. One should also keep in mind that in the Middle Ages a book, every book, within its frame of reference, was meant to serve a practical purpose as an essential aid to the student and the author was always under a moral obligation to improve and update his work as best he could.

Let us take as an example the commentary of Rashi to the Pentateuch. Over one hundred complete manuscripts of this work exist today and many more are extant in fragmentary form. It is astonishing to see how diverse all these texts are. They differ, for the most part, in richness of style and verbosity, while remaining faithful to the actual exegetical content and context. But comparison of the manuscripts shows also that they have many additional and/or missing paragraphs. Prof. Elazar Touitou recently proposed the revolutionary thesis that whatever is not found in all Rashi manuscripts should be considered unoriginal and a later addition.[3] He argued that no one would dare omit anything from the original, though some scribes would have been ready to make additions (presumably with a graphic note or sign, which could have fallen out with time). This thesis was refuted by Prof. Avraham Grossman, who proved that many original paragraphs whose authenticity is testified to by R. Shemaya, Rashi's devoted pupil, in his handwritten copy of Rashi's commentary (ms. Leipzig 1) and in his own commentary are missing in many manuscripts.[4] Indeed, Touitou's position was untenable even without Grossman's manuscript proof, because the many purely stylistic variants mentioned above make the possibility of scribal intervention implausible and point clearly to Rashi himself as their author. Contrary to common opinion, Rashi did not aim his commentary at simple folk, who would probably not have been able even to understand his Hebrew, but to a limited elite group of French and German scholars for whom he produced a constantly improved version of his commentary, done either by himself or by intimate pupils such as R. Shemaya, R. Simha, and the great Rashbam, who studied "before him" and acted upon his orders and wishes, very much like literary secretaries of modern times.

Another possibility must be taken into account here; namely, that Rashi read out his commentary to students of his inner circle and they "copied" or, rather, "recorded" his words in their copybooks, with slight stylistic variations caused by individual differences of inner mental listening. Substantial evidence

[3] E. Touitou, "Concerning the Presumed Original Version of Rashi's Commentary on the Pentateuch" (Heb.), *Tarbiz* 56 (1987), pp. 211–242.

[4] A. Grossman, "Marginal Notes and Addenda of R. Shemaya and the Text of Rashi's Biblical Commentary" (Heb.), *Tarbiz* 60 (1990), pp. 67–98. See now Touitou's reply, "Does Ms. Leipzig 1 Really Reflect an Authentic Version of Rashi's Commentary on the Pentateuch?" (Heb.), *Tarbiz* 61 (1991), pp. 61–84.

for a scriptorium origin of our medieval Hebrew literature does not exist, but personal copy-books of the type described here might well have been in use in eleventh to twelfth-century Franco-German communities. I must add here that recently I have found proof that Rashi wrote an earlier version of his commentary to the Pentateuch and that the current version, with all its variants, is a shortened version of the original, much longer, commentary, which was heavily abridged by the author himself.

Rashi was not the inventor of this type of open book. His great German teachers R. Isaac b. R. Judah and R. Isaac ha-Levi, and their teachers, the great German rabbis of the first half of the eleventh century, heads of the Mayence yeshiva (starting with the famous Rabbenu Gershom Me'or ha-Golah), did very much the same, as can easily be seen from the well-known *Perush Rabbenu Gershom Me'or ha-Golah* on a number of talmudic tractates. This commentary, the first of its kind to be written in Europe, originally covered most of the Talmud, but it was soon surpassed and superseded by the classic talmudic commentary of Rashi, and fell into total disuse, with the exception of a few tractates that were not dealt with by Rashi. This work carries the name of Rabbenu Gershom Me'or ha-Golah though he did not actually write it, because he conceived and initiated it in his role as the founder and first principal of the yeshiva in Mayence. During almost a century of activity, the academy in Mayence labored through the Talmud many times over, its heads supervising the ongoing process of rewriting and re-editing the "official" commentary; adding to and subtracting substantively from it from generation to generation, as can be deduced from the differences between the few manuscripts still in existence.[5] I cannot discuss here in depth the many aspects of this type of open book, but I must add that this work is not the only example of its kind. The same sages who endeavored to create this Talmud commentary took pains to do the same for the Midrash, for the ancient *piyyutim* and probably also for all other literary works that were studied at the time as part of the official curriculum of the academy. Eleventh-century German commentaries on the *piyyutim* and on some *midrashim* are still extant in manuscript and they reflect the same literary phenomenon.

This type of open book was common to both Franco-Germany and to Spain, Moslem, and Christian alike, as we shall soon see. But the Franco-German scholars brought the technique to the peak of its development, by applying the principle with equal energy to other classical and semi-classical books that they had not themselves authored, including the authoritative Talmud itself, which was actually "opened" by them. Correcting versions of the Talmud in response to various kinds of logical and philological considerations was widespread in France and Germany, and the same approach was applied with

[5] I. Ta-Shma, "Rabbenu Gershom Me'or ha-Golah's Commentary on the Talmud" (Heb.), *Kiryat Sefer* 53 (1978), pp. 356–367.

no less ease to all other books of lesser standing, accepted there as worthy of study.[6] And if this attitude was tolerated with regard to other people's books, how much more was it considered necessary with regard to one's own original compositions.

Two main types of revision were current in medieval Hebrew literature: one arising from personal, internal progress and development, the other from external coercion. The first type is found mostly in early works, which were rethought by their authors at a more advanced stage of their lives. Changes of this type affected, in most cases, specific sentences or paragraphs of the original, leaving the main body of text intact. A classic example would be Maimonides' *Commentary on the Mishnah*, finished and made public when he was only of thirty and emended regularly throughout the rest of his life—three more-or-less distinct versions were actually published and are still in existence.[7] In these revisions Maimonides was probably able to achieve control of the text in his immediate vicinity, but not farther afield. When the reliability of the text seemed especially important to him, as in his *Mishneh Torah*—which, as a major code of law, could hardly tolerate inaccuracies—Maimonides went to the trouble of marking his personal endorsement on the parchment or authorizing a member of his household to check the manuscript and mark his endorsement. A somewhat different example is the *Halakhot Rabbati* by R. Isaac Alfasi.[8] This classic was composed in North Africa during the second third of the eleventh century and disseminated by releasing copies of it to a select group of disciples who served as rabbis in the cities of North Africa and Muslim Spain. Alfasi kept revising his opinions for the remaining forty years of his life, but by updating this inner group of disciples who had received the original copies, he could be sure that his corrections would be inserted in most of the existing copies, each disciple keeping track by himself of all further copies that he commissioned. Needless to say, the technique was probably effective only as long as R. Alfasi was alive and active; but as time passed by, the proliferation and diffusion of copies got out of control and numerous variants appeared in the academies, many of which are still extant.

Other examples belonging to this category are the large collections of novellae to the Talmud written by the Spanish rabbis Solomon b. Aderet

[6] I. Ta-Shma, "The Library of the Ashkenazi Sages in the Eleventh to Twelfth Centuries" (Heb.), *Kiryat Sefer* 60 (1985), pp. 298–309 and id., "Addenda" (Heb.), *Kiryat Sefer* 61 (1986), pp. 581–582. See also Ta-Shma, "The Library of the French Sages," in *Rashi 1040–1990. Hommage a Ephraim E. Urbach. Congres Europeen des Études Juives*, ed. G. Sed-Rajna (Paris: Cerf, 1993), pp. 535–540.

[7] S. Liebermann, *The Laws of the Palestinian Talmud* (Heb.) (New York: Jewish Theological Seminary of America, 1947), pp. 6–15; Rabbi J. Kafih, *Introduction to His Hebrew Translation of Maimonides' Mishnah Commentary* (Jerusalem 1963).

[8] I. Ta-Shma, "Jewish Judiciary and Law in the Eleventh and Twelfth Centuries in Spain" (Heb.), *Shenaton ha-Mishpat ha-Ivri* 1 (1974), pp. 353–372.

(Rashba) and Yomtov Ashbili (Ritba) toward the end of the thirteenth century. These two great scholars stood at the head of two large *yeshivot* and wrote down their novellae year in and year out, as they taught the various tractates in an annual cycle. When the academy studied the same tractate again, these authorities added to, or sometimes retracted from, their earlier novellae. In this case the new "edition" was not really meant to replace the old one, but rather to improve it and to serve side by side with it. Today we find many examples of such "parallel" novellae in the surviving manuscripts.

Changes could also be caused by criticism, as when a literary opponent claimed that a work was, to a greater or lesser degree, in error. Such criticism, once it was made public by copying, provoked a literary response in which the author either admitted the correction, rejected it, polemicized against his opponent, or apologized for a misunderstanding or a scribal error. Errata could, of course, be discovered by the author himself, who would certainly wish to clear them up as soon as possible. In both cases, whether as the result of external criticism or his own decision, the author would take steps to improve his original work, either by rewriting and releasing it to the public as a new edition, or by writing a short summary of the main points requiring discussion or correction. Both techniques have their limitations: the first is very lengthy, slow and costly, the second is cryptic and puzzling to most readers.

An unusual and noteworthy method of revision was used by the Provencal rabbi Abraham b. David, the famous Rabad of Posquieres. This great man was engaged in a life-long altercation with his colleague R. Zerahya of Lunel, each criticizing the other's work throughout their long lives. Rabad of Posquieres, who was prone by nature to constant revision of his earlier opinions, adopted a singular method of emending and re-editing his books to take account of his own changes of opinion and/or his acceptance of outside criticism. He formulated alternative sentences, sometimes extending to full paragraphs, to be inserted by the reader (or by the professional copyist) in place of the retracted sentence (or paragraph). The new sentences had the same opening and closing words as the original, and were carefully formulated so as to thread easily and naturally into the original text. By exchanging the new material for the old, the owner of a manuscript could easily and cheaply upgrade his book. This may seem to us to be the most practical solution to the problem, but, in fact, it was not very much in vogue because it created an embarrassing problem, as evidenced by Rabad himself. Rabad's new text, which read so fluently as a natural replacement of the original, entirely hid the fact that it had come about as a response to R. Zerahya's criticism (whose name was mentioned nowhere in the replacement paragraph). By accepting R. Zerahya's criticism and correcting his original text accordingly, Rabad made R. Zerahya's critical treatise look absurd to anyone having before his eyes only the revised "original," and not knowing that it was really not "original" at all. R. Zerahya penned some very sharp comments on this practice when he found out what had happened. As is well known, Rabad rewrote some of his books as many as three times, changing his halakhic views time and again and concealing behind the revisions many covert and tacit answers to open criticisms aimed at him by colleagues and opponents.

Rabbi Zerahya himself stood at the opposite end of the spectrum of revision. His major work, a critique of the halakhic code of R. Isaac Alfasi, was in process of being written for almost fifty years, kept in the meantime in its author's desk, in semi-privacy, before it was allowed to be copied and made public. This large and most extensive *magnum opus* is entirely homogeneous, with almost no internal contradictions and hardly any changes of mind. We know that R. Zerahya did show his book to an inner circle of pupils and intimate friends with whom he held discussions and who quote him here and there in their own books, which appeared long before R. Zerahya's work was published. These were mostly oral quotations that can easily be located in the subsequently published volumes. Zerahya himself quotes, again orally, the views of the members of this group and these quotations can now, in certain instances, be located in their books, some of which were made available to the world at large only after R. Zerahya's death.[9]

The second major type of rewriting current in medieval manuscripts was externally coerced. Sometimes a book was so much in demand that the author was persuaded to let it out of his hands prematurely, pending the publication of the full, mature text at some time in the future. This happened, for example, to R. Yeruham b. Meshulam of Provence, who wrote his well-known book *Meisharim* on monetary laws in Spain, ca. 1340. In his introduction he tells us that the book, which greatly facilitated the work of the judges and was the first of its kind available, was in such demand that it was literally snatched out of his hands and he, therefore, apologizes to readers who may find later, to their surprise, that other, much improved versions are extant.

Another interesting example of this phenomenon is found in some of Avraham Ibn Ezra's commentaries to certain books of the Bible and in many of his *opuscula minora*, which were re-written time and time again, with interesting variations, because the author was a wandering scholar and constantly on the move. Wherever he visited, he was asked for one or more of his books. Sometimes he left behind his one and only copy or, because he wanted to conceal or censor his own views, he wrote a special version for the occasion.

[9] These antithetical behaviors and their historical implications are explained at some length in my book *Rabbinic Literature in Twelfth-Century Provence* (Jerusalem: Mosad Ha-Rav Kook, 1993), pp. 129–135 (Heb.).

Originally published in
Bulletin of the John Rylands University Library of Manchester, 75, no.3 (1993).

CHAPTER 14

THE STUDY OF AGGADAH AND ITS INTERPRETATION IN EARLY RABBINIC LITERATURE

The study of the aggadic sections of the Talmud, through the Middle Ages and up to the beginning of our modern period, has its own history, completely separate and different from the parallel history of the study of talmudic halakhah. The history of talmudic commentary describes a linear, uninterrupted process, progressing rapidly from elementary glossaries to the most sophisticated levels of erudition and intellectual achievement, as outlined in my work on the history of talmudic commentary.[1] The aggadic sections of the Talmud were handled in a totally different manner and the history of this area does not conform in any way to the general rules governing the rest of the Talmud.

Needless to say, such special attention to the many scattered aggadic sections in the Talmud, viewing them all in their totality as a separate literary entity requiring its own specialized methodological approach, is obviously unique to our modern period. Medieval scholars—in whom we are interested here—did not see it that way. The general medieval approach to history, ancient and contemporary, and to the study of sacred literature—the authoritative carrier of historical information—was very fragmented in nature, treating individual events as separate units, unrelated to and entirely independent of previous ones. The comprehension of history as a rationally explicable continuum, a cause-and-effect series of events, interpreting the individual event in the light of the larger historical setting, was completely unknown, much as there was no apprehension of a unified and fully integrated personality:

> Medieval science denied coherence in human character and behavior, envisioning man simply as a collection of attributes, with more or less independent status. This perceptual mode made it impossible for chroniclers to view character in its totality, and thus to establish any workable approach to the problem of individual personality.

[1] I. Ta-Shma, *Talmudic Commentary in Europe and North Africa: 1000–1400* (Jerusalem: Magnes Press I–II, 1999–2000).

This sentence is quoted from Mrs. Gabrielle Spiegel's article.[2] I also refer the reader to Willie Brandt's outstanding book on the parallel mode of interpreting individual events in complete isolation from their relevant historical context.[3] A similarly fragmented approach to the aggadic material of the Talmud impeded its development as compared to the rapid and most impressive progress of parallel work on halakhic commentary. Unfolding part of this slow and hesitant process is the main interest of the present chapter. I shall narrow my study to Talmud commentators alone, in whose work the subject should find its clearest expression, although there are other intellectual groups whose work should be considered in this context, such as preachers, Bible commentators, and ethical writers.

We shall consider the post-Geonic Era only. The Geonim did not create a systematic, self-initiated Talmud commentary, and whatever they had to say—and they certainly had quite a lot to say—was always in reply to a specific query. In any case, geonic material pertaining to aggadah is quite rare, and even anti-Karaite material, which was much in demand, dealt mainly with halakhic subjects. When asked to clarify actual aggadic material, they answered very briefly, frequently adding a short note to the effect that since the query touched on *divrei aggadah*, it was not worthwhile to waste one's time on it. We shall, nevertheless, encounter geonic material in its secondary use by the early North African commentators Rabbenu Hananel and Rabbenu Nissim.

There was always a big difference, in many major respects, between North African and Central European Talmud commentaries, from their early beginnings. Rabbenu Hananel, Rabbenu Nissim, and Rabbenu Gershom Me'or ha-Golah (all three of them flourished in the first half of the eleventh century) were the first to write a premeditated, clear, standard, and full-scale commentary to the three normally studied *sedarim*, *ad usum studentorum*, striving to forestall potential obstacles, to make things easier and clear the way for future students. Although there were great structural and methodological disparities between them, all three took a revolutionary step forward in the long history of *talmud Torah* independently of each other, each following a completely different course, technique, and method and achieving different cultural results. The subject is treated in great detail in the first volume of my aforesaid book, but aggadah was not considered in that volume, and I wish to develop it here.

R. Nissim Gaon (d. 1065) wrote three separate works in which he commented upon the Talmud:

1. *Sefer Mafte'akh Man'ulei ha-Talmud*, translated at a very early date from the original Arabic into Hebrew, and printed in the Rom edition of the Talmud (Vilna 1880) to tractates *Berakhot*, *Shabbat*, and *Eruvin*.

[2] G.M. Spiegel, "Political Utility in Medieval Historiography: A Sketch," *History and Theory* 14 (1975), pp. 314–325.

[3] Willie Brandt, *The Shape of Medieval History: Modes of Perception* (New Haven 1966).

The book records the location of many references to Tannaitic and Amoraic material quoted in the Talmud without such indication. R. Nissim says that this is a big stumbling block, hindering the understanding of the original and central context of the cited sayings, thus preventing the smooth study of the *sugya*.

2. The second book is a current running commentary to some tractates of the Talmud, known to us only through a few remaining fragments in the Geniza. This commentary rendered a direct and full-fledged paraphrase of the *sugya* in the author's words, enlarging upon it according to what he felt was required.
3. The third book, *Megilat Setarim*, is a collection of a few hundred paragraphs devoted to different talmudic subjects, dealing with a variety of topics in halakhah, aggadah, theology, midrash, and folkloric matter.

Rabbenu Hananel, for his part, wrote a single, comprehensive, running commentary to the three *sedarim*, well known to all, although never printed before its first publication in the Rom Talmud, 1880. It was also extant before that throughout a multitude of secondary medieval literature. Rabbenu Hananel's commentary raises many problems and there are major variations between its medieval Italian manuscript tradition, preserved in the printed version, and the somewhat different tradition reaching us from the Mediterranean Geniza. However, basically they all represent the same book, which can be defined as a partial paraphrase to the Talmud, skipping over much of the talmudic text that Rabbenu Hananel considered was "easy to understand" or "self-understood" and, therefore, needed no further elaboration. As is well known, Rabbenu Hananel quotes regularly and freely from the *Talmud Yerushalmi* in order to complement the Babylonian *sugya*; he also draws heavily on Rabbenu Hai Gaon.

Now, both authors, Hananel and Nissim, do refer to some of the aggadic material along the way. However, if we try to determine which part of the aggadic material draws their attention and calls for their added commentary, we easily discover that they confront themes that were in vogue in current Jewish-Moslem polemics and/or in the Rabbanite-Karaite literary war. All other aggadic material, irrelevant to these polemics, was not commented upon by them, but just mechanically quoted or simply skipped over. As it is clear that the "polemic" material forms just a small fraction of the total talmudic aggadah, and even that small quantity is commented upon along strictly religio-philosophical technical lines—never demonstrating any psychological, aesthetic, or literary insights—one can fairly conclude that eleventh-century North African commentators were practically uninterested in improving the student's understanding of aggadic material as such.

This does not mean, of course, that people, in general, were not interested in aggadah. We know that other types of Jewish scholars, such as poets, Bible commentators, preachers, and ethical writers were certainly interested in aggadic material, as is clear from R. Samuel Hanagid's ethical writings, and Rabbenu Bakhye's *Chovot ha-Levavot*, which made remarkably advanced use of such talmudic material. All it means is that students of the *beit ha-midrash*, studying for professional matriculation as future rabbis, *dayyanim*, and heads of *yeshivot*, did not see the aggadic sections of the Talmud as part of their academic provisio. Unless it had some relevance for the socially important polemics with their Moslem or Karaite neighbors, they would probably never be required by their future audiences to answer in-depth questions about normal, neutral, talmudic aggadah. While such a conclusion is undoubtedly correct, one must admit that the aggadic sections in Hananel and Nissim, limited as they are in scope and space, do lend a certain air of open-mindedness, a slight touch of literary and aesthetic interest, and an overall contemplative mood to their otherwise rather dry, technical, and unsophisticated halakhic commentary.

Let us now consider some examples from Hananel and Nissim. According to a well-known *sugya* in *Berakhot*, R. Yishmael the High Priest ascended to the heavens, where he saw the Almighty sitting on his throne, crowned with his phylacteries. God asked R. Yishmael to bless him and, indeed, R. Yishmael did as he was asked. Such talk cannot be ignored by any normal commentator as it literally cries out to high heaven. Surely enough, Hananel hastens to assure us that it should not be taken literally. No man in his right senses, says Rabbenu Hananel, would ascribe corporeality of any kind to God, in direct contradiction to clear-cut, biblical dogma. The scene, to be sure, was visionary. It never happened in reality and R. Yishmael must have undergone a spiritual experience in his mind, his heart, or his imagination; alternatively, it may have happened in a dream. What he actually "saw"—if one is to use this unfitting word—was the *Demut ha-Kavod*, and I shall not elaborate here on the nature of that semi-spiritual, created being. We know now that all this was taken from R. Hai Gaon, as in many other cases in Hananel's commentary, but that does not detract from its import as part of Hananel's work, through which it became widespread among later generations.

A few pages later in *Berakhot*, the Talmud presents a vivid description of God as wailing in tears and crying out in anger for having set fire to his temple. In the same vein, Hananel is again quick to reject the strong anthropomorphic thrust of the episode, by adding the magic word כביכול to the text and proposing, as an alternative, that this too happened in a dream or was otherwise a virtual reality. All in all, there are more than a dozen instances of similar exegesis throughout Hananel's commentary.

Rabbenu Nissim was sensitive to these polemical topics in the Talmud and to many other, less obvious ones. For example, his analysis of the *sugya* of "עשה דוחה לא תעשה" a complicated *sugya* in *Yevamot*, which seems to have triggered an ancient Moslem, anti-Jewish complaint over the obscure theological issue of whether God can change his mind and retract upon his formerly expressed views and commandments. If he could do that, then his Torah could not be considered eternal, being subject to possible changes at any time in the future. If a positive commandment can overrule a previous, independent, negative commandment—so the argument ran—then the way should be open for many other heretical ideas. Rabbenu Nissim, therefore, explains that that is not the case. A positive commandment does not cancel a contradictory negative commandment. The positive commandment is valid on condition that there be no negative commandment to contradict it; otherwise it does not apply.

Let us now consider the problem before us. Many, if not the lion's part of, aggadic passages in the Talmud are bizarre and seem to be far removed from normal human experience, exhibiting extreme human behavior; describing fantastic situations; reporting unbelievable dialogues and strange religious disputations with Gentiles; transmitting imaginary folklore and magic lore; using extreme anthropomorphic terms; or setting dubious moral standards. There is no need to mention specific examples and some will emerge later on. How is it possible, then, that while the study of the halakhah was constantly improved and intensely developed, generation after generation, from the early eleventh century until the end of the fourteenth century and later, the aggadah was left almost untouched, its commentary progressing very slowly, until the fourteenth century. Even then no real breakthrough was achieved until the sixteenth century. One obvious reason is, of course, that the aggadah is intrinsically "unimportant," as it has no practical consequences in real life. This would be true as regards North Africa and Spain, but it would not apply to Franco-German Jewry, because they did attach halakhic significance to purely aggadic passages—as was adequately demonstrated in Avraham Grossman's article[4] and further argued in my article on the subject.[5]

But, indeed, to describe the extent of aggadic commentary in eleventh to twelfth-century Franco- Germany, that is, by *Perushei Magentza* (Rashi, Rashbam, Rabbenu Tam, and R. Isaac of Dampierre) I would use one single word: nothing. They exhibited not even a minimal interest in polemical topics that attracted the attention of their North African colleagues. Let's take Rashi for example. Rashi never ignores or skips over an aggadic passage. He will always be there to translate or explain difficult words or phrases, to answer obvious technical difficulties, and to clarify an obscure text, but he never seems to be taken aback—or at least surprised—by whatever he may read in the *aggadeta*. He adheres strictly to the plain, verbal meaning of the text and follows the ancient glossatory technique of adding short sublinear clarifications to the

[4] A. Grossman, "The Roots of *Kiddush Hashem* in Early Germany," in *Sanctity of Life and Martyrdom*, eds. Y. Gafni and A. Ravitsky [in memory of Amir Yekuti'el] (Jerusalem 1993), pp. 99–130 (Heb.).

[5] I. Ta-Shma, "Suicide and Homicide: On *Kiddush Hashem*" in *Jews against the Cross*, eds. Yom-Tov Assis et al. (Jerusalem 2000), pp. 150–157.

text—a technique totally abandoned by Rashi himself when dealing with normative halakhic material—in an entirely unsophisticated or, perhaps one should rather say, naive manner. For a simple example: *Berakhot* 51: "R. Yishma'el said: Suri'el the Prince of the Inner Court told me three things..." and Rashi comments: "R. Yishma'el ascended the high heaven using a holy name [as is written] in *Beraita de-Ma'ase Merkava*." And in *Sanhedrin* 65, on the famous story about R. Hanina and R. Oshaya who studied *Sefer Yetzira* every Friday and thereby created a living calf, Rashi comments: "And it is not an act of magic, but the act of God, by the use of His Holy Name." The stories themselves do not seem to call for an extra commentary. The only question that would weigh on the student is technical: How could these individuals perform such a celestial journey? The answer is plain and simple: by using a holy name, as we read in *Baraita de-Ma'ase Merkava*. It is interesting to note that Rabbenu Hananel, as quoted in *Yikhussei Tana'im ve-Amora'im*, says that R. Yishmael could speak with angels by using a holy name, but not that he could or actually did ascend to heaven by using a name.

I want to make myself clear. There is no real difference between the early North African commentators and the early Franco-German ones. They all ignore aggadic passages: Hananel and Nissim by simply skipping over them—thus giving the impression that such passages were probably passed over and ignored in the *beit ha-midrash* itself—and Rashi by commenting upon philological, verbal, and technical difficulties alone, as though there were no other much more important difficulties to solve. It is true, though, that the North African commentators do treat aggadic passages that are relevant to the current inter-religious polemics of their times, mainly striving to ward off their apparent anthropomorphic implications, whereas Rashi and his predecessors do not oppose anthropomorphic trends of thought and tend to accept such talmudic examples at their face value. As I have shown in a separate article,[6] R. Isaiah di Trani clearly testified that the Franco-German sages believed in an anthropomorphic Godhead, because they considered themselves totally bound to the literal meaning of the Bible, accepting other, more advanced interpretations as an added value, but not as invalidating the plain and primary reading. And as the Gentile environment, too, obviously did not find anything wrong with anthropomorphism—their god Jesus professing to have performed a full personal anthropomorphic course—there was no need for eleventh to twelfth-century Franco-German commentators to apologize in any way for such talk encountered in the Talmud.

I would like to digress and use the opportunity to clarify a relevant side issue. Contrary to current scholarship, which considers the Franco-German anthropomorphic attitude as being in total polar opposition to the Maimonidean conception of an abstract and formless Deity, the truth is quite different.

6 di Trani, *Kiryat Sefer* 64 (1992), pp. 751–753 (Heb.).

Ashkenazi anthropomorphism is only one of many options, an option testified by the Bible to be real at times and at will. So is the abstract phase one of the many options open to God of his free will. The idea is that God is at complete freedom to appear in any form agreeable to him—including an abstract formless form—and no philosophical principle can limit his free will. Thus, an extremely abstract Maimonidean description of God could be as acceptable to Rashi as an anthropomorphic one. I shall leave that as it is, and return to my main theme.

The main point I wish to stress is that as long as you profess confidence in a plain literal meaning of your traditional and authoritative literature, you cannot really progress toward an improved, more profound understanding of your texts. This is true independently of the question as to the original meaning of the texts. The original meaning could have been anything or everything; but once cardinal value has been attached to the plain meaning, no alternative understanding can possibly take its place, even though the validity of such alternative understandings in a parallel mode to the basic, literal, unshakable *peshat* meaning will be acknowledged. This tendency was most characteristic for the eleventh to thirteenth centuries, as is clear to anyone who has read Kieckhefer's study of medieval magic and witchcraft, according to which the first signs of a change became recognizable only toward the end of the thirteenth century.[7] The profound belief in magic, astrology, divinations, ghosts, evil spirits, etc. in the Middle Ages stemmed from a basic belief in the plain literal meaning of ancient authoritative texts, and not the other way round. This is true both for Gentile Europe and for medieval Jewish culture. Scholars are in the habit of emphasizing the outstanding quasi-modern inclination of Jewish medieval Bible commentators in eleventh to twelfth-century France, such as R. Joseph Kara, Rashi, and Rashbam, toward *peshat*, even extreme and sometimes critical *peshat*, as if it were an indication of an enlightened approach to the texts compared to the classical midrashic approach. But in reality there was nothing outstanding about it: it was a dominant contemporary attitude toward ancient traditional and authoritative texts. It contributed little to the development of Bible commentary in general, although it improved the understanding of individual phrases and verses. The shortcomings of such an attitude are apparent in the parallel, exegetical work performed by the same great luminaries on the aggadic sections of the Talmud. Under Islamic domination, eleventh-century North African Talmud commentators were forced to alienate themselves from the literal *peshat* reading of certain problematical passages, thereby opening the way for a more refined, more theologically sublime, reading of the text, although that reading need not have been the historically correct one. In Christian Europe, even that minimal pressure did not exist. As a

7 R. Kieckhefer, *Magic in the Middle Ages* (Cambridge University Press, 1989).

result, Spanish Talmud commentators were the first to move forward in interpreting the aggadah, toward the end of the thirteenth century.

An important step forward was taken by Rashba, R. Solomon b. Aderet, the famous Barcelona rabbi (d. 1310), and a disciple of Nahmanides, R. Moses b. Nahman. Rashba composed a special book on talmudic aggadah, one of the best commentaries ever and completely separate from his classic commentary to the Talmud. The book on the aggadah is, strictly speaking, not the first of its type, since earlier Geronese kabbalists, R. Ezra and R. Azri'el, did write a similar work. But R. Ezra's work is actually not a commentary at all and R. Azri'el's work was addressed to a very small and restricted circle of fellow kabbalists, as explained by Prof. Tishby in his excellent introduction to his edition of their work. Therefore, Rashba's work on the aggadah should be regarded as the first of its genre. The book has reached us in fragmentary form, scarcely 150 pages for the whole Talmud.[8] Rashba did not write a systematic book but a haphazard collection of *ad hoc* commentaries that he decided at some point to put together and publish as a book. There is still quite a lot of unpublished material in manuscript unnoticed by scholars, mainly in fifteenth-century, pre-exile, Spanish and Egyptian semi-halakhic manuscripts. These manuscripts testify to a second re-awakening of interest in talmudic aggadah, not incidentally in a Spanish environment again, some one hundred fifty years after the Rashba.

As is well known, the Rashba wrote many responsa on biblical and talmudical stories and aggadic passages, and there is no doubt that the subject aroused a lively public interest at the time. The Rashba admits that biblical story-telling and talmudic aggadic passages have an inner covert meaning that sometimes actually takes priority over the plain, literal meaning; that plain, literal meaning serves only as a cover or defense against unskilled and improper treatment. Here again, as in Rabbenu Hananel and Rabbenu Nissim some two hundred fifty years before, inter-religious tension played an important role, and the newly emergent kabbalah was a primary factor in the background—actually, in the forefront—of the novel literary phenomenon. The real immediate incentives were quite different: the undermining of absolute confidence in the plain, literal *peshat* meaning of the biblical texts; the adoption of rational, more natural, attitudes toward faith, characteristic of the thirteenth century; and the application of neo-classical, allegoristic, exegetical tools that enabled one to adhere to the holy texts while at the same time denying their plain, far from credible, literal meaning. The great controversy over allegory and its relationship to Maimonidean philosophy and Bible exegesis was at its peak toward the end of Rashba's life; he himself became one of its central protagonists and his aggadah commentary was an integral part of the issue.

Rashba was the first talmudic commentator whose concentrated efforts on talmudic aggadah reached us to a great measure, but he was not the first on the

[8] A. Feldman, ed., *Perushei ha-Aggadot la-Rashba* (Jerusalem 1991).

historical arena. An obscure rabbinic figure, R. Isaac b. Yedaya, was actually the first to dedicate a tremendous effort to explicate, exclusively aggadic material included in the Talmud (and separately in the midrash), but his extraordinary large books—over one thousand pages in all—are now lost, except for some manuscript fragments, some two hundred pages, kept in some American and European libraries. The author, a Provencal rabbi, mistakenly thought by some to be Yedaya ha-Penini's son, flourished around the middle of the thirteenth century and was probably a disciple of the famous Rabbenu Meshulam of Beziers. As he was interested only in the aggadic material in the Talmud, he should be categorically differentiated from the classical genre of Talmud commentators. A "professional" Talmud commentator, dealing with the Talmud in its halakhic totality, tries to reach the "objective" *peshat* of the text lying before him, while the "interested," exclusive aggadah commentator is much more subjective in his work; he chooses his selection of texts carefully and seeks to discover an inner meaning in them that will best fit his preconceived theological and ethical creeds. R. Isaac and his books were carefully studied in great detail by M. Saperstein, and his careful work is an outstanding contribution to the study of aggadah commentary in the Middle Ages.[9]

Maimonidean philosophy and theology were clearly a primary motive power behind these new trends, but in our narrow and immediate context—that is, Maimonides' role in the achievement of a significant step forward in interpreting the aggadah—I would more specifically highlight the new horizons that he opened in the field of understanding the aggadah, which is a major Maimonidean contribution to medieval Jewish culture entirely independent of his overall and global influence on that culture.

In his *Moreh Nevukhim* Maimonides quoted, and made intensive use of, many *midrashim* and individual aggadic sayings cited in the Talmud, molding them in a clever and sophisticated way to serve his unique personal philosophical or ethical goals, and to encourage reading and interpreting them in such a manner. His readings are always interesting and insightful; many of them are original, although rarely revolutionary. Of course, Maimonides himself was quite aware of the unique and creative nature of his readings, frequently openly praising and specifically underlining their novelty, originality, and profundity. He also developed an accomplished literary theory according to which the inner meanings of many aggadic passages—the so-called "golden apples"—lie hidden beneath an artistic, semi-transparent, filigree silver cover, through which talented scholars can gain a clear glimpse of the inner truth, the hidden message, and then decode and interpret it correctly. His original approach to aggadah opened new vistas, sharpened the ancient allegorical techniques, and made them into modern and forceful exegetical tools, arousing renewed atten-

[9] M. Saperstein, *Decoding the Rabbis: A 13th-Century Commentary on the Aggada* (Cambridge: Harvard University Press, 1980).

tion and intellectual interest in talmudic aggadah. The concept gained universal popularity among medieval scholars of all sorts and types, and its literary residues are found all over medieval rabbinic literature. Maimonides had planned to write a special work on midrash and aggadah, which would have been the first of its sort ever written, but after having begun, he changed his mind, as he explains in his introduction to the *Moreh*, and it is clear that the subject of interpreting midrash and aggadah haunted him throughout his life. It would not be an exaggeration to say that his specific contribution to the study of midrash and aggadah was more profound than his general influence on Jewish religious thought.

Direct Maimonidean influence was felt mainly in thirteenth-century Spain and Provence, but in Germany and Northern France it met with strong opposition. Indirect influences were much more widespread. Many rabbis were opposed to many of his specific ideas and principles, as well as to many of his readings in halakhah and in aggadah. At the same time, however, they were captivated by his novel, exegetical attitude toward midrash and aggadah in general and they imitated his methods while following different, more personal routes. Nachmanides' commentary to the Torah is a very good example. While sharply opposing many Maimonidean explanations of biblical material, he adopted his open and creative attitude toward traditional literary material and was the first Bible commentator to apply relevant circumstantial, psychological, and literary considerations in reading about and evaluating biblical personages and their life stories. Nachmanides' disciples, mainly Rashba and R. Aharon ha-Levi, quote Maimonides' aggadic interpretations from the *Moreh Nevukhim* with deep appreciation, some of which sound quite trivial to modern ears, but aroused much interest and appreciation at the time, representing first examples of their type and being original and of an avant-garde nature. Take for an example Maimonides' original understanding of the somewhat enigmatic saying "הרהורי עבירה קשים מעברה." Maimonides explains that by impure thoughts the sinner makes improper use of his mind—which is a higher, more sanctified, part of his self—than by sinning simply through the mundane flesh. Prof. S. Abramson has written a detailed article on the most unusual career of this explanation in medieval literature, and the same could be shown to be true on many other original explanations put forth by Maimonides.[10] Another excellent example would be Maimonides' explanation of the punishment apparently imposed upon Adam and Eve, to which Prof. Pines dedicated a special article.[11] There are many other examples of the kind.

[10] See S. Abramson, "Ma'amar Chazal U-Perusho" [A Rabbinic Saying and Its Interpretation] (Heb.), *Molad* 68 (1971), pp. 421–429.

[11] S. Pines, "Truth and Falsehood versus Good and Evil: A Study in Jewish and General Philosophy in Connection with *The Guide of the Perplexed*," Part 1, Ch. 2, in I. Twersky, ed., *Studies in Maimonides* (Harvard University Press, 1990), pp. 95–157.

There is no doubt that Maimonides' *Moreh Nevukhim*, which was actually a partial fulfillment of his plan to write a commentary on the aggadah, opened the way, showing the potential and the beauty of such exegesis. Of course, Maimonides himself was following the classic Spanish tradition that did not accept the priority of the *peshat* principal over other, more sophisticated exegetical techniques, which were deemed compulsory for the interpretation of the many biblical and talmudic anthropomorphisms. His influence was felt mainly in the Spanish and Provencal environment in the thirteenth and fourteenth centuries (for which the Me'iri is one of the best representatives) and in the later fifteenth century, reawakening of the interest in aggadah, in pre-exilic Spain. Parallel developments in the Ashkenazic intellectual circles were much postponed, hardly presentable before the sixteenth century.

The first talmudic commentator who integrated systematic aggadic interpretations into his running commentary to the Talmud was R. Menahem ha-Me'iri. He treated mainly the more acceptable "light" *aggadot* for further—mainly ethical and educational—elaboration, keeping aloof from the irrational and bizarre type of *aggadot*. In such cases he does not hesitate, many times, to entirely change the meaning of the saying with such dexterity that the reader is completely unaware of what has happened.[12] With all its limitations, the fact that Ha-Me'iri integrated systematic aggadic interpretations into his running commentary to the Talmud clearly indicates that the academies became more interested in aggadic topics as an integral part of their regular Talmud studies, a typical characteristic of fourteenth-century rabbinic literature.

A great drive for aggadic commentary was achieved in the first half of the fourteenth century by the Toledan R. Isaac Abuhav, a disciple of R. Asher b. Yehiel (the famous Rosh), in his book *Menorat ha-Ma'or*. This book and its follower of the same name by R. Israel Al-Naqawa (end of the fourteenth century) are both dedicated wholly to aggadic material, presenting it in a pseudo-halakhic form, as though it dealt with normative, halakhic issues. Abuhav—who wrote halakhic works as well—emphasizes that there are two groups of Talmud students: those who spend their days in *pilpulim*—hair splitting argumentations—over theoretical halakhic issues and others who are more interested in deciding the practical halakhah. Both of them, he complains, neglect completely the study of aggadah, as though it lacked any practical—educational and ethical—projection. Although *Menorat ha-Ma'or* does not include commentarial deliberations and advanced interpretations, it is the first rabbinic book calling attention to aggadah as an important category of studies for Talmud students; a real revolution in the academy.

[12] For further details and examples, see Ta-Shma, *Talmudic Commentary*, n. 1, Part II, pp. 198–200.

CHAPTER 15

RABBI JONAH GERONDI

SPIRITUALITY AND LEADERSHIP

The second third of the thirteenth century witnessed a dramatic change in the Jewish leadership of Aragon and Catalonia. The historical process has been outlined in full detail and excellently explained—in all its social, economic, and religious aspects—by B. Septimus.[1] The revolutionary change, headed by the great rabbis Moses b. Nachman (Nachmanides) and Jonah b. Abraham Gerondi, brought about the downfall of the aristocratic, secular *nesi'im* and the rise to power of the foremost rabbis and *talmidei hakhamim* of the time. This change determined the historical image of Spanish Jewry for at least one hundred fifty years and is thus described by Septimus:

> The victory of the party...marks a major transition in the history of the Jewish community of Barcelona. The form of its government is no longer an aristocratic regime dominated by courtiers, but rather an elected government dominated by scholars and merchants. The spiritual world of the dominant group is now informed less by literary "court culture" and philosophical rationalism than by profound study of Talmud and Kabbalah.

Elsewhere in the same article Septimus hints at the "profound influence of Franco-German talmudic culture and Provencal Kabbalah that set Nachmanides and his circle on a cultural course so different from that of the *nesi'im*."[2] This crucial element has been fully elaborated in my article on Ashkenazi Hasidism in Spain.[3] I showed that R. Jonah Gerondi was, in effect, a disciple of *Hasidei Ashkenaz*, having been educated at the French, Torah center of Evreaux, which was a branch of German Pietism in France. I pointed out the literary evidence for this upbringing of R. Jonah, and the close affinity between

[1] B. Septimus, "Piety and Power in 13th Century Catalonia," in *Studies in Medieval Jewish History and Literature* I, ed. I. Twersky (Cambridge, Mass. and London 1971), pp. 197–230.

[2] Ibid., p. 213.

[3] I. Ta-Shma, "Ashkenazi Hasidism in Spain: Rabbi Jonah Gerondi – The Man and His Work" (Heb.), in *Exile and Diaspora: Studies in the History of the Jewish People*, eds. A. Mirsky et al. (Jerusalem 1988), pp. 165–194.

his ethical writings and parallel works by foremost German Pietists. It is, therefore, important to realize that practically every element of the Catalonian revolution carries a distinctive Ashkenazi character: positing greatness in Torah as a central requirement for communal leadership rather than aristocratic lineage; preference for an economic background—trade and commerce—as a better qualification for communal leadership than "court culture" and connections; subordination of all elected communal functionaries to the rule of the spiritual, talmudic leaders at their collective forum, the *beth din*; candid demonstration of a deep social sensitivity and concern for the economic welfare of the poor and the weak; honest and outspoken abhorrence of greed, avarice, and addiction to luxury; deep concern for a full and equal talmudic-rabbinic education for all; and the establishment of a varied system of *yeshivot*. All these elements and many others are typically Ashkenazi, and they are all part of the Catalan revolution and belong to R. Jonah's Franco-German intellectual background.

There is, however, one point of considerable importance that needs further elaboration. It is not clear exactly how the Maimonidean controversy was connected to this communal upheaval. The dates do coincide more or less and we do, indeed, know that the Barcelona *nesi'im* were followers of Maimonides and his philosophical teachings and that they were engaged in a bitter fight with a group of Provencal "anti-rational" sages over the Maimonidean issue. It is also quite true that R. Jonah Gerondi was a member of this Provencal group and that he apparently had to flee from Provence to Barcelona, where he could contact local friends and kinsmen who opposed the *nesi'im*. Nevertheless, it is quite doubtful whether the two issues have much to do with each other, as is Septimus' contention. It seems that although R. Jonah was at first firmly opposed to Maimonidean rationalism and philosophy, he had changed his mind by the early 1240s. He discontinued his struggle against Maimonides and advocated his halakhic positions with enthusiasm. This opinion was first expressed by R. Hillel of Verona, who tells us that after witnessing the burning of the Talmud in Paris in 1240, R. Jonah tended to see in it a punishment from heaven for inciting the Christian inquisition to burn the *Moreh Nevukhim* on the grounds of heresy. According to his story, R. Jonah whole-heartedly repented the deed and dedicated himself to an intensive study of the Maimonides for the rest of his life. He also planned to go to *Eretz Israel* to ask forgiveness on Maimonides' tomb, but he was delayed in Toledo, where he met with a violent death of an unspecified nature. As is well known, the story met with much disbelief among scholars of medieval Jewish history, led by I. Baer, who penned a detailed critique of it and the skepticism has continued to this day among most scholars, including Septimus himself.[4]

[4] I. Baer, *A History of the Jews in Christian Spain* (Tel Aviv 1959), p. 485, n. 60, (Heb.).

In my article on R. Jonah, I argued for the plausibility of this story and brought interesting proof to show that R. Jonah did, indeed, dramatically change his attitude toward the study of Maimonides in his later years. While his large, early book *Aliot* on the tractate *Bava Batra* scarcely contains any mention of Maimonides' *Yad ha-Hazakah*, in later years, when he headed the Toledo yeshiva, he taught his pupils the *Yad ha-Hazakah* regularly, as can be easily seen by even a cursory survey of *Talmidei Rabbenu Yona*, his commentary to numerous tractates. A similar change of attitude is also clearly discernible in R. Meir Abulafia, the contemporaneous rabbi of Toledo, as was pointed out and explained by Septimus himself.[5]

There is hardly any need to emphasize the great admiration Nachmanides had for Maimonides and his ambivalent attitude toward the philosophical aspects of the latter's work. Nachmanides was R. Jonah's main ally in laying the foundations for and executing the communal revolution in Aragon. R. Jonah and Nachmanides were both followers of the Franco-German school of their time. Perplexity and hesitation seem to have characterized the German attitude toward Maimonides in the first third of the thirteenth century, unlike the generally positive attitude taken by the French Tosafists. Nevertheless, there is no question that a major change of opinion must have occurred in Germany, as well, around the 1240s, enabling Maharam of Rotenburg, early in the second half of the thirteenth century, to state that one should follow Maimonides' halakhah "everywhere," unless it is explicitly opposed by a decision made by a consensus of Tosafists (a very rare occurrence, according to Maharam). It is very difficult to imagine Nachmanides exploiting the Maimonidean inclinations of the *nesi'im* in his fight against them, nor does it make much sense to say this about Rabbenu Jonah. The simple fact is that Maimonidean halakhic influence in Spain grew to no end precisely in the years following Nachmanides' (and R. Jonah's) communal revolution, as is clear from Jonah Ibn Bahlul's halakhic treatise in verse.[6]

In fact, the entire treatise, written in the year 1254, is dedicated to a sweeping demonstration of the great improvements achieved in the field of halakhah since the adoption of *Mishneh Torah* as the principle halakhic guide in Spain. True enough, these two personalities were kabbalists; in fact, Nachmanides was a leading—though silent—kabbalist, but this does not necessarily mean that they were opposed, in any way, to philosophy. On the contrary, they could both be devout—though silent—philosophers at the same time, and there would still be no contradiction in terms or in anything else.

5 B. Septimus, *Hispano-Jewish Culture in Transition* (Cambridge, Mass. and London 1982), pp. 54–58.

6 Idem, "Kings, Angels or Beggars: Tax Law and Spirituality in a Hispano-Jewish Responsum," in *Studies in Medieval Jewish Literature* II, ed. I. Twersky (Cambridge, Mass. and London 1984), pp. 310–311.

My question is: Were these two kabbalists, Nachmanides and R. Jonah, pro or anti-philosophy? Or were they, perhaps, neutral? Were their true, inner attitudes toward philosophy on a par with their declared, public attitudes? Is it possible that they were actually "esoteric" philosophers in much the same way that we know them to be esoteric kabbalists? Did they, too, think—as we do—that these two categories of thought were radically and hopelessly opposed to each other? My impression is that neither of the two men studied philosophy from Arabic texts, although Nachmanides could read the language[7] and probably R. Jonah could as well (but Jospe's proof for such knowledge, from the evidence of R. Hillel of Verona, is not persuasive. R. Hillel does not mention R. Jonah by name; he just says, "my teacher who taught me natural sciences," and this teacher need not have been R. Jonah or even Jewish. The term *beit ha-midrash* mentioned therein will easily cover Gentile schools as well. Neither do Sermonetta and Harvey, both mentioned in Jospe's article, refer to the name of R. Jonah in this episode). Hebrew translations of Aristotelian philosophy did not exist in the first half of the thirteenth century. But even if my impression happens to be correct and it then follows that neither man had taken a systematic course on the subject, they still knew its contents very well, probably from Maimonides' works, and they could—and certainly did—form an opinion about its worth and status as theology.

It seems that a major aspect of the "kabbalah versus philosophy" controversy in Provence and Spain has been completely neglected or misunderstood in modern research. Reading, for example, the very learned description of the extremely polarized theological views of these two sects and their immediate religious and social results in I. Baer's classical book on the history of Jewish Spain mentioned above,[8] one cannot avoid feeling that Baer left an important part of the issue out of his book: a clarification of the objective academic and religious attitudes of the great talmudic scholars of Spain toward philosophy and kabbalah—namely, R. Jonah and Nachmanides, the deciders of the halakhah and the heads of the great talmudic academies. The chapter is occupied with a comparison of the two men in terms of their influence upon daily life and their outlook on life. There is a detailed analysis of the events leading up to R. Solomon b. Aderet's ban on the premature study of philosophy and the *Moreh Nevukhim* and a study of the ban's actual contents, accompanied by a short report on R. Jonah's activity in the matter.

One might raise an objection here that Baer was a historian, not a philosopher and, therefore, was interested in ideas only insofar as they exerted actual influence on historical events. But the crucial point is that Baer left the entire rabbinic sphere out of his book, *The History of the Jews in Christian Spain* [!]

[7] R. Jospe, "Rambam and Arabic" (Heb.), *Tarbiz* 62 (1987), pp. 67–94.

[8] n. 4, pp. 141–178.

He omitted the academies (*yeshivot*): the institution, the curriculum, the pupils, and the literary creativity, all of which were of central importance in the history of the Jews in Spain until the expulsion. R. Solomon b. Aderet, R. Yom-Tov b. Abraham of Seville, and other rabbinic leaders are all mentioned in Baer's book in the sole context of their activities as communal and political leaders. Yet these scholars were all first-class talmudists who headed large academies—many students of which came from abroad—and in this capacity composed unusually profound commentaries to many tractates of the Talmud and interpreted most of the Talmud nearly twenty-five times over during a period of approximately one hundred years. Large portions of their work exist to this day, copied and later printed, time and again, to fulfill Talmud students' undying desire to consult them. All these scholars were first, second, or third-generation pupils of Nachmanides, who was himself mainly a talmudist and halakhist and whose huge literary work deals mainly with halakhah and talmudic literature. These rabbis were the leaders of their time not only in communal and political affairs, but primarily as heads of important academies in which hundreds of talented people studied Talmud, preparing themselves for future local leadership.

Baer dealt with the question of how "philosophers," that is, scholars dedicated to the study of philosophy, and "kabbalists," dedicated to the study of kabbalah, regarded their respective vocations and totally neglected the study of the main intellectual pursuits of these times: the yeshiva and talmudic studies. One should always remember that both philosophers and kabbalists represented minority elite groups, almost esoteric in nature, while the main intellectual endeavors were openly directed toward talmudic-rabbinic studies. The ratio of newly written books on philosophy and kabbalah of this period compared to those on halakhah is at least 1 : 10 in quantity and 1 : 100 in their long-term influence on future generations. One should also remember that all great spiritual leaders of Spanish Jewry in the thirteenth to fourteenth centuries, since R. Jonah's revolution, were, first of all, talmudic scholars and *poskim*, filling their public posts because they were known to be great talmudic scholars.

Baer knew all this, of course, but he failed to grasp that this talmudic mainstream was also an ideological "school," with a well-defined attitude toward life and toward the two colleague "schools" and with a much greater effect on social and communal style and outlook than they had. In his book there is no information whatever on the special historical character of the rabbinate in Spain, its inner ideological world, its academies, or its literature and leadership in Christian Spain. It is as if all this was of no importance to the understanding of the sad chain of events that took place in Spain during the fourteenth and fifteenth centuries. It is hard to believe that in Baer's *History* there is no mention at all of the most important spiritual creation of the Jews in Spain: the many large sets of novellae to the Talmud. There are hundreds of volumes in number, written and rewritten by scores of first-rank scholars (most of them quiet kabbalists!) over a century of intensive study with hundreds and thousands of yeshiva students, most of it lost to us today, but the remainder of which is still very relevant to over one hundred thousand modern *talmidei hakhamim*.

Professor G. Scholem was, of course, much more sophisticated than Baer was, and in his lectures he warned his pupils against easy simplifications of the subject.[9]

> Relationships between Kabbala—as a movement of specific religious tendencies, therefore—and the world of philosophic enlightenment coming from Spain and the East, and whose trends are opposed, in a great measure, to what the Kabbala aims at defending; these relationships still need clarification. This contradiction is known from historians[!], but is nevertheless not so simple.

Scholem further illustrates the problem by describing the historic spiritual image of R. Abraham b. David, who seems to be interested—rather, immersed—in both subjects at the same time, and then says:

> We do not feel that these persons faced any sense of tension between the two; on the contrary: there is no discrepancy here when we read these different sources. I do not mean to say that there is no conflict between them. But as far as they were concerned, there was no conflict here. They acted in full harmony within themselves.

Scholem dedicates a lot of space to explaining how such a contradiction could, indeed, be entertained by the same people, his central idea being that both philosophy and kabbalah are "ideologies" in the sense that they both try to explain—or, rather, apologize for—notions that arose naturally in the past, in an "organic" manner, but have become problematic under outside attacks by the Karaites and the Christians, and, therefore, demand an explanation. Being both "ideologies"—that is, explanations and, in fact, apologetics intended to back up a natural, or vital, way of life that came under heavy attack and was losing meaning—they still differ from each other, because philosophy uses allegory and kabbalah uses the language of symbolism, which is on a different plane, comfortably compatible with allegory.

I do not mean to discuss Scholem's view here, but it is worth noting that:

1. the problem of the apparent psychological compatibility of the extreme opposites of philosophy and kabbalah seems to have troubled Professor Scholem enough to extract a lengthy and detailed observation from him, which was nevertheless left here *in medias res*, so to speak, but is more fully developed in his *Major Trends*,[10] (first lecture, chapter 7).

[9] G. Scholem, *The Kabbalah in Provence* (Jerusalem 1966).

[10] Idem, *Major Trends in Jewish Mysticism* (New York 1961), chapter 7.

2. Scholem confronted the problem when he was discussing the Provencal R. Abraham b. David, the Ravad, and his group. Ravad was, indeed, one of the first kabbalists, but he was first and foremost the leading halakhist of Provence in the last quarter of the twelfth century.
3. Scholem did not form a connection between points (1) and (2), and although he extensively explained the different mental attitude of kabbalists and philosophers toward the world of halakhah,[11] he never touched on the other side of this coin: the attitude of the leading halakhists toward philosophy and kabbalah. As did Baer, Scholem also assumed a total separation between the three faculties.

Halakhah is an ideology in the same sense that kabbalah or philosophy is, and within it different trends struggle, as they do within the latter. All three: kabbalah, philosophy, and halakhah are highly intellectual occupations, engaging elite groups of well-read and well-bred people, with the important social difference that halakhists were always the traditional spiritual and communal leaders, enjoying, by *consensus omnium*, theoretical and tactical superiority over their fellow kabbalists and philosophers. All three groups had fixed opinions on the virtues and shortcomings of the other two, and although they all accepted halakhah as a binding practice, they each understood its spiritual meaning and message differently. In his lecture that was quoted earlier, Scholem understands halakhah and aggadah to be authentic, organic expressions of Judaism, whereas philosophy and kabbalah purport to be its ideological "explanation." But in late twelfth-century Provence and Spain, under the historical stress of Karaite and Christian attacks, halakhah, too, functioned as an "explanation" of Jewishness—if not of Judaism—and it was recommended that all three be studied in mutual confrontation, so as to better understand the various current attitudes to the main doctrines of their ideologies. Admittedly, philosophy and kabbalah are systems of thought from which many practices are derived, and halakhah is a system of practices from which many ideas are derived; but that does not mean that they are not on an equal footing as explanatory ideologies.

An accurate and patient reading of the classical halakhic books of the Spanish rabbis will show, if I am not mistaken, that from Nachmanides and R. Jonah onward, the leading Spanish sages accepted philosophy as a valid "science"; were well-versed in its central, important books and handbooks; and adopted its terminology, its unique logic, its regard for allegory, and most of its conclusions. In an article I wrote on halakhic decisions in Spain,[12] I had the opportunity to clearly show how leading Provencal and Spanish scholars, from the

[11] Idem, pp. 28–30.

[12] I. Ta-Shma, "Philosophical Considerations for Halakhic Decision-Making in Spain" (Heb.), *Sefunot* 3/18 (1985), pp. 99–110.

eleventh century to the fourteenth, all used pure philosophical terms and logic in their halakhic discussions, a phenomenon that was unparalleled in the Ashkenazi rabbinate. A respect for philosophy, in all its branches, was felt by Spanish rabbis long before kabbalah appeared on the scene, and it remained there after its appearance. R. Jonah was an expert psychologist in his time, and his commentaries to *Mishlei* and tractate *Avot* reflect a perfect and very detailed knowledge of this branch of philosophy. However, these rabbis were opposed to lifelong and systematic study of philosophy, in the same way that they were opposed to a lifelong study of any other "science," such as medicine or astronomy. They believed that all important information can—and should—be learned directly from the Torah, to the study of which they demanded lifelong dedication. All of the leading rabbis of Spain, from R. Jonah and Nachmanides to the end of the fourteenth (actually, fifteenth) century, were more than well-versed in philosophy and wrote philosophical treatises (and sometimes books) in no less a measure than most of them knew kabbalah and had deep respect for it. On the other hand, they did not encourage the study of philosophy—or kabbalah—nor did they encourage the study of any other science, because they saw talmudic-halakhic studies to be the main "Jewish" intellectual occupation.

Another question is, of course, locating the relevant references in the voluminous halakhic literature of Spanish origin, which seems to be completely empty of non-halakhic material. But this is actually far from the case. Let me present a few examples to illustrate my point, in particular, one paragraph in R. Aharon of Barcelona's commentary to tractate *Berakhot*, which is dedicated to our topic. R. Aharon was a pupil of Nachmanides—as were most other rabbinic leaders of that age—and a famous talmudist, who wrote commentaries on many tractates and on the *halakhot* of R. Isaac Alfasi. He was also a lifelong halakhic antagonist of his famous colleague and co-rabbi, Solomon b. Aderet, the Rashba. He is, therefore, an excellent representative of the said "third ideology" and will also serve as an indication for further research.

The paragraph quoted here is written as a commentary to the *mishnah* in *Berakhot* 5:4: *Ha-omer al ken tzipor yagi'u rakhamekha...meshatkin oto* ("He who says [in his cantorial prayer] 'your mercy reaches to the bird's nest'... must be silenced at once"), because this interpretation of the biblical commandment of *shilu'akh ha-ken*[13] ("To drive away the mother bird from the nest") is wrong; [cf. *Bavli Berakhot* 35a]. This chapter in the *Mishnah* presents a welcome opportunity for R. Aharon to discuss, at some length, the problem of *ta'amei ha-mitzvot*, that is, the reason for the biblical commandments, which was a very central—and crucial—issue for kabbalah, philosophy, and halakhah students alike. R. Aharon says that "his brother" explained the reason for *shilu'akh ha-ken* to be a demonstration of God's General Providence toward animal genres, in contrast to his Personal Providence toward humans. He then

13 Deut 22:6–7.

says that this is also the reason behind the commandment *oto ve-et beno*, prohibiting the slaughtering of an animal and its offspring on the same day. The reason for the commandment to keep Sabbath is to instill in us the cognition and belief in Creation, and the commandment to make a parapet for our roofs[14] was given in order to teach us that a man must do whatever he can to avoid danger and then leave the rest to the will of God. Similarly, we apply to doctors for medical help, thus doing our best, yet knowing that final results are up to God's will. The commandment to put salt on all our sacrifices is meant to consolidate our belief in the realization of all the divine promises to our nation, which is also the reason for the commandment *gid ha-nashe*, "the thigh sinew."

He then says that

> the whole Torah is to be explained according to these lines, [teaching] true creeds and opinions, true promises, values and benefits that are [woven and incorporated] in the different laws of prohibition and uncleanliness. And if some [of these explanations] are not mentioned, they were concealed for our good, and the "concealed" advantages—good practices and right opinions—reach us automatically....Everything which was absolutely proved to be true by the study of the motion of the celestial spheres [that is, Aristotelian physics], and whose explanation is true, like the existence of God, his unity and superiority over all "separate intellects," is included in the biblical doctrine of the immortality of the soul, and embodied, in part, in the biblical phenomenon of prophecy. For all other things, on which there is still no final proof, such as creation *ex nihilo*, and the rest of the things [posited in the Torah], the Torah itself is proof enough. On things for which no final proof can be produced, a man should listen to the evidence of the Torah, which is fully trustworthy. Thus, a man who busies himself with the study of the Torah, attains truth without having to enter into deep enquiries, which are hidden techniques, full of obstacles, because the ways of God are far above theirs. And I intend, please God, to write a special pamphlet on this subject, so that I can explain in it matters that I have worked out myself, or heard [from others].

This unique paragraph demands our attention. First of all, I must point out that each and every one of the reasons for the various commandments enumerated in it was taken, word for word, from the classical book *Sefer ha-Hinukh*, wrongly attributed to many authors, among them R. Aharon himself. As we have seen, R. Aharon quotes the authority of his brother for that which follows, and this is absolute proof that the author of *Sefer ha-Hinukh* is R. Pinchas of Barcelona, Aharon's elder brother and a close friend of Nachmanides. This has been elaborated upon in great detail in my article on the authorship of *Sefer ha-Hinukh*.[15]

14 Deut 22:8.

15 I. Ta-Shma, "The True Author of *Sefer ha-Hinukh*" (Heb.), *Kiryat Sefer* 56 (1980), pp. 787–790.

R. Aharon argues that there really is no point in dedicating time and effort to studying philosophy. The essence of philosophy and its unique virtue lies in its ability to construct logical and, therefore, irrefutable proofs to a series of basic assumptions, both physical and metaphysical. Yet the basic truths that are thus deliberated on in philosophical works are all embodied in the Torah, and whoever studies Torah will arrive at the same results, without treading the difficult and complicated path of philosophy, which has its own theological dangers and pitfalls. Not only will a person end up with the same results, but an additional series of truths, for which no proof has ever been produced by logical methods will also be known to him upon the evidence of the Torah. Aristotelian philosophy and Maimonides' *Moreh Nevukhim* are clearly hinted at and there is, of course, no question that R. Aharon knew the book. In order to make this point clear and to ensure that his hints are not misread, R. Aharon hastened to quote a paragraph from the *Moreh* (1:59)—quoting Maimonides by name but not *Moreh Nevukhim*—dealing with the neighboring section of Talmud *Berakhot*. This is one of the relatively few quotations from the *Moreh* in rabbinic literature, and it deals with Maimonides' original interpretation of the talmudic parable, or allegory, about a king who was praised for owning much silver instead of gold.

On the other hand, it is obvious that R. Aharon was a kabbalist as well, being a pupil of Nachmanides and a friend of all the other pupils of Nachmanides, who are all known to us as kabbalists. But we can go further than that and say that R. Aharon actually knew parts of the Zohar, as is evident from the a comparison of two paragraphs discussed in my book *Ha-Nigleh she-Banistar*.[16]

The fact that these two paragraphs are, indeed, copied from one another is evident from the strange mistake found in both of them, of using the Aramaic nouns *atvan* ["letters"] and *teivin* ["words"] in an inverted, most unusual manner. R. Aharon ha-Levi of Barcelona died around the years 1300–1305, that is about twenty years or more after the writing of the Zohar, and he is thus the one who made use of the Zohar and not the other way round. Notice, too, that his sentence "The beginning of this Alphabet [*El Adon*] on *Shabbat* two first letters, and so forth, is quite meaningless, because the other alphabet, for the week days [*El Barukh*], was not mentioned at all in the paragraph, while the Zohar did, indeed, start its discussion with the Alphabet for the week days, and was, therefore, right to begin this sentence with the words "the praise of *Shabbat*," and so forth.

There is an outstanding example in which R. Aharon makes use of indubitable philosophical speculation to advance his mystical argument. In his exegesis to the somewhat strange formula of the monthly blessing of the moon, R. Aharon says that it deals with the topic of resurrection, its content being that

[16] I. Ta-Shma, *Ha-Nigleh she-Banistar – The Halakhic Residue in the Zohar* (Tel Aviv 2001), pp. 30, 67.

the dead will rise physically from their graves, each person with the same body he had before he died and functioning exactly as he used to function: consuming food, engaging in sexual intercourse, and so on. But this time everyone will be able to squeeze the maximum from his body and, therefore, live for a long time. Nevertheless, when each body in its turn is exhausted, it will metamorphose from a normal, four-element, fleeting, base material into a celestial body of eternal existence, like all other sphere-material above the moon. This doctrine by itself is a unique mixture of the Maimonidean idea of resurrection as an intermediate, second-chance stage between bodily existence in this world and a completely spiritual world-to-come, with the Saadian idea of a simple, full, one-stage, bodily resurrection following immediately after this world.

The reference to the full biological function of the resurrected limbs is obviously meant to answer Maimonides' critique of their apparent superfluity. The comment about the "celestial" metamorphosis of the body in the "final" world-to-come and its connection to the original nature of Adam and the "Tree of Life" was originally conceived by his teacher, Nachmanides, in *Shaar Ha-Gemul*.[17] The surprising—to my knowledge, unparalleled—part of the thesis, however, lies in the logical argument given to prove its case. R. Aharon says that the hierarchical "Ladder of Being," from top to bottom, progresses thus: Separate Intellects > Eternal Physical Intellects = Spheres > Temporal Physical Intellects finally to be metamorphosed into Eternal Physical Intellects = Man > Temporal Physical Bodies = Animals > Flora. Now, if resurrection is to be understood as a clear spiritual phase, then man must occupy a place in the hierarchy above the spheres, and this is "impossible." This hierarchy is taken, of course, from Maimonides' *Mishneh Torah* (*Yesodei ha-Torah* 3:9–11) and it is used in an original way to refute the Maimonidean creed of spiritual resurrection.

We encounter here a central talmudic figure, well-versed in Maimonidean philosophy, generally adopting its information, speculations, and conclusions on physics and metaphysics as true "science" and, therefore, binding, but at the same time advocating serious reservations as to the possible implications that this might, or might not, have on determining specific Jewish dogma—which to him were much nearer to mystical speculation than to philosophical rationalism. Philosophy is very useful as a system of thought and reliable enough as a natural science, but it is inadequate—perhaps worthless—as a pontifex in the deep waters of the supernatural. In this realm one must make careful use of "accepted" (kabbalistic) knowledge, passed from generation to generation, and kept secret by a select few. The Torah offers a safe shortcut to valid philosophical wisdom and is, therefore, a much preferred alternative to it; but kabbalah is the only possible course to be taken when studying supernatural orders of existence, which are entirely beyond philosophy's horizon.

All this, and far more, stands out clearly in the classical *Sefer ha-Hinukh*,

[17] Nachmanides, *Sha'ar ha-Gemul*, vol. 2, ed. C. Chavel (Jerusalem 1964), p. 305.

which was written, anonymously, by R. Pinchas, the brother of our Aharon ha-Levi, who quotes him generously in his commentary to *Berakhot*, as we have seen. R. Pinchas was the older brother, more or less the same age as Nachmanides—who died, however, before him—and a great admirer of Nachmanides, though not actually his pupil. R. Pinchas wrote commentaries to many tractates of the Talmud, most of them already lost, but only a very few biographical facts about him are known to us. *Sefer ha-Hinukh* (The Book of Education) defines and counts the traditional 613 commandments in the Pentateuch, according to the order of the weekly portions read in the synagogue each Sabbath. Every commandment is first defined, then explained as to its roots; afterward the major talmudic-halakhic details of the commandment are given; and, finally, the book mentions the persons under its obligation, whether it is always valid or dependent upon certain conditions, etc. The book is addressed to beginners, mainly young boys, the author's own son explicitly included, and is meant to capture their attention and constructively fill up some of their free time on Sabbath, when they usually waste their time in unruly conduct in the streets. All this is expressly said by the author himself in his enlightening introduction and many times more in the book itself, when the opportunity arises.

We are interested mainly in the explanatory parts of the book—the roots of every commandment. The halakhic part of the book is most interesting, but will not occupy us here. In it, the author strives to acquaint his young readers with the main talmudic precepts relevant to each commandment and he sometimes enters upon a detailed discussion, mentioning controversies and dissenting opinions. It is quite clear that imparting talmudic knowledge is one of the central goals of the book. The same—and much more so—applies to the explanatory part of the book. This part is a classical representative for the large and ubiquitous literary genre of *ta'amei ha-mitzvot*, giving various reasons and reasonings for the 613 commandments of the Torah, many of them strange, sometimes even bizarre, and removed from common sense.

This branch of literature occupied the minds of many Jewish scholars of all schools, with each person trying to explain the commandments in accordance with his own intellectual tendencies toward philosophy, mysticism, grammar and syntax, allegory, or whatever else it might have been. Maimonides dedicated much space in his *Moreh Nevukhim* to this subject, seeing the biblical war against idolatry as the main rational key to the riddle. Kabbalists, on the other hand, found here a large field for their mystical speculation and endeavored to explain everything upon mystical grounds. Especially active in this field was the Geronese school of kabbalists in the first half of the thirteenth century, which concentrated most of its intellectual and literary effort around the topic of *ta'amei ha-mikra*, undoubtedly in response to Maimonides' parallel philosophic endeavor.[18]

[18] Important information on this point is to be found in J. Katz, "Halacha and Kabbala— First Contacts" (Heb.), *Zion* 44 (1980), pp. 159–170.

In his *Sefer ha-Hinukh*, R. Pinchas regularly quotes by name only two authors: Maimonides and Nachmanides. His book is actually founded upon them and he quotes them, by name or anonymously, on every page. Between the two, Pinchas is more strongly oriented toward Maimonides, as is clear to everyone versed in this book and as he himself says, on a rare occasion when he prefers Nachmanides' view: "I explained this chapter [on libation wine] following Nachmanides, contrary to my habit in the rest of the book, in which I always preferred Maimonides' view, but here I saw that the biblical sentence reads more fluently this way..." (Number 112).

The reason R. Pinchas preferred Maimonides is obvious. Occupying oneself with finding reasons for the *mitzvot* has always had its dangers, mainly a fear lest people say that under modern conditions the reasons are irrelevant and the commandments meaningless and, therefore, superfluous. As was explained, *Sefer ha-Hinukh* was intended for young readers and beginners, and, therefore, the reasons given for the various commandments were always rational, ethical, relevant, simple, straightforward, and easy to grasp and identify with. As he himself says:

> The roots of this commandment [not to sacrifice leaven and honey] are hidden, and it is impossible to find even the slightest clue for [them]. But, because I have already announced at the beginning of my book, that my intention in writing down these "reasons" was to give the young boys a pretaste [an appetizer] and accustom them to an orderly study, and because the words of the Torah do have reasons and utility, which the young boys may comprehend only according to their limited capacities, let them better get whatever they can so that the Torah will not seem to them an unintelligible book, lest they kick [it] out, abandoning it forever. Therefore, I shall write whatever comes to me at first thought, and let no one criticize me, who knows my purpose (Number 126).

Many commandments were, therefore, explained to be motivated by the same reasons, trying to achieve the same goals, and the author warns his readers not to wonder why one commandment is not enough in such cases—the basic idea being that the mind is always directed by deeds, and not vice versa:

> Hearken my son...man is always tending according to his deed, and his heart and thoughts are always in post factum accordance with his deeds, whether good or bad. Even a wicked man, whose thoughts are evil all day, if he concentrate his efforts on studying Torah and keeping *mitzvot*, though his heart be far from it, he will automatically change for the better, his deeds overcoming, as it were, his instincts. For the hearts are carried after the deeds. And if a man be righteous and pious, wholly intent on Torah and *mitzvot*, if he busy himself with disgraceful matters—let us say, the king put him on such business—if he will actually be busy through the day fulfilling his dirty job, he will eventually turn bad, and with the time become thoroughly wicked..." (Number 20 and many more).

In spite of his declared tendency to popularize when the author faces an important commandment, one that occupies a central place in the Pentateuch and/or is instinctively felt to be so, the author takes special care not to misguide his young readers into accepting his simplistic, inadequate explanation as the full truth of the matter and then says that the simple, rational—perhaps stereotyped—reason just proposed is barely enough for true understanding and that fuller, better explanations are known to the kabbalists; but he never elaborates further. Sometimes he says that the boys would meet with it when they grow up and sometimes not even that. For example, after giving a symbolic interpretation of the sacrifices, saying that they are to show us that material animal life, without the added intellectual components, is worthless and so forth, he ends with these words:

> And as to the various sacrifices and the different rules for their slaughtering and blood-throwing...and other variant details, if we were to explain them according to their simple meaning [the way we did up to here] we shall be talking nonsense, and, generally speaking, even in what we said on the over-all meaning of the sacrifices, we can actually not find our hands and feet without the help of the kabbalists, to whom we bow in all such matters (Number 95).

Additional references to kabbalistic knowledge can be found in many places throughout the book, e.g., "About the details [i.e., of the commandment not to sacrifice on the Golden Altar anything but the daily incense] we have no idea or apprehension at all, and if you press me hard for an answer I shall say...but I have heard that the kabbalists have outstanding reasons and deep secrets for each and every detail" (Number 104; cf. also *Yibbum*, Number 554).

The author is also very careful not to misguide the reader into accepting Maimonidean reasons—quoted according to the author's general policy, just not explained—in the few cases where Nachmanides takes elaborate pains to refute them. That is, he will not risk oversimplifications when they may obscure, perhaps forever, important alternative principles, and he will take steps to avoid such dangers by simply telling the beginner to be aware and to inquire further when he is older and in a better position to understand.

There is, of course, no question at all where the author's stakes lie. He is a full-fledged kabbalist, a devout follower of Nachmanides, who knows and always remembers that certain knowledge is to be sought with the kabbalists but that their knowledge is not appropriate for the education of the many. He, therefore, makes extensive use of Maimonides' views and methods, popularizing and simplifying them, and at the same time warns the reader, from time to time, that there are higher, "inner" explanations that the reader might be able to discover for himself in the future. This does not imply that he thought little of his "simplified" explanations. On the contrary, R. Pinchas says that both Maimonides and Nachmanides thought that the commandments were given to us for our benefit, not for their Giver's benefit, and, therefore, calculating the special benefit that each one of them is supposed to yield, even a part of it, is an integral part of the commandment, even when we lack any clue as to its meaning (Number 537). Maimonides and Nachmanides are both "reliable witnesses, two pillars of the world, great sages, possessing purified intellects and being themselves kabbalists" (*u-vesitrei ha-Torah mekubalim*; ibid.).

He did not admire Maimonides merely as a man and a philosopher but he also respected his background philosophy, which he—as did all of Nachmanides' other pupils—knew from its presentation in the *Moreh Nevukhim*. In Number 33 he explains the "root" of *Shabbat* as signifying the principle of creation "in contrast to the opinion of philosophizers, who are loathsome to us for it, who think that everything existed as an integral part of His existence." The few following sentences are a direct adaptation of *Moreh Nevukhim* 2:31. In Number 25, speaking about the commandment to believe in God, he explains that "belief entails not only an inner conviction but also the mouth expressing what the heart believes to be true, even if one has to give up one's life for doing so." And he continues:

> And if he will be privileged [later on] to progress in the ladder of wisdom, and his heart will understand—and his eyes see—with an absolute proof [*mofet hotekh*] that his belief was really true and above doubt...then he will be fulfilling this commandment in the best possible way [*mitzvah min ha-muvkhar*].

Rabbi Pinchas is, of course, siding here with Maimonides (*Sefer ha-Mitzvot* 1), who counts belief in God as the first biblical commandment, in the face of the obvious question: How can anyone fulfill this commandment before he actually does believe in God? To which comes R. Pinchas' surprising answer that the obligation to believe in God means, basically, verbal admission, even without an adequate inner conviction. But when one does get one's absolute philosophical [or mystical-kabbalistic?] proof, he will then be fulfilling this commandment *min ha-muvkhar*. I think that there can be no doubt but that the author of these sentences had sincere trust in both philosophy and kabbalah, as he hinted at both of them by making use of an ambiguous phrase (*mofet hotekh*), which technically comes from the realm of philosophy but could still serve as any other sort of "proof."

Sefer ha-Hinukh is an excellent prosopographical example of a central rabbinic figure from Nachmanides' and R. Jonah's circles. All the great rabbinic figures of the next generation—R. Aharon ha-Levi of Barcelona, R. Solomon b. Aderet, R. Yom Tov b. Abraham of Seville, R. Crescas Vidal, and others—were all of the type called in rabbinic literature of the time *Hakham ha-Kolel*, a comprehensive scholar, a sort of omniscient scholar expected by everyone to have a thorough knowledge of every branch of Jewish wisdom and what is near to it. Rashba and Ritva were quite knowledgeable philosophers, as is clear from their books, and they were both keen on kabbalah as well, concerning which they kept very quiet, in the tradition of their teacher Nachmanides. So were probably all their Spanish colleagues, too. Nachmanides taught that our Torah includes in it, in many different ways, all the true information—on whatever subject—being taught by the different teachers and schools. One who dedicates himself to the study of the Torah and succeeds in one's efforts is, therefore, bound to know automatically every true bit of scientific information and the correct philosophical conclusions that have been reached, after much travail, by systematic philosophers. As a direct result of this, Nachmanides' personal attitude to philosophy was more negative than those of all other rabbis who came after him. They adopted both kabbalah and philosophy, seeing no essential conflict between them and, in clear cases of a clash, took the side of kabbalah. There were, of course, personal differences in this matter, as in other matters, and it is clear that Rashba and Ritva both used philosophical materials to a far greater degree than did R. Aharon ha-Levi. Sages such as R. Pinchas of Barcelona seem to be much more balanced, publicly advocating philosophical positions but at the same time hinting at the more important esoteric kabbalah. Yet, on the whole, they were positively biased toward philosophy. The bitter fight between proponents of kabbalah and those of philosophy was fought by "professionals," that is, sages who dedicated their lives and intellectual powers to the one sole spiritual pursuit—either kabbalah or philosophy. In their extremity and in their exclusion of other, more neutral studies kabbalah and philosophy are bitter enemies, but to the mainstream rabbis, who dedicated their intellectual powers to Talmud and halakhah, both kabbalah and philosophy were acceptable, honorable, and open to dispute. To what extent? The answer to that differed from person to person: some were more inclined toward kabbalah, and others might sometimes have preferred philosophic speculation, but I cannot name even one leading talmudic scholar in Spain who rejected philosophy in principle, from Nachmanides to the rabbis in the time of the Expulsion, although most of them were, apparently, inclined toward kabbalah.[19]

[19] An outstanding example of the extent to which kabbalah and philosophy could be integrated by Nachmanides into perfect harmony can be much better appreciated reading Moshe Halbertal's excellent article, "Esoteric Doctrine of the Hidden Miracle – The Layers of Being in the Teaching of Nahmanides" in *Kabbalah – Journal of the Study of Jewish Mystical Texts* 7, eds. D. Abrams and A. Elqayam (2002), pp. 257–280.

Originally published in
Jewish Mystical Leaders and Leadership in the 13th Century
M. Idel and M. Ostow, eds. Jerusalem

CHAPTER 16

PROFESSOR KATZ ON HALAKHAH AND KABBALAH

The late Professor Yaakov Katz blazed new trails in the study of Jewish history in a variety of areas. One of the most interesting was his series of pioneering studies—there are six of them—on the historical relationship between halakhah and kabbalah. Prof. Katz lived to a ripe old age, and there was no decline whatsoever in the quality of his work till his death at ninety-four. He published the articles to which we are referring in his old age, between the ages of around seventy-five and eighty. Five of them appeared almost simultaneously, between 1979 and 1982, and the last was published in 1984. We will be concerned mainly with the first two articles: "Halakhah and Kabbalah—First Contacts"[1] and "Halakhic Rulings in the Zohar."[2] Three important articles were devoted to the relationship between halakhah and kabbalah in the generations after the "discovery of the Zohar"; one article on that very subject[3] and two others concerned with specific examples: "*Tefillin* on the Intermediate Days of Festivals"[4] and "Levirate Marriage and *Halitzah* in the Post-Talmudic Period."[5] The subject of the sixth article, "Halakhah and Kabbalah as Rival Subjects of Study," is somewhat different, and I will not deal with it here.

Despite the wide publicity achieved at the time, the series of articles aroused no reaction, positive or negative, and it had no echoes in subsequent historical research. In his ground-breaking work, *Kabbalah—New Perspectives*,

[1] Katz, "Halakhah and Kabbalah—First Contacts" (Heb.), *Zion* 44 (1979) [= *Yitzhak F. Baer Memorial Volume)*, pp. 148–172.

[2] Idem, "Halakhic Statements in the *Zohar*" (Heb.), *Tarbiz* 50 (1980–1981), pp. 405–422.

[3] Idem, "Post-Zoharic Relations between Halakhah and Kabbalah" (Heb.), *Da'at* 4 (1980), pp. 57–74.

[4] Idem, "*Tfillin* on the Half-Holidays—An Example of the Channels of Kabbalistic Influence" (Heb.), *Seventh World Congress of Jewish Studies* (Jerusalem 1977), pp. 191–213.

[5] Idem, "Levirate Marriage and *Halitza* in Post-Talmudic Times" (Heb.), *Tarbiz* 51 (1981–1982), pp. 59–106.

Prof. Moshe Idel dedicated four lines to it, at the very end of chapter 1, "Remarks on Kabbalah Scholarship," and I quote:

> Finally, the relationship between Kabbala and such classical Jewish literary genres as Midrash and Halakha, has been largely neglected by modern scholarship, an outstanding exception being Jacob Katz's recent pioneering treatment of the relationship between Kabbalah and Halakha.[6]

But no further information is given, and the results of this pioneering effort remain unnoticed. Prof. Katz's historical, religious, and social writings inspired detailed descriptions and summaries, as well as substantial discussions while he was still alive, and they continue to do so today. Some of those discussions were critical, others more friendly to Katz's ideas. Various historians took part in these discussions, some devoting important articles to his views on such subjects as the history of Hungarian Jewry, the history of Orthodoxy, harbingers of Zionism, Jewish-Christian relations during the last few centuries, and so on. However, his articles on the general development of halakhah in the Middle Ages and its interrelationship with society and environment, including his research on the relationship between halakhah and kabbalah in particular, stimulated no reaction and were not even summarized in succinct form. Prof. Katz was deeply interested in the history of halakhah. It was one of his research subjects throughout his life and he published extensively in the field (besides his series on halakhah and kabbalah), but it elicited no response from historians except for the excellent work of his student, Prof. Haim Soloveitchik, whose work more than touches on Katz's theories. Most scholars' interest in and understanding of the subject are quite limited. However, it is quite surprising that scholars of kabbalah, too, have ignored Prof. Katz's series of articles. After all, these more than one hundred pages offer novel and interesting observations, carefully and precisely phrased, on subjects intimately bound up with kabbalistic literature. I am not a historian by profession, and certainly not a scholar of kabbalah, but I am deeply interested in the history and development of halakhah in the Middle Ages. For this reason, I would like to try and fill the gap myself, namely, to summarize Katz's views on the question of halakhah and kabbalah and to offer a brief response.

The main new subject brought up for discussion in these articles may be summarized in a single sentence: How was halakhah integrated into the kabbalistic literature of various periods, and how did the resulting mix, in turn, influence halakhic praxis? The first two articles deal with the first part of the question, the three others with the "feedback." As stated, I will adhere to the first part only, that is, the ways in which halakhah was integrated into kabbalistic literature. Katz essentially splits this terse question into a string of more

6 I. Idel, *Kabbalah—New Perspectives* (New Haven 1988), p. 16.

detailed inquiries: What parts of halakhah appear in kabbalistic literature? Can one discern any historical development in the integration process? What is the halakhic level of that integration and of the person, or group of persons, responsible for it? Can one differentiate between different levels of achievement in the course of time? What was the contribution of the integration to halakhic theory, if at all, and what was its purpose? How much innovative, original creativity was involved? Were there any unique features in the kabbalists' perception of halakhah beyond their special symbolic interpretation?

Katz's first article, "First Contacts," opens with *Sefer ha-Bahir*, the first book of kabbalah, and advances step by step, through R. Isaac the Blind and R. Ezra of Gerona, up to, but not including, the Zohar. The role of halakhah in the Zohar, which is the zenith of the study and its major desideratum, is the subject of the entire second article. The last three articles deal, directly and indirectly, also with the study of the Zohar, but they are concerned with the "feedback"—the influence of kabbalistic halakhah on halakhic praxis. Thus, Prof. Katz's research in the field covers the relationship between kabbalah and halakhah from first to last, from *Sefer ha-Bahir* almost to the present. His account of the overarching historical development of this relationship runs as follows.

In *Sefer ha-Bahir* we find references to more than a dozen *mitzvot* mentioned explicitly in the Torah. The book refers to them by name, citing one or more verses from the relevant biblical passage and reinterpreting them in a manner entirely at variance with the plain meaning and intention of the text, through "destructive" exegesis in the spirit of kabbalistic symbolism and its usual concerns. We do not know why these particular *mitzvot*, rather than many others, were chosen and mentioned in the book, but it is quite clear that those chosen were *mitzvot* to which the sages themselves had already attributed some semi-mystical intent, such as the precepts of *tefillin* and *tzitzit*, which the rabbis said were worn by God, himself. This ancient interpretative substrate made it easier to introduce interpretations in the spirit of the new kabbalistic symbolism.

Two generations later we find R. Isaac the Blind going further and modifying the end formula of the last benediction in the Grace after Meals,[7] based not on halakhic grounds but entirely on kabbalistic considerations—quite an

[7] I do not intend here to go into details of the *halakhot* that Katz discusses, but content myself with a few brief remarks. In this context, S. Abramson took a different approach in his book, *Inyanot be-Sifrut ha-Ge'onim* (Jerusalem 1974), pp. 150–155, where he discusses the subject at great length and states categorically that the prayer in question is the Eighteen Benedictions and not the Grace after Meals; what the *Magen Avraham* had to say on the subject, Abramson believes, was exceptional. In this connection, however, Prof. Katz was right. At the time, Abramson was unaware of what R. Isaac of Acre wrote in *Me'irat Einayim*, which clearly indicates the existence of an early tradition explicitly referring to Grace after Meals, as Katz wrote.

exceptional procedure in the traditional world of halakhah. R. Ezra of Gerona, who wrote a long chapter on the 613 *mitzvot* and their reasons, adheres closely to those *mitzvot* already "presumed" by kabbalists. Indeed, these *mitzvot* do receive special attention from R. Ezra, but he also expands and supplies kabbalistic explanations for other *mitzvot*, not previously held to be such. What is more important is that we find R. Ezra concerning himself with small, petty details of the law, even the most minor minutiae, to which he assigns regular meaning and function in the conceptual world of the kabbalah. As time goes on, this tendency becomes more pronounced, and the Zohar does not hesitate to take an active part in actually deciding the halakhah between two, or more, competing views and even contains previously unknown halakhic innovations, though Katz points out that not everything generally thought to be an innovation of the Zohar is, indeed, new, and that a considerable part of such "innovations" originated in earlier Halakhic traditions.

When Prof. Katz initiated the discussion of how halakhah was woven into kabbalah, he took advantage of his considerable proficiency in the Talmud and his profound scholarship and thorough acquaintance with the world of halakhah, with its special concepts and unique patterns of thought. Presumably, it was the lack of these skills, or of most of them, that prevented previous scholars from entering this field of research. They tacitly assumed that halakhah and kabbalah reflect parallel and detached realms of thought and knowledge that never intersect. They were perceived as two different views, or ideologies, of the content of the world of religious praxis, each view assigning a different conceptual significance to the same system of positive and negative *mitzvot*. Kabbalah, indeed, considers itself subordinate in all practical respects to the strictest commandments of halakhah, but at the same time believes the entire halakhic system to derive most of its inner meaning from the kabbalistic world of symbols and entities. The differences between the two views lie in the field of ideas, thought and symbol and have nothing to do with practical observance that is ruled, as all agree, by the absolute dictates of halakhah.

Prof. Katz disputed this supposed dichotomy. He showed that kabbalah incorporates many disputed halakhic questions and offers its own rulings, relating not only to disputes that had already, ostensibly, been resolved in the past, but also to disagreements concerning issues current at the time. Moreover, at times its ruling contradicts the generally accepted one, having been reached in a new, specifically kabbalistic way, sometimes constituting an innovative, creative approach to halakhah.

Furthermore, Katz showed that kabbalah enlisted in its service not only general principles of widespread halakhah, but delved into its most minute details. In addition, as far as the sefirotic symbolism attached to them was concerned, it most surprisingly accorded equal treatment and sefirotic importance to all categories of halakhah—biblical law (*de'orayta*), rabbinic law (*de-rabbanan*), and custom (*minhag*)—regardless of their quite different halakhic force and status. According to Katz, the kabbalah considers halakhah, any part of halakhah, to be meaningful only in its all-inclusive totality, as a round and "finished product" in its accepted practice, ignoring the many legal differences and nuances in the background. Katz rightly stresses that it is here, in relation to the small details of the *mitzvot*, that the attitudes of philosophers to the world of halakhah differ essentially from those of the kabbalists. While medieval philosophers also considered themselves subordinate to halakhah and its dictates, endeavoring to explain the underlying reasons for various *mitzvot* and to assign them a rational meaning, they could not consistently explain the myriad minutiae of the *mitzvot*— those fine details that make up the main content and significance of each *mitzvah* but must remain obscure and inexplicable, as Maimonides explicitly admits in his *Guide of the Perplexed*. The kabbalists, on the other hand, joyfully embraced all those details, considering them all of equal and precise sefirotic importance, without arranging them in any hierarchy of intrinsic significance. By thus penetrating to the most basic substrate, as it were, of the halakhic system, by assigning value and meaning to each and every detail of religious observance, major or minor, the kabbalists showed no hesitation—and, in fact, succeeded in an almost natural way—in innovating hitherto unknown details and gestures, playing a creative, original role in renewing the theoretical and practical aspect of halakhah.

At this point, Prof. Katz raises the following point: "From now on, we are justified in asking whether, in such innovations, halakhic considerations played any part whatever, or whether they fell by the wayside as a consequence of the proclivity to kabbalistic interpretation." After discussing several issues and examples, Katz reaches the conclusion that the motive for this creativity came exclusively from the force of kabbalistic exegesis; halakhic considerations were never brought into play by the author of the Zohar, who, Katz believes, was a rather mediocre halakhist and never achieved the level of a halakhic authority. This is why one finds various well-known examples in the Zohar of religious laws diametrically opposed to accepted talmudic tradition—serious deviations regarding which, in Katz's words, "no great halakhic authority would ever have erred..., even when half asleep."

Katz's views of the matter may thus be summarized as follows. In a gradual process, which lasted about one hundred years, from the first advent of kabbalah on the historical stage in *Sefer ha-Bahir*, at the end of the twelfth century, till the completion of the Zohar at the end of the thirteenth century, the new movement of kabbalah became increasingly involved, qualitatively as well as quantitatively, in halakhic matters. At the first stage, kabbalists assigned mystical significance to an increasing number of *mitzvot* in the framework of kabbalistic symbolism. Next, they totally took over to their domain the entire body of halakhah as practiced in real life, with no consideration for the inner hierarchy of biblical, rabbinic, and customary law. Later on, they even had no scruples about changing the wording of benedictions on the basis of kabbalistic considerations and ruling on various disputes and practices. At the end of the process they acted quite independently, feeling free to create new halakhic details and new ceremonies—driven not by halakhic pretensions, but by motives and interests stemming from kabbalistic interpretation. Kabbalah, as it were, appropriated halakhah from the outside, without any inner authority or ability based on halakhic proficiency.

Notwithstanding the superficial purport of the thesis, the main importance and significance of these views pertain, I believe, primarily to the history of halakhah in the period of the Zohar and later on, and not so much to the history of kabbalah. This was, indeed, Prof. Katz's intention, for he was concerned all his life with the various social and religious aspects of the study of halakhah, while kabbalah interested him only as far as it affected those aspects of halakhah. Nevertheless, a more careful look at the conclusions of his research may raise further directions of inquiry, which may well have important historical conclusions in the area of kabbalah research as well.

A central question in Prof. Katz's general approach to the relationship between halakhah and kabbalah is the extent of creative innovation to be found in the Zohar. In the course of his research, Katz proposed two mutually contradictory findings. He himself realized the inner tension between them, but nevertheless insisted that they coexist, complementing rather than contradicting each other. On the one hand, he maintained that halakhic creativity—that is, the creation of new ritual and halakhic details, unprecedented in the past—was the peak of the kabbalah's active intervention in the world of halakhah. However, the second side of this coin was the argument, or rather discovery, that many innovations normally credited to kabbalah are actually ancient traditions, though it is not always easy to trace them today in pre-zoharic literature and one must sometimes simply rely on impressions, lacking real proof.

On the face of it, the second thesis cancels out the first, for if it is true, there is no more any measure of innovation present. Katz was aware of the apparent contradiction and, therefore, phrased his double thesis as follows:

> Even if a careful examination should prove that many rulings attributed to the Zohar have their sources elsewhere, and the Zohar only put its stamp on them and promoted their dissemination, it is still true that it considerably expanded the scope of ritual and ruled concerning *halakhot* that were questionable or disputed prior to its time.

However, this rather tepid formulation is not necessarily correct. Indeed, if the origin of those laws, customs, and ritual details is elsewhere, their being mentioned in the Zohar does not necessarily imply any zoharic ruling, "stamp" or the like; all it implies is that those laws, etc., were practiced in the social circle of the author of the Zohar, so that what is reflected in the Zohar is the accepted practice of his cultural and halakhic environment, not his personal halakhic rulings. It should be noticed that halakhic matters figure in the Zohar only as required by the kabbalistic content invested in them, and most of them are referred to only in passing. In such cases it seems clear that no deliberate halakhic decision or ruling on any level is involved, but only existing circumstances. After all, it was Prof. Katz himself who always stressed the secondary role of the great luminaries of Jewish scholarship in the development of halakhah, in contrast to the decisive role of traditional Jewish society that, guided by an inner religious sensitivity, carefully sifted out the permitted from the forbidden, discarding some practices and admitting others, thus determining for itself proper halakhic norms. Only after such customs had taken root and become common practice among the many were they brought to the professional, authoritative attention of halakhic luminaries, who generally tended to sanction accepted customs, though at times improving upon them or, more rarely, abolishing them. So why should we interpret halakhic matters in the Zohar as straightforward halakhic rulings, rather than reflections of generally accepted norms?

The following simple illustration will suffice. Katz devoted a whole article to the history of the wearing of *tefillin* on the Intermediate Days of a festival—one of the series of six articles under discussion here.[8] He points out there that R. Isaac Karo, uncle of R. Joseph Karo, who lived in the last generation before the expulsion from Spain, wrote that the universal practice in Spain was to follow the rulings of R. Asher b. Yehiel (the Rosh), who wore *tefillin* on the Intermediate Days; however, ever since Spanish scholars had found an injunction in the Zohar forbidding the practice, they rejected the Rosh's ruling. This is, indeed, a good example of the considerable authority attributed by some scholars to the Zohar in Spain during the second half of the fifteenth century. However, Katz's statement "The ruling of the Zohar in the matter of *tefillin* on the Intermediate Days of festivals received attention at an early stage" is untenable. Katz himself shows in the same article that, while the Rosh's ruling agrees with the halakhic tradition of Franco-Germany, all the great Spanish scholars, up to and during the Rosh's lifetime, unanimously agreed that one should not wear *tefillin* on the Intermediate Days; it was the Rosh who changed the ancient Spanish practice from his time on, by virtue of his great personal and public authority. The Zohar, however, which was written around the time of Nachmanides, followed the accepted custom of all Spanish scholars up to and including its own time, thus forbidding *tefillin* on the Intermediate Days in conformity with what was customary in that part of the Jewish world. It seems self-evident that the Zohar was by no means ruling or settling some previous controversy, but simply expressing what was accepted at that time. The author of the Zohar could not, of course, have known that the Rosh would come to Spain some thirty or forty years later, reject the accepted Spanish custom and reverse the ruling. Only scholars of later generations, such as R. Isaac Karo, on the eve of the expulsion, who were familiar with the Rosh's

[8] n. 4.

practice and with that of their own country, might have regarded the zoharic injunction as a halakhic ruling that could reverse an existing situation.

To return to our main subject: The question is, then, how much creative, original innovation is discernible in the halakhic component of the Zohar, that halakhic—or semi-halakhic—component for which we know of no literary or other precedent and which may be considered the Zohar's own creation, and what is the real extent of that component? Now, despite the importance of this question, a much more important question should be asked, I believe. It concerns the halakhic component of the Zohar that is clearly derived from some outside source, whether by way of halakhic ruling as seen by Katz or as an accepted practice of the environment, as might be argued were it not for Katz's work. Can one point to some common source for those practices or, at least, to some underlying basis common to all or most of them? Or were these elements culled from different sources and simply included if they agreed with the needs of the appropriate kabbalistic interpretation? Katz did not deal with this important question, which will now occupy us.

Truth to tell, the fifteen examples that Katz adduced to demonstrate the existence of an earlier source for *halakhot* previously believed to have been innovated by the Zohar, all originate in Ashkenazi custom and in halakhic literature written in the sphere of Franco-German Jewish culture. Katz did not notice this point (or ignored it as accidental and insignificant), being troubled, rather, by a question of principle: How could the Zohar, written by Moses de Leon in Spain, have drawn on an Ashkenazi source? As he wrote, after claiming that a single example could be shown to have possibly been derived from an Ashkenazi source: "The Zohar's adoption of what was probably an Ashkenazi custom [namely, that the levites wash the priests' hands before the priestly blessing.—I.T.S.] should not surprise us, for many Ashkenazi customs were known before that time in Spain, as will be demonstrated in the following case," namely, the recitation of the words *el melekh ne'eman* before the *Shema*, a subject that I had already dealt with in much detail and associated with the Zohar, and Katz, indeed, cited my work to prove his point. However, as already noted, not only these two but all Katz's examples of early origins come from Franco-Germany, and even while reading his article I decided to try and examine the phenomenon in depth. It quickly became apparent that a proper examination could not be carried out without a thorough check of the whole book of the Zohar, to locate all its submerged halakhic matters, including questions of liturgy, which actually demand separate treatment.

As such an extensive project was out of the question, I confined myself to the explicit occurrences of such themes in the Zohar, the result being my little book *Ha-Nigleh she-Banistar*,[9] which was devoted entirely to that subject.

[9] I. Ta-Shma, *Ha-Nigleh she-Banistar—The Halakhic Residue in the Zohar* (Tel Aviv 2001) (Heb.).

That inquiry clarified the extent to which the Ashkenazi rite figures in the Zohar. The basic halakhah of the Zohar is unmistakably Spanish, almost always following Maimonides. This is the case, for example, for the aforementioned injunction against wearing *tefillin* on the Intermediate Days of festivals; and the same holds for the basic liturgy of the book. Nevertheless, there are many details of laws and rules occurring in the Zohar that originate in Ashkenazi practice and in Franco-German rabbinic literature. After the book had been published, I found further very interesting examples of this phenomenon, and published them in two special articles in the English-language journal *Kabbalah*, edited by my friend Dr. Daniel Abrams, and later included in the second edition of the book.

The phenomenon in question clearly indicates the degree of Ashkenazi influence on the circle of the Zohar—not ideological, philosophical, or mystical influence in any way, but the immediate, practical influence of everyday religious ritual, whose myriad details combine to form what is usually known as the "Ashkenazi rite." While I am by no means arguing that all the Ashkenazi rite, with all its details and minutiae, was absorbed into the Zohar—and there is certainly no proof of such extensive absorption—we nevertheless have a large body of Franco-German life experience inside Spain. This is, to my mind, the most important message to emerge from the analysis of Katz's series of articles, though it appears there not explicitly but implicitly. In my above-mentioned book I wrote at length of the broader significance of this discovery for our understanding of the background and immediate message of the Zohar, also noting further points of contact between the book and various Ashkenazi elements reflected in it. Here, however, I am concerned solely with the content of Katz's research and with my reactions to it.

At the beginning of this chapter I referred to Katz's central observation that the kabbalists concerned themselves with halakhah in its final form, as actually practiced, paying no attention to underlying theoretical elements; they considered it a single, unified corpus, homogeneous in structure, with equal strength and importance attributed to general principles and details alike. They assign precise kabbalistic-sefirotic meanings to all components of the relevant halakhah in equal degree, completely ignoring the tripartite hierarchic structure and inner subdivision of halakhah into levels of strictness—biblical law, rabbinic law, and custom. This approach rightly surprised Prof. Katz, for any person taking such a position reveals himself as not much of a scholar; not prepared for or capable of considering every law against the background of the complex scholarly debate underlying it, but rather taking a short-cut to mystical-symbolic interpretation by treating all components equally. If I am not mistaken, this perplexity was the main reason for Katz's ultimate conclusion that the author of the Zohar was not an accomplished scholar. The difficulty inherent in this conclusion is, of course, the tremendous familiarity with the Talmud and the Midrash obvious from every page of the Zohar. This familiarity relates mostly to aggadic material, so there is no obstacle to our viewing the author of the Zohar as well-versed in aggadah but not a professional scholar, therefore, preferring to avoid complicated and superfluous analyses of halakhic questions. This is more or less Prof. Katz's conclusion, as we have already seen.

I believe, however, that the real solution to this puzzle is quite different. Basically, the zoharic approach to halakhah is the typical one of the Ashkenazi halakhist, which is quite different from the widespread classical, geonic-Spanish, approach. The world of Ashkenazi halakhah assigned a very important place to custom, far beyond that implied by the usual talmudic norm, which treats custom as the lowest rung on the ladder of halakhic importance. In the Ashkenazi world of values, however, custom heads the hierarchy, in the simple sense that it has the power to supplant accepted law in the spirit of the rule "custom circumvents the law." I discussed this principle at great length in my book *Minhag Ashkenaz ha-Kadmon*, where I pointed out that the basis for this approach came from *Eretz Israel* and elaborated on its historical and literary background.[10]

The common talmudic hierarchy—biblical, rabbinic, custom—expresses the level of severity from the standpoint of punitive measures, that is, the attitude toward a person who transgresses the law; it does not reflect the degree of importance of the individual details of the *mitzvah* for a person who observes it faithfully. With regard to this positive aspect, custom had pride of place in Ashkenazi halakhic tradition; in essence, it was observance of the traditions of ancestral custom, passed down from one generation to the next in all their minute detail, that constituted religious observance—not observance of the specific law *per se*. In different places, where the observance of a given *mitzvah* was governed by different customs, local Jews were obligated to observe it in exactly the same way as their ancestors had observed it there, unchanged. This approach was a radical, mental about-face for anyone schooled in the classical talmudic way of thinking, as well as its later manifestations in geonic literature and the works of the Spanish authorities, from Maimonides to the *Shulhan Arukh*. On the other hand, it represents an elementary religious-cultural reality for anyone familiar with medieval Franco-German rabbinic literature. Its implications are still with us to this day in the Ashkenazi *haredi* society. I cannot possibly describe the whole extent of the Ashkenazi approach here—in the book just mentioned, I needed almost one hundred pages to develop a proper discussion of all its details. However, my few words here should suffice to resolve much of the surprise expressed by Prof. Katz at finding Ashkenazi material in the Zohar. In the classical Ashkenazi perception, custom does not reflect mere folkloristic episodes and popular culture—these are viewed by

10 I. Ta-Shma, *Early Franco-German Ritual and Custom* (Jerusalem 1992) (Heb.).

halakhah with some disdain and treated at best patiently, like a stepchild. On the contrary, custom as prevalent among the people is the main content of each *mitzvah*; the slightest deviation from custom is forbidden, even if it seems to contradict halakhah. In fact, the basic form of every *mitzvah* is the form in which it is observed in that particular place. Essentially, Prof. Katz's observation of the unscholarly nature of zoharic halakhah is the best illustration of its Ashkenazi character.